Lecture Notes in Computer Science   12549

More information about this subseries at http://www.springer.com/series/7408

Maria Christakis · Nadia Polikarpova ·
Parasara Sridhar Duggirala ·
Peter Schrammel (Eds.)

Software Verification

12th International Conference, VSTTE 2020
and 13th International Workshop, NSV 2020
Los Angeles, CA, USA, July 20–21, 2020
Revised Selected Papers

 Springer

Editors
Maria Christakis
MPI-SWS Kaiserslautern
Kaiserslautern, Germany

Nadia Polikarpova ⓘ
University of California, San Diego
La Jolla, CA, USA

Parasara Sridhar Duggirala ⓘ
Computer Science
University of North Carolina at Chapel Hill
Chapel Hill, NC, USA

Peter Schrammel ⓘ
Engineering and Informatics
University of Sussex
Brighton, UK

ISSN 0302-9743   ISSN 1611-3349   (electronic)
Lecture Notes in Computer Science
ISBN 978-3-030-63617-3   ISBN 978-3-030-63618-0   (eBook)
https://doi.org/10.1007/978-3-030-63618-0

LNCS Sublibrary: SL2 – Programming and Software Engineering

This Springer imprint is published by the registered company Springer Nature Switzerland AG
The registered company address is: Gewerbestrasse 11, 6330 Cham, Switzerland

VSTTE 2020 Preface

This volume contains the papers presented at the 12th Working Conference on Verified Software: Theories, Tools, and Experiments (VSTTE 2020), held virtually during July 20–21, 2020. The working conference was co-located with the 32nd International Conference on Computer-Aided Verification (CAV 2020).

The Verified Software Initiative (VSI), spearheaded by Tony Hoare and Jayadev Misra, is an ambitious research program for making large-scale verified software a practical reality. VSTTE is the main forum for advancing the initiative. VSTTE brings together experts spanning the spectrum of software verification in order to foster international collaboration on the critical research challenges.

There were 14 submissions to VSTTE 2020, with authors from 9 countries. The Program Committee consisted of 36 distinguished computer scientists from all over the world. Each submission was reviewed by three Program Committee members in single-blind mode. In order to obtain domain-specific expertise, we also involved one external reviewer, Frédéric Recoules. After a comprehensive discussion on the strengths and weaknesses of papers, the committee decided to accept nine papers. The technical program also included three invited talks by Prof. Bor-Yuh Evan Chang (University of Colorado Boulder and Amazon, USA), Prof. Isil Dillig (The University of Texas at Austin, USA), and Prof. Xi Wang (University of Washington, USA).

This was our first time running a virtual conference, and we greatly appreciate the help we got from CAV 2020 organizers, in particular, the workshop chair Zvonimir Rakamaric. We are thankful to EasyChair for providing an easy and efficient mechanism for submission of papers, management of reviews, and eventually in the generation of this volume.

October 2020

Maria Christakis
Nadia Polikarpova
Natarajan Shankar

VSTTE 2020 Organization

General Chair

Natarajan Shankar   SRI International, USA

Program Chairs

Maria Christakis   MPI-SWS, Germany
Nadia Polikarpova   University of California, San Diego, USA

Program Committee

Christel Baier	TU Dresden, Germany
Nikolaj Bjorner	Microsoft, USA
Supratik Chakraborty	IIT Bombay, India
Maria Christakis	MPI-SWS, Germany
Eva Darulova	MPI-SWS, Germany
Ankush Desai	Amazon, USA
Gidon Ernst	Ludwig Maximilian University of Munich, Germany
Grigory Fedyukovich	Princeton University, USA
Pietro Ferrara	JuliaSoft SRL, Italy
Jean-Christophe Filliatre	CNRS, France
Carlo A. Furia	USI - Università della Svizzera Italiana, Switzerland
Patrice Godefroid	Microsoft, USA
Marieke Huisman	University of Twente, The Netherlands
Rajeev Joshi	Amazon, USA
Dejan Jovanović	SRI International, USA
Akash Lal	Microsoft, India
Nuno P. Lopes	Microsoft, UK
Peter Müller	ETH Zurich, Switzerland
Jorge A. Navas	SRI International, USA
Andrei Paskevich	Université Paris-Sud, LRI, France
Hila Peleg	University of California, San Diego, USA
Nadia Polikarpova	University of California, San Diego, USA
Christopher M. Poskitt	Singapore Management University, Singapore
Zvonimir Rakamaric	The University of Utah, USA
Philipp Ruemmer	Uppsala University, Sweden
Christian Schilling	IST Austria, Austria
Rahul Sharma	Microsoft, Singapore
Julien Signoles	CEA LIST, France
Graeme Smith	The University of Queensland, Australia
Michael Tautschnig	Queen Mary University of London, UK

Tachio Terauchi	Waseda University, Japan
Caterina Urban	Inria, France
Thomas Wies	New York University, USA
Kirsten Winter	The University of Queensland, Australia
Valentin Wüstholz	ConsenSys Diligence, Germany
Damien Zufferey	MPI-SWS, Germany

NSV 2020 Preface

The 13th International Workshop on Numerical Software Verification (NSV 2020) was held virtually during July 20–21, 2020. NSV 2020 was co-located with the 32nd International Conference on Computer-Aided Verification (CAV 2020).

Numerical computations are ubiquitous in digital systems: Supervision, prediction, simulation, and signal processing rely heavily on numerical calculus to achieve desired goals. Design and verification of numerical algorithms has a unique set of challenges, which set it apart from the rest of software verification. To achieve the verification and validation of global properties, numerical techniques need to precisely represent local behaviors of each component. The implementation of numerical techniques on modern hardware adds another layer of approximation because of the use of finite representations of infinite precision numbers that usually lack basic arithmetic properties, such as commutativity and associativity. Finally, the development and analysis of cyber-physical systems (CPS), which involve the interacting continuous and discrete components, pose a further challenge. It is hence imperative to develop logical and mathematical techniques for the reasoning about programmability and reliability. The NSV workshop is dedicated to the development of such techniques.

This year, the NSV workshop hosted a special session on numerical computations in machine learning. The topics included performance vs accuracy trade-offs, reliability, robustness, and co-design of hardware and software for numerical computations in machine learning frameworks.

A highlight of NSV 2020 is the presence of high-profile invited speakers from computer science, control theory, and industry: Naresh Shanbhag (University of Illinois at Urbana-Champaign, USA) talked about "Minimum Precision Requirements of Deep Neural Networks"; Zachary Tatlock (University of Washington, USA) and Pavel Panchekha (The University of Utah, USA) talked about "Towards Numerical Assistants"; and Nikos Aréchiga (Toyota InfoTechnology Center, USA) gave a talk on "Automatic Testing and Falsification with Dynamically Constrained Reinforcement Learning". Regarding the contributed papers, NSV 2020 received seven submissions, of which each received three reviews, and four of them were accepted.

We would like to thank the CAV organizers, in particular, the workshop chair Zvonimir Rakamaric, for their support and the organization of the video conferencing and messaging system, and the Steering Committee, in particular Sergiy Bogomolov, for allowing us to organize NSV 2020.

September 2020

Parasara Sridhar Duggirala
Peter Schrammel

NSV 2020 Organization

Program Chairs

Parasara Sridhar Duggirala   University of North Carolina at Chapel Hill, USA
Peter Schrammel   University of Sussex and Diffblue Ltd., UK

Program Committee

Assalé Adjé   University of Perpignan - Domitian, France
Stanley Bak   Safe Sky Analytics, USA
Sylvie Boldo   Inria, France
Lucas Cordeiro   The University of Manchester, UK
Aaron Dutle   NASA, USA
Ashutosh Gupta   IIT Bombay, India
Ichiro Hasuo   National Institute of Informatics, Japan
Xiaowei Huang   The University of Liverpool, UK
Manuel Mazo   Delft University of Technology, The Netherlands
Martin Nyx Brain   City University of London, UK
Tatjana Petrov   University of Konstanz, Germany
Laura Titolo   National Institute of Aerospace, USA
Jana Tumova   KTH Royal Institute of Technology, Sweden
Xiang Yin   Shanghai Jiao Tong University, China

VSTTE 2020 Invited Talks

Goal-Directed Static Analysis and Software Frameworks

Bor-Yuh Evan Chang

University of Colorado Boulder and Amazon, USA

Abstract. Static analysis is about computing a global over-approximation of a program's behavior from its source code. But what if most of its code is missing or unknown? Analyzing app code developed against modern software frameworks for mobile or the web is essentially this situation. To create apps that behave as expected, developers must follow complex and often implicit programming protocols imposed by the framework. So what makes static analysis of apps hard is largely what makes programming them hard: the specification of the programming protocol is unclear, and the control flow is complex, asynchronous, dynamic, and higher-order. In this talk, I present some of our efforts in developing tools and techniques for analyzing such code motivated by real-world application domains. In particular, in such situations, we have seen benefits to moving our focus beyond the global reasoning engine to apply goal-directed analysis in support of tasks like alarm triage, demand-driven refinement, and evidence generation.

Bio. Bor-Yuh Evan Chang is an Associate Professor of Computer Science at the University of Colorado Boulder and an Amazon Scholar. He is interested in tools and techniques for building, understanding, and ensuring reliable computational systems. His techniques target using novel ways of interacting with the programmer to design more precise and practical program analyses. He is a recipient of an NSF CAREER award (2010).

Formal Methods for Database Application Evolution

Isil Dillig

The University of Texas at Austin, USA

Abstract. Database applications typically undergo several schema changes during their life cycle due to performance and maintainability reasons. Such changes to the database schema not only require migrating the underlying data to a new schema but also re-implementing large chunks of the application code that query and update the database. In this talk, we describe how formal methods can simplify (and ensure the correctness of) evolving database applications. Specifically, we first describe our work on verifying equivalence between database applications that operate over different schema, such as those that arise before and after schema refactoring. Next, we describe how to use this verification procedure to solve the corresponding synthesis problem: That is, given a database application and a new schema, how can we automatically generate an equivalent program over this new schema?

Bio. Isil Dillig is an associate professor at the computer science department of the University of Texas at Austin where she leads the UToPiA research group. Her main research interests are program analysis and verification, program synthesis, and automated logical reasoning. She obtained all her degrees (BS, MS, PhD) at Stanford University. Isil is a 2015 Sloan Fellow and a recipient of an NSF CAREER award.

Automated Verification of Systems Software with Serval

Xi Wang

University of Washington, USA

Abstract. This talk will give an overview of Serval, a framework for developing automated verifiers for systems software. Serval builds on the Rosette solver-aided language to provide an extensible infrastructure for creating verifiers by lifting interpreters under symbolic evaluation, and a systematic approach to identifying and repairing verification performance bottlenecks using symbolic profiling and optimizations. Using Serval, we build automated verifiers for the RISC-V, ARM, x86, LLVM, and BPF instruction sets. We report our experience of retrofitting CertiKOS and Komodo, two systems previously verified using Coq and Dafny, respectively, for automated verification using Serval. In addition, we apply Serval to the BPF just-in-time compilers in the Linux kernel, uncovering more than 30 new bugs.

Bio. Xi Wang is an associate professor in the Paul G. Allen School of Computer Science & Engineering at the University of Washington. He received his PhD from MIT, and B.E. and M.E. from Tsinghua. His research interests are in building secure and reliable systems. He contributed to the STACK tool for finding undefined behavior bugs in C programs, the Yggdrasil toolkit for writing file systems with push-button verification, and the Serval framework for automated verification of systems software.

NSV 2020 Invited Talks

Minimum Precision Requirements of Deep Neural Networks

Naresh Shanbhag

University of Illinois at Urbana-Champaign, USA

Abstract. The accuracy, energy, and latency of deep neural network (DNN) implementation is a strong function of the precision of its weights, activations and computation. Determining the minimum precision requirements of DNNs is made difficult by the inherent complexity of such networks. Hence, much of the work in literature is ad-hoc, e.g., pruning, binarization, and others.

This talk address the problem of determining minimum precision requirements of DNNs with theoretical guarantees on its inference accuracy by seeking answers to the following two questions: 1) What are the minimum precision requirements of a dot product kernel in order to meet a specific accuracy requirement at its output? We show that the commonly used Bit-Growth Criterion (BGC) for precision assignment in digital accelerators is overly conservative and propose a Minimum Precision Criterion (MPC) that achieves the same signal-to-quantization noise ratio (SQNR) as BGC but with much lower precision; and 2) What are the minimum precision requirements of a DNN to meet a specific network accuracy? We show that the minimum precision requirements for activations and weights trade-off with each other and show that a minimum precision network obtained using our approach has lower complexity than binarized networks at iso-accuracy. Finally, we employ the above two insights to determine the precision limits of the recently proposed in-memory computing (IMC) architectures which exhibit an interplay between quantization and analog circuit noise.

Towards Numerical Assistants

Zachary Tatlock[1] and Pavel Panchekha[2]

[1]University of Washington, USA
[2]University of Utah, USA

Abstract. The last few years have seen an explosion of work on tools that address numerical error in scientific, mathematical, and engineering software. The resulting tools can provide essential guidance to expert non-experts: scientists, mathematicians, and engineers for whom mathematical computation is essential but who may have little formal training in numerical methods. It is now time for these tools to move into practice.

Practitioners need a "numerical workbench" that not only succeeds as a research artifact but as a daily tool. We describe our experience adapting Herbie, a tool for numerical error repair, from a research prototype to a reliable workhorse for daily use. In particular, we focus on how we worked to increase user trust and use internal measurement to polish the tool. Looking more broadly, we show that community development and an investment in the generality of our tools, such as through the FPBench project, will better support users and strengthen our research community.

Automatic Testing and Falsification with Dynamically Constrained Reinforcement Learning

Nikos Aréchiga

Toyota InfoTechnology Center, USA

Abstract. We consider the problem of using reinforcement learning to train adversarial agents for automatic testing and falsification of cyberphysical systems, such as autonomous vehicles, robots, and airplanes. In order to produce useful agents, however, it is useful to be able to control the degree of adversariality by specifying rules that an agent must follow. For example, when testing an autonomous vehicle, it is useful to find maximally antagonistic traffic participants that obey traffic rules. We model dynamic constraints as hierarchically ordered rules expressed in Signal Temporal Logic, and show how these can be incorporated into an agent training process. We prove that our agent-centric approach is able to find all dangerous behaviors that can be found by traditional falsification techniques while producing modular and reusable agents. We demonstrate our approach on two case studies from the automotive domain.

Contents

VSTTE 2020

SARL: OO Framework Specification for Static Analysis

Pietro Ferrara[1](✉) and Luca Negrini[1,2]

[1] Ca' Foscari University of Venice, Venice, Italy
pietro.ferrara@unive.it
[2] JuliaSoft SRL, Verona, Italy
luca.negrini@juliasoft.com

Abstract. Semantic static analysis allows sound verification of program properties, that is, to prove that a given property holds for all possible executions. However, modern object-oriented applications make heavy use of third-party *frameworks*. These provide various functionalities (like libraries), as well as an extension of the execution model of the program. Applying standard models to statically analyze software relying on such frameworks could be potentially unsound and imprecise.

In this paper we introduce SARL, a domain-specific language which allows one to specify the runtime behaviors of frameworks of object-oriented programs. Such specifications can be then applied to automatically generate annotations on program components of the application to model the framework runtime environment. In addition, SARL specifications document which aspects of a framework are supported by the static analyzer and how. We adopted SARL to model WindowsForms and ASP.NET, two of the most popular .NET frameworks in an existing industrial static analyzer (Julia). We then analyzed the three most popular GitHub repositories using these frameworks, comparing the results with and without SARL. Our experimental results show that the application of SARL sensibly improved the precision and soundness of the analysis without affecting its runtime performances.

1 Introduction

Static analysis allows one to prove properties of computer programs without executing them. Such properties vary from the absence of runtime errors to functional correctness.

Object-oriented software makes extensive use of third party libraries and frameworks, avoiding the re-implementation of common functionalities in favor of reusable and highly tested code already widely used. In object-oriented software, a library is a collection of classes, methods, etc. that implements some standard functionalities, and that can be called by the application. Instead, software frameworks represent a wider concept: *"A software framework provides a standard way to build and deploy applications. (...) Software frameworks may include support programs, compilers, code libraries, tool sets, and application*

© Springer Nature Switzerland AG 2020
M. Christakis et al. (Eds.): NSV 2020/VSTTE 2020, LNCS 12549, pp. 3–20, 2020.
https://doi.org/10.1007/978-3-030-63618-0_1

programming interfaces (APIs) which bring together all the different compo-nents to enable development of a project or system." [25]. Frameworks have been applied to various contexts. For instance, ASP.NET [9] allows a devel-oper to implement and deploy a web application, while WindowsForms [14] is designed to easily build desktop applications with modern UIs. Therefore, each framework provides a specific execution model.

Static analyzers may raise alarms on generated code or specific framework components, since these usually follow non-standard patterns that are hardly detectable by and might confuse the analyzers. Moreover, frameworks often offer ad-hoc execution models, that might rely on specific configuration files. Not being aware of these behaviors might lead to unsoundly ignoring relevant portions of the application code, or to consider too many methods as candidates for the reflective calls to preserve soundness.

Nowadays, there are dozens of software frameworks (like Spring and Lombok in Java, or ASP.NET and WindowsForms in C#), each one with its own execu-tion model, and new ones keep emerging. This represents a challenge for static analyzers, since customers expect the analysis to be up-to-date with modern technologies, while the effort of modeling even a single framework might not be negligible. Furthermore, to keep amplifying the range of supported frameworks, there is the need for a flexible mean to model new ones, as well as to improve the knowledge of the analyzer on already-known frameworks. Finally, new versions of the same framework might require different models. It is therefore essential to document which parts of a framework are supported and how to keep the models updated when new versions are released.

Contribution. In this paper we present SARL (Static Analysis Refining Lan-guage), a domain-specific language which allows one to easily instruct a static analyzer about the execution model of a framework to *improve* the results in terms of both precision and soundness. SARL targets statically type-safe, object-oriented programming languages (C# and Java in particular). These languages offer a construct which allows to add metadata to object-oriented components, describing their characteristics. We will generically refer to it as *annotation*.

SARL adopts annotations as the key mean to instruct the analyzer about both the structure and the execution model of the application under analysis. The goal of SARL is to produce a set of rules, called *framework specification*, that describes the behavior of a framework. Such description is then automatically applied to a program to produce a collection of annotations on it that the static analyzer is able to interpret and exploit during the analysis (e.g., when building the call graph of the program or approximating the heap structure).

Since we want to apply the SARL specification and extract the annotations on the target application *before* the analysis starts, framework specifications must be evaluated syntactically on the analyzed application without any semantic knowledge of the program. At this stage, no information about the dynamic types of the program's values is known, as well as the effective targets of methods calls. Hence, the content of framework specifications needs to be designed using static types and call targets.

SARL has been interfaced with Julia, an abstract interpretation based static analyzer of Java bytecode whose analyses consider a wide range of annotations. Born as a Java analyzer, Julia has been recently extended to analyze .NET (CIL) bytecode as well [13].

Therefore, we applied SARL to model two popular .NET frameworks (WindowsForms and ASP.NET), and we present, for each of these frameworks, the results of Julia analyses on the 3 most popular GitHub repositories of projects relying on these frameworks. In particular, we study how the analysis improved in terms of precision and soundness when using the SARL specification w.r.t. the original Julia analysis. The experimental results show that for programs widely relying on a framework (WindowsForms) the improvement is dramatic (SARL specification removed between 35.3% and 74.5% of false alarms), while when only a small portion of a program exploits a framework (ASP.NET) the benefit is restricted to that (between 1.6% to 4.3%). Moreover, since SARL specifications collect all framework support into a single file, a readable representation of what has been covered and how can be easily generated. Julia includes this representation as part of its own documentation[1].

The rest of the paper is structured as follows. Section 1.1 reports a first example of a SARL specification modeling ASP.NET. Section 2 discusses the related work, while Sect. 3 reports the overall architecture of the Julia static analyzer. Section 4 introduces another specification, targeting WindowsForms, and uses it to describe all the constructs of SARL, together with its complete grammar. Section 5 reports the benefits obtained when applying SARL specifications to six applications using WindowsForms and ASP.NET, while Sect. 6 concludes.

1.1   Example SARL Specification

Consider the specification for the ASP.NET [9] framework contained in Fig. 1, where namespaces have been omitted for the sake of compactness. ASP.NET is a Microsoft framework used to build web applications written in C#. It comes in various flavors, like *WebForms* and *MVC*. As most web application frameworks, applications written with ASP.NET have an execution model fairly different from the one of a standard application. In fact, a wide variety of methods are invoked from the external environment, such as page and graphical event handlers. This means that a static analyzer would not find explicit calls to these methods, considering them (as well as all other methods invoked directly or indirectly) as not reachable. Moreover, graphical objects are usually stored in fields, enabling the runtime environment to access them for initialization. Since those interactions are not part of the program, a static analyzer might suggest to replace those fields with local variables (if it is referenced in only one method), or to remove them completely (if no explicit accesses are found in the code). The specification of Fig. 1 describes both these features (as well as marking few other methods as reachable), providing metadata (as annotations supported by Julia), in a concise and self-explanatory manner: it is applied when a .NET program contains

---

[1] https://static.juliasoft.com/docs/2.7.0.3/frameworks.html.

1   **rule**: **rte** ".net"
2   **rule**: **superclass** HttpApplication
3   **predicate**: isControl = *cls* −> *subtypeOf*:: "Control"
4   **predicate**: isNestedComponent = **and**(*fld* −> *type* **satisfies** isControl, *fld* −>
     definingClass **satisfies** isControl)
5   **predicate**: isEventHandler = **and**(*mtd* −> basicReturnType:: "void", **and**(*mtd* −>
     numberOfParameters:: 2, **and**(*mtd* −> *hasParameter* **and**(*par* −> *index*:: 0, *par*
     −> *type*:: "Object"), *mtd* −> parameter **and**(*par* −> *index*:: 1, *par* −> *type*.
     subtypeOf:: "EventArgs")))))
6   **predicate**: isWebViewExecute = **and**(*mtd* −> basicReturnType:: "void", *mtd* −> *name*
     :: "Execute")
7   **predicate**: isGetAppInstance = **and**(*mtd* −> *returnType.subtypeOf*:: "HttpApplication",
     mtd −> *name*:: "get_ApplicationInstance")
8   **specification**: **annotate** *mtd* **with** EntryPoint **if and**(*mtd* −> *definingClass* **satisfies**
     isControl, **satisfies** isEventHandler)
9   **specification**: **annotate** *fld* **with** ExternallyRead, Injected **if satisfies** isNestedComponent
10 **specification**: **annotate** *mtd* **with** EntryPoint **if and**(*mtd* −> *definingClass.subtypeOf*::
     "WebPageExecutingBase", **and**(*mtd* −> *numberOfParameters*:: 0, **or**(**satisfies**
     isWebViewExecute, **satisfies** isGetAppInstance)))
11 **specification**: **annotate** *mtd* **with** EntryPoint **if and**(*mtd* −> *definingClass*::*startsWith* "
     _ASP.FastObjectFactory", **and**(*mtd* −> *name*::*startsWith* "Create_ASP_", **and**(
     mtd −> *returnType*:: "System.Object", *mtd* −> *numberOfParameters*:: 0)))

Fig. 1. ASP.NET specification

at least one *HttpApplication*, which is the base class for ASP.NET applications
(lines 1 and 2). Then, fields representing runtime-managed objects (subtypes
of the *Control* class) are identified and marked (line 9) as externally read and
written (that is, injected), while event handlers, web page creation factories, and
other standard framework methods are considered as entry point (lines 10–11).

This information is needed in order to build up a sound approximation of
the execution of ASP.NET applications. For instance, event handlers are usually not public, but they are implicitly executed by the framework. Therefore,
these methods would be considered as unreachable by a semantic static analyzer,
potentially leading to both false positives (e.g., warnings about unreachable event
handlers) and negatives (e.g., missing warnings on the code implementing of the
event handler). Instead, by annotating them as entry points, SARL instructs the
analyzer (and the call graph constructor in particular) to consider them as externally called with arbitrary values. In this way, the analysis will produce alarms
on the code directly or indirectly executed by the method (removing false negatives), and remove warnings about unreachable event handlers (removing false
positives). Similarly, ASP.NET stores objects representing UI components in
(usually private) fields that are written and read by the framework itself. Usually such fields are never written in the application, and sometimes not even
read. For instance, in the first case, a semantic static analyzer would consider
these fields as always null, potentially producing both false positives (e.g., nullness alarms when the object stored in the field is dereferenced) and negatives
(e.g., on the code of a branch of an if-then-else statement that is guarded by

a nullness check on the field, thus considered as deadcode). These imprecisions of the analysis are removed once these fields are annotated as externally written (injected), since the analyzer will consider that they might be assigned with arbitrary values.

As one can see from this brief example, SARL allows to easily specify to which programs the specification should be applied, a set of predicates (improving the readability and reusability of the specification), and a set of specification rules to annotate program components as well as libraries. This specification will later be used in Sect. 5 to refine the results of Julia on applications that use ASP.NET.

2 Related Work

Several static analyzers, like Julia and FindBugs [15] allow a developer to instruct the analysis about specific runtime behaviors of a framework through annotations. The goal of SARL is to automatically produce these annotations and apply them to the code under analysis. In this way, SARL decouples the framework specification from the program.

Specification languages such as the Java Modeling Language [17] allow to specify pre- and post-conditions and object invariants following the design-by-contract methodology. Different verification tools can then check if the program satisfies the given specification. Therefore, these languages are aimed at specifying the properties of interests that one might want to check on a program, rather than the behavior of frameworks (that is the goal of SARL).

SLIC is a specification language developed about two decades ago "designed to specify the temporal safety properties of APIs implemented in the C programming language" [10]. Similarly to SARL, SLIC was designed to specify the behavior of libraries, and in particular safety temporal requirements of the APIs. Instead, SARL is focused towards object-oriented frameworks that might both provide external libraries and modify the runtime execution model of the program, and it targets various safety and security properties of such programs.

Previous works [11,23] relied on hardcoded knowledge of specific framework features, hence building an a priori model for each framework. However, handling new frameworks required a modification of the analysis engine, expanding both the size and complexity of the product and requiring a developer with expertise both in the framework itself and on static analysis. Moreover, this solution did not provide a fast and reliable way for supporting new software frameworks, and it did not document which features of a specific framework are taken into account by the analysis and how.

More recent works exploited a framework's configuration files. These files often restrict the possible executions, allowing to (almost always) precisely resolve the targets of reflective calls in the framework. F4F [22] aimed at building an application-specific model of the framework's behavior automatically, and this can be used by the analysis to react accordingly to modifications of the execution model made by the framework itself. However, building a model generator for each framework does not keep the actual pace of releases of new frameworks, and each analysis needs to be modified to be model-aware during its execution. Concerto [16] combined mostly-concrete interpretations of the framework code and abstract interpretation of application code, providing sound and accurate analysis on the overall program. Both of the above approaches targeted frameworks whose behavior depends on some application-specific configuration files, and that is not the case for any framework. Moreover, the code from the framework itself needs to be submitted to the analysis, and this will eventually slow down the analyzer due to the significantly larger amount of code to analyze. Also notice that, if the format of the configuration file changes among different versions of the same framework, a new parser for such a file must be built, and the logic of the newly introduced constructs must be embedded into the analyzer.

StubDroid [8] built up data flow summaries of Android libraries for taint analyzers. If on the one hand such approach is completely automatic, on the other hand it is specific for taint analysis and it required an ad-hoc static analysis in order to infer the data flow summaries. While SARL framework specifications might be automatically inferred with static and dynamic analyses, this is not the focus of this paper and is left as future work. Averroes [7] introduced a new approach that, starting from the code of application and libraries, built up a placeholder library that soundly approximates the library behaviors. The construction of the placeholder library relied on the separate compilation assumption, and it handles reflection. Such an approach sensibly improved the efficiency of the analysis without affecting its precision and soundness. However, more recent frameworks rely on ad-hoc runtime environments that extends the execution model of the programming languages. These runtime environments are outside the code of the library, and therefore they cannot be handled with this approach.

3 Julia

Julia's analyses are interprocedural (that is, they consider the flow of control and information from callers to callees and vice-versa) and abstract the heap (that is, they consider the flow of data through heap writes and reads). This is essential to perform semantic static analyses, such as information flow or sound nullness analysis.

In Julia, the model of the program under analysis is built by a so-called class analysis, that infers the possible runtime dynamic types of the variables and stack elements. Julia uses the one defined in [19], which has been shown to be a reasonable trade-off between precision and cost. The construction of such model of the program is called *extraction* in Julia, since methods are extracted and then analyzed only if they are actually called in the program. The extraction starts from a set of entry points, that, by default, are all the public methods of the analyzed application. However, as an input of the analysis the user can specify other entry point modes, and in particular (i) only standard entry point methods (e.g., *main* and servlet methods), (ii) only explicit entries (that is, methods annotated as *@EntryPoint*), or (iii) all public and protected methods.

For the sake of simplicity, in the rest of the paper we consider only the default mode. Julia includes various static analyses (e.g., sound nullness analysis [20], taint analysis [12] and data-size analysis [21]).

Being born as a Java analyzer, Julia acquired knowledge on widespread Java frameworks during the years. However, frameworks behaviors have been hardcoded throughout various analysis components, making it hard to understand and document which aspects of each framework has been covered and how. Instead, Julia has no hardcoded model for C# frameworks. Thus, our initial effort targets this area.

Annotations. As of version 2.7.0.3, Julia defines more than 70 annotations with various meanings[2]. Some of them are used to provide context about how the application interacts with the external environment (e.g., *@EntryPoint* states that a method could be called from outside the program, while *@Injected* states that a field or a parameter could be written by an external source), while the majority of them are used to provide information to a specific checker (e.g., *@SqlTrusted* is used to instruct the Injection checker that untrusted data should not flow into that location since it will end up in a database, while *@NonNull* states that a field or a method's return value are never *null*). Finally, *@SuppressJuliaWarnings* instructs Julia that a certain kind of warning should not be reported on the annotated component (either a field, method, constructor, class, method parameter, or local variable).

Each annotation has a different scope, and thus, a different impact on the analysis: *@EntryPoint* will be exploited during the construction of the call graph, but its effect will be propagated throughout the whole analysis (i.e., additional reachable code will be considered); *@SqlTrusted* instead will only be used during the execution of the taint analysis based checkers (the Injection checker is the most popular, but other ones exist). Thus, a *framework specification* could be logically split into sections, each one having effects on a different set of checkers.

4   The SARL Language

The goal of SARL is to allow a user to specify a set of rules (called *framework specification*) representing how the framework affects the runtime behavior of a program. Such specification will then be exploited by a static analyzer to improve its precision and soundness. In particular, we rely on annotations to pass this information. Therefore, these should be expressive enough to represent these runtime behaviors. Throughout this paper, we need annotations to specify: (i) when a method might be called by the framework runtime (*@EntryPoint* in Julia), (ii) when a field is read or written by the framework runtime (*@ExternallyRead* and *@Injected* in Julia), (iii) when the warnings on a specific component (e.g., method or field) should be suppressed (*@SuppressJuliaWarnings* in Julia, *@SuppressWarnings* in Java), and (iv) properties related to specific analyses (e.g., *@AutoClosedResource* of the CloseResource analysis in Julia).

---

[2] The documentation of the available annotations is available at https://static.juliasoft.com/docs/2.7.0.3/annotations.html.

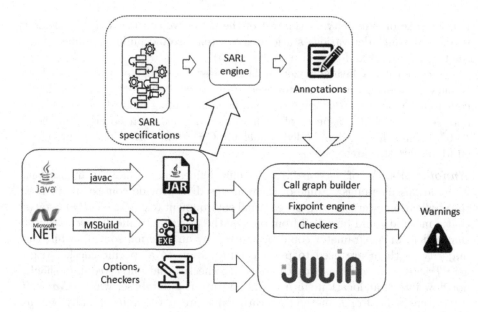

Fig. 2. Schema of Julia's architecture with SARL

Building a *framework specification* can be achieved with two different approaches. One can acquire knowledge about the framework itself, understanding its model of execution and how it interacts with the application code. Then, the acquired knowledge needs to be converted into a SARL specification, by understanding how each framework feature may impact the various analysis modules. While this approach ensures that every peculiarity of the framework has been taken into account, the number and heterogeneity of software frameworks makes it hard to achieve, since one should possess knowledge on both the analyzer *and* the framework. Another approach consists into iteratively analyzing software that rely on the target framework, inspecting the analysis results searching for evidence of the lack of framework knowledge by the analyzer (e.g., unreachable methods that are instead invoked by the framework, no injection-related warning on a web application, . . .) and fixing them in the specification. This approach is highly dependent on how representative the software is in exploiting the framework's functionalities, but can nevertheless be a good starting point. Both SARL instances presented in this paper have been built following the latter approach.

Figure 2 depicts the overall architecture of our approach, and how this interfaces with the Julia static analyzer. Given a framework specification and an application to be analyzed, the SARL engine (represented inside the dotted rectangle) produces a set of annotations. These are then serialized to an XML file and passed together with all the other inputs of the analysis (analyzed code, analysis options and checkers to run) to the analyzer. Further developments will bring the SARL engine inside the analyzer itself, making the identification of frameworks and the generation of extra annotations a fixed step of the analysis lifecycle.

1   **rule: rte** ".net"
2   **rule: superclass** Form
3   **predicate:** isComponent = *cls* −> *subtypeOf*:: "IComponent"
4   **predicate:** isDisposable = *fld* −> *type.subtypeOf*:: "IDisposable"
5   **predicate:** isNestedComponent = **and**(*fld* −> *type* **satisfies** isComponent, *fld* −>
     definingClass **satisfies** isComponent)
6   **predicate:** isGeneratedFormField = **and**(*fld* −> *definingClass.subtypeOf*:: "
     ContainerControl", **and**(*fld* −> hasAccessor:: "private", **and**(*fld* −> name:: "
     components", *fld* −> *type.subtypeOf*:: "IContainer")))
7   **specification: annotate** *fld* **with** ExternallyRead, Injected **if satisfies** isNestedComponent
8   **specification: annotate** *fld* **with** AutoClosedResource **if or**(*fld* −> *type.subtypeOf*:: "
     ContainerControl", **and**(**satisfies** isDisposable, *fld* −> *definingClass* **satisfies**
     isComponent))
9   **specification: annotate** *fld* **with** NonNull, ExternallyRead, Injected **if satisfies** "
     isGeneratedFormField";
10 **library: annotate** *mtd* **with** ResourceThatDoesNotNeedToBeClosed **if** *cls* Brushes *mtd*
     matches "get_.*()LSystem/Drawing/Brush;"
11 **library: annotate** *mtd* **with** ResourceThatDoesNotNeedToBeClosed **if** *cls* Pens *mtd*
     matches "get_.*()LSystem/Drawing/Pen;"
12 **library: annotate** *mtd* **with** ResourceThatDoesNotNeedToBeClosed **if** *cls* Process *mtd* "
     GetCurrentProcess()LSystem/Diagnostics/Process;"

Fig. 3. WindowsForms specification

Running Example: Windows Forms. Before discussing SARL formally, we introduce another SARL specification targeting WindowsForms [14], a framework to build GUIs of C# desktop applications. Usually, these are developed through the designer included in Visual Studio, which places a pointer to each graphical component in private fields initialized by the generated code, causing the analyzer to raise a high number of warnings about field usage (stating that a field can be replaced by a local variable, or that the value written inside a field is never read later). Moreover, each graphical component in WindowsForms implements the *IDisposable* interface (which represents objects that should be disposed when no longer needed, since they could hold handles to non-managed resources that needs to be manually released) and it is disposed by the framework runtime. Figure 3 reports the specification of WindowsForms (as in Sect. 1.1, namespaces have been omitted for compactness), that will be used to explain SARL constructs.

Language Definition. SARL is built over five basic components: *rules, implications, specifications, predicates*, and *library specifications*. Rules embed information to detect if a given application relies on the framework. The specification is applied if and only if the condition specified in the rules holds. Core components (implications, specifications and predicates) allow one to define the conditions required to apply an annotation to a program member. Finally, library specifications allow to generate annotations also on non-application classes (that is, classes that come from a supporting library or the system runtime).

General structure

⟨SARL⟩ ::= ⟨RULES⟩
          ((⟨IMPL⟩
          | ⟨PREDICATE⟩
          | ⟨SPEC⟩
          | ⟨LIB⟩))*
⟨RULES⟩ ::= (*rule:* (⟨RULE_RTE⟩ |
                      ⟨RULE_CODE⟩))*
⟨RULE_RTE⟩ ::= ⟨R_RTE⟩
⟨RULE_CODE⟩ ::= ⟨R_ANN⟩
              | ⟨R_SUPER⟩
              | ⟨R_TYPE⟩
⟨IMPL⟩ ::= *implication:* ⟨ANN⟩
          implies ⟨ANN⟩ (,⟨ANN⟩)*
⟨PREDICATE⟩ ::= *predicate:* ⟨ID⟩ = ⟨C_CHAIN⟩
⟨SPEC⟩ ::= *specification:* annotate ⟨T⟩ *with* ⟨ANN⟩
          (, ⟨ANN⟩)* *if* ⟨C_CHAIN⟩
⟨LIB⟩ ::= *library:* annotate ⟨T⟩
          with ⟨ANN⟩ (,⟨ANN⟩)*
          if ⟨SIG⟩

Rules

⟨R_RTE⟩ ::= *rte* ((⟨R_OP⟩)? ⟨STRING⟩)
⟨R_ANN⟩ ::= *annotation* ((⟨R_OP⟩)? ⟨QNAME⟩
⟨R_SUPER⟩ ::= *superclass* ((⟨R_OP⟩)? ⟨QNAME⟩
⟨R_TYPE⟩ ::= *uses type* ((⟨R_OP⟩)? ⟨QNAME⟩

Conditions

⟨C_CHAIN⟩ ::= ⟨NT_TYPE⟩ ->
              ⟨NT_OP⟩(⟨OPT⟩)?.⟨NT_COND⟩
            | ⟨T_TYPE⟩ -> ⟨T_OP⟩ ⟨VALUE⟩ | ⟨L_COND⟩
⟨L_COND⟩ ::= | *satisfies* ⟨ID⟩ | *not*(⟨C_CHAIN⟩)
            | *and*(⟨C_CHAIN⟩,⟨C_CHAIN⟩)
            | *or*(⟨C_CHAIN⟩,⟨C_CHAIN⟩)

⟨NT_COND⟩ ::= ⟨NT_OP⟩ . ⟨NT_COND⟩
            | ⟨NT_OP⟩⟨OPT⟩ ::⟨T_COND⟩
            | (⟨NT_OP⟩)? ::⟨T_COND⟩
            | ⟨NT_OP⟩⟨L_COND⟩
⟨T_COND⟩ ::= (⟨T_OP⟩)? ⟨VALUE⟩
⟨OPT⟩ ::= /⟨ID⟩ /

Targets

⟨T⟩ ::= *cls* | *fld* | *mtd* | *par*
⟨SIG⟩ ::= *cls* ⟨QNAME⟩ (*fld* ⟨T_OP⟩ ⟨STRING⟩
        | *mtd* ⟨T_OP⟩ ⟨STRING⟩
        | (*par* ⟨NUMBER⟩)?)?

Types

⟨NT_TYPE⟩ ::= *cls* | *ann* | *var* | *mtd* | *fld*
⟨T_TYPE⟩ ::= *str* | *int*

Operators

⟨R_OP⟩ ::= *equals* | *startsWith* | *endsWith* | *contains*
⟨T_OP⟩ ::= *equals* | *startsWith* | *endsWith*
         | *contains* | *matches*
⟨NT_OP⟩ ::= *definingMethod* | *name* | *index* | *type*
          | *basicType* | *hasAnnotation*
          | *definingClass* | *returnType*
          | *basicReturnType* | *hasVariable*
          | *hasAccessor* | *hasOptionValue*
          | *hasParameter* | *subtypeOf*
          | *containsMethod* | *containsField*
          | *numberOfParameters*

Program members identifiers

⟨ANN⟩ ::= ⟨QNAME⟩ ((⟨MEMBER⟩
        (, ⟨MEMBER⟩)*))?
⟨MEMBER⟩ ::= ⟨ID⟩ = ⟨STRING⟩
⟨QNAME⟩ ::= ⟨ID⟩ (. ⟨ID⟩)*
⟨ID⟩ ::= [a-zA-Z] | [_a-zA-Z]([_a-zA-Z0-9])*

Values

⟨VALUE⟩ ::= ⟨STRING⟩ | ⟨NUMBER⟩
⟨STRING⟩ ::= " .* "
⟨NUMBER⟩ ::= 0 | [1-9]([0-9])*

Fig. 4. SARL's grammar

Figure 4 defines the complete syntax of SARL, while Fig. 5 formalizes the semantics of the various components. During the formalization, we consider a program p as a set of classes; each class is a tuple (n, A, F, C) where n is the name of the class, while A, M and F are the set of annotations, fields and methods of the class, respectively. An annotation is a tuple $(n, \wp(n \times str))$, with n being a full qualified name and $\wp(n \times str)$ being the set of members, represented as a pair of name and string value. A field is a tuple $(n, t, A, \wp(str))$, where n is the name, t is the type, A is the set of annotations, and $\wp(str)$ is the set of accessors. A method is a tuple $(n, t, A, \wp(str), P, V)$, where n is the name, t is the return type, A is the set of annotations, $\wp(str)$ is the set of accessors, P is the set of parameters, and V is the set of local variables. A parameter is a tuple (n, t, A, i), with n being the name, t being the type, A being the set of annotations, and i being the index of the parameter. A variable instead is a pair (n, t) with n being the name and t being the type. Each element of the formalization could be subscripted with a letter stating if it refers to a class c, a field f, a method m, or a parameter p.

The semantics, that will be discussed in the rest of this section, relies on a set of standard operators over the different object-oriented program components. For the sake of simplicity, from now on we denote with ⟨XS⟩ sequences or sets of ⟨X⟩ components.

Rules. A rule ⟨RULE⟩ defines a condition to be satisfied to apply a specification. Rules express conditions on either the analysis ⟨RULES_RTE⟩, or the code ⟨RULES_CODE⟩. Rules semantics is defined in the first five definitions of

$$hold(((\langle RULES\_RTE\rangle, \langle RULES\_CODE\rangle), p) \Leftrightarrow \begin{cases} \langle RULES\_RTE\rangle = \emptyset \vee \exists r \in \langle RULES\_RTE\rangle : hold(r, p) \\ \wedge \\ \langle RULES\_CODE\rangle = \emptyset \vee \exists r \in \langle RULES\_CODE\rangle : hold(r, p) \end{cases}$$

$$hold(\langle R\_RTE\rangle, p) \Leftrightarrow holdString(extractRTE(p) \; \langle R\_OP\rangle \; \langle STRING\rangle))$$
$$hold(\langle R\_ANN\rangle, p) \Leftrightarrow \exists n \in extractAnn(p) : holdString(n \; \langle R\_OP\rangle \; \langle QNAME\rangle))$$
$$hold(\langle R\_SUPER\rangle, p) \Leftrightarrow \exists n \in p : n' \in extOrImpl(n) : holdString(n' \; \langle R\_OP\rangle \; \langle QNAME\rangle))$$
$$hold(\langle R\_TYPE\rangle, p) \Leftrightarrow \exists n \in extractType(p) : holdString(n \; \langle R\_OP\rangle \; \langle QNAME\rangle))$$

$$impl(\langle IMPL\rangle, p) = \bigcup_{(n_c, A_c, F, M) \in p} \left\{ \begin{array}{l} (n_c, A_c \cup ann(A_c, \langle IMPL\rangle), F', M') : \\ F' = \bigcup_{f \in F} (n_f, t_f, A_f \cup ann(A_f, \langle IMPL\rangle), C_f), \\ M' = \bigcup_{m \in M} \left\{ \begin{array}{l} (n_m, t_m, A_m \cup ann(A_m, \langle IMPL\rangle), C_m, P'_m, V_m) : \\ P'_m = \bigcup_{p \in P_m} (n_p, i_p, A_p \cup ann(A_p, \langle IMPL\rangle), i_p) \} \end{array} \right\} \end{array} \right\}$$

$$ann(A, \langle ANN\rangle \; implies \; \langle ANNS\rangle) = A \cup \begin{cases} \emptyset & if \; \langle ANN\rangle \notin A \\ \langle ANNS\rangle & if \; \langle ANN\rangle \in A \end{cases}$$

$$lib(\langle LIB\rangle, p) = \bigcup_{(n_c, A_c, F, M) \in p} \left\{ \begin{array}{l} (n_c, A_c \cup addLA(\langle LIB\rangle, n_c), F', M') : \\ F' = \bigcup_{f \in F} (n_f, t_f, A_f \cup addLA(\langle LIB\rangle, f), C_f), \\ M' = \bigcup_{m \in M} \left\{ \begin{array}{l} (n_m, t_m, A_m \cup addLA(\langle LIB\rangle, m), C_m, P'_m, V_m) : \\ P'_m = \bigcup_{p \in P_m} (n_p, t_p, A_p \cup addLA(\langle LIB\rangle, p), i_p) \} \end{array} \right\} \end{array} \right\}$$

$$addLA(\langle LIB\rangle, s) = \begin{cases} \langle ANNS\rangle & if \; typeOf(s) = \langle T\rangle \wedge checkSignature(s, \langle SIG\rangle) \\ \emptyset & otherwise \end{cases}$$

$$spec(\langle SPEC\rangle, p) = \bigcup_{(n_c, A_c, F, M) \in p} \left\{ \begin{array}{l} (n_c, A_c \cup cond(\langle SPEC\rangle, (n_c, A_c, F, M)), F', M') : \\ F' = \bigcup_{f \in F} (n_f, t_f, A_f \cup cond(\langle SPEC\rangle, f), C_f), \\ M' = \bigcup_{m \in M} \left\{ \begin{array}{l} (n_m, t_m, A_m \cup cond(\langle SPEC\rangle, m), C_m, P'_m, V_m) : \\ P'_m = \bigcup_{p \in P_m} (n_p, t_p, A_p \cup cond(\langle SPEC\rangle, p), i_p) \} \end{array} \right\} \end{array} \right\}$$

$$cond(\langle SPEC\rangle, s) = \begin{cases} \langle ANNS\rangle & if \; typeOf(s) = \langle T\rangle \wedge chain(s, \langle C\_CHAIN\rangle) \\ \emptyset & otherwise \end{cases}$$

Fig. 5. Semantics of **SARL** statements, where $< i >_k$ represents element i of k (e.g.., n_m represents the name of method $m \in M$)

Fig. 5. Analysis rule $\langle R\_RTE\rangle$ defines the runtime environment (e.g., .NET or Java) of the framework. Instead, code rules define what should be found inside the application to apply a specification, in particular identifying some specific types (either as supertype - $\langle R\_SUPER\rangle$, or as type in a member signature - $\langle R\_TYPE\rangle$), or annotations from the library ($\langle R\_ANN\rangle$).

Example. The first two lines of the specification of WindowsForms in Fig. 3 define the $\langle RULES\rangle$. In particular, this specifies to apply the framework to applications whose (i) runtime environment is set to *.net* (line 1), and (ii) at least one class inherits from (or implements) *Form* class (line 2).

Implications. $\langle IMPL\rangle$ specifies that a given annotation $\langle ANN\rangle$ implies a set of other annotations. Then, if a program member is annotated with the first annotation, it is automatically annotated with all the other annotations (definitions of *impl* and *ann* in Fig. 5). This can be useful in situations where the developers have used annotations from the libraries to get some functionalities in their code, and these annotations semantically imply some other annotations supported by the analyzer, or when a framework searches a program member through reflection by searching all annotated members. For example, if a Java method is annotated with JAX-RS's *javax.ws.rs.GET* annotation, it will eventually be called from the external environment to handle an HTTP GET request. Hence, such method has to be considered an entry point of the analysis. Thus, relatively to Julia, an implication between *@GET* and *@EntryPoint* is needed.

Predicates. ⟨PREDICATE⟩ lets one assign an arbitrary name ⟨ID⟩ to a condition ⟨C_CHAIN⟩ (later defined in this Section), in order to avoid rewriting it multiple times. For example, one might define predicate *isGetter* whose condition identifies a getter method. Once such predicate is defined, its name can be used in any other condition instead of rewriting the actual condition.

Example. For instance, line 5 of the WindowsForms specification in Fig. 3 defines the *isNestedComponent* predicate. This holds if and only if the type of the given field satisfies predicate *isComponent* (that is, it is a subtype of *IComponent* as defined at line 3), and the class defining the field satisfies *isComponent* as well (that is, it is a subtype of *IComponent*).

Specifications. This is the core component of SARL. A specification lets one specify a condition on a program member that, when satisfied, causes a set of annotations to be generated on that program member. Thus, all such members have to be iterated when evaluating a specification. This construct enables one to identify members depending on their structure, as well as the one of their related members. This goes beyond the simple reflective access (e.g., the one offered by library specifications described below), allowing one to identify members in a very precise manner. ⟨SPEC⟩ consists of the type ⟨T⟩ of program member we want to annotate, one or more annotations ⟨ANN⟩, and a condition ⟨C_CHAIN⟩ that states when these have to be applied (definition of *spec* in Fig. 5, where *typeOf* returns the type - class, field, method, or parameter - of a program component). For example, when analyzing a Unity [24] application, each *Start* method of classes that extends *UnityEngine.MonoBehaviour* should be considered as an entry point for the analysis, since such method will be called by the Unity engine to perform the setup of the component. This can be achieved using a specification that has *mtd* as target, contains *@EntryPoint* as annotation, and as condition the *and* of the two aforementioned conditions (method's name and parent class).

Example. For instance, line 9 of WindowsForms specification (Fig. 3) specifies to annotates all fields satisfying *isNestedComponent* field with *@ExternallyRead* and *@Injected*.

Conditions. ⟨C_CHAIN⟩ may be (i) the application of a predicate (via its name), (ii) a logical operator (*and, or, not*) applied to other conditions, (iii) a non-terminal operator followed by a further condition, or (iv) a terminal operator followed by a constant value where *str* and *int* represent strings and integers, respectively. Conditions are grouped in chains, where operators are applied to navigate among the properties of program members (e.g., starting from a class, one could navigate to a parameter of one of its supertype's methods). The ability to navigate through program members enables the definition of syntactic conditions that corresponds to how a framework might search for a program member to interact, both by searching instances of particular types or by retrieving members annotated with a given framework annotation. The formalization of the check of these conditions is represented by function *chain* in Fig. 5 and left implicit for the sake of simplicity (mostly standard checks of standard OO properties). Notice that, if one omits an operator, the default one will be applied, depending on the program member that is currently under evaluation.

Library Specifications. In object-oriented software, most of the code is contained in libraries providing standard features to the application. However, libraries contain code which could need SARL generated annotations, since their methods or fields could require additional knowledge. However, library code is usually much bigger than the application code, and iterating over it would lead to a huge overhead. In this context, SARL does not provide complex conditions, but it simply allows one to check the signature of a program member and annotate it. Therefore, $\langle$LIB$\rangle$ consists of the type $\langle$T$\rangle$ of program member we want to annotate, one or more annotations $\langle$ANN$\rangle$, together with the signature $\langle$SIG$\rangle$ of the target program member. When applied, this leads to adding the given annotations to all the program members whose signature fulfills the specified signature (definition *lib* in Fig. 5, where *checkSignature* checks if two signatures represent the same element, and *typeOf* returns the type - class, field, method, or parameter - of a program component). Notice that, even if this component was specifically designed to operate on library code, it can be used also to annotate application code, avoiding the iteration on all program members by loading them through reflective calls.

Example. Line 10 of WindowsForms specification (Fig. 3) specifies to annotate with *@ResourceThatDoesNotNeedToBeClosed* all the getter methods of class *Brushes* that return a *Brush* instance, since these are system-wide objects handled by the runtime, and therefore should not be manually closed by the program.

SARL Application. Figure 6 reports the algorithm for applying a SARL specification to a program. In particular, given a specification $\langle$SARL$\rangle$, and a program composed of an application a and a library l (both represented as set of classes), it applies the specification if and only if the rules set $\langle$RULES$\rangle$ is satisfied on the application a (line 4). If this is the case, it then sequentially applies all the specifications $\langle$SPEC$\rangle$ (lines 5–6), libraries $\langle$LIB$\rangle$ (lines 7–9), and implications $\langle$IMPL$\rangle$ (lines 10–12) contained in the SARL specification $\langle$SARL$\rangle$. Note that, while specifications $\langle$SPEC$\rangle$ are applied only to the application, library specifications $\langle$LIB$\rangle$ and implications $\langle$IMPL$\rangle$ are applied to both the application and the library part of the program. In this way, SARL allows adding information about the libraries of the framework, and not only to model the effects of the framework runtime model on the application.

```
1: function APPLYSARL((a, l), ⟨SARL⟩)
2:     rte ← ⟨RULES_RTE⟩ ∈ ⟨RULES⟩ ∈ ⟨SARL⟩
3:     code ← ⟨RULES_CODE⟩ ∈ ⟨RULES⟩ ∈ ⟨SARL⟩
4:     if hold((rte, code), a) then
5:         for ⟨SPEC⟩ ∈ ⟨SARL⟩ do
6:             a ← spec(⟨SPEC⟩, a)
7:         for ⟨LIB⟩ ∈ ⟨SARL⟩ do
8:             a ← lib(⟨LIB⟩, a)
9:             l ← lib(⟨LIB⟩, l)
10:        for ⟨IMPL⟩ ∈ ⟨SARL⟩ do
11:            a ← impl(⟨IMPL⟩, a)
12:            l ← impl(⟨IMPL⟩, l)
13:     return (a, l)
```

Fig. 6. Application of a SARL specification to a program

Table 1. Analyzed applications

Framework	Application	Version	Stars	Rank	LOCs	Time with	Time without
WindowsForms	Shadowsocks [4]	4.1.6	49768	1	12788	2'23"	2'14"
WindowsForms	ShareX [5]	12.4.1	13045	11	99191	5'24"	5'24"
WindowsForms	CefSharp [3]	73.1.130	7109	36	17863	2'01"	1'59"
ASP.NET	SignalR [2]	2.4.1	8067	18	49182	4'24"	4'36"
ASP.NET	AspnetBoilerplate [1]	4.5.0	8476	23	87288	6'15"	6'08"
ASP.NET	Umbraco [6]	8.0.2	2995	139	130384	11'09"	11'03"

5 Experimental Results

SARL has been interfaced with the Julia static analyzer, version 2.7.0.3, as specified in Fig. 2. The SARL specification parser relies on JavaCC[3], while the semantics has been natively implemented in Java and passed to Julia through external (i.e., specified in an XML file rather than the application code) annotations.

In this Section, we analyze, for both WindowsForms and ASP.NET, the 3 most popular applications publicly available in GitHub that rely on these frameworks. We adopt as a metric of the popularity of a repository its number of stars. For each application we took the last stable release in the repository. All the statistics refer to the status of GitHub on June 28th, 2020. Each application has been analyzed with and without the framework specification. We report as lines of code (LOC) the number of physical lines of code reported by Locmetrics on the C# source files (with *cs* file extension) of the different applications in GitHub. Therefore, we consider only the code of the application, and not the libraries.

For each application, we compared the results of the analyses with and without SARL, investigating the number of warnings added or removed by the latter

---

[3] https://javacc.org/.

Table 2. Difference in warnings on WindowsForms analyses

	Shadow.	ShareX	CefSharp
Warn. w/o spec.	730	5471	465
Common (%)	473 (64.8%)	1397 (25.5%)	241 (51.8%)
Added (%)	0 (0%)	6 (0.1%)	0 (0%)
Removed (%)	257 (35.2%)	4074 (74.5%)	224 (48.2%)

Table 3. Warnings removed on WindowsForms applications

Warning	SS		SX		CS	
	A	R	A	R	A	R
ResourceNotClosedAtEndOfMethod	0	8	0	98	0	32
CloseableNotStoredIntoLocal	0	202	0	2802	0	124
FieldShouldBeReplacedByLocals	0	32	0	958	0	50
FieldIsOnlyUsedInConstructors	0	0	0	1	0	0
UselessAssignmentToDefaultValue	0	7	0	83	0	6
TestIsPredetermined	0	4	0	66	0	6
UnreachableInstruction	0	4	0	66	0	6
SetStaticInNonStaticWarning	0	0	6	0	0	0

analysis. Each of such warnings has been manually investigated to ensure that no true positives were lost with our approach, and that new warnings can be accounted on the introduction of new entry points causing the analysis of previously unreachable code.

Table 1 reports the applications we selected, where column **Framework** reports the framework it uses, **Application** the name of the analyzed application, **Version** the analyzed version (taken from GitHub, thus directly associated with a commit that can be used for reproducibility), **Stars** the number of stars of the repository, **Rank** the rank of the repository among the C# ones, **Time with** and **Time without** the analysis time with and without the application of the framework specification (considering also the time needed for applying the specification to the application), respectively. All the analyses were executed on a r5.xlarge Amazon Web Service machine. These instances feature a Xeon Platinum 8000 series (Skylake-SP) processor with a sustained all core Turbo CPU clock speed of up to 3.1 GHz and 32 GB of RAM.

5.1 WindowsForms

Table 2 reports, for each application, the number of warnings with Basic checkers without the SARL specification, and the number of common, added and removed warnings when applying the specifications presented in Fig. 3 of Sect. 4. The result highlight that even small specifications can have a major impact on the

Table 4. Difference in warnings on ASP.NET analyses

	SignalR	ANB	Umbraco
Warn. w/o spec.	681	552	1729
Common (%)	658 (96.6%)	544 (98.6%)	1658 (95.9%)
Added (%)	1 (0.1%)	0 (0%)	0 (0%)
Removed (%)	23 (3.4%)	8 (1.4%)	71 (4.1%)

results of the analyses, removing a huge portion of false alarms issued due to the lack of knowledge by the analyzer. We will focus on the removed warnings only, since the 6 ones added in ShareX analysis are all real alarms which reside in methods that were previously considered dead code (thus not analyzed).

Table 3 reports the warnings removed (columns **R**) and added (**A**) when applying the WindowsForms specification to Shadowsocks (column **SS**), ShareX (**SX**) and CefSharp (**CS**), grouped by warning type. The specification targeted mostly disposable graphical objects stored into fields. The majority of the warnings (4403 out of 4556, that is, 96%) refers to these components, and we focus the following discussion on them.

5.2   ASP.NET

Table 4 reports, for each analyzed application, the number of warnings with a standard analysis (without the SARL specification) executing Basic checkers all together, and the number of common, added and removed warnings when performing the same analyses with the specifications presented in Fig. 1 of Sect. 1.1 (**ANB** is a shortcut for AspnetBoilerplate). It is noticeable that the results on ASP.NET applications are less pervasive that the ones on desktop applications: this is due to the nature of those projects which are rather libraries (SignalR and AspnetBoilerplate) or content providers (Umbraco), and they contain very few Web pages based on ASP.NET.

Table 5 reports the warnings removed (**R**) and added (**A**) when applying the ASP.NET specification to SignalR (**SR**), AspnetBoilerplate (**AB**) and Umbraco (**UM**) grouped by warning type. As for WindowsForms results, we will not discuss the added warnings since they are true alarms on methods that were previously considered dead code.

6   Conclusion

In this paper, we introduced SARL, a domain specific language which allows one to specify the execution model of a framework. Such information is used to instruct a static analyzer about the model of execution of a framework. This approach enables the support of new frameworks through a readable and documentable model without modifying the code of the analysis engine, since it

Table 5. Warnings removed on ASP.NET applications

Warning	SR		AB		UM	
	A	R	A	R	A	R
FieldNeverUsed	0	6	0	0	0	1
FieldReadWritten	0	0	2	0	0	0
Uncalled	0	17	0	10	0	70
PossibleInsecureCookieCreation	1	0	0	0	0	0

is applied to the analyzed application producing annotations that agnostically instruct the analyzer about the runtime environment. Furthermore, we applied this approach to six real-world applications dealing with two different frameworks, studying how the number of false alarms was reduced thanks to their respective specifications. Experimental result show that, even with extremely concise SARL specifications, all false alarms previously issued due to the lack of knowledge on these frameworks by the Julia static analyzer were successfully removed. The percentage of false alarms removed by SARL specifications highly varies depending on how much code relies on the frameworks (that is, from a minimum of 1.6% on AspnetBoilerplate to a maximum of 74.5% of ShareX).

Currently, we are working on the application of SARL to other frameworks, and in particular to Java Lombok [18], .NET Xamarin [26] and Unity [24].

References

1. Asp.net boilerplate. https://github.com/aspnetboilerplate/aspnetboilerplate
2. Asp.net signalr. https://github.com/SignalR/SignalR
3. Cefsharp. https://github.com/cefsharp/CefSharp
4. Shadowsocks for windows. https://github.com/shadowsocks/shadowsocks-windows
5. Sharex. https://github.com/ShareX/ShareX
6. Umbraco CMS. https://github.com/umbraco/Umbraco-CMS
7. Ali, K., Lhoták, O.: AVERROES: whole-program analysis without the whole program. In: Castagna, G. (ed.) ECOOP 2013. LNCS, vol. 7920, pp. 378–400. Springer, Heidelberg (2013). https://doi.org/10.1007/978-3-642-39038-8_16
8. Arzt, S., Bodden, E.: Stubdroid: automatic inference of precise data-flow summaries for the android framework. In: Proceedings of ICSE 2016. IEEE (2016)
9. ASP.NET (2018). https://www.asp.net/
10. Ball, T., Rajamani, S.: Slic: a specification language for interface checking (of c). Technical report. MSR-TR-2001-21, January 2002
11. Centonze, P., Naumovich, G., Fink, S.J., Pistoia, M.: Role-based access control consistency validation. In: ISSTA (2006)
12. Ernst, M.D., Lovato, A., Macedonio, D., Spiridon, C., Spoto, F.: Boolean formulas for the static identification of injection attacks in Java. In: Davis, M., Fehnker, A., McIver, A., Voronkov, A. (eds.) LPAR 2015. LNCS, vol. 9450, pp. 130–145. Springer, Heidelberg (2015). https://doi.org/10.1007/978-3-662-48899-7_10

13. Ferrara, P., Cortesi, A., Spoto, F.: Cil to Java-bytecode translation for static analysis leveraging. In: Proceedings of FormaliSE 2018. Springer (2018)
14. Forms, W.: (2018). https://docs.microsoft.com/it-it/dotnet/framework/winforms/
15. Hovemeyer, D., Pugh, W.: Finding bugs is easy. SIGPLAN Not. **39**, 12 (2004)
16. Toman, J., Grossman, D.: Concerto: a framework for combined concrete and abstract interpretation. In: Proceedings of the ACM on Programming Languages, vol. 3 (2019)
17. Leavens, G.T., Baker, A.L., Ruby, C.: JML: a Java modeling language. In: Formal Underpinnings of Java Workshop 1998 (1998)
18. Lombok (2018). https://projectlombok.org/
19. Palsberg, J., Schwartzbach, M.I.: Object-oriented type inference. In: Proceedings of OOPSLA 1991. ACM Press (1991)
20. Spoto, F.: Nullness analysis in Boolean form. In: Proceedings of SEFM 2008. IEEE (2008)
21. Spoto, F., Mesnard, F., Payet, E.: A termination analyzer for java bytecode based on path-length. ACM Trans. Program. Lang. Syst. (TOPLAS) **32**(3), 1–70 (2010)
22. Sridharan, M., Artzi, S., Pistoia, M., Guarnieri, S., Tripp, O., Berg, R.: F4f: taint analysis of framework-based web applications. In: Proceedings of the 2011 ACM International conference on Object-Oriented Programming, Systems, Languages, Languages, and Applications, vol. 16, pp. 1053–1068 (2011)
23. Tripp, O., Pistoia, M., Fink, S.J., Sridharan, M., Weisman, O.: TAJ: effective taint analysis of web application. In: PLDI. ACM (2009)
24. Unity (2018). https://unity3d.com/
25. Wikipedia: Software framework. https://en.wikipedia.org/wiki/Software_framework
26. Xamarin (2018). https://visualstudio.microsoft.com/xamarin/

QPR Verify: A Static Analysis Tool for Embedded Software Based on Bounded Model Checking

Marko Kleine Büning[1(✉)], Carsten Sinz[1], and David Faragó[2]

[1] Karlsruhe Institute of Technology (KIT), Karlsruhe, Germany
{marko.kleinebuening,carsten.sinz}@kit.edu
[2] QPR Technologies, Karlsruhe, Germany
farago@qpr-technologies.de

Abstract. We present the tool QPR Verify, which is an extension of the bounded model checking approach implemented in the tool LLBMC. QPR Verify is designed to verify industrial embedded software in C and C++ and focuses on runtime errors like arithmetic overflow or invalid memory access. The requirements of verifying industrial embedded software motivated a number of features tuned towards both functionality and usability, for instance providing code traces for each runtime error, better performance and scalability, and a flexible CLI and GUI. Besides new features, we discuss the architecture of QPR Verify and it's functionality, using a case study from the embedded system domain.

1 Introduction

Embedded software is employed in an increasing number of safety and security critical systems; automotive, aerospace and medical devices are well-known examples. Case studies about the cost of such software errors [24] demonstrate the necessity of tools that are tuned for the verification of industrial code. As opposed to open-source, industrial software often needs a more elaborate approach, with state based modelling and implementation, partly code generation, multi-variance, and Data-Range-Specifications, following the AUTOSAR architecture and standards like ISO 26262 and MISRA. Our search for such projects in the open-source space only led to small projects by Bosch, which we included in this article, and https://github.com/GENIVI, which has its focus on architecture and multimedia, not safety-critical code.

Verifying static analysis tools currently employed in industrial practice can be divided into two categories: tools based on Abstract Interpretation (AI) [7,8,23] and tools based on Bounded Model Checking (BMC) [4,9,12,16,19]. Abstract interpretation tools are already established in application areas such as automotive or avionics, because with a suitable AI domain (often the interval domain) they scale quite well. Bounded model checking approaches using bitvector and array theories are generally more precise but lack scalability, which is the main reason why they are still not frequently applied in industry. *QPR Verify* is built

© Springer Nature Switzerland AG 2020
M. Christakis et al. (Eds.): NSV 2020/VSTTE 2020, LNCS 12549, pp. 21–32, 2020.
https://doi.org/10.1007/978-3-030-63618-0_2

as an extension of the bounded model checker LLBMC [19] with the aim to keep high precision while increasing scalability and performance to be usable for industry sized projects. This has been done in the startup QPR Technologies, which focused on static code analysis with high Quality, Precision and Reliability. We investigated challenges and requirements for the verification of industrial embedded sequential software, which guided our development and implementation of QPR Verify. The main contributions of QPR Verify are:

1. User-friendly setup for larger projects and encompassing automatic generation of runtime checks on the source code level, as opposed to the LLVM intermediate representation (LLVM-IR) level, as is done in many tools.
2. Preprocessing analysis to increase scalability and fast feedback through a lightweight syntactic analysis.
3. Program slicing to minimize the source code to be checked, to increase scalability.
4. Structural abstractions that partition the verification problem for the bounded model checker, to increase scalability.
5. Detailed verification reports, including exact error traces in C (and partially C++).

The structure of this article is as follows: Sect. 2 presents the challenges and requirements of industrial software verification. Based on these challenges, Sect. 3 gives an overview of our tools' architecture. Section 4 demonstrates the usage and special features of QPR Verify. Section 5 gives an evaluation on an industrial software project, Bosch's BMI160 driver [20]. Section 6 concludes.

2   Challenges and Requirements for the Verification of Industrial Embedded Software

Generally, every verification tool has to balance the competing criteria of scalability versus precision and completeness. This challenge grew further over the last years because the size of safety-critical embedded software increased dramatically. For example, the software running on board a Boeing 787 encompasses roughly 8 millions lines of code, in a Chevrolet Volt the size is around 40 millions [22], with more and more safety-critical features. Software verification can hardly keep up with this trend. Through a market research with 30 companies [3] and several proof of concepts on industrial projects, we derived the following criteria to rate the industrial applicability of an analysis tool (Bessey et al. came to similar conclusions [1]):

REQ-SetUp   How laborious is the setup of the verification tool for the software project to be analyzed?

REQ-Precision   Which language features are covered, with how much precision?

REQ-Assertion   Are user assertions supported?

REQ-Enviroment	Can the (hardware and software) environment of the program be simulated?
REQ-Specificity	How many incorrect analysis results (false positives and false negatives) occur?
REQ-Information	How much information is supplied about detected faults?
REQ-Scalability	Does the tool scale in the size and complexity of the checked code, i.e. does it have sufficiently low runtime and space requirements?
REQ-Incrementally	Can analysis be performed incrementally, i.e. in iterations of increased precision or successive code changes?
REQ-Languages	Are multiple programming languages supported?

We will refer to those requirements when describing the tool's architecture and its features in more detail. Furthermore, we compare QPR Verify to other state-of-the-art tools based on these requirements.

Embedded software often contains loops with a fixed number of iterations; we make use of this by computing a suitable unroll bound for each such loop. Often many global variables occur in embedded software, e.g., for system configuration; we support modeling restrictions on these variables by our Data Range Specifications (DRS), see Sect. 4. Furthermore, often no dynamic memory allocation is allowed (e.g., enforced by the MISRA-C standard); this influenced the selection of checks implemented in QPR.

Related Work. There is a large number of tools performing static analysis of software written in C and C++. Tools based on AI techniques are most dominant for the industrial application of safety-critical embedded software, with Polyspace [23], Astrée [8], IKOS [2] and CRAB [11] being widely used implementations. Abstract interpretation approaches gain their scalability mostly through the abstraction of value domains but therefore lose the information about specific values that lead to errors. This can potentially produce a large amount of false positives.

Bounded Model Checking approaches are more precise and the underlying SAT/SMT solver produces exact error values and a lower amount of false positives. As trade-off, they often lack the scalability to verify large programs.

Current tools based on the BMC approach like CBMC [16] and ESBMC [10] are very precise but often not tuned towards the application of large industry projects. For example, it is hard to control and see which checks are actually performed at each program location, and sometimes code modifications are needed on the input to make it parsable by the tool. Thus, the support for complete C-features (REQ-Precision), easy set-up (REQ-SetUp) and abstraction methodologies (REQ-Scalability) are limited for those approaches. There are frameworks trying to combine different techniques: The tool Sea-Horn [12] scales up its analysis using a combination of abstract interpretation and property directed reachability (PDR) to generate loop invariants. Frama-C [9] and VeriAbs [4] also combine different solving techniques as portfolio solvers. They provide a range of

functionalities, but do not explicitly tackle the scalability of BMC. Approaches
taking this direction typically try to minimize the formulas for BMC, e.g. lifting
the assertions closer to the entry point of analysis [17] or abstracting loops [5].
QPR Verify takes another approach and abstracts the problem on a structural
level. Theoretical foundations for the semantic of LLVM-based modularization
and structural abstractions can be found in [14], while this paper concentrates
on the tool. The closest tool performing such abstractions is BLITZ [6], which
uses underapproximated preconditions of functions to partition the program into
smaller sub-problems that can be solved incrementally. While they increase the
scalability of BMC, the underapproximation of preconditions can lead to false
negatives, which are particularly undesirable for industrial verification. The general techniques of function and loop summaries [15] serve a similar purpose.

3   Architecture of QPR Verify

The architecture of QPR Verify is intended to support the criteria from Sect. 2
and to offer an automatic approach ranging over multiple stages: from source
code compilation over preprocessing by lightweight static analysis, encoding and
solving, to the user friendly display of verification results.

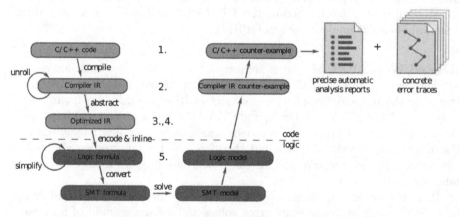

Fig. 1. Architectual layers of QPR Verify and LLBMC.

Verification Process. QPR Verify analyses the given source code in the following stages, depicted on the left part of Fig. 1, along the downward arrows:

1. QPR Verify **automatically detects properties to be checked** by travers-
   ing the abstract syntax tree (AST) of a given C (or C++) program. Currently,
   this stage (called *Murphy*) marks program locations where the program's
   behavior might be undefined, as well as all user-defined assertions (see REQ-
   Assertion). The check categories currently supported by QPR Verify and more
   details are presented in Sect. 4.1.

2. The program under analysis is then **compiled to LLVM-IR**. For this, our extension of *Clang* additionally emits an IR-level assertion for each check established in the first step. Operating on LLVM-IR, other languages besides C and C++ that can be translated to LLVM-IR (e.g. Rust) could easily be covered by LLBMC, too (see REQ-Languages).[1]

3. To reduce the verification workload, **lightweight syntactic analysis** is applied to the inserted checks (see REQ-Scalability). It performs less precise, but more scalable checks during compile time to supersede the subsequent BMC checks (e.g., based on bit-width arguments).

4. In the preparation step, the **problem is abstracted and partitioned** according to user-provided settings. A slicing algorithm also incorporating memory abstraction removes unnecessary instructions. To handle the trade-off between REQ-Precision and REQ-Scalability, QPR Verify offers three modes of verification: *global analysis*, *local analysis* and *call abstraction analysis*, where the latter two partition the program using structural abstractions. The user chooses the set of checks to be analyzed, and may opt to enable IR-level optimizations to increase scalability, see Sect. 4.2.

5. The code produced in step 3 is **analyzed using the bounded model checking** technique implemented in LLBMC. This step may be performed an arbitrary number of times with different configurations and abstractions, enabling incremental analysis to increase precision (see REQ-Incremental).

On the right part of Fig. 1, the results produced in the previous steps are translated back to the C (or C++) level and compiled into a **verification report** consisting of a list of check results and an interactive graphical presentation of the error traces produced by LLBMC (see REQ-Information). The error traces are presented as traces within the source code of the analyzed program, thus hiding all aspects from lower layers of Fig. 1 (esp. LLVM-IR) from the user.

4   Application of QPR Verify

Besides a GUI-based report, QPR Verify is implemented as a suite of command-line utilities, facilitating the integration of static code analysis in automated development workflows. Furthermore, we reduced the effort required to set up the analysis by aiming to provide a "push button" solution requiring minimal user intervention while still providing advanced options for experienced users. We will demonstrate the workflow of QPR Verify step-wise from a user perspective. For this, we describe the most important commands from the CLI, which can be called manually or over a QPR script file.

4.1   Setup and Preprocessing

The first, and often underestimated, step for verification is the setup of the tool and software project to be verified. QPR Verify offers out-of-source con-

---

[1] We also extended LLBMC to handle rarely-supported constructs such as variadic functions.

figurations: The first step is to create an empty folder and initialize it for the verification with QPR Verify. With the command

$$qpr\ init\ \texttt{<root-directory>} \tag{1}$$

giving the root directory of the project to be verified, a verification task is set up. Compiler options can be added by

$$qpr\ add\text{-}compiler\text{-}option\ \texttt{<option>} \tag{2}$$

The files of the project are then either added by

qpr find-source-files	(including files in root-directory) or	(3)
qpr add-source-files <files>	(including a list of files).	(4)

QPR Verify finds all necessary source and header files to compile the program. We additionally included a set of standard libraries in QPR that can be referenced when the software under test is written for a system that substantially deviates from the system QPR Verify is running on. In QPR, external functions can be either treated as uninterpreted functions or are reported as an error when called; if another behavior is intended, data range specifications (DRS) [18] or stubs have to be added manually. Data range specification are an implemented mechanism to specify bounds on global variables and function parameters. These turned out to be sufficient for many environment modeling.

Afterwards, QPR creates a bitcode file for the program, while automatically detecting properties to be checked. Currently, this stage marks program locations where the program's behavior might be undefined as specified in the C language standard [13], as well as all user-defined assertions. The *check categories* currently supported by QPR Verify are:

- **Arithmetic overflows:** Overflow of signed arithmetic operations such as addition, multiplication, division, or pre- and post-decrement and -increment.
- **Illegal shift operations:** Left and right shifts of negative values, shifts by an amount that is larger than the bit-width of the first operand, and shift overflows (cf. C99 standard, Sec. 6.5.7).
- **Division by zero** for the division and modulo operations.
- **Type casts:** A type cast of a signed integer to a smaller bit-width is implementation-defined behavior.
- **Non-initialized local variables:** Reading uninitialized memory locations is undefined behavior. (Limited support)
- **Array index out of bounds:** For arrays, where the bound can be determined from the declared type, we check for out-of-bound indices.

The checks were selected based on feedback from embedded systems practitioners and the market research mentioned in Sect. 2. For example, the index for dynamic arrays (an information not provided by C) are not tracked because most arrays in embedded software are fixed size. Memory is modeled according to the model of the used bounded model checker, in our case LLBMC [21].

In the context of QPR Verify, a *check* denotes a property of the program to be analyzed, and is implemented as an assert intrinsic on the LLVM level. Fundamentally, a check result can be `safe`, `unsafe` or `indeterminate` and may be further qualified depending on the mode of analysis. Check results that have a potential to be a false positive (due to abstractions) resp. false negative (due to the unroll limit) are marked with a *conditional* flag, i.e. `cond. safe` resp. `cond. unsafe`.

As a fast preprocessing step, lightweight *syntactic analysis* is applied to the inserted checks to reduce the overall verification workload. In many cases, checks can be analyzed efficiently on the syntactic level, for instance undefined behavior in integer-arithmetic expressions involving only constants. So a check C pertaining to an operation O is *safe* rsp. *unsafe* if a check result for C can be established by obtaining the operands of O via compile-time evaluation and directly showing the safety of C rsp. a violation of C's condition. While our implementation of syntactic analysis does not improve scalability for hard verification problems, it does significantly reduce the overall workload put on the model checker and yields results much faster. In our experience, more than two thirds of the checks in industrial code can be analyzed conclusively using our syntactic analysis.

The check insertion, compilation, and syntactic analysis are all performed by issuing the two commands `qpr murphy` and `qpr compile`. The result is a list of checks for all properties which have been prepossessed by the syntactic analysis, leaving checks in the categories `safe`, `unsafe` and `indeterminate`. This indeterminate checks, representing harder verification tasks, can then be solved sequentially or in parallel with different solving strategies.[2]

4.2 Solving Strategies and Abstractions

QPR Verify offers different solving strategies to verify the remaining checks. All strategies use LLBMC; they differ in entry points, memory assumptions and check activation. Most configuration options apply for the whole project and are set by `qpr configure-project <name>:<value>`. The configuration options with the largest impact are

- *AnalyzeChecksIndividually*, which disables grouping checks together, i.e. runs an individual verification per check
- *EnableSlicing*, which can be used only together with *AnalyzeChecksIndividually*, to activate a memory-abstracting slicing algorithm that removes all instructions expendable for the current check (i.e. the verification task).
- *Loop-Unroll-Bound*, which specifies how often to unroll loops Clang did not unroll by itself (i.e. for which Clang could not infer the maximum amount of iterations).
- *Data Range Specifications*, which specify restrictions on the domain of global variables and function parameters [18] (see REQ-Environment).

---

[2] We have implemented an experimental parallel version of QPR Verify based on MPI; first experiments show promising results of increased scalability.

In all analysis modes, previous errors on a path do not shadow subsequent errors, which is important in practice to avoid repeated runs after fixing an error. Thus, when an error occurs, the path is not truncated at the error location. Instead the computed variable is set to an undefined value for subsequent checks.

Global Analysis. The basic mode of analysis with QPR Verify is called *global analysis*. It is the standard bounded model checking approach, where the program is encoded as a whole.

Let P be the program under analysis and C be a check or group of checks in P. With global analysis, QPR Verify checks whether C holds for all execution paths starting at the main function. If there is an execution path violating C, the check result **unsafe** is added to the check result set of C. If C is shown to hold for all such execution paths, the check result **globally safe** is added to the set of C's check results. However, if some execution path was truncated during analysis, e.g. due to a loop bound having been reached, the check result added for C is further qualified corresponding to the reason for the path truncation. The analysis can be performed by setting the entry point (default value is the function "main") and then starting the analysis:

$$\texttt{qpr configure-project EntryPoint:<function-name>} \qquad (5)$$

$$\texttt{qpr analyze-globally} \qquad (6)$$

Local Analysis. *Local analysis* uses *structural abstractions* to partition the program into smaller modules [14]. The approach iterates through all functions in P and starts the analysis with a function F as the entry point. The call-environment (input parameter and memory) of F are over-approximated by setting them to undetermined values. The analysis only verifies checks that are located within F, but still takes called functions within F into account. The check results are assigned analogously to global analysis; however, the check result is called **safe** rsp. **cond. unsafe**. Using local analysis greatly reduces the verification's computational effort. However, since the semantics of function calls are taken into account (but not their correctness properties, i.e. their checks), local analysis is still an interprocedural analysis and may require considerable resources for large programs. The analysis is simply started by a single command and no entry points have to be specified: **qpr check-all-functions-locally**.

Since no assumption about the calling context is made in local analysis, **safe** without further qualifications (such as "loop bound reached") is the strongest safety guarantee that can be established with QPR Verify, since the checked property cannot be violated for any calling context of F. However, the results **safe** with qualifications and **cond. unsafe** are only valuable to the QA engineer when F may actually be an entry point of the source code, e.g. a library API function. Otherwise, the result needs to be refined by adjusting the analysis parameters (such as the loop bound), by preconditions or by using a global analysis taking into account the calling context of F.

Call Abstraction Analysis. The call abstraction analysis is a local analysis that abstracts away calls to functions outside of the chosen entry point function F. We only keep checks (assertions) in function F, and abstract away all function calls that exceed a user defined call depth (called *havoc-limit*). When abstracting a function call without any further knowledge, an over-approximation of its behavior has to be assumed. Next to the return value (if existent), memory content (including global variables) can be altered by the called function, and thus are assumed to be arbitrary.

$$\texttt{qpr configure-project HavocLimit:<positive number>}, \qquad (7)$$

$$\texttt{qpr check-all-functions-with-call-abstraction}. \qquad (8)$$

Incremental Analysis. All checks can be performed incrementally to refine check results by combining the above-mentioned analyses. Checks that are set to safe or to unsafe do not need to be checked again. Checks with a different status (indeterminate or cond. unsafe/safe) are rechecked by successive analyses, which can be performed manually or over available scripts.

4.3   Error Traces and Result Display

The results produced in the previous step are compiled into a report consisting of a list of check results and an interactive graphical presentation of the error traces produced by LLBMC. The error traces are presented as traces within the source code of the analyzed program, thus hiding all aspects related to LLVM-IR from the user. The user interface allows to step forwards and backwards through the trace, where the former direction is similar to a source level debugger.

Fig. 2. QPR client providing a project overview (center), check information (left) and detailed error traces (right).

5   Evaluation

While QPR Verify has been used to verify projects of around 160 KLoC [14], we will demonstrate the usage of QPR Verify on a smaller, more presentable example that demonstrate the iterative usage[3]. We chose the open-source library BMI160-Driver [20] implemented by the Robert Bosch GmbH. It has 135 functions and

---

[3] Instructions to replicate the results and experiment with QPR in a prepared VM, can be found under https://baldur.iti.kit.edu/qpr/QPR_Verify-2020-info.txt.

around 2000 LoC and implements a sensor API. As a library module it does not have a main function. Thus, we are performing different configurations of the local analysis. We ran QPR with a loop bound of 5. This parameter can be incrementally increased to further refine the analysis, as is typical for BMC.

Table 1 displays results for three individual analysis runs and one running these three approaches incrementally one after each other. The first, "Checks Combined", performs a local analysis which groups checks by function. All checks inside a function are encoded together with the source code into one formula. Erroneous checks are then deactivated through *activation literals* to get information about the status of individual checks. In "Checks Individually & Slicing" each check is analyzed on its own and backwards slicing is applied with respect to the check location. "Call Abstraction" performs the above described call abstraction analysis. In the last line, "Incremental Analysis", all three analysis are run successively.

Table 1. Results of 4 solving approaches on 2593 checks of BMI160-Driver.

Approach/Results	Safe	Cond. Safe	Cond. Unsafe	Unsafe	Indeter.	Time
Checks combined	2051 (79%)	447 (17%)	95 (4%)	0	0	124 s
Checks individually & Slicing	2376 (92%)	5 (0%)	212 (8%)	0	0	201 s
Call abstraction	2460 (95%)	23 (1%)	0	0	110 (4%)	365 s
Incremental analysis	2469 (96%)	29 (1%)	95 (3%)	0	0	690 s

The three different approaches have different strengths and weaknesses. While the call abstraction leads to the most checks categorized as `safe`, it produces a high number of `indeterminate` results. Running the three analysis incrementally after each other produced the best result. 96% of the checks were proven to be `safe`. 1% (29) `cond. safe` with respect to a loop bound and 3% (95) are `cond. unsafe` with respect to the entry point and other abstractions needed.

With standard BMC approaches, it is very difficult to perform such analysis of an API driver. Using for example CBMC, one has to manually extract function names and then iteratively activate and deactivate single checks to then gather detailed information.

6   Conclusion and Future Work

We have presented QPR Verify, a static analysis tool based on software bounded model checking with a focus on industrial application. We devised requirements for the verification of industrial embedded software and implemented QPR Verify accordingly. Based on the bounded model checking approach, the tool produces precise verification results, while providing a range of abstractions and solving strategies for a scalable analysis. New features like a fast syntactical analysis, data range specifications, different solving strategies and the support of a wide range of C features are implemented to fulfill industrial requirements. Providing additional information for checks, like error traces, in an interactive GUI should make the tool applicable for a wide user base.

References

1. Bessey, A., et al.: A few billion lines of code later: using static analysis to find bugs in the real world. Commun. ACM **53**(2) (2010)
2. Brat, G., Navas, J.A., Shi, N., Venet, A.: IKOS: a framework for static analysis based on abstract interpretation. In: Giannakopoulou, D., Salaün, G. (eds.) SEFM 2014. LNCS, vol. 8702, pp. 271–277. Springer, Cham (2014). https://doi.org/10.1007/978-3-319-10431-7_20
3. Bährle, R.: Market analysis of safety-critical software in the automotive industry. Master's thesis, Karlsruhe Institue of Technologie (2016). https://baldur.iti.kit.edu/qpr/Marktanalyse-baehrle.pdf
4. Darke, P., et al.: VeriAbs: verification by abstraction and test generation. In: Beyer, D., Huisman, M. (eds.) TACAS 2018. LNCS, vol. 10806, pp. 457–462. Springer, Cham (2018). https://doi.org/10.1007/978-3-319-89963-3_32
5. Chimdyalwar, B., Darke, P., Chavda, A., Vaghani, S., Chauhan, A.: Eliminating static analysis false positives using loop abstraction and bounded model checking. In: FM 2015: Formal Methods, pp. 573–576 (2015)
6. Cho, C.Y., D'Silva, V., Song, D.: Blitz: compositional bounded model checking for real-world programs. In: ASE, pp. 136–146. IEEE (2013)
7. Cousot, P., Cousot, R.: Abstract interpretation frameworks. J. Logic Comput. **2**(4), 511–547 (1992)
8. Cousot, P., et al.: The ASTREÉ analyzer. In: Sagiv, M. (ed.) ESOP 2005. LNCS, vol. 3444, pp. 21–30. Springer, Heidelberg (2005). https://doi.org/10.1007/978-3-540-31987-0_3
9. Cuoq, P., Kirchner, F., Kosmatov, N., Prevosto, V., Signoles, J., Yakobowski, B.: Frama-C. In: Eleftherakis, G., Hinchey, M., Holcombe, M. (eds.) SEFM 2012. LNCS, vol. 7504, pp. 233–247. Springer, Heidelberg (2012). https://doi.org/10.1007/978-3-642-33826-7_16
10. Gadelha, M.R., Monteiro, F., Cordeiro, L., Nicole, D.: ESBMC v6.0: verifying C programs using k-induction and invariant inference. In: Beyer, D., Huisman, M., Kordon, F., Steffen, B. (eds.) TACAS 2019. LNCS, vol. 11429, pp. 209–213. Springer, Cham (2019). https://doi.org/10.1007/978-3-030-17502-3_15
11. Gange, G., Navas, J.A., Schachte, P., Søndergaard, H., Stuckey, P.J.: An abstract domain of uninterpreted functions. In: Jobstmann, B., Leino, K.R.M. (eds.) VMCAI 2016. LNCS, vol. 9583, pp. 85–103. Springer, Heidelberg (2016). https://doi.org/10.1007/978-3-662-49122-5_4
12. Gurfinkel, A., Kahsai, T., Komuravelli, A., Navas, J.A.: The SeaHorn verification framework. In: Kroening, D., Păsăreanu, C.S. (eds.) CAV 2015. LNCS, vol. 9206, pp. 343–361. Springer, Cham (2015). https://doi.org/10.1007/978-3-319-21690-4_20
13. ISO: C99 Standard (ISO/IEC 9899:1999). International Organization for Standardization, Geneva, Switzerland, December 1999

14. Kleine Büning, M., Sinz, C.: Automatic modularization of large programs for bounded model checking. In: Ait-Ameur, Y., Qin, S. (eds.) ICFEM 2019. LNCS, vol. 11852, pp. 186–202. Springer, Cham (2019). https://doi.org/10.1007/978-3-030-32409-4_12

15. Kroening, D., Sharygina, N., Tonetta, S., Tsitovich, A., Wintersteiger, C.M.: Loop summarization using state and transition invariants. Formal Method Syst. Des. **42**(3), 221–261 (2013)

16. Kroening, D., Tautschnig, M.: CBMC – C bounded model checker. In: Ábrahám, E., Havelund, K. (eds.) TACAS 2014. LNCS, vol. 8413, pp. 389–391. Springer, Heidelberg (2014). https://doi.org/10.1007/978-3-642-54862-8_26

17. Lai, A., Qadeer, S.: A program transformation for faster goal-directed search. In: 2014 Formal Methods in Computer-Aided Design, pp. 147–154. IEEE (2014)

18. MathWorks: Polyspace code prover. Matlab & Simulink (2017)

19. Merz, F., Falke, S., Sinz, C.: LLBMC: bounded model checking of C and C++ programs using a compiler IR. In: Joshi, R., Müller, P., Podelski, A. (eds.) VSTTE 2012. LNCS, vol. 7152, pp. 146–161. Springer, Heidelberg (2012). https://doi.org/10.1007/978-3-642-27705-4_12

20. Bosch Sensortec GmbH, BMI160 Sensor Driver (2016). https://github.com/BoschSensortec/BMI160_driver

21. Sinz, C., Falke, S., Merz, F.: A precise memory model for low-level bounded model checking. In: Proceedings of the 5th International Conference on Systems Software Verification, p. 7. USENIX Association (2010)

22. Staron, M.: Automotive Software Architectures - An Introduction. Springer, Cham (2017). https://doi.org/10.1007/978-3-319-58610-6

23. Wissing, K.: Static analysis of dynamic properties - automatic program verification to prove the absence of dynamic runtime errors. GI Jahrestagung (2007)

24. Wolf, M.: Embedded software in crisis. Computer **49**(1), 88–90 (2016)

Verified Translation Between Purely Functional and Imperative Domain Specific Languages in HELIX

Vadim Zaliva[1]([⊠]) [ID], Ilia Zaichuk[2] [ID], and Franz Franchetti[1] [ID]

[1] Carnegie Mellon University, Pittsburgh, PA, USA
vzaliva@cmu.edu
[2] Taras Shevchenko National University, Kyiv, Ukraine

Abstract. HELIX is a formally verified language and rewriting engine for generation of high-performance implementation for a variety of numerical algorithms. Based on the existing SPIRAL system, HELIX adds the rigor of formal verification of its correctness using the Coq proof assistant. It formally defines a series of domain-specific languages starting with *HCOL*, which represents a computation data flow. HELIX works by transforming the original program through a series of intermediate languages, culminating in LLVM IR. In this paper, we will focus on three intermediate languages and the formally verified translation between them. Translation between these three languages is non-trivial, because each subsequent language introduces lower-level abstractions, compared to the previous one. During these steps, we switch from pure-functional language using mixed embedding to a deep-embedded imperative one, also introducing a memory model, lexical scoping, monadic error handling, and transition from abstract algebraic datatype to floating-point numbers. We will demonstrate the design of these languages, the automatic reification between them, and automated proofs of semantic preservation, in Coq.

1 Introduction

With the current level of sophistication of hardware architectures, the problem of high-performance implementation of numerical algorithms becomes challenging for manual implementation even when using optimizing compilers and is often solved by specialized code generation systems, such as SPIRAL [13].

Developed over the last 20 years, the SPIRAL system has been used to generate, synthesize, and autotune programs and libraries. It works by translating rule-encoded high-level specifications of mathematical algorithms into highly optimized/library-grade implementations. SPIRAL has been used to formalize a variety of computational kernels from the signal and image processing domain, including graph algorithms, robotic vehicle control, software-defined radio (SDR), numerical solution of partial differential equations. SPIRAL is capable of generating code for multiple platforms ranging from mobile devices

© Springer Nature Switzerland AG 2020
M. Christakis et al. (Eds.): NSV 2020/VSTTE 2020, LNCS 12549, pp. 33–49, 2020.
https://doi.org/10.1007/978-3-030-63618-0_3

and multicore (desktop and server) processors to high-performance and super-computing systems [7].

When SPIRAL is applied to generate high-performance libraries used in mission critical software, the question arises as to what kind of assurances could be made about the correctness of the generated code. The goal of HELIX, as a part of the High Assurance SPIRAL project [5,11], is to formally prove of the correctness of SPIRAL optimizations and code generation using Coq proof assistant.

Both SPIRAL and HELIX work by transforming an original formula through a series of intermediate languages, culminating in machine code, as shown in Fig. 1. The translation steps correspond to different levels of abstraction:

1. Mathematical formula
2. The dataflow (SPIRAL: OL language, HELIX: $HCOL$ language)
3. The dataflow with implicit loops: (SPIRAL: Σ-OL language, HELIX: Σ-$HCOL$ language
4. Imperative program: (SPIRAL: iCode language, HELIX: $FHCOL$ language)
5. Mainstream programming language code: (SPIRAL: C Program, HELIX: LLVM IR program)

The dataflow language is very close to mathematical notation and can represent a wide class of relevant mathematical formulae. As a first step, SPIRAL attempts to deconstruct the original expression into simpler expressions, which, combined by a function composition, represent a data-flow graph of the computation [8]. The resulting expression is then translated into another language, called Σ-OL which adds the implicit representation of iterative computations. Next, the Σ-OL expression is rewritten using a series of rewrite rules, driven by the extensive knowledge base of SPIRAL's optimization algorithms, into a shape which lends itself to generating the most efficient code for the target platform. Subsequently, an Σ-OL expression is compiled into an intermediate imperative language. By doing this, SPIRAL converts the dataflow graph into a sequence of loops and arithmetic operations. Finally, an intermediate imperative language representation, after some additional transformations, yields a C program which is compiled with an optimizing compiler, producing an executable high-performance machine code implementation of the original expression.

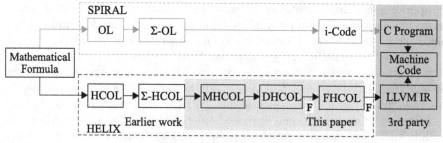

Legend: F-*future work*

Fig. 1. SPIRAL/HELIX transformation stages

This paper describes the design of a part of the HELIX system, a formally verified version of SPIRAL. Implementing such a system broadly consists of defining and formalizing all intermediate languages, writing translators between them, and proving semantic preservation of each such translation. The scope of this paper is shown by the shaded box labeled "This paper" of Fig. 1. The definition of *HCOL* and *Σ-HCOL* languages and proving correctness of their translation was addressed in previous papers: [16,17]. This paper focuses on *MHCOL*, *DHCOL*, and *FHCOL* languages. Unlike SPIRAL, HELIX uses LLVM IR instead of C as the last intermediate translation step. This decision was based on the ease of formally proving the semantics preservation of this step. Some features that SPIRAL relies upon still have no adequate formalization in CompCert [10], the most developed formally verified C compiler. On the other hand Vellvm [19] project provides almost all LLVM IR formalization we require. Even though we already developed the *FHCOL* to LLVM IR compiler, its design and verification will be addressed separately in future papers.

The main contributions we present in this paper are:

1. Demonstration of a working approach to semantics-preserving, two-step translation from a mixed-embedded dependently-typed purely functional language to a deep-embedded imperative one.
   (a) The initial translation of *Σ-HCOL* into an intermediate *MHCOL* language lowering the abstraction level by introducing lower-level data representation and error handling.
   (b) Subsequent compilation of *MHCOL* into *DHCOL* language. Formalization of memory model, type system, evaluation contexts, and small-step operational semantics of the target language. Mapping algebraic abstraction of partial computations via sparse vectors into independent memory updates. Formalizing and proving the notion of semantic preservation between *MHCOL*'s denotational semantics and *DHCOL*'s small step operational semantics.
2. Demonstration of a framework for switching from abstracted *reals* and *natural numbers* to IEEE 754 floating-point numbers and fixed bit-length machine integers. Our approach with two versions of the same language parameterized by different types provides a convenient framework for numerical stability and overflow-safety proofs.

2   The Approach

We start with *Σ-HCOL* language. It is a purely functional *operator language* with mixed embedding in Coq and is built around the concept of *operators* from multi-linear algebra, which are defined as maps on vector spaces [6]. It operates on finite length sparse vectors of abstract *carrier type*. Our intermediate goal is to compile it (via intermediate languages) into an imperative *DHCOL* program suitable for LLVM IR translation. This undertaking involves several distinct challenges:

1. Translating a purely functional program into imperative language.
2. Mapping the layout of Σ-$HCOL$ data to $DHCOL$ memory and variables.
3. Mapping Σ-$HCOL$ sparse vector abstraction to partially initialized memory blocks.
4. Switching from mixed to deep embedding.
5. Handling errors.
6. Switching from *carrier type* to IEEE 754 floating-point numbers.
7. Switching from natural numbers to fixed bit-length machine integers.
8. Proving semantic equivalence between the original Σ-$HCOL$ expression and the generated $DHCOL$ program.

In this paper, we will discuss how these challenges were addressed, what technical decisions were made, and the lessons learned. The translation is performed via series of intermediate languages, as shown in Fig. 1.

With each step, the level of abstraction moves from purely mathematical operations on abstract algebraic types down towards LLVM IR instructions operating on registers and memory locations. The semantic preservation is proven from each language to the next one in the chain.

Our source Σ-$HCOL$ [17] language is mixed-embedded in Coq and purely functional. The main data type is a finite length sparse vector of *carrier type* values. Σ-$HCOL$ programs have no error handling, since potential error situations, like out-of-bounds vector index access, are eliminated by strong, dependent typing.

In Σ-$HCOL$, we use sparse vectors as an abstraction for partial computations. Each operator can perform a computation of some elements of a vector, leaving others undefined. To perform algebraic transformations on Σ-$HCOL$ expressions, sparsity is rigorously tracked, but sparse (undefined) vector elements are assigned implicit "default" value [17]. While such default values are used in algebraic equational theory that supports underlying Σ-$HCOL$ rewriting rules, they are not supposed to contribute to the final result, which must depend solely on dense (defined) elements of input vectors.

The 15 Σ-$HCOL$ operators are listed with their informal descriptions below:

1. `IdOp` – no-op.
2. `Embed i n` – Takes an element from a single-element input vector and puts it at a specific index in a sparse vector of given length.
3. `Pick i` – Selects an element from the input vector at the given index and returns it as a single element vector.
4. `Scatter f` – Maps elements of the input vector to the elements of the output according to an index mapping function f. The mapping is *injective* but not necessarily *surjective*. That means the output vector could be sparse.
5. `Gather f` – Works in a similar manner to `Scatter`, except the index mapping function f is used in the opposite direction – to map the output indices to the input ones.
6. `SHPointwise f` – Similar to the `map` function in Haskell.

7. `SHBinOp f` – Similar to the `map2` function in Haskell, applied to the first and the second half of the input vector.
8. `SHInductor n f` – Iteratively applies given function `f` to the input `n` times.
9. `liftM_HOperator hop` – "lifts" *HCOL* operators, so they can be used in *Σ-HCOL* expressions.
10. `HTSUMUnion sop1 sop2` – A higher-order operator applying two operators to the same input and combining their results (discussed in more detail below).
11. `SafeCast sop` – A higher-order operator, wrapping another *Σ-HCOL* operator. While it does not change the values, computed by the wrapped operator, it adds a monadic wrapper to track sparsity properties.[1]
12. `UnSafeCast sop` – Similar to `SafeCast` but uses a different monadic wrapper (See footnote 3).
13. `IUnion f (fam: {x:nat|x<n} → SHOperator)` – Iteratively applies indexed family of *n* operators to the input and combines their outputs element-wise using the given binary function `f`. This is an abstraction for parallel loops.
14. `IReduction f (fam: {x:nat|x<n} → SHOperator)` – Similar to `IUnion` but without assumption of non-overlapping sparsity.
15. `SHCompose sop1 sop2` – Functional composition of operators.

Let us consider more closely the example of the *Σ-HCOL* operator, `HTSUMUnion`. It is a higher-order operator parameterized by the two operators, `f` and `g`. Given an input vector, the operator applies them both to the vector and combines their results using *vector union*, as shown in Fig. 2.

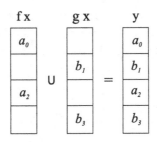

Fig. 2. `HTSUMUnion` in *Σ-HCOL*

In *structurally correct Σ-HCOL* expression, it is guaranteed (proven) that both inputs to such a union will have disjoint sparsity patterns which guarantees that we will never try to combine two non-sparse elements. The *structural correctness* property is an invariant of the previous steps in the HELIX processing chain, and the *Σ-HCOL* expressions that we are dealing with are guaranteed to satisfy it.

---

[1] The details of our monadic approach to sparsity tracking are out of scope of this paper, but discussed in detail in [17].

3   *MHCOL*: An Intermediate Language

Sparse vectors in Σ-*HCOL* are an algebraic abstraction for *memory blocks*. We make this explicit in an intermediate mixed-embedded language, *MHCOL* (M stands for *memory*). Each memory block is represented as a dictionary in which the keys are memory offsets and the values are memory values of a carrier type. There is no mapping for keys corresponding to sparse values.

An examples of both representations is shown in Fig. 3. It shows a sparse vector with three initialized elements, A, B, and C, and a dictionary with three corresponding keys.

0	A
1	
2	B
3	C

0 →A
2 →B
3 →C

Sparse vector   Dictionary

Fig. 3. Sparse vectors as dictionaries

HTSUMUnion in *MHCOL* is shown in Fig. 4. Each of the two operators f and g, applied to the input vector x, produces a corresponding dictionary, and the two dictionaries have disjoint keys: $[0; 2]$ and $[1; 3]$, respectively. They are then combined into the final resulting dictionary y.

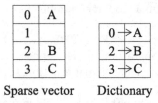

Fig. 4. HTSUMUnion in *MHCOL*

With this change of data representation, we move away from the algebraic nature of Σ-*HCOL* towards a lower-level representation. In this representation, an actual value must be associated with a key in a dictionary before it can be accessed. Trying to access an uninitialized key is an error. It means that *MHCOL* operators could return errors and thus have a type: mem_block $\rightarrow$ option mem_block. However, we prove that our translation of structurally correct Σ-*HCOL* programs produces *MHCOL* programs that do not err when applied to sufficiently initialized memory blocks.

Like in Σ-*HCOL*, we use *mixed embedding* [4] (a combination of *shallow* and *deep embedding*) to represent *MHCOL* operators. The following record type is used (we assume the reader is familiar with Coq):

```
Record MSHOperator {i o: ℕ} : Type := mkMSHOperator {
        mem_op: mem_block → option mem_block;
        mem_op_proper: Proper ((equiv) ⟹ (equiv)) mem_op;
        m_in_index_set: FinNatSet i;
        m_out_index_set: FinNatSet o; }.
```

It is indexed by dimensions of input and output memory blocks. The fields include: a function implementing the operation on memory blocks which can fail (returning None); a *proper morphism* [3] for this function with respect to the setoid equality equiv (required because the carrier type is abstract); and the two sets which define input and output memory access patterns.

All *MHCOL* operator implementations must satisfy certain *memory safety* properties. We have formulated these properties as the typeclass, MSHOperator_Facts, and proven instances of it for all operators. This is a similar approach to what we took with Σ-*HCOL*, but the properties are different:

1. When applied to a memory block with all memory cells in m_in_index_set mapped to values, mem_op will not return an error.
2. The mem_op must assign a value to each element with index in m_out_index_set and must not assign a value to any element with index not in m_out_index_set
3. The output block of mem_op is guaranteed to contain no values at indices outside of operators' declared output size.

The semantic equality for a pair of Σ-*HCOL* and *MHCOL* operators is defined as the SH_MSH_Operator_compat typeclass. It ensures that they have the same dimensionality, the same input and output patterns (index sets), and structural correctness of Σ-*HCOL* and *MHCOL* operators (by the presence of respective SHOperator_Facts and MSHOperator_Facts instances). In addition to these properties, the main semantic equivalence statement to be proven is:

```
mem_vec_preservation:
∀ (x:svector i),
    (∀ (j: ℕ) (jc: j < i), in_index_set sop (mkFinNat jc) → Is_Val (Vnth x jc))
    →
    Some (svector_to_mem_block (op sop x)) = mem_op mop (svector_to_mem_block x)
```

Informally it could be stated as:

For any vector which complies with the input sparsity contract of the Sigma-HCOL operator, an application of the *MHCOL* operator to such vector, converted to a memory block, must succeed and return a memory block which must be equal to the memory block produced by converting the result of the Σ-*HCOL* operator.

For regular operators, SH_MSH_Operator_compat instances could be proven directly. For higher-order operators, the proofs are predicated on

SH_MSH_Operator_compat assumptions for all operators involved. Some operators may have additional prerequisites. For example, for HTSUMUnion, output index sets of f and g must be disjoint.

Translation from Σ-HCOL to MHCOL, is implemented using the Coq meta-programming plugin, TemplateCoq [2]. For translated programs, we use proof automation to prove that SH_MSH_Operator_compat holds between the original and the compiled programs. This approach is known as *translation validation*.

4 *DHCOL*: An Imperative Language

The next language in the translation sequence is called *DHCOL* (D stands for *deep-embedded*). While Σ-HCOL and MHCOL have one-to-one correspondence between the operators, this no longer holds true for Σ-HCOL to DHCOL. DHCOL is a lower-level language, so each MHCOL operator is translated into not one but a sequence of DHCOL operators. Another distinction is that DHCOL is *deep embedded*. However, a more important difference is that it is no longer *functional* but *imperative*. The execution model assumes an *environment* (variables) and memory. The operators can have side effects, modifying the memory but not the environment.

The language design decisions for *DHCOL* were guided by the needs of an intermediate representation language between MHCOL and LLVM IR. It is not meant to be a general-purpose programming language and contains only features required to represent DHCOL programs. By constraining it in such way, we have kept it small and made it easier to prove statements about it.

Our earlier example, HTSUMUnion operator, could be viewed imperatively as a sequential execution of two operators and a combination of their results. Since output key index sets are guaranteed not to overlap, these operators could be computed independently (or even in parallel) and could write to the same output dictionary, as shown in Fig. 5, without the risk of overwriting each others' results.

Finally, because we need to work with multiple memory blocks, we organize them into a *memory*, which is just a dictionary of memory blocks. Such a two-level hierarchical memory model is very similar to the memory model used in CompCert [10] and Vellvm [19].

In addition to memory, there is an *evaluation context* which holds all variables in scope. Variables are typed and can hold natural numbers, *carrier type* values, and memory pointers.

We provide *small-step operational semantics* of DHCOL by an evalDSH Operator: evalContext $\rightarrow$ DSHOperator $\rightarrow$ memory $\rightarrow$ fuel $\rightarrow$ option (err memory) function which, given an *evaluation context*, a memory state, and an operator, returns a modified memory state. It uses *fuel* to make it easier to prove that it always terminates. It should be noted that a semantic step is expressed as a transition between memory states. The environment stays unchanged, and operator side effects are limited to modifying memory values. The reason for that is the design of the language; variables are statically scoped and are in *single static assignment* (SSA) form.

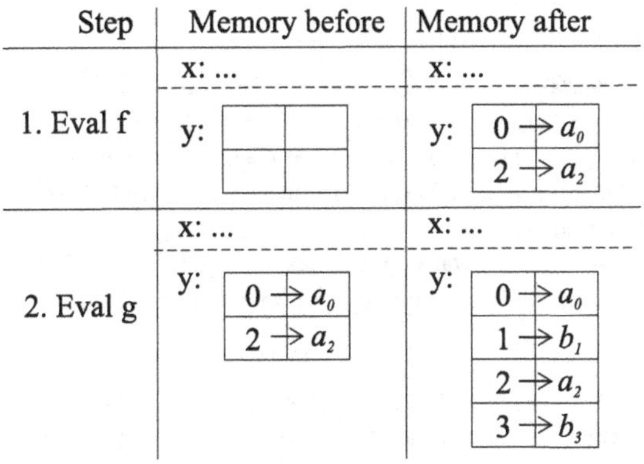

Step	Memory before	Memory after
1. Eval f	x: ... y: (empty 2x2 block)	x: ... y: $0 \mapsto a_0$ / $2 \mapsto a_2$
2. Eval g	x: ... y: $0 \mapsto a_0$ / $2 \mapsto a_2$	x: ... y: $0 \mapsto a_0$ / $1 \mapsto b_1$ / $2 \mapsto a_2$ / $3 \mapsto b_3$

Fig. 5. HTSUMUnion in $DHCOL$

The reification of $MHCOL$ to $DHCOL$ is also implemented using Template Coq. In addition to operators, we translate arithmetic expressions on natural numbers and carrier type values. During expression translation, we enforce the restriction that only supported operations like + are allowed. A high-level reification and validation approach is discussed in [18].

The reification process is then invoked with the Run TemplateProgram (reifySHCOL shcol "dhcol") command in Coq. It translates Σ-$HCOL$ expression shcol and creates a new definition with the name dhcol initialized with its $DHCOL$ translation.

4.1   Definition

$DHCOL$ expressions are made up of variables from an evaluation context (referenced by de Bruijn indices), operations (e.g., + and −), and constants. There are four types of expressions: NExpr - expressions on natural numbers; AExpr - expressions of carrier type values; PExpr - pointer expressions; and MExpr - memory block expressions. The first two, NExpr and AExpr, evaluate to natural and carrier type values, respectively. The latter two, PExpr and MExpr, both evaluate to memory blocks. The variables in the evaluation context are typed and could have one of three types: *natural numbers, carrier type* values, or *pointers to memory blocks*.

The are ten $DHCOL$ operators, defined by an inductive type shown in Listing 1.1.

```
Inductive DSHOperator :=
| DSHNop (* no-op *)
| DSHAssign (src dst: MemVarRef) (* memory cell assignment *)
| DSHIMap (n: N) (x_p y_p: PExpr) (f: AExpr) (* indexed [map] *)
| DSHBinOp (n: N) (x_p y_p: PExpr) (f: AExpr) (* [map2] on two halfs of [x_p] *)
| DSHMemMap2 (n: N) (x0_p x1_p y_p: PExpr) (f: AExpr) (* [map2] *)
(* recursive application of [f]: *)
| DSHPower (n:NExpr) (src dst: MemVarRef) (f: AExpr) (initial: CT.t)
(* evaluate [body] [n] times. Loop index will be bound during body
eval: *)
| DSHLoop (n:N) (body: DSHOperator)
(* allocates new uninitialized memory block and makes the pointer to it
    available in evaluation context at de Bruijn index 0 while the [body] is evaluated: *)
| DSHAlloc (size:NT.t) (body: DSHOperator)
(* initialize memory block indices [0-size] with given value: *)
| DSHMemInit (size:NT.t) (y_p: PExpr) (value: CT.t)
(* copy memory blocks. Overwrites output block values, if present: *)
| DSHMemCopy (size:NT.t) (x_p y_p: PExpr)
| DSHSeq (f g: DSHOperator) (* execute [g] after [f] *).
```

Listing 1.1. *DHCOL* operator type

4.2   Proof of Semantics Preservation

While the regular *MHCOL* operators translate to a single *DHCOL* instruction, the higher-order operators translate into a sequence of instructions, with place-holders filled with *DHCOL* translations of their respective parameters. For example, *MHCOL*'s (MSHIReduction i o n z f op_family) operator is compiled to the following *DHCOL* program:

```
DSHSeq
  (DSHMemInit o y_p z)
  (DSHAlloc o (DSHLoop n (DSHSeq dop_family (DSHMemMap2 o y_p' (PVar 1) y_p' df)))))
```

The parameters of MSHIReduction above are: the dimensions of the input and the output vectors (i and o respectively), the size n of the operator family op_family, and initialization value z. In *DHCOL*, df and dop_family correspond to f and op_family, respectively, translated to *DHCOL*.

Operators DSHAlloc and DSHLoop introduce two new variables: the pointer to newly allocated memory block and the loop index. Inside the loop they are referenced by their respective de Bruijn indices as (PVar 1) and (PVar 0). The dop_family takes the loop index to access the family operator member to evaluate on each iteration which is then executed writing output to temporary memory block. The output of MSHIReduction is assumed to be written to a memory block referenced by variable y_p, and y_p' is the same variable with the de Bruijn index increased by two (to accommodate for the loop index and a new variable, holding a reference to the newly allocated temporary memory block).

We want to prove that our translation from *MHCOL* to *DHCOL* preserves the semantics. As with other HELIX languages, we use automated *translation validation* approach. To allow automatic proof of translation results, we need to prove correctness lemmas for each *MHCOL* operator and its *DHCOL* representation. Then, these lemmas could be applied recursively, hierarchically descending the structure of the *MHCOL* reified expression.

The first step in the process is to formalize the notion of semantic equivalence between the purely functional language with denotational semantics (*MHCOL*) and the imperative language with operational semantics (*DHCOL*). Each *MHCOL* operator is a function $x \mapsto y$ where x and y are memory blocks.[2] It is a *pure function* without side effects, whose output y depends on x and other variables in scope. On the other hand, a *DHCOL* translation of this *MHCOL* operator is an imperative program that can read variables available in the *evaluation context*, and it also can read and modify the memory. One block from this memory will correspond to x, and some other block will correspond to y. Being a translation of a pure function, the operator can modify only y. The formalization of the class of *DHCOL* programs representing pure functions is expressed as DSH_pure typeclass:

```
Class DSH_pure  (d: DSHOperator) (y: PExpr) := {
    mem_stable: forall σ m m' fuel,
        evalDSHOperator σ d m fuel = Some (inr m') ->
        forall k, mem_block_exists k m <-> mem_block_exists k m';

    mem_write_safe: forall σ m m' fuel,
        evalDSHOperator σ d m fuel = Some (inr m') ->
        (forall y_i , evalPexp σ y = inr y_i ->
                memory_equiv_except m m' y_i)
}.
```

It has the following two properties:

o *memory stability* states that the operator does not free or allocate any memory blocks
o *memory safety* states that the operator modifies only the memory block referenced by the pointer variable y, which must be valid in the environment, σ.

Now, we can proceed to formulate the semantic equivalence between an *MHCOL* operator and a "pure" *DHCOL* program. Since the *MHCOL* part of this relation is a function, we need to universally quantify on all possible inputs. Since *DHCOL* operators read and modify memory, the input and output of this function must correspond to some existing memory blocks. In *DHCOL* memory, locations could be accessed via pointer variables only, so we state that there are two pointer variables in the evaluation context corresponding to the input and output memory block locations. For convenience, we define semantic equivalence as a type class parameterized by the respective *MHCOL* and *DHCOL* operators, the evaluation context, and by the name of the input and output pointer variables in this context. Additionally, the purity of the *DHCOL* operator must be guaranteed by providing a DSH_pure instance.

---

[2] We omit error handling for now.

```
Class MSH_DSH_compat
     {i o: ℕ} (σ: evalContext) (m: memory)
     (mop: @MSHOperator i o) (dop: DSHOperator)
     (x_p y_p: PExpr) '{DSH_pure dop y_p} := {
     eval_equiv: ∀ (mx mb: mem_block),
         (lookup_Pexp σ m x_p = inr mx) → (lookup_Pexp σ m y_p = inr mb) →
         (h_opt_opterr_c
             (λ md m' ⇒ err_p (λ ma ⇒ SHCOL_DSHCOL_mem_block_equiv mb ma md)
                        (lookup_Pexp σ m' y_p))
         (mem_op mop mx)
         (evalDSHOperator σ dop m (estimateFuel dop))); }.
```

In the listing above, h_opt_opterr_c deals with error handling. While mem_op
has simple error reporting via option type, evalDSHOperator has two-level error
handling, distinguishing between running out of fuel and other errors. The equality is defined if both operators err (for whatever reason) or both succeed, in
which case, their results must satisfy a provided sub-relation. The sub-relation
(expressed via lambda) does additional error handling via err_p to ensure that
y_p lookup succeeds in m'. Finally, the equality is reduced to the predicate
SHCOL_DSHCOL_mem_block_equiv relating mb, ma, and md.

   Figure 6 shows the origin of these values in a case where no errors occur.
Legend: σ is an evaluation context, m and m' are memory states before and after
execution of the evalDSHOperator. The ma corresponds to a memory block in m'
referenced by y_p. The md is the result of applying the *MHCOL* operator to mx.

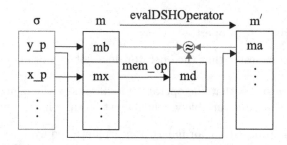

Fig. 6. *DHCOL* and *MHCOL* equality relation

To understand this relation, we must recall, that in *Σ-HCOL*, sparse vectors
represent the results of partial computation. Sparse elements correspond to as
yet uncomputed values, while dense elements are already computed. Performing
a union of the resulting sparse vectors represents the combining of several partial computations. Replacing immutable vectors with mutable memory blocks
allows us to replace the operation of combining computation results with a simple memory update. Following this reasoning, the result of the *MHCOL* operator
application (called md, where "d" stands for *delta*) is a memory block containing values only at the indices that we need to update. The values at all other

indices must remain unchanged. On the other hand, in *DHCOL*, we know the memory state before the operator evaluation and the updated state after it has been evaluated. Thus, `SHCOL_DSHCOL_mem_block_equiv` represents the relation between:

○ `mb` - memory state of the output block before *DHCOL* execution
○ `ma` - memory state of the output block after *DHCOL* execution
○ `md` - values of changed output block elements after *MHCOL* evaluation

This relation is implemented via the element-wise relation, `MemOpDelta`, which is lifted to memory blocks as `SHCOL_DSHCOL_mem_block_equiv`:

```
Definition SHCOL_DSHCOL_mem_block_equiv (mb ma md: mem_block) : Prop
:= ∀ i, MemOpDelta
       (mem_lookup i mb)
       (mem_lookup i ma)
       (mem_lookup i md).


Inductive MemOpDelta (b a d: option CarrierA) : Prop :=
| MemPreserved: is_None d → b = a → MemOpDelta b a d
| MemExpected: is_Some d → a = d → MemOpDelta b a d
```

Informally, it could be stated as:

For all memory indices in `md` where a value is present, the value at the same index in `ma` should be the same. For indices not set in `md`, the value in `ma` should remain as it was in `mb`.

Once we have proven `SH_MSH_Operator_compat` instances for all *MHCOL* operators and their corresponding *DHCOL* equivalents, we can automatically generate proof for the result of any *MHCOL* to *DHCOL* translation as an instance of this class top top-level *MHCOL* and *DHCOL* expressions. During this proof automation, we need to recursively descend on an *MHCOL* expression. The reason for this is that mapping between the two is not injective, and compiling two different *MHCOL* operators could result in similar *DHCOL* constructs not easily distinguishable by simple matching on the structure. Whereas *MHCOL* operators could be uniquely matched.

5   Connecting the Dots: From *FHCOL* to LLVM IR

Dealing with floating-point numbers presents a distinct set of challenges. Instead of introducing floating-point numbers from the very start, we work on an abstract data type (generalized reals) up to and including *DHCOL* language. Switching to floating-point numbers is done by introducing yet another intermediate language, *FHCOL* (F stands for *floating-point*), which operates on IEEE 754 numbers. *FHCOL* and *DHCOL* share the same memory model, but elements are now IEEE 754 *floats* instead of values of the abstract *carrier type*. This is still a higher level than that of the Vellvm memory model, which deals with bytes. However, the

FHCOL memory model can be unambiguously mapped to the Vellvm memory model.

We apply a similar treatment to integers used in arithmetic expressions to calculate memory indices. Since the indices are non-negative by definition, we represent the integers as *natural numbers* in all intermediate languages up to *FHCOL*, where we replace them with int64.

The translation between *DHCOL* and *FHCOL* is trivial, since both languages are implemented as module instances parameterized by different types (for floats and integers). They both a members of a language family indexed by numeric types. This approach allows us to easily define both language syntax and semantics without code duplication. It also allows some lemmas to proven for both languages generally. The translation from *DHCOL* to *FHCOL* is implemented in Gallina.

5.1   Correctness Proof Using Numerical Analysis

The relation in the real domain between the results of the evaluation of the structurally similar expressions in these two languages could encapsulate all numerical analysis properties, such as error bounds and numerical stability.

For integers, we need to perform a very simple bounds check to avoid integer overflows in the arithmetic expressions. The ranges of arithmetic expressions could be estimated based on the ranges of their components. In *DHCOL*, these components are either constants or loop indices. Since loop indices are also bound by constant loop dimensions, overflow analysis is possible.

For floating-point numbers, we identified three approaches. None have yet been implemented, and all represent future research directions.

1. Offline Uncertainty Propagation. In the most general case, an uncertainty propagation approach could be applied [9]. Using it, we can estimate error bounds for compiled *FHCOL* expressions. Unfortunately, in many cases, the error bounds are too large to be useful for practical applications. This analysis could be very easily plugged into our verification framework at the *DHCOL* to *FHCOL* verification step.

2. Problem-Specific Error Estimation. One of the primary intended uses of HELIX is to validate cyber-physical systems. In such settings, the problem domain could inform additional physical constraints which will allow us to provide stronger guarantees, such as tighter error bounds. Therefore, instead of trying to solve this problem in general, we will allow users to plug in their own reasoning, by providing a lemma which guarantees that for a particular expression and its value ranges, the floating-point approximation meets the user's given criteria. This analysis could be implemented by a user and plugged into our verification framework at the *DHCOL* to *FHCOL* verification step.

3. Online Uncertainty Propagation. This approach is similar to the Abstract Interpretation on interval domain, where the values are represented as intervals which are computed at runtime. The result of the computation is not a single value but an interval. Because it is computed for concrete values, it is usually much narrower than one estimated using offline uncertainty propagation. In some cases, it could be proven that it is smaller than the *machine epsilon* of the floating-point representation, collapsing the output interval into a single floating-point number. The price of this approach is that additional computations have to be performed at runtime affecting the performance. The unique advantage of HELIX here is that such computations could be compiled into highly efficient parallelized and vectorized code using SPIRALs optimizations. For this approach, we will introduce yet another language named *IHCOL* which replaces the abstract data type with an interval represented as two IEEE floating point numbers for its bounds. Compared to other approaches, implementing this approach will require greater changes to HELIX, including a new LLVM compiler and its verification.

5.2   Compiling to LLVM IR

Finally, *FHCOL* is compiled into LLVM IR language. A compiler from *FHCOL* to LLVM IR was implemented using Template Coq. To prove semantic equivalence of *FHCOL* programs and their IR translations, we rely on the VELLVM project, which provides formal semantics of IR. The proof involves interaction trees [15], and detailed discussion of it is beyond the scope of this paper.

5.3   Implementation Details and Related Work

There are also many smaller but useful language design and proof techniques not covered in this paper due to space constraints. Presently HELIX consists of 43,393 lines of Coq code. Examples of such techniques include proof automation, monadic error handling, meta-programming translation techniques, dealing with imperative programs with "holes" in the presence of de Bruijn indices (using resolvers), among others. Interested readers are encouraged to see the HELIX source code at https://github.com/vzaliva/helix.

There are several projects for certified compilation from functional to imperative languages. *CertiCoq* translates Gallina programs to CompCert's *Clight*. The goal is much more ambitious than ours, as the aim is to translate not a domain specific language like *Σ-HCOL* but a dependently typed general purpose language. Interestingly, all three guiding principles cited in [1] also apply to our approach. Some of their transformation steps could be related to ours. For example, going from dependently typed *Σ-HCOL* to *MHCOL*, we perform nominal *type erasure*. However, there are some differences at later stages. For example, unlike HELIX, they use a continuation-passing style representation. They prove compiler correctness, while we rely on automated translation validation.

Another related project is *CakeML*, which also targets a subset of a general-purpose language (Standard ML). Unlike HELIX, *CakeML* uses higher-order logic (HOL) to specify *functional big-step semantics* [12]. There are similarities with our approach, as we also use a *definitional interpreter* [14] written in Gallina, to define the semantics of the higher-order language, *FHCOL*. The main differences are: small-step versus big-step semantics and translation validation versus certified compilation. Additionally our programs can not diverge, and while we technically use *fuel* to simplify termination checking, it is different from the *clock* usage in CakeML.

6   Conclusions and Future Work

Our successful completion of this penultimate verification step in the HELIX translation chain brings us one step closer to our final goal of completing HELIX, a formally verified end-to-end high performance code synthesis system based on SPIRAL.

The main contribution of this work is demonstration of an approach to verified translation from mixed-embedded purely functional operator language (*Σ-HCOL*) to deep-embedded imperative language (*DHCOL*) via an intermediate language (*MHCOL*). We have gradually introduced and proven: error handling, a memory model, and evaluation contexts. Our proof approach constrains each language program by a set of properties (*structural correctness* for *Σ-HCOL*, *memory safety* for *MHCOL*, and *purity* for *DHCOL*), using them to prove each translation step. Such properties carry some useful information from step to step in a generic but usable form. For example, when we introduce error handing in *MHCOL*, we prove a property under which no errors would occur in *MHCOL* programs translated from *structurally correct Σ-HCOL*. Similarly, in *DHCOL*, a program can modify arbitrary memory blocks, but we recognize a subset of *DHCOL* programs representing pure functions which have no side effects beyond modifying a single output memory block.

Future work will include the two main directions: First, completing the proof of translation chain by proving the last step of LLVM IR code generation. We made significant progress in this direction jointly with the Vellvm team and expect to finish and publish the results shortly. The second direction is related to floating-point related proofs using one of the strategies outlined in Sect. 5.1. We feel that we did most of preparatory work defining all languages and proof frameworks required to successfully complete this step. It must be noted that the remaining part of the work belongs mostly to the field of numerical analysis rather than formal methods and programming languages.

References

1. Anand, A., et al.: CertiCoq: a verified compiler for Coq. In: The Third International Workshop on Coq for Programming Languages (CoqPL) (2017)
2. Anand, A., Boulier, S., Cohen, C., Sozeau, M., Tabareau, N.: Towards certified meta-programming with typed TEMPLATE-COQ. In: Avigad, J., Mahboubi, A. (eds.) ITP 2018. LNCS, vol. 10895, pp. 20–39. Springer, Cham (2018). https://doi.org/10.1007/978-3-319-94821-8_2

3. Castéran, P., Sozeau, M.: A gentle introduction to type classes and relations in Coq, Technical Report hal-00702455, version 1 (2012)
4. Chlipala, A.: Formal reasoning about programs (2017). http://adam.chlipala.net/frap
5. Franchetti, F., et al.: High-assurance spiral: end-to-end guarantees for robot and car control. IEEE Control Syst. **37**(2), 82–103 (2017). https://doi.org/10.1109/MCS.2016.2643244
6. Franchetti, F., de Mesmay, F., McFarlin, D., Püschel, M.: Operator language: a program generation framework for fast kernels. In: Taha, W.M. (ed.) DSL 2009. LNCS, vol. 5658, pp. 385–409. Springer, Heidelberg (2009). https://doi.org/10.1007/978-3-642-03034-5_18
7. Franchetti, F., et al.: SPIRAL: extreme performance portability. Proc. IEEE **106**(11), 1935–1968 (2018). Special Issue on From High Level Specification to High Performance Code
8. Franchetti, F., Voronenko, Y., Püschel, M.: Formal loop merging for signal transforms. In: Proceedings of the 2005 ACM SIGPLAN Conference on Programming Language Design and Implementation, PLDI 2005, pp. 315–326. ACM, New York (2005). https://doi.org/10.1145/1065010.1065048
9. Higham, N.J.: Accuracy and Stability of Numerical Algorithms, 2nd edn. Society for Industrial and Applied Mathematics, Philadelphia (2002)
10. Leroy, X., Appel, A., Blazy, S., Stewart, G.: The CompCert memory model, version 2. Technical report, INRIA (2012)
11. Low, T.M., Franchetti, F.: High assurance code generation for cyber-physical systems. In: IEEE International Symposium on High Assurance Systems Engineering (HASE) (2017)
12. Owens, S., Myreen, M.O., Kumar, R., Tan, Y.K.: Functional big-step semantics. In: Thiemann, P. (ed.) ESOP 2016. LNCS, vol. 9632, pp. 589–615. Springer, Heidelberg (2016). https://doi.org/10.1007/978-3-662-49498-1_23
13. Püschel, M., et al.: SPIRAL: code generation for DSP transforms. Proc. IEEE **93**(2), 232–275 (2005). https://doi.org/10.1109/JPROC.2004.840306
14. Reynolds, J.C.: Definitional interpreters for higher-order programming languages. In: Proceedings of the ACM Annual Conference, vol. 2, pp. 717–740. ACM 1972. Association for Computing Machinery, New York (1972). https://doi.org/10.1145/800194.805852
15. Xia, L., et al.: Interaction trees. In: Proceedings of the 47th Annual ACM SIGPLAN-SIGACT Symposium on Principles of Programming Languages (POPL 2020). ACM, New York (2020)
16. Zaliva, V., Franchetti, F.: Formal verification of HCOL rewriting (2015). http://www.crocodile.org/lord/Formal_Verification_of_HCOL_Rewriting_FMCAD15.pdf
17. Zaliva, V., Franchetti, F.: HELIX: a case study of a formal verification of high performance program generation. In: Proceedings of the 7th ACM SIGPLAN International Workshop on Functional High-Performance Computing, FHPC 2018, pp. 1–9. ACM, New York (2018). https://doi.org/10.1145/3264738.3264739
18. Zaliva, V., Sozeau, M.: Reification of shallow-embedded DSLs in Coq with automated verification. CoqPL, Cascais, Portugal (2019). http://www.crocodile.org/lord/vzaliva-CoqPL19.pdf
19. Zhao, J.: Formalizing the SSA-based compiler for verified advanced program transformations. Ph.D. thesis

Automatic Detection and Repair of Transition-Based Leakage in Software Binaries

Konstantinos Athanasiou[✉], Thomas Wahl, A. Adam Ding, and Yunsi Fei

Northeastern University, Boston, MA, USA
athanasiou.k@northeastern.edu

Abstract. The effectiveness of masking as a countermeasure against information leakage in cryptographic ciphers is contingent upon individual instructions leaking information independently. An example of dependent leakage is *transition-based leakage*: side-channels can leak data proportional to the exclusive-or of the old and the new value during a register write, despite proper first-order masking. In this paper we present a technique to detect and repair transition-based leakage. Our detection technique symbolically executes a binary to relate the old and new values during a register write. We then combine existing analyses to check for, and quantify, any leakage caused by the write. Our repair module closes a leak by flushing the affected register before writing it.

We also present a fully automated detection and repair tool called BATTL, which is the first to our knowledge to operate at the binary level and is thus sensitive to decisions at any compilation stage that may affect security. We evaluate BATTL against first-order secure implementations of the AES block cipher, and of a secure multiplicative inversion algorithm. BATTL identified a number of transition-based leakages, some with high leakage amounts. Our countermeasure removes all first-order leakages with only moderate runtime overhead.

Keywords: Side channels · Masking · Transition-based leakage

1 Introduction

The security of cryptographic algorithms, such as block ciphers, against crypto attacks, i.e. attacks that exploit how differences in the input correlate with the algorithm's output, is a well-studied problem [20]. Side-channel attacks use physical measurements of cryptographic implementations, such as timing, power consumption, and electromagnetic emanations [17,21,22], to recover the ciphers' secret, demonstrating that "correct" implementations of the cryptographic algorithms do not guarantee their security.

Countermeasures against such attacks are thus critical. The most widely used such measure, the *masking* of software, is a form of secret sharing that splits a secret in $d+1$ shares such that the joint distribution of any d shares is statistically independent of the secret. The implementation has to be refactored to compute its results over $d+1$ shares. If applied correctly, masking guarantees order-d security: any combination of d intermediate results of the implementation is statistically independent of the secret.

Work supported by the US National Science Foundation under award no. SaTC-1563697.

M. Christakis et al. (Eds.): NSV 2020/VSTTE 2020, LNCS 12549, pp. 50–67, 2020.
https://doi.org/10.1007/978-3-030-63618-0_4

These guarantees rest, however, on the *independent leakage assumption* [27]: the intermediate points in the computation should leak independently. Prior work has established that this assumption does not always hold [1,9]. In software implementations, physical effects that occur when a register's old value is overwritten with a new value give rise to leakage that depends on both values, a phenomenon known as *transition-based leakage* (TBL). Balash et al. experimentally demonstrated that a first-order ($d = 1$) secure implementation that splits its secret in ($d + 1 = 2$) shares, leaks the value of a secret to a first-order attacker (that observes $d = 1$ intermediate results) [1]. The leakage assessment required only a small number of power traces, which was collected and analyzed in a few minutes. Effectively, the paper showed that TBL incurs a reduction of the security order by a factor of 2: an attacker can now in effect observe (some) pairs of intermediate results. The same authors suggest that TBL can be averted simply by doubling the masking order. This approach, although easy to enforce, incurs a non-trivial performance overhead compared to the original cryptographic algorithm.

Prior work has proposed to instead address this problem using a modified compiler [31]: by determining pairs of program values that may cause TBL and taking this into account when assigning registers, it prevents TBL-inducing overwrites to begin with. This technique is light-weight and efficient to execute on a given input program. On the down-side, it comes with a heavy implementation cost: modifying a compiler's register allocation is non-trivial and compiler-specific, as it doesn't readily transfer to different compilation toolchains. Furthermore, this prior approach cannot account for leakages introduced during later compilation stages (e.g. linking).

In this paper, instead of analyzing the masked source code or an intermediate representation of it, we propose to analyze the compiled *binaries* of first-order masked programs. Our technique uses symbolic execution to locate register overwrites whose combined leakage involves all shares of the secret. We refer to these writes as *potential* TBLs. To check for statistical dependence of the potential leakage on the secret, we employ a secret dependence detection scheme that utilizes existing approaches [18,32] and quantifies the leakage intensity. If non-zero, we speak of *genuine* TBL.

Operating at the binary level, our technique detects leakages irrespective of whether they are present at the source code, or were introduced at some stage during the compilation. As an example, we show in this paper instances of leakage introduced during compiler optimizations, undetectable for source-code analyses. Our technique is also compiler-agnostic, allowing us to present experiments with different compilers and to compare the leakage characteristics of code generated by them. The technique is implemented in a publicly available tool called BATTL ("Binary Analysis Tool for Transition-based Leakage" [5]), which relies on the angr binary analysis platform [30].

If genuine TBL is detected in the binary, BATTL recompiles the masked program into assembly code, and applies to it a countermeasure based on register flushing. Given a register overwrite that causes genuine TBL, we assign a constant value to the register before the overwrite. At the end, the detection technique can be re-applied to the repaired binaries. In our experiments we confirmed that the flushing countermeasures indeed eliminated the detected leakages, and did not introduce new ones. This is not possible using the compiler-modification strategy proposed in [31].

2 Background and Problem Formalization

2.1 Abstract State Machines

We introduce a simple abstract state machine model, "machine" for short, to study the different leakage models of software implementations. Let V be a set of *values*, and $A \subseteq V$ a set of *addresses*. A machine *state* s is a mapping $s: A \to V$ from addresses to values; we denote by S the set of all such states. For $s \in S$ and $a \in A$, notation $s(a)$ therefore denotes the value stored at address a. Let $R \subseteq S \times S$ be a *transition relation*, formalizing the possible state changes of the machine. An *execution* of the machine is a sequence of states $s_0, s_1, s_2, \ldots$ such that, for all $i \geq 0$, $(s_i, s_{i+1}) \in R$. The initial state s_0 contains the set of machine inputs I.

2.2 Leakage Modeling

The leakage behavior of a state or a transition is formalized using *leakage models*: functions assigning to each state, or each transition, a mapping from addresses to leakage measures. Let $\boxplus$ denote bit-wise XOR.

Definition 1. *The **value-based leakage function** $V_L: S \to (A \to V)$ and the **transition-based leakage function** $T_L: R \to (A \to V)$ are defined by*

$$V_L(s) = \{(a, s(a)) : a \in A\}, \qquad and \qquad (1)$$
$$T_L(s, s') = \{(a, s(a) \boxplus s'(a)) : a \in A\}. \qquad (2)$$

For traceability, we denote XOR used to compute leakage (such as in T_L) by $\boxplus$, while XOR used in source code is denoted $\oplus$. Our definition of V_L above can simply be written as the identity function: $V_L(s) = s$; we write it in the form (1) to emphasize the contrast with (2). In practice, leakage functions often return more abstract measures of the value $s(a)$ stored at some address a, such as its Hamming weight [23]. Our definition is stronger, as it assumes the exact value $s(a)$ is leaked.

The (leakage) *trace* of an execution $t = s_0, s_1, s_2, \ldots$ is obtained by lifting the application of the leakage function from states to traces for VBL and from pairs of states in R to traces of TBL, resulting in:

$$t_{V_L} = V_L(s_0), \quad V_L(s_1), \quad V_L(s_2), \quad \ldots$$
$$t_{T_L} = \qquad\quad T_L(s_0, s_1), \quad T_L(s_1, s_2), \quad \ldots$$

2.3 Masking and Threat Model

Masking [8] is a form of secret sharing [29] in which a secret k is split into *shares* that can be combined using a suitable function to recover the secret. We consider order-d Boolean masking, which uses $d + 1$ share variables, called *(secret) shares*, computed by introducing d shares distributed uniformly at random, and defining the $(d + 1)^{st}$ share as $k_d = k \oplus k_0 \oplus \ldots \oplus k_{d-1}$. The secret thus satisfies $k = k_0 \oplus \ldots \oplus k_d$. Masking is a countermeasure against *differential power analysis* on cryptographic algorithms [21], aimed at making every intermediate measure leaked by the machine appear random.

The plaintext, the secret, the random variables that give rise to the shares, and potentially additional random variables form the input set I of a machine implementing a cryptographic algorithm.

Definition 2. *The result of a leakage function f_L **statistically depends** on the secret if there exist secret values k, k' and a plaintext value p such that the distributions of values of f_L over all choices of the random inputs differ between inputs (k, p) and (k', p).*

We assume the standard Differential Power Analysis threat model [21]: the adversary has physical access to the machine, can provide plaintext inputs, can measure power consumption when executing over the secrets, can measure execution time and knows the implemented algorithm. She does not know the secret values in the implemented algorithm.

Definition 3. *An **execution** of a machine is **first-order secure** under leakage function f_L if each measure generated by f_L along its trace is statistically secret-independent.*

In this paper we focus on the problem of determining whether an execution of a given masked software is first-order secure under TBL. If not, we devise countermeasures that repair the leakage, while preserving the functional semantics of the program.

3 Motivating Example

3.1 Transition-Based Leakage

Compilers are known to compromise software security properties, due to the abstraction gap between source and binary code [12]. Physical resource allocation epitomizes this gap. The compiler maps program variables to physical locations, e.g. registers, which are not present in the source code. This has consequences: *transition-based leakage* [1,9], a known phenomenon in processors that occurs when a register's contents is updated, can accidentally be introduced by a compiler agnostic to the abstraction gap.

We use the *secure inversion* of a shared secret [28] to demonstrate this phenomenon in software binaries. Secure inversion, shown in Algorithm 1, is used in software implementations of the AES S-Box, parameterized by the order d of the masking applied to the source code. Secure multiplication, shown in Algorithm 2, is used inside secure inversion to multiply two shared secrets of size 1 byte each.

We consider the first call to SecMul in Algorithm 1 (Line 3) with symbolic arguments $z = (x_0^2 \oplus r, x_1^2 \oplus r)$ and $x = (x_0, x_1)$, where $x = x_0 \oplus x_1$ is the shared secret and r the random value introduced after the first call to RefreshMasks. We focus on the first time Line 4 of Algorithm 2 is executed. To illustrate TBL, we inspect the ARM assembly of the source code, which is shown in Listing 1.1 of Fig. 1: Line 1 sets up the first call to the `spamul` function, called in Line 2 to compute the product $a_0 \times b_1 := (x_0^2 \oplus r) \times x_1$; Lines 3–5 compute the leftmost XOR prioritized by the parentheses, i.e. $r_{0,1} \oplus (a_0 \times b_1) := r_{0,1} \oplus (x_0^2 \oplus r) \times x_1$; Lines 6–14 set up the second call to `spamul` at Line 15, which computes $a_1 \times b_0 := (x_1^2 \oplus r) \times x_0$.

Figure 2 depicts the register file contents after executing Lines 1 and 14 of Listing 1.1. Following the ARM calling convention, register `r1` holds the second argument

Algorithm 1. SecInv: secure inversion of shared secret x in $GF(2^8)$.	**Algorithm 2.** SecMul: secure multiplication of shared secrets x and y.
Require: $\mathbf{x} = (x_0, \ldots, x_d)$ s.t. $\oplus_i x_i = x$ **Ensure:** $\mathbf{y} = (y_0, \ldots, y_d)$ s.t. $\oplus_i y_i = x^{-1}$ 1: **for** i from 0 to d **do** $z_i := x_i^2$ 2: RefreshMasks($\mathbf{z}$) 3: $\mathbf{y} := $ SecMul($\mathbf{z}, \mathbf{x}$) 4: **for** i from 0 to d **do** $w_i := y_i^4$ 5: RefreshMasks($\mathbf{w}$) 6: $\mathbf{y} := $ SecMul($\mathbf{y}, \mathbf{w}$) 7: **for** i from 0 to d **do** $y_i := y_i^{16}$ 8: $\mathbf{y} := $ SecMul($\mathbf{y}, \mathbf{w}$) 9: $\mathbf{y} := $ SecMul($\mathbf{y}, \mathbf{z}$)	**Require:** $(a_0, \ldots, a_d)$ and $(b_0, \ldots, b_d)$ s.t. $\oplus_i a_i = a$ and $\oplus_i b_i = b$ **Ensure:** $(c_0, \ldots, c_d)$ s.t. $\oplus_i c_i = a \times b$ 1: **for** i from 0 to d **do** 2: **for** j from $i + 1$ to d **do** 3: $r_{i,j} \in_R GF(2^n)$ 4: $r_{j,i} := (r_{i,j} \oplus a_i \times b_j) \oplus a_j \times b_i$ 5: **for** i from 0 to d **do** 6: $c_i := a_i \times b_i$ 7: **for** j from 0 to $d, j \neq i$ **do** 8: $c_i := c_i \oplus r_{i,j}$

to `spamul`, i.e. x_1 in Line 3 and x_0 in Line 14. The overwrite of register r1 caused by the `mov` instruction in Line 14 involves both shares of $\mathbf{x}$ in a single instruction. This fact alone does not yet indicate a secret leakage; we refer to it as a *potential* leak. To determine whether the leak is *genuine*, we use the leakage model function T_L (introduced in Sect. 2.2), i.e. the XOR between the old and new values of the register write [1,9]. The potential leak observed at Line 14 measures as $x_1 \boxplus x_0 = x$ and constitutes a genuine leak of the value of x as the secret and the leakage expression are directly related.

To see that the presence of all shares of a secret in a leakage expression is not sufficient for genuine leakage, consider the first call to `spamul`: its return value $(x_0^2 \oplus r) \times x_1$ is stored in register r2 (not shown in Listing 1.1). The load at Line 7 overwrites r2 with a constant value and forms the potential TBL $(x_0^2 \oplus r) \times x_1 \boxplus \text{0x7ffefd74}$. This leakage is not genuine since the random variable r eliminates any statistical dependence between the leakage expression and the secret $\mathbf{x}$. The goal of this paper is to detect genuine TBL, and to protect against it using countermeasures.

3.2 Complications Ahead: Value-Based Leakage

Ignoring security concerns during compilation can not only introduce TBL, as seen in Sect. 3.1, but can in fact sabotage the very leakage protection that source-code transformations like masking are supposed to provide. To see this, consider Line 4 of Algorithm 2 and its corresponding *optimized* ARM assembly, shown in Listing 1.2 of Fig. 1. The two calls to `spamul` are inlined and computed in parallel in Lines 1–9. After executing the load instruction at Line 10, registers r6 and r2 hold the two products computed in Line 4 of SecMul, namely $(x_0^2 \oplus r) \times x_1$ and $(x_1^2 \oplus r) \times x_0$ respectively, and register r3 the fresh random value $r_{0,1}$. In Lines 11 and 12, the compiler decides to exploit the associativity of XOR and change the order of operations, creating the expression $(x_0^2 \oplus r) \times x_1 \oplus (x_1^2 \oplus r) \times x_0$ for the symbolic value computed at Line 11. This expression is statistically dependent on the secret x (the random variable r cancels out and provides no protection). The resulting VBL demonstrates how the protection provided by the source-code level masking was inadvertently destroyed by an optimization that obliviously rewrote an expression.

```
1   mov    r1, r3
2   bl     spamul
3   mov    r3, r0
4   eors   r3, r4
5   uxtb   r4, r3
6   ldr    r3, [r7, #24]
7   ldr    r2, [r7, #12]
8   add    r3, r2
9   ldrb   r0, [r3, #0]
10  ldr    r3, [r7, #28]
11  ldr    r2, [r7, #8]
12  add    r3, r2
13  ldrb   r3, [r3, #0]
14  mov    r1, r3
15  bl     spamul
```

Listing 1.1: Default asm (-O0)

```
1   ldrb   r2, [r2, #256]
2   ldrb   r3, [r3, #256]
3   ubfx   r6, r6, #7, #1
4   ubfx   r0, r0, #7, #1
5   orrs   r1, r5
6   and    r6, r6, r4, asr #7
7   and    r0, r0, r1, asr #7
8   mul    r6, r6, r2
9   mul    r2, r0, r3
10  ldrb   r3, [ip, #1]
11  eors   r2, r6
12  eors   r3, r2
13  strb   r3, [sp, #30]
14  ldrb   r2, [sp, #4]
```

Listing 1.2: Optimized asm (-O2)

Fig. 1. Assembly code for Line 4 of Algorithm 2 (SecMul) generated by default compiler flags (left) and optimization flags (right)

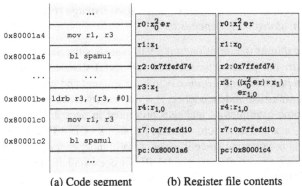

(a) Code segment   (b) Register file contents

Fig. 2. (a) Code segment of Listing 1.1 causing transition-based leakage after executing the instruction highlighted red. (b) Register file contents after executing the first mov instruction (left), and after executing the highlighted mov instruction (right), which ultimately causes the leakage. (Color figure online)

While VBL due to compiler optimizations is not the main object of our study, it has important repercussions on the detection and repair of TBL: Line 14 of Listing 1.2 loads the constant value 0x7ffefd74 to register r2 and produces the TBL $(x_0^2 \oplus r) \times x_1 \oplus (x_1^2 \oplus r) \times x_0 \boxplus 0x7ffefd74$, which is statistically dependent on x. While technically a TBL, the leakage is already present in the value stored in register r2 and is unrelated to the confluence of all shares of a secret during the overwrite. We require for a potential TBL to be genuine, not only that the $\boxplus$ between the old and the new value of the register be statistically dependent on the secret, but also that neither value have genuine value-based leakage. Line 9 of Listing 1.2 is an example of a genuine TBL as it satisfies all these conditions. We formally define all these concepts in Sect. 4. This distinction also becomes relevant when it comes to eliminating the leakage as the TBL countermeasure we present in Sect. 5 is designed to disrupt said confluence of shares and will thus not repair TBLs that are in fact due to value-based leaks.

The latter type must be repaired using its own dedicated techniques, e.g. by preventing the above-mentioned unsafe expression rewriting.

4   Detection of Transition-Based Leakage

4.1   Potential and Genuine Leakage

We extend the definition of the abstract machine of Sect. 2.1 to a *symbolic* machine: let V_{sym} denote the set of *symbolic values* (expressions) over program inputs, A_{sym} the set of *symbolic addresses* (address variables), S_{sym} the set of *symbolic states* and R_{sym} the set of symbolic transitions. Let $Sh(k)$ be the set of shares into which the secret k is split, i.e. such that $\bigoplus_{k_i \in Sh(k)} k_i = k$. The shares are part of the symbolic input variables I_{sym}, i.e. $Sh(k) \subseteq I_{sym}$. Let $vars(v)$ be the set of symbolic variables in expression v.

Definition 4. *A **potential value-based leakage (PVBL)** is a pair $(s, a) \in S_{sym} \times A_{sym}$ such that $Sh(k) \subseteq vars(s(a))$. A **genuine value-based leakage (GVBL)** is a PVBL (s, a) such that $V_L(s)(a)$ statistically depends on k.*

Definition 4 captures the intuition that a VBL satisfies the necessary leakage condition of being *share-complete*: it must contain all secret shares. Our motivation to distinguish between *potential* and *genuine* is to have a sound and quick (although partial) way of checking statistical independence: it is implied by share-incompleteness.

We revisit some examples of leakages presented in Sect. 3. For a shared secret x such that $x_0 \oplus x_1 = x$ and a random value r, $(x_0^2 \oplus r) \times x_1$ is a PVBL since it is share-complete, but it is not genuine since it is statistically independent of x. In contrast, the PVBL $(x_0^2 \oplus r) \times x_1 \oplus (x_1^2 \oplus r) \times x_0$ is a GVBL: it does statistically depend on x. We discuss in Sect. 6 how to check this dependence condition.

Definition 5. *A **potential transition-based leakage (PTBL)** is a triple $(s_{i-1}, s_i, a) \in R_{sym} \times A_{sym}$ such that*

(i) $Sh(k) \subseteq vars(s_{i-1}(a)) \cup vars(s_i(a))$, and
(ii) neither (s_{i-1}, a) nor (s_i, a) is a GVBL.

*A **genuine transition-based leakage (GTBL)** is a PTBL (s_{i-1}, s_i, a) such that the term $T_L(s_{i-1}, s_i)(a)$ statistically depends on k.*

Note how we design our notion of (P)TBL to depend on GVBL, in order to exclude leakages attributable to VBL (see Sect. 3.2). Under the above definitions, the leakage $(x_0^2 \oplus r) \times x_1 \oplus (x_1^2 \oplus r) \times x_0 \boxplus 0x7ffefd74$ from the overwrite of register r2 discussed in Sect. 3.2 is not a GTBL since the lhs of $\boxplus$ (the old value of r2) is (already) a GVBL.

4.2   Detection of Genuine Transition-Based Leakage

Following the definitions of Sect. 4.1, our TBL detection must be able to decide share-completeness and statistical dependence. We make use of forward symbolic execution to check for share-completeness by keeping track of the *symbolic transitions*, i.e. pairs containing the symbolic values of a location at two consecutive symbolic states.

```
1        0x22:mov r8, #0
2        0x24:mov r0, r9
3        0x26:ldrb r1, [r6, r8]
4        0x2a:mul r0, r0, r1
5        0x2e:mov r1, r10
6        0x30:mov r4, r0
7        0x32:ldrb r0, [r5, r8]
8        0x36:mul r0, r0, r1
9        0x3a:add r8, r8, #1
10       0x3c:cmp r8, #2
11       0x40:bne 0x24
```

Listing 1.3: ARM assembly program fragment. Symbolic inputs $a0, $a1, $b0, $b1 are stored in registers/locations r9, 0x7d, r10, 0x8d, resp. Registers r5, r6 hold the location addresses 0x7d, 0x8d. Symbols #0, #1, #2 denote constants.

Table 1. Symbolic transitions generated by executing Listing 1.3. *Address* is the address of an instruction in the listing, *Location* is the name of the instruction's target register. Symbols c_1, c_2, c_3 denote constants.

Address	Location	Symbolic Transition (old, new)
0x24	$r0	$(c_1, \$a0)$
0x26	$r1	$(c_2, \$b1)$
0x2a	$r0	$(\$a0, \$a0 * \$b1)$
0x2e	$r1	$(\$b1, \$b0)$
0x30	$r4	$(c_3, \$a0 * \$b1)$
0x32	$r0	$(\$a0 * \$b1, \$a1)$
0x36	$r0	$(\$a1, \$a1 * \$b0)$

Consider Listing 1.3, the two secrets $a and $b and their corresponding sets of shares $Sh(\$a) = \{\$a0, \$a1\}$, $Sh(\$b) = \{\$b0, \$b1\}$. Table 1 lists the transitions generated by symbolically executing Listing 1.3. The instructions at Lines 2,3,6 don't generate interesting transitions because their target registers r0, r1, r4 contain constants before the instruction and thus no shares. The target registers of instructions at Lines 4 and 8 hold secret shares both before and after the transition; however, the before and the after value together do not involve *all* shares of secret $a, nor all shares of $b. Only instructions at Lines 5 and 7 involve all shares of one of the secrets (in red) and qualify as share-complete. Application of a leakage function to the contents of an address of a symbolic state generates a symbolic leakage expression. We need a leakage analysis method that can decide whether this expression statistically depends on the secret variable. Various techniques and metrics for qualitative and quantitative analysis of statistical dependence have been proposed in the literature [7, 16, 18, 19]. For now we present our GTBL detection method in a form parametric in the dependence analysis; we instantiate this parameter in Sect. 6.

Algorithm 3 shows our GTBL detection scheme implementing Definition 5. It uses the abstract predicate *SecretDep*(l) that decides whether a given symbolic leakage expression l statistically depends on the secret. The algorithm is *lazy* in the sense that it delays the (potentially expensive) secret dependence checks, in favor of the (syntactic) share-completeness checks: Line 1 checks condition (i) in Definition 5. The symmetric blocks starting in Lines 3 and 6 check condition (ii), by first determining share-completeness of the respective VBL expression and then, if necessary, check for statistical dependence on the secret, still for VBL. In Line 9 we know the TBL is potential; to determine its genuineness we must perform a secret dependence check.

Algorithm 3 is used at every step of the forward symbolic execution, to classify whether the location that is written to during that step constitutes a GTBL. The number of GTBL checks is thus linear in the number of states along the execution (instead of quadratic, as it would be for the alternative method of checking for second-order

---

Algorithm 3. GTBL checker

Require: Symbolic state s_i and its predecessor s_{i-1}, address a written at s_i.
Ensure: True if (s_{i-1}, s_i, a) is a GTBL; False otherwise.
1: **if** $(s_{i-1}(a), s_i(a))$ is share-incomplete **then**
2:     **return** False
3: **if** $s_{i-1}(a)$ is share-complete **then**
4:     **if** $SecretDep(V_L(s_{i-1})(a))$ **then**
5:         **return** False
6: **if** $s_i(a)$ is share-complete **then**
7:     **if** $SecretDep(V_L(s_i)(a))$ **then**
8:         **return** False
9: **return** $SecretDep(T_L(s_{i-1}, s_i)(a))$

```
10   ldr    r3, [r7, #28]
11   ldr    r2, [r7, #8]
12   add    r3, r2
13   ldrb   r3, [r3, #0]
14   mov    r1, #0
15   mov    r1, r3
16   bl     spamul
```

Listing 1.4: Flushing instruction eliminating the GTBL of L. 14 in List. 1.1.

```
7    and    r0, r0, r1, asr #7
8    mov    r7, #0
9    mov    r7, r6
10   mov    r6, #0
11   mul    r6, r7, r2
12   mov    r7, #0
13   mul    r2, r0, r3
```

Listing 1.5: Flushing gadget eliminating the GTBL of L. 8 in List. 1.2.

protection, by considering all possible pairs of states). Absence of GTBLs along the execution implies that the latter is first-order secure under TBL.

5   Repair of Transition-Based Leakage

TBL violates the independent leakage assumption via a register overwrite that combines the value computed at the current step and the value last stored in the register. To eliminate the TBL, it therefore suffices to disconnect the confluence of the two values by *flushing* the contents of the overwritten register. The flushing countermeasure has to be applied before the register write (i.e. before the *definition*, in compiler terminology) that manifests the leakage, yet after the previous definition of the same register. We refer to the TBL-inducing register as TBL register. Additionally, to guarantee that the original program's I/O semantics is maintained (correctness requirement), flushing has to be applied *after* the last read (i.e. *use*) of the TBL register, to ensure that uses see the original contents instead of the flushed ones.

Simply inserting a *flushing instruction*, such as one that sets the contents of the TBL register to 0 right before the leaky instruction, guarantees in most cases that the above conditions are met, and results in a straightforward and efficient countermeasure. Listing 1.4 shows how a flushing instruction eliminates the GTBL described in Sect. 3.1.

The flushing instruction approach assumes that the last use of the TBL register occurs at a different, earlier instruction in the program. This assumption is violated in the case of instructions that both use and define the TBL register, which we refer to as *update instructions*. Listing 1.5 shows a *flushing gadget* for repairing the TBL of the

---

Algorithm 4. Flushing Countermeasure

Require: Instruction I whose target register is to be flushed.
Ensure: Sequence of instructions that is I/O equivalent to I and GTBL-free.
  1: $r_d := Def(I)$
  2: **if** $r_d \notin Use(I)$ **then**
  3:     **return** Flush(r_d); I
  4: **else**
  5:     r_t := Dead()
  6:     $I_0; I_1 := Split(I, r_t)$
  7:     **return** Flush(r_t); I_0; Flush(r_d); I_1; Flush(r_t)

---

update instruction **mul** r6, r6, r2 at Line 8 of Listing 1.2. The gadget splits the instruction and eliminates the use of the TBL register r6, as follows. First, it transfers the old contents of r6 to an unused register, namely r7, in Line 9 of Listing 1.5.[1] Second, it performs the flush of the TBL register (Line 10). Third, it modifies the original leaky instruction, by replacing r6 on the right-hand side (the use) by r7 (Line 11), so that the modified instruction is equivalent to the original update. Finally, and critically, the gadget must rule out that r7 accidentally introduce leakage through its previous or future contents. Therefore, r7 is flushed at Lines 8 and 12.

We formalize our flushing countermeasure in Algorithm 4, which takes as input an instruction I whose target register is to be flushed, and makes use of the following subroutines:

Def(I):   the register instruction I defines;

Use(I):   the set of registers instruction I uses;

Flush(r):   given register r, return the instruction **mov** r, #0;

Split(I, r_t):   given an update instruction I (**opc** ra, ra, rb) and a temporary
            register r_t, return an I/O-equivalent sequence of two instructions
            (**mov** rt, ra; **opc** ra, rt, rb) that eliminate the use of
            the target register of I, by using the temporary register instead;

Dead():   an available register, i.e. one that is not used along any path between
          the instruction we are flushing and its next definition.

Theorem 6. *Application of the flushing countermeasure (Algorithm 4) to each GTBL-induc-ing instruction of an assembly program P results in an I/O-equivalent and GTBL-free assembly program P_f.*

Proof (Sketch): I/O-equivalence follows easily from the subroutine specifications given above. Flushing eliminates each GTBL (s_{i-1}, s_i, a) by splitting it into its corresponding non-genuine VBLs (s_{i-1}, a) and (s_i, a), and the zero leakage VBL (s_f, a), where s_f is the state introduced by Flush. $\square$

---

[1] If an unused register is not available, we free a used register, by spilling its contents to memory.

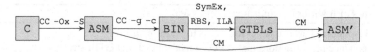

Fig. 3. BATTL's GTBL detection and repair pipeline. Arrows indicate the invocation of the components mentioned above them; boxes indicate the intermediate results produced by BATTL's flow.

6   BATTL: Binary Analysis for Transition-Based Leakage

6.1   Implementation

We have implemented the detection and repair of transition-based leakage in BATTL, our BINARY ANALYSIS TOOL FOR TRANSITION-BASED LEAKAGE [5], written in Python and C. Figure 3 shows the toolflow of BATTL. It expects a masked C program, compiles it to binary, reports the detected GTBLs, and outputs an I/O-equivalent and TBL-free masked assembly (asm) program. BATTL is parametric to the compiler used for generating the binary and asm programs, and requires no compiler modifications.

Detection. BATTL's symbolic execution component (SymEx) is built on top of the `angr` binary analysis platform [30] and uses the latter's symbolic execution engine on the compiled binaries to generate symbolic transitions. BATTL is imported as a library in user provided *drivers*, which are python programs specifying the inputs and secrets of the binary. We use two complementary techniques, in order of increasing hardness and precision, for the implementation of *SecretDep*. First, we adapt the *rule-based* approach of Gao et al. [18] to operate on bitvector expressions. This rule-based system (RBS) statically checks the symbolic leakage expressions for semantic properties that imply the distribution class they fall into, namely one of three classes: (i) RUD, denoting a random-uniform distribution; (ii) SID, denoting a secret-independent distribution, or (iii) UKD, denoting an unknown distribution. Class RUD is a subset of SID; both permit the conclusion of leakage-freedom. A UKD expression, however, may or may not leak; in this sense, RBS is incomplete.

To resolve this incompleteness, our implementation of *SecretDep* resorts to a second technique, the *Information Leakage Amount* (ILA) metric function [32]. ILA quantifies how much one secret value is distinguishable from the remaining secret values, by computing the averaged square of the L_2-distances of the Hamming weights of the f_L-measures that each different value of the secret gives rise to. ILA maps a symbolic expression to a real number in the range $[0, 4]$ that signifies its leakage intensity. Zero ILA implies that the expression doesn't statistically depend on the secret; in this case *SecretDep* returns False. Positive ILA implies dependence on the secret; higher values indicate more leakage and thus easier exploitability. The upper bound of 4 derives from the number of bits of the secret variable divided by 2: we have 1-byte secrets, stored in 32-bit machine integers.

The calculation of ILA involves exhaustive enumeration of the possible values of the secret and random variables of the leakage expression and can therefore be expensive. Our implementation of *SecretDep*, which returns the ILA value (rather than just a

Boolean value, as suggested by Algorithm 3), uses a sampling-based approach to compute ILA for expressions with 4 or more variables. The ILA computation component is implemented as a C embedding in the original source code of the analyzed program.

Repair. The flushing countermeasure of Sect. 5 is implemented as a component of BATTL named CM. In BATTL's pipeline we instruct the compiler to generate the (possibly optimized) assembly code to which we add debug information and then compile to an executable binary. BATTL detects the binary's GTBLs and using debug information it reports the asm source lines and instruction that cause the GTBLs. The instructions and the assembly code are the input of CM, which applies the flushing countermeasure. To accommodate the Dead subroutine required by the flushing gadgets without the need of spilling, we perform a register liveness analysis during the SymEx phase.

6.2 Evaluation

We evaluate BATTL by attempting to validate the following hypotheses.

H1: Genuine TBLs naturally occur in first-order secure implementations;
H2: GTBL is not restricted to specific compilation toolchains or options;
H3: GVBLs appear in binaries obtained from masked source code due to "careless" optimizations; they influence the number of reported GTBLs;
H4: Flushing countermeasures are effective and incur only small overhead on the original implementation.

We present a thorough analysis of the above hypotheses using BATTL. We are not aware of other tools that are able to identify TBL at the binary level. The prior work on compiler-based elimination of TBL [31], which operates on llvm IR, does not offer a publicly available implementation.

Benchmarks. We test these hypotheses against benchmarks from two algorithms: SecInv [28] (shown in Sect. 3) and a masked version of AES [10, 11, 33]. Both algorithms are parametric in the protection order d, which we set to $d = 1$ since we focus on the detection of first-order TBL. While SecInv is nominally part of the AES SBox, the implementation of AES used in the evaluation of BATTL makes use of the *common share* [10] and *randomness reduction* [33] approaches and performs improved mask refreshing [11].[2] The SecInv benchmark is therefore not part of the AES benchmark.

Our benchmarks consist of binaries generated from C implementations of SecInv ($\approx$100 LOC) and AES ($\approx$500 LOC) that target the ARM Cortex-M3 family of microprocessors and vary along two orthogonal axes: the optimization level (O0–O2) and the compilation toolchain (gcc, llvm). SecInv operates on 1 secret key byte, and AES on 16 secret key bytes. We instruct BATTL to symbolically execute the full SecInv binaries and identify leaks of its secret key. In the case of the AES binaries we stop after executing the first AES round (the algorithm consists of 10 rounds in total) and check for leaks stemming from the first key byte.[3]

---

[2] https://github.com/knarfrank/Higher-Order-Masked-AES-128.

[3] BATTL can be configured by the user to check for any number of bytes of the secret key. We choose one, the first, for presentation purposes.

Table 2. Rows 1–4: Potential and genuine TBL summary for SecInv and AES. #PTBL is the total number of PTBLs. The fraction of PTBLs shown to be secret-independent using the RBS is given in row #RUD/SID, that of PTBLs shown secret-independent using the ILA metric in row #ILA=0, and that of PTBLs shown to leak genuinely on account of a positive ILA in row #GTBL. Rows #RUD/SID, #ILA=0, #GTBL add up to row #PTBL. Rows 5–7: Wall-clock running time of BATTL's components. Rows RBS and ILA report the total runtime spent on the analysis of all PTBLs of each benchmark.

	SecInv (d=1)						AES (d=1)					
	gcc			llvm			gcc			llvm		
	-O0	-O1	-O2	-O0	-O1	-O2	-O0	-O1	-O2	-O0	-O1	-O2
1: #PTBL	442	262	194	309	200	121	156	92	113	108	90	92
2: #RUD/SID	263	143	106	222	132	71	121	67	85	87	69	75
3: #ILA=0	43	20	12	17	23	19	4	8	6	6	9	9
4: #GTBL	136	99	76	70	45	31	31	17	22	15	12	8
5: SymEx	1m57s	21s	20s	53s	27s	19s	6m08s	2m5s	2m27s	2m47s	1m55s	1m38s
6: RBS	3s	4s	3s	4s	2s	1s	1s	1s	1s	1s	1s	1s
7: ILA	4h26m	1h45m	1h4m	2h3m	1h56m	1h4m	1h53m	57m32s	46m29s	32m19s	36m22s	23m48s

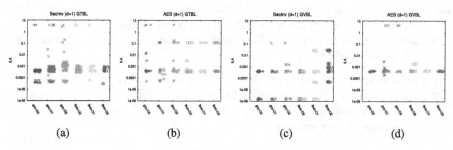

(a)   (b)   (c)   (d)

Fig. 4. Scatter plots of GTBLs and GVBLs for SecInv and AES benchmarks; each point represents a genuine leakage with the ILA value reported on the vertical axis.

Experimental Results. Table 2 summarizes the numbers of TBL leaks reported by BATTL across all benchmarks. It confirms **H1** and **H2** and shows that first-order source-code protection does not avert first-order TBL, as BATTL identified GTBLs across *all* configurations of optimization options and compiler toolchains. Figure 4 displays the distribution of different leakage amounts across the different experiments and different leakage points (code locations). We see that in most benchmarks the manifested leakage can be large. All of the SecInv benchmarks except for llvm-O2 have at least one GTBL case near the maximum ILA value of 4, which is easily exploitable by an adversary [32]. For AES, 2/6 benchmarks show ILA values of 4, with the rest having a large count of GTBLs with ILA ≈ 0.1. Our experiments also suggest that llvm-generated binaries show fewer TBL points, with smaller ILA values, than those generated by gcc, for both algorithms across all flags, essentially providing a more narrow attack surface. As a possible explanation, we observed on our benchmarks that llvm aggressively unrolled loops and generated larger basic blocks and, therefore, altogether larger

Table 3. Performance analysis of repaired benchmarks. Columns FI, FG show the number of flushing instructions and flushing gadgets per benchmark, respectively. Columns CC show the number of clock cycles of the repaired benchmarks. Columns (%) show the percentage increase in cycles between the original and the repaired benchmarks.

	SecInv (d=1)							AES (d=1)						
	gcc				llvm				gcc				llvm	
	FI	FG	CC	(%)	FI	FG	CC	(%)	FI	FG	CC	(%)	FI	FG	CC	(%)
-O0	16	4	6640	7.58	8	3	4978	7.65	8	5	36847	5.47	3	4	28757	3.73
-O1	12	5	1856	19.88	8	2	2688	9.38	7	5	11599	9.24	1	3	13422	1.38
-O2	9	13	1645	15.74	11	2	1086	6.08	7	4	10781	7.96	4	2	9666	0.33

binaries. We believe this code layout approach leads to fewer TBLs as it (accidentally) promotes the use of more registers in a basic block.

Our experiments were performed on first-order source-code secure implementations and might therefore be expected by the unaware programmer to be free of value-based leakage. Our findings contradict this expectation and confirm **H3**: for SecInv the two points with ILA ≈ 0.12 in Fig. 4c for gcc-O1/O2 correspond to the VBL due to expression reordering (explained in Sect. 3.2). llvm-O1/O2 also shows measurable leakage with ILA ≈ 0.02. For AES, Fig. 4d gcc-O1/O2 shows full leakage of the secret due to VBL with ILA ≈ 4. The remaining points in Fig. 4d have very small ILA values obtained via sampling, indicating that they might in fact be leak-free. The llvm compiler fares strictly better than gcc, regarding re-introduction of VBL. We attribute this to differently implemented expression rewriting (-ftree-reassoc, -reassociate flags) in the two toolchains.

Analysis Performance. Table 2 summarizes BATTL's performance. For each benchmark, we execute BATTL on a single core of a desktop Intel-i7-4770@3.40 GHz with 16 GB RAM. Block cipher code consists of loops with a constant number of iterations and lacks input-dependent control-flow variations. As a result, SymEx doesn't suffer from path explosion; its runtime variations across benchmarks result from the different program sizes. angr's engine scaled well with increasing expression size: no benchmark required more than 6 GB of RAM for its analysis.

BATTL spends a negligible amount of time on the RBS module; the ILA module dominates the time required for deciding *SecretDep* for PTBLs. For each benchmark, the number of ILA checks is equal to the sum of i) #PTBL – #RUD/SID and ii) the number of ILA checks performed when determining the set of PTBLs caused by GVBL. The runtime of each ILA check depends on the number of variables present in the leakage expression (see Sect. 6.1).

Flushing Countermeasure and Overhead. We have used CM to flush all the GTBLs of our benchmarks in the compiler-generated assembly. We use the internal clock cycle counter of ARM Cortex-M3 [24] to measure the number of clock cycles of one invocation of SecInv and one round of AES, shown in Table 3. CM eliminates GTBLs without an increase in the masking order and incurs small performance overhead, confirming **H4**. For comparison, we have measured second-order ($d = 2$) implementations to incur more than a 100% overhead. The difference in clock cycles between SecInv and AES is due to the larger size of the latter, which naturally results in longer execution times. SecInv is subject to larger overheads (%) compared to AES. Per Table 2, SecInv has a larger amount of GTBLs and consequently requires more flushing instructions and flushing gadgets, to eliminate the leakage. Spilling was required in 14/24 of the flushing gadgets applied to the AES benchmarks (it was never required in SecInv).

The slowdown (%) incurred by our countermeasure is comparable to that reported by the earlier compiler-based approach [31]. In contrast to that work, we can apply BATTL to the final repaired binary to confirm the effectiveness of our countermeasure. (Note that Theorem 6 applies only to the repaired assembly (ASM' in Fig. 3) and does not account for possible interference by later compilation stages, such as the linker.)

7 Related Work

The majority of related work targets the VBL model. They use formal techniques to verify the correctness of masking countermeasures [3,7,13,15,18] and correct-by-construction approaches that automatically mask the source code, either at compile time [4,6,25], or synthesized independently [14]. Some of the verification techniques can in principle be extended to the TBL model by verifying second-order masking (since a second-order secure implementation is free of first-order TBL, as shown in [1]), although their experimental evaluations show that the analysis does not scale [7,18].

One can think of our technique, dedicated to TBL, as a *focused* second-order analysis: instead of considering all pairs of intermediate variables, only those that constitute consecutive assignments to the same register are investigated. This vastly reduces the complexity of the analysis from quadratic to linear in the length of the execution path. Based on forward symbolic execution, our technique is a form of (path-)bounded analysis: it reports all leakages up to the point of the symbolic execution. It is suitable for code with modest control-flow variations, or code with loops of a constant number of iterations. Block ciphers, the main target of power attacks, enjoy such characteristics.

Only recent work has considered the issue of TBL explicitly [2,26,31]. The work closest to ours is the correct-by-construction approach of Wang et al. [31]. They present a sound static analysis (based on the same rule system [18] used in BATTL) that is applied on the llvm IR. To avoid considering all pairs of instructions in the IR (which lacks register information) they use additional static analysis to overapproximate pairs of instructions that share registers, and apply the rule system to these pairs. Any pair classified as UKD is considered sensitive. To eliminate leaks that could arise from sensitive pairs, they add constraints to the register allocation and DAG combination passes of llvm to disallow register overwrites and to eliminate update instructions respectively.

The notion of *sensitive pair* [31] is an overapproximation of our notion of PTBL (the latter are precise in terms of register overwrites) and can thus not prove the existence of leakages, only their absence. Being a purely static analysis, their approach favors efficiency over precision. Their technique incurs small, if any, performance overhead. However, it is (i) susceptible to interference from the compilation framework after the countermeasure passes are applied, and (ii) bound to their modified `llvm` compiler. As our analysis is performed on binaries, BATTL doesn't suffer from the above issues: it can be run on the repaired binaries to confirm the absence of compiler interference, and it is compiler agnostic. The refined definition of a GTBL that accounts for leakages due to GVBLs and is unique to our methodology, crucially influences the security guarantees of countermeasures specialized for TBL. BATTL reports such cases to the user and doesn't apply countermeasures to them, since they would anyway be ineffective. The user is responsible for eliminating the GVBL that induces the TBL, before starting a fresh round of detection and repair. Wang et al. do not distinguish cases of TBL due to VBL that cannot be eliminated by TBL-specific countermeasures and as a result the binaries they produce are subject to leakage.

MaskVerif [2], a tool based on a relational verification approach [3], is aimed at the analysis of (very) high-order software implementations under VBL and TBL. It requires transformation of the masking algorithm to some intermediate representation, contrary to our approach that operates directly on binary programs. It is geared towards circuit implementations that operate on Boolean variables and therefore doesn't handle software implementations. These shortcomings are common among previously proposed methods: they operate on intermediate representations such as `llvm` IR [7,18,31] or other internal languages [2] and target Boolean programs [2,18]. Work that, like ours, operates on ARM assembly does not handle TBL or high-order implementations [13].

ASCOLD [26] is a tool for detecting transition-based leakages in AVR assembly. It keeps track of register overwrites and conservatively reports all cases that are share-complete. This leads to a vast amount of false positive leakage reports and unnecessary overhead when attempting to apply countermeasures. ASCOLD is restricted in the programs it can handle. It has been used on hand-written assembly code and supports but a fragment of the AVR assembly instruction set and it cannot be applied to arbitrary, compiler-generated binaries. Both MaskVerif and ASCOLD rely on manual insertion of countermeasures to TBL.

8 Conclusion and Future Work

We have presented a technique for the automated detection of transition-based leakage in software binaries, and a countermeasure for their repair. Our analysis showed that such leakage is prevalent in block ciphers and of high intensity among different compiler configurations. Our countermeasure was able to eliminate the reported leakages with a moderate performance overhead. By operating on binaries, our detection approach is sensitive to any leaks introduced by a leakage-oblivious compilation chain.

We leave the detection of transition effects through *memory writes*, in addition to register writes, as an immediate step for future work. In terms of repair, we believe that by using information provided by the forward symbolic execution we can devise even smaller gadgets that don't require flushing of registers used to temporarily hold values.

References

1. Balasch, J., Gierlichs, B., Grosso, V., Reparaz, O., Standaert, F.-X.: On the cost of lazy engineering for masked software implementations. In: Joye, M., Moradi, A. (eds.) CARDIS 2014. LNCS, vol. 8968, pp. 64–81. Springer, Cham (2015). https://doi.org/10.1007/978-3-319-16763-3_5

2. Barthe, G., Belaïd, S., Cassiers, G., Fouque, P.-A., Grégoire, B., Standaert, F.-X.: maskVerif: automated verification of higher-order masking in presence of physical defaults. In: Sako, K., Schneider, S., Ryan, P.Y.A. (eds.) ESORICS 2019. LNCS, vol. 11735, pp. 300–318. Springer, Cham (2019). https://doi.org/10.1007/978-3-030-29959-0_15

3. Barthe, G., Belaïd, S., Dupressoir, F., Fouque, P.-A., Grégoire, B., Strub, P.-Y.: Verified proofs of higher-order masking. In: Oswald, E., Fischlin, M. (eds.) EUROCRYPT 2015. LNCS, vol. 9056, pp. 457–485. Springer, Heidelberg (2015). https://doi.org/10.1007/978-3-662-46800-5_18

4. Barthe, G., et al.: Strong non-interference and type-directed higher-order masking. In: Proceedings of the 2016 ACM SIGSAC Conference on Computer and Communications Security, pp. 116–129. ACM (2016)

5. BATTL: Binary Analysis Tool for Transition-Based Leakage. https://gitlab.com/athanasiou.k/BATTL

6. Bayrak, A.G., Regazzoni, F., Brisk, P., Standaert, F.X., Ienne, P.: A first step towards automatic application of power analysis countermeasures. In: Proceedings of the 48th Design Automation Conference, pp. 230–235. ACM (2011)

7. Bayrak, A.G., Regazzoni, F., Novo, D., Ienne, P.: Sleuth: automated verification of software power analysis countermeasures. In: Bertoni, G., Coron, J.-S. (eds.) CHES 2013. LNCS, vol. 8086, pp. 293–310. Springer, Heidelberg (2013). https://doi.org/10.1007/978-3-642-40349-1_17

8. Chari, S., Jutla, C.S., Rao, J.R., Rohatgi, P.: Towards sound approaches to counteract power-analysis attacks. In: Wiener, M. (ed.) CRYPTO 1999. LNCS, vol. 1666, pp. 398–412. Springer, Heidelberg (1999). https://doi.org/10.1007/3-540-48405-1_26

9. Coron, J.-S., Giraud, C., Prouff, E., Renner, S., Rivain, M., Vadnala, P.K.: Conversion of security proofs from one leakage model to another: a new issue. In: Schindler, W., Huss, S.A. (eds.) COSADE 2012. LNCS, vol. 7275, pp. 69–81. Springer, Heidelberg (2012). https://doi.org/10.1007/978-3-642-29912-4_6

10. Coron, J.-S., Greuet, A., Prouff, E., Zeitoun, R.: Faster evaluation of SBoxes via common shares. In: Gierlichs, B., Poschmann, A.Y. (eds.) CHES 2016. LNCS, vol. 9813, pp. 498–514. Springer, Heidelberg (2016). https://doi.org/10.1007/978-3-662-53140-2_24

11. Coron, J.-S., Prouff, E., Rivain, M., Roche, T.: Higher-order side channel security and mask refreshing. In: Moriai, S. (ed.) FSE 2013. LNCS, vol. 8424, pp. 410–424. Springer, Heidelberg (2014). https://doi.org/10.1007/978-3-662-43933-3_21

12. D'Silva, V., Payer, M., Song, D.: The correctness-security gap in compiler optimization. In: 2015 IEEE Security and Privacy Workshops (SPW), pp. 73–87. IEEE (2015)

13. El Ouahma, I.B., Meunier, Q.L., Heydemann, K., Encrenaz, E.: Symbolic approach for side-channel resistance analysis of masked assembly codes. In: Security Proofs for Embedded Systems (2017)

14. Eldib, H., Wang, C.: Synthesis of masking countermeasures against side channel attacks. In: Biere, A., Bloem, R. (eds.) CAV 2014. LNCS, vol. 8559, pp. 114–130. Springer, Cham (2014). https://doi.org/10.1007/978-3-319-08867-9_8

15. Eldib, H., Wang, C., Schaumont, P.: Formal verification of software countermeasures against side-channel attacks. ACM Trans. Softw. Eng. Methodol. (TOSEM) **24**(2), 11 (2014)

16. Eldib, H., Wang, C., Taha, M., Schaumont, P.: QMS: evaluating the side-channel resistance of masked software from source code. In: Proceedings of the 51st Annual Design Automation Conference, pp. 1–6. ACM (2014)

17. Gandolfi, K., Mourtel, C., Olivier, F.: Electromagnetic analysis: concrete results. In: Koç, Ç.K., Naccache, D., Paar, C. (eds.) CHES 2001. LNCS, vol. 2162, pp. 251–261. Springer, Heidelberg (2001). https://doi.org/10.1007/3-540-44709-1_21

18. Gao, P., Zhang, J., Song, F., Wang, C.: Verifying and quantifying side-channel resistance of masked software implementations. ACM Trans. Softw. Eng. Methodol. (TOSEM) **28**(3), 16 (2019)

19. Gierlichs, B., Batina, L., Tuyls, P., Preneel, B.: Mutual information analysis. In: Oswald, E., Rohatgi, P. (eds.) CHES 2008. LNCS, vol. 5154, pp. 426–442. Springer, Heidelberg (2008). https://doi.org/10.1007/978-3-540-85053-3_27

20. Knudsen, L.R., Robshaw, M.: The Block Cipher Companion. Springer Science & Business Media, Heidelberg (2011). https://doi.org/10.1007/978-3-642-17342-4

21. Kocher, P., Jaffe, J., Jun, B.: Differential power analysis. In: Wiener, M. (ed.) CRYPTO 1999. LNCS, vol. 1666, pp. 388–397. Springer, Heidelberg (1999). https://doi.org/10.1007/3-540-48405-1_25

22. Kocher, P.C.: Timing attacks on implementations of Diffie-Hellman, RSA, DSS, and other systems. In: Koblitz, N. (ed.) CRYPTO 1996. LNCS, vol. 1109, pp. 104–113. Springer, Heidelberg (1996). https://doi.org/10.1007/3-540-68697-5_9

23. Mangard, S., Oswald, E., Popp, T.: Power Analysis Attacks: Revealing the Secrets of Smart Cards, vol. 31. Springer, Boston (2007). https://doi.org/10.1007/978-0-387-38162-6

24. Cortex-M4 Technical Reference Manual: Data watchpoint and trace unit. http://infocenter.arm.com/help/index.jsp?topic=/com.arm.doc.ddi0337h/BIIFBHIF.html

25. Moss, A., Oswald, E., Page, D., Tunstall, M.: Compiler Assisted Masking. In: Prouff, E., Schaumont, P. (eds.) CHES 2012. LNCS, vol. 7428, pp. 58–75. Springer, Heidelberg (2012). https://doi.org/10.1007/978-3-642-33027-8_4

26. Papagiannopoulos, K., Veshchikov, N.: Mind the gap: towards secure 1st-order masking in software. In: Guilley, S. (ed.) COSADE 2017. LNCS, vol. 10348, pp. 282–297. Springer, Cham (2017). https://doi.org/10.1007/978-3-319-64647-3_17

27. Renauld, M., Standaert, F.-X., Veyrat-Charvillon, N., Kamel, D., Flandre, D.: A formal study of power variability issues and side-channel attacks for nanoscale devices. In: Paterson, K.G. (ed.) EUROCRYPT 2011. LNCS, vol. 6632, pp. 109–128. Springer, Heidelberg (2011). https://doi.org/10.1007/978-3-642-20465-4_8

28. Rivain, M., Prouff, E.: Provably Secure Higher-Order Masking of AES. Cryptology ePrint Archive, Report 2010/441 (2010), https://eprint.iacr.org/2010/441

29. Shamir, A.: How to share a secret. Commun. ACM **22**(11), 612–613 (1979). https://doi.org/10.1145/359168.359176

30. Shoshitaishvili, Y., et al.: SOK: (state of) the art of war: offensive techniques in binary analysis. In: IEEE Symposium on Security and Privacy (2016)

31. Wang, J., Sung, C., Wang, C.: Mitigating Power Side Channels during Compilation. arXiv preprint arXiv:1902.09099 (2019)

32. Zhang, L., Ding, A.A., Fei, Y., Luo, P.: A unified metric for quantifying information leakage of cryptographic devices under power analysis attacks. In: Iwata, T., Cheon, J.H. (eds.) ASIACRYPT 2015. LNCS, vol. 9453, pp. 338–360. Springer, Heidelberg (2015). https://doi.org/10.1007/978-3-662-48800-3_14

33. Zhang, R., Qiu, S., Zhou, Y.: Further improving efficiency of higher order masking schemes by decreasing randomness complexity. IEEE Trans. Inf. Forensics Secur. **12**(11), 2590–2598 (2017)

BanditFuzz: A Reinforcement-Learning
Based Performance Fuzzer
for SMT Solvers

Joseph Scott[1]([⊠]), Federico Mora[2], and Vijay Ganesh[1]

[1] University of Waterloo, Waterloo, ON, Canada
{joseph.scott,vijay.ganesh}@uwaterloo.ca
[2] University of California, Berkeley, USA
fmora@cs.berkeley.edu

Abstract. Satisfiability Modulo Theories (SMT) solvers are fundamental tools that are used widely in software engineering, verification, and security research. Precisely because of their widespread use, it is imperative we develop efficient and systematic methods to test them. To this end, we present a reinforcement-learning based fuzzing system, BanditFuzz, that learns grammatical constructs of well-formed inputs that may cause performance slowdown in SMT solvers. To the best of our knowledge, BanditFuzz is the first machine-learning based performance fuzzer for SMT solvers.

BanditFuzz takes the following as input: a grammar G describing well-formed inputs to a set of distinct solvers (say, a target solver T and a reference solver R) that implement the same specification, and a fuzzing objective (e.g., aim to maximize the relative performance difference between T and R). BanditFuzz outputs a list of grammatical constructs that are ranked in descending order by how likely they are to increase the performance difference between solvers T and R. Using BanditFuzz, we constructed two benchmark suites (with 400 floating-point and 300 string instances) that expose performance issues in all considered solvers, namely, Z3, CVC4, Colibri, MathSAT, Z3seq, and Z3str3. We also performed a comparison of BanditFuzz against random, mutation, and evolutionary fuzzing methods and observed up to a 81% improvement based on PAR-2 scores used in SAT competitions. That is, relative to other fuzzing methods considered, BanditFuzz was found to be more efficient at constructing inputs with wider performance margin between a target and a set of reference solvers.

1 Introduction

Over the last two decades, many sophisticated program analysis [20], verification [24], and bug-finding tools [13] have been developed thanks to powerful Satisfiability Modulo Theories (SMT) solvers. The efficiency of SMT solvers significantly impacts the efficacy of modern program analysis, testing, and verification tools. Given the insatiable demand for efficient and robust SMT solvers, it is

© Springer Nature Switzerland AG 2020
M. Christakis et al. (Eds.): NSV 2020/VSTTE 2020, LNCS 12549, pp. 68–86, 2020.
https://doi.org/10.1007/978-3-030-63618-0_5

imperative that these infrastructural tools be subjected to extensive correctness and performance testing and verification.

While there is considerable work on test generation and verification techniques aimed at correctness of SMT solvers [7,11], we are not aware of previous work aimed at automatically generating inputs that expose performance issues in these complex and sophisticated tools.

One such approach is (relative) performance fuzzing[1], which can be defined as follows: methods aimed at automatically and efficiently generating inputs for a program-under-test T such that the performance margin between the program T and a set of other program(s) R that implement the same specification is maximized.

Reinforcement Learning (RL) Based Performance Fuzzing: Researchers have explored many methods for performance fuzzing of programs, including blackbox random and mutation fuzzing [25]. While blackbox approaches are cheap to build and deploy, they are unlikely to efficiently find inputs that expose performance issues. The reason is that purely blackbox approaches are oblivious to input/output behavior of programs-under-test. A whitebox test generation approach (such as some variation of symbolic analysis) is indeed suitable for such a task, but they tend to be inefficient for a different reason, namely, the path explosion problem. In particular, for complex systems like SMT solvers, purely whitebox performance fuzzing approaches are unlikely to scale.

By contrast, the paradigm of RL is well suited for this task of performance fuzzing, since RL methods are an efficient way of navigating a search space (e.g., a space of inputs to programs), guided by corrective feedback they receive via historical analysis of input/output (I/O) behavior, of programs-under-test. Further, they can be low-cost since they interact with programs-under-test in a blackbox fashion.

In this paper, we introduce an RL-based fuzzer, called BanditFuzz, that improves on traditional fuzzing approaches by up to a 81% improvement for *relative performance* fuzzing. That is, relative to other fuzzing methods considered in this paper, BanditFuzz is more efficient at constructing inputs with wider performance margins between a target and a set of reference solvers.

The metric we use for comparing various fuzzing algorithms considered in this paper is the PAR-2 score margins used in SAT competitions [29]. Using BanditFuzz, we generated a database of 400 inputs that expose relative performance issues across a set of FP solvers, namely, CVC4 [4], MathSAT [16], Colibri [30], and Z3 [18], as well as 300 inputs exposing relative performance issues in the Z3seq (Z3's official string solver [18]), Z3str3 [6], and CVC4 string solvers [26].

Description of BanditFuzz: BanditFuzz takes as input a grammar G that describes well-formed inputs to a set P of programs-under-test (for simplicity, assume P contains only two programs, a target program T to be fuzzed, and a reference program R against which the performance of T is compared), a fuzzing

---

[1] We use the terms "relative performance fuzzing" and "performance fuzzing" interchangeably in this paper.

objective (e.g., aim to maximize the relative performance margin between a target and a set of reference solvers). BanditFuzz outputs a ranked list of *grammatical constructs* (e.g., syntactic tokens, expressions, keywords, or combinations thereof, over the input language described by G) in the descending order of ones that are most likely to trigger a performance issue, as well as actual instances that expose these issues in the programs-under-test. (It is assumed that Bandit-Fuzz has blackbox access to programs in the set P and that all programs in the set P have the same input grammar G.)

Briefly, BanditFuzz works as follows: BanditFuzz generates well-formed inputs that adhere to the input grammar G, mutates them in a grammar-preserving manner, and uses RL methods to perform a historical analysis of the I/O behavior of the programs in P, in order to learn which grammatical constructs are most likely to cause performance issues in the programs in P. By contrast, traditional mutation fuzzers choose or implement a *mutation operator* at random and are oblivious to the behavior of the programs-under-test.

BanditFuzz reduces the problem of how to optimally mutate an input to an instance of the multi-arm bandit (MAB) problem, well-known in the RL literature [44, 46]. The crucial insight behind BanditFuzz is the idea of automatically analyzing the history of a target solver's performance, and using this analysis to create a list of grammatical constructs in G, and ranking them based on how likely they are to be a cause of a performance issue in the solver-under-test. Initially, all grammatical constructs in G are treated as uniformly likely to cause a performance issue by BanditFuzz's RL agent. BanditFuzz then randomly generates a well-formed input I, to begin with, and runs all the programs in P on the input I. In each of the subsequent iterations of its feedback loop, BanditFuzz mutates the input I from its previous iteration using the ranked list of grammatical constructs (i.e., the agent performs an action) and runs all solvers in P on the mutated version of the input I. It analyzes the results of these runs to provide feedback (i.e., rewards) to the RL agent in the form of those constructs that are most likely to cause relative performance difference between the target program T with respect to the reference program R. It then updates and re-ranks its list of grammatical constructs with the goal of maximizing its reward (i.e., increasing the relative performance difference between the target and reference solvers in P). The process continues until the RL agent converges to a ranking or runs out of resources.

Key Features of BanditFuzz: A key feature of BanditFuzz that sets it apart from other fuzzing and systematic testing approaches is that, in addition to generating inputs that reveal performance issues, it isolates or localizes a cause of performance issue, in the form of a ranked list of grammatical tokens that are the most likely cause of a performance issue in the target solver-under-test. This form of localization is particularly useful in understanding problematic behaviours in complex programs such as SMT solvers.

Contributions:

First RL-Based Performance Fuzzer for Floating-Point and String SMT Solvers: We describe the design and implementation of the first

RL-based fuzzer for SMT solvers, called BanditFuzz. BanditFuzz uses RL, specifically MABs, in order to construct fuzzing mutations over highly structured inputs with the aim of maximizing a fuzzing objective, namely, the relative performance difference between a target and a reference solver. To the best of our knowledge, using RL in this way has never been done before. Furthermore, as far as we know, BanditFuzz is the first RL-based performance fuzzer for SMT Solvers.

Extensive Empirical Evaluation of BanditFuzz: We provide an extensive empirical evaluation of our fuzzer for detecting relative performance issues in SMT solvers and compare it to existing techniques. That is, we use our fuzzer to find instances that expose large performance differences in four state-of-the-art floating-point (FP) solvers, namely, Z3, CVC4, MathSat, and Colibri, as well as three string solvers, namely, Z3str3, Z3 sequence (Z3seq), and CVC4 solvers (as measured by PAR-2 score [29]). BanditFuzz outperforms existing fuzzing algorithms (such as random, mutation, and genetic fuzzing) by up to an 81% increase in PAR-2 score margins, for the same amount of resources provided to all methods. We also contribute two large benchmark suites discovered by BanditFuzz that contain a combined total of 400 for the theory of FP and 300 for the theory of strings that the SMT community can use to test their solvers.

2 Preliminaries

Reinforcement Learning: There is a vast literature on reinforcement learning, and we refer the reader to the following excellent surveys and books on the topic [44–46]. As discussed in the introduction, the reinforcement learning paradigm is particularly suited for modelling mutation fuzzing, whenever an online corrective feedback loop makes sense in the fuzzing context. In this paper, we specifically deploy multi-armed bandit (MAB) algorithms [44], a class of reinforcement learning algorithms, to learn mutation operators (functions that perform a syntactic modification on well-formed inputs in a grammar-preserving fashion).

Reinforcement learning algorithms are commonly formulated using *Markov Decision Processes* (MDPs) [39, 42, 46], a 4-tuple of states S, actions A, rewards R, and transitions T. The multi-armed bandit (MAB) problem is a common reinforcement learning problem based on a stateless MDP (or more precisely, a single state $S = \{s_0\}$) and a finite set of actions A. Due to the nature of the problem, there is no learned modelling of transitions T. What remains to be learned, is the unknown probability distribution of rewards R over the space of actions A. In the context of MAB, actions are often referred to as arms (or bandits[2]).

---

[2] The term bandit comes from gambling: the arm of a slot machine is referred to as a one-armed bandit, and multi-arm bandits referred to several slot machines. The goal of the MAB agent is to maximize its reward by playing a sequence of actions (e.g., slot machines).

In this paper, we exclusively consider the case where rewards are sampled from an unknown Bernoulli distribution (rewards are $\{0,1\}$). The MAB agent attempts to approximate the expected value of the Bernoulli distribution of reward for each action in A. The MAB learns a *policy* – a stochastic process of how to select actions from A. The learned policy balances the exploration/exploitation trade-off, i.e., a MAB algorithm selects every action an infinite number of times in the limit. Still, it selects the action(s) with the highest expected reward more frequently.

While we implemented three solutions to the MAB problem into BanditFuzz, we focus on only one in this paper, namely, *Thompson Sampling*. Thompson Sampling builds a Beta distribution for each action in the action space. Beta distributions are a variant of Gamma distributions and have a long history. We refer the reader to Gupta et al. on Beta and Gamma distributions [21]. Intuitively, a Beta distribution is a continuous approximation of an underlying Bernoulli distribution approaching the same mean (p parameter) in the limit. It is maintained by updating the parameters $\alpha - 1$ (the samples of 1) and $\beta - 1$ (the samples of 0) from the underlying Bernoulli distribution.

In Thompson sampling, the agent maintains a Beta distribution for each action. The agent samples each action's distribution, and greedily picks its arm based on the maximum sampled value. Upon completing the action, α is incremented on a reward. Otherwise, β is incremented. For more on Thompson sampling, we refer to Russo et al. [40].

Satisfiability Modulo Theories and the SMT-LIB Standard: Satisfiability Modulo Theories (SMT) solvers are decision procedures for first-order theories such as integers, bit-vectors, floating-point, and strings that are particularly suitable for verification, program analysis, and testing [5]. The SMT-LIB is an initiative to standardize the language and specification of several theories of interest. In this paper, we exclusively consider solvers, whose quantifier-free FP and string decision procedures are being actively developed at the time of writing of this paper.

Quantifier-Free Theory of Floating Point Arithmetic (FP): The SMT theory of FP was first proposed by Rümmer et al. [38] with several recent revisions. In this paper, we consider the latest version, by Brain et al. [10]. The SMT-LIB FP theory supports standard FP sorts of 32, 64, and 128 bit lengths with their usual mantissa and exponent bit vector lengths, and also allows for arbitrary width sorts with appropriate mantissa and exponent lengths. The theory includes common predicates, operators, and terms over FP. We refer the reader to the SMT-LIB standard for details on the syntax and semantics of FP theory. In this paper, we consider the following set of operators: {fp.abs, fp.neg, fp.add, fp.mul, fp.sub, fp.div, fp.fma, fp.rem, fp.sqrt, fp.roundToIntegral}, set of predicates: {fp.eq, fp.lt, fp.gt, fp.leq, fp.geq, fp.isNormal, fp.isSubnormal, fp.isZero, fp.isInfinite, fp.isNaN, fp.isPositive, fp.isNegative}, and rounding terms {RNE, RNA, RTP, RTN, RTZ}. Semantics of all operands follow the IEEE754 08 standard [17].

Quantifier-Free Theory of Strings: The SMT-LIB standard for the theory of strings is currently in development [14]. The draft has a finite alphabet Σ of characters, string constants and variables that range over Σ^*, integer constants and variables, as well as the functions {str.++, str.contains, str.at, str.len, str.indexof, str.replace, re.inter, re.range, re.+, re.*, re.++, str.to_re}, and predicates {str.prefixof, str.suffixof, str.in_re}. We further clarify that this list was carefully selected to include only those that are supported amongst all solvers considered in this paper.

Software Fuzzing: A Fuzzer is a program that automatically generates inputs for a target program-under-test. Fuzzers may treat the program-under-test as a whitebox or blackbox, depending on whether they have access to the source code. Unlike random fuzzers, a mutation fuzzer takes as input a database of inputs of interest and produces new inputs by mutating the elements of the database using a mutation operator (a function defining a syntactic change). These mutation operators are frequently stochastic bit-wise manipulations in the case of model-less programs or grammar-preserving changes for model-based programs [15,27,31,49]. Other common fuzzing approaches include genetic and evolutionary fuzzing solutions. These approaches maintain a population of input seeds that are mutated or combined/crossed-over using a genetic or evolutionary algorithm [23,36,41].

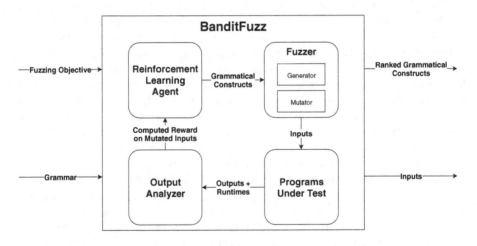

Fig. 1. Architecture of BanditFuzz

3   BanditFuzz: An RL-Based Performance Fuzzer

In this section, we describe our technique, BanditFuzz, a grammar-based mutation fuzzer that uses reinforcement learning (RL) to efficiently isolate grammatical constructs of an input that are the cause of a performance issue in a solver-under-test. The ability of BanditFuzz to isolate those grammatical constructs that trigger performance issues, in a blackbox manner, is its most interesting feature. The architecture of BanditFuzz is presented in Fig. 1.

3.1 Description of the BanditFuzz Algorithm

BanditFuzz takes as input a grammar G that describes well-formed inputs to a set P of solvers-under-test (for simplicity, assume P contains only two programs, a target program T to be fuzzed, and a reference program R against which the performance or correctness of T is compared), a fuzzing objective (e.g., aim to maximize the relative performance difference between target and reference solvers) and outputs a ranked list of grammatical constructs (e.g., syntactic tokens or keywords over G) in the descending order of ones that are most likely to cause performance issues. We infer this ranked list by extrapolating from the policy of the RL agent. It is assumed that BanditFuzz has blackbox access to the set P of the solvers-under-test.

The BanditFuzz algorithm works as follows: BanditFuzz generates well-formed inputs that adhere to G and mutates them in a grammar-preserving manner (the instance generator and mutator together are referred to as fuzzer in Fig. 1) and deploys an RL agent (specifically a MAB agent) within a feedback loop to learn which grammatical constructs of G are the most likely culprits that cause performance issues in the target program T in P.

BanditFuzz reduces the problem of how to mutate an input to an instance of the MAB problem. As discussed earlier, in the MAB setting an agent is designed to maximize its cumulative rewards by selecting the arms (actions) that give it the highest expected reward, while maintaining an exploration-exploitation tradeoff. In BanditFuzz, the agent chooses actions (grammatical constructs used by the fuzzer to mutate an input) that maximize the reward over a period of time (e.g., increasing the runtime difference between the target solver T and a reference solver R). It is important to note that the agent learns an action selection policy via a historical analysis of the results of its actions over time. Within its iterative feedback loop (that enables rewards from the analysis of solver outputs to the RL agent), BanditFuzz observes and analyzes the effects of the actions it takes on the solvers-under-test. BanditFuzz maintains a record of these effects over many iterations, analyzes the historical data thus collected, and zeroes-in on those grammatical constructs that have the highest likelihood of reward. At the end of its run, BanditFuzz outputs a ranked list of grammatical constructs which are most likely to cause performance issues, in descending order. In the fuzzing for relative performance fuzzing mode, BanditFuzz performs the above-described analysis to produce a ranked list of grammatical constructs that increase the difference in running time between a target solver T and a reference solver R.

3.2   Fuzzer: Instance Generator and Grammar-Preserving Mutator

BanditFuzz's fuzzer (See Architecture of BanditFuzz in Fig. 1) consists of two sub-components, namely, an instance[3] generator and a grammar-preserving mutator (or simply, mutator). The instance generator is a program that randomly samples the space of inputs described by the grammar G. The mutator is a program that takes as input a well-formed G-instance and a grammatical construct δ and outputs another well-formed G-instance.

Instance Generator: Here we describe the generator component of Bandit-Fuzz, as described in Fig. 1. Initially, BanditFuzz generates a random well-formed instance using the input grammar G (FP or string SMT-LIB grammar) via a random abstract syntax tree (AST) generation procedure built into StringFuzz [7]. We generalize this procedure for the theory of FP.

The FP input generation procedure works as follows: we first populate a list of free 64-bit FP variables and then generate random ASTs that are asserted in the instance. Each AST is rooted by an FP predicate whose children are FP operators chosen at random. We deploy a recursive process to fill out the tree until a predetermined depth limit is reached. Leaf nodes of the AST are filled in by randomly selecting a free variable or special constant. Rounding modes are filled in when required by an operator's signature. The number of variables and assertions are parameters to the generator and are specified for each experiment.

Similar to the generator in StringFuzz, BanditFuzz's generation process is highly configurable. The user can choose the number of free variables, the number of assertions, the maximum depth of the AST, the set of operators, and rounding terms. The user can also set weights for specific constructs as a substitute for the default uniform random selection.

Grammar-Preserving Mutator: The second component of the BanditFuzz fuzzer is the mutator. In the context of fuzzing SMT solvers, a mutator takes a well-formed SMT formula I and a grammatical construct δ as input, and outputs a *mutated* well-formed SMT formula I' that is like I, but with a suitable construct (say, γ) replaced by δ. The construct γ in I could be selected using some user-defined policy or chosen uniform-at-random over all possible grammatical constructs in I. In order to be grammar-preserving, the mutator has to choose γ such that no typing and arity constraints are violated in the resultant formula I'. The grammatical construct δ, one of the inputs to the mutator, may be chosen at random or selected using an RL agent. We describe this process in greater detail in the next subsection.

On the selection of a grammatical construct, an arbitrary construct of the same type (predicate, operator, or rounding mode, etc.) is selected uniformly at random. If the replacement involves an arity change, the rightmost subtrees are dropped on a decrease in arity, or new subtrees are generated on the increase in arity.

For illustrative purposes, we provide an example mutation here. Consider a maximum depth of two, fixed set of free FP variables (x_0, x_1), limited rounding

---

[3] We use the terms "instance" and "input" interchangeably through this paper.

Algorithm 1. BanditFuzz's Performance Fuzzing Feedback Loop. Also refer to BanditFuzz architecture in Figure 1.

```
 1: procedure BANDITFUZZ(G)
 2:     Instance I ← a randomly-generated instance over G              ▷ Fuzzer
 3:     Run target solver T and reference solver(s) R on I
 4:     Compute PerfScore(I)                                   ▷ OutputAnalyzer
 5:     θ = 2· Solver timeout
 6:     while fuzzing time limit not reached and PerfScore(I) < θ do
 7:         construct ← RL AGENT picks a grammatical construct        ▷ RL Agent
 8:         I' ← Mutate I with construct                              ▷ Fuzzer
 9:         Run target solver T and reference solver(s) R on I'
10:         if PerfScore(I', P) > PerfScore(I, P) then        ▷ OutputAnalyzer
11:             Provide reward to RL AGENT for construct
12:             I ← I'
13:         else
14:             Provide no reward to AGENT for construct
15:         end if
16:     end while
17:     return I and the ranking of constructs from RL AGENT
18: end procedure
```

mode set of $\{RNE\}$, and an asserted equation:

$$(fp.eq\ (fp.add\ RNE\ x_0\ x_1)(fp.sub\ RNE\ x_0\ x_1)).$$

If the agent elects to insert $fp.abs$ there are two possible results:

$$(fp.eq\ (fp.abs\ x_0)(fp.sub\ RNE\ x_0\ x_1)),\quad (fp.eq\ (fp.add\ RNE\ x_0\ x_1)(fp.abs\ x_0)).$$

For further analysis, consider the additional asserted equation:

$$(fp.eq\ (fp.abs\ x_0)(fp.abs\ x_1)),$$

if the agent elects to insert $fp.add$, then there are four[4] possible outputs:

$$(fp.eq\ (fp.add\ RNE\ x_0\ x_0)(fp.abs\ x_1))$$
$$(fp.eq\ (fp.add\ RNE\ x_0\ x_1)(fp.abs\ x_1))$$
$$(fp.eq\ (fp.abs\ x_0)(fp.add\ RNE\ x_1\ x_0))$$
$$(fp.eq\ (fp.abs\ x_0)(fp.add\ RNE\ x_1\ x_1))$$

In these examples, the reason why the possible outputs may seem limited is due to type and arity preservation rules described above. As described below, the fuzzer would select one of the mutations in the above example in a manner that maximizes expected reward (e.g., the fuzzing objective such that the performance difference between a solver-under-test and a reference solver is increases).

---

[4] This is assuming only the RNE rounding mode is allowed, otherwise each of the below expressions could have any valid rounding mode resulting in 20 possible outputs.

3.3   RL Agent and Reward-Driven Feedback Loop in BanditFuzz

As shown in Fig. 1, the key component of BanditFuzz is an RL agent (based on Thompson sampling) that receives rewards and outputs a ranked list of grammatical constructs (actions). The fuzzer maintains a policy and selects actions from it ("pulling an arm" in the MAB context), and appropriately modifies the current input I to generate a novel input I'. The rewards are computed by the Output Analyzer, which takes as input the outputs and runtimes produced by the solver-under-test S and computes scores and rewards appropriately. These are fed to the RL agent; the RL agent tracks the history of rewards it obtained for every grammatical construct and refines its ranking over several iterations of BanditFuzz's feedback loop (see Algorithm 1). In the following subsections, we discuss it in detail.

Computing Rewards for Performance Fuzzing: We describe BanditFuzz's reward computation for performance fuzzing in detail here, and display the pseudo-code for it in Algorithm 1 (see also the architecture in Fig. 1 to get a higher-level view of the algorithm). Initially, the fuzzer generates a well-formed input I (sampled uniformly-at-random). BanditFuzz then executes both the target solver T and reference solver R on I and records their respective runtimes (it is assumed that both solvers may produce the correct answer with respect to input I or timeout). BanditFuzz's OutputAnalyzer module then computes a score, PerfScore, defined as

$$\text{PerfScore}(I) := \text{runtime}(I, T) - \text{runtime}(I, R)$$

where the quantity $\text{runtime}(I, T)$ refers to the wall clock runtime of the target solver T on I, and $\text{runtime}(I, R)$ the runtime of the reference solver R on I. If the target solver reaches the wallclock timeout, we set $\text{runtime}(I, T)$ to be $2 \cdot timeout$—PAR-2 scoring in the SAT competition. In the same iteration, BanditFuzz mutates the input I to a well-formed input I' and computes the quantity $\text{PerfScore}(I')$. Recall that we refer to the mutation inserted into I to obtain I' as γ.

The OutputAnalyzer then computes the rewards as follows. It takes as input I, I', quantities $\text{PerfScore}(I)$, and $\text{PerfScore}(I')$, and if the quantity $\text{PerfScore}(I')$ is better than $\text{PerfScore}(I)$ (i.e., the target solver is slower than the reference solver on I' relative to their performance on I), the mutations γ gets a positive reward, else it gets a negative reward. Recall that we want to reward those constructs which make the target solver slower than the reference one. The reward for all other grammatical constructs remains unchanged.

The rewards thus computed are fed into the RL agent. The bandit then updates the rank of the grammatical constructs. The Thompson sampling bandit analyzes historically, the positive and negative rewards for each grammatical construct and computes the α and β parameters. The highest-ranked construct γ is fed into the fuzzer for the subsequent iteration. This process continues until the fuzzing resource limit has been reached.

4 Results: BanditFuzz vs. Standard Fuzzing Approaches

In this section, we present an evaluation of BanditFuzz vs. standard performance fuzzing algorithms, such as random, mutational, and evolutionary.

4.1 Experimental Setup

All experiments were performed on the SHARCNET computing service [3]: a CentOS V7 cluster of Intel Xeon Processor E5-2683 running at 2.10 GHz. We limited each solver to 8 GB of memory without parallelization. Otherwise, each solver is run under its default settings. Each solver/input query is ran with a wallclock timeout of 2500 s.

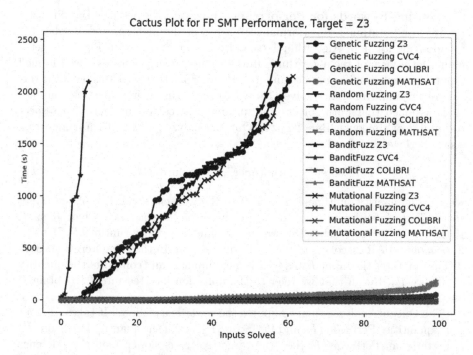

Fig. 2. Cactus Plot for targeting the Z3 FP Solver against reference solvers CVC4, Colibri, and MathSAT. As seen above, BanditFuzz has larger performance margins against the target solver (Z3), compared to the other fuzzing algorithm within a given time budget.

Baselines: We compare BanditFuzz with three different widely-deployed fuzzing loops that are built on top of StringFuzz [7]: random, mutation, and genetic fuzzing. We describe the three approaches below. We extend StringFuzz to floating-point, as described in Sect. 3.2. All baselines generate and modify inputs via StringFuzz's generator and transformer interface.

Random Fuzzing – Random fuzzers are programs that sample inputs from the grammar of the program-under-test (we only consider model-based random fuzzers here). Random fuzzing is a simple yet powerful approach to software fuzzing. We use StringFuzz as our random fuzzer for strings and extend a version of it to FP as described in Sect. 3.2.

Mutational Fuzzing – A mutation fuzzer typically mutates or modifies a database of input seeds in order to generate new inputs to test a program. Mutation fuzzing has had a tremendous impact, most notably in the context of model-less program domains [15,27,31,49]. We use StringFuzz transformers as our mutational fuzzer with grammatical constructs selected uniformly at random. We lift StringFuzz transformer's to FP as described in Sect. 3.2.

Genetic/Evolutionary Fuzzing – Evolutionary fuzzing algorithms maintain a population of inputs. In every generation, only the *fittest members of the population* survive, and new members are created through random generation and mutation [36,41].

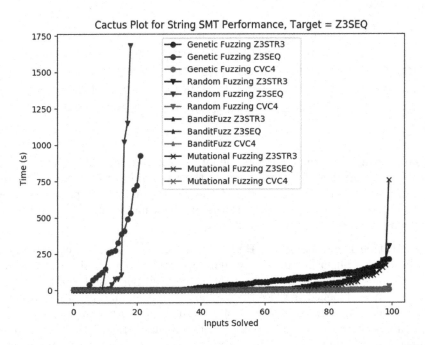

Fig. 3. Cactus Plot for targeting the Z3seq string solver against reference solvers CVC4 and Z3str3. As seen above, BanditFuzz has larger performance margins against the target solver (Z3), compared to the other fuzzing algorithm within a given time budget.

We configure StringFuzz to generate random ASTs at random with five assertions. Each formula has one check-sat call. Each AST has depth three with five string/FP constants[5].

4.2 Quantitative Method for Comparing Fuzzing Algorithms

We run each of the baseline fuzzing algorithms and BanditFuzz on a target solver (e.g., Z3's FP procedure) and a set of reference solvers (e.g., CVC4, Colibri, MathSAT) for 12 h to construct a single input with maximal difference between the runtime of the target solver and the reference solvers. We repeat this process for each fuzzing algorithm 100 times. We then take and compare the highest-scoring instance for each solver for each fuzzing algorithm.

Table 1. PAR-2 Score Margins of the returned inputs for considered fuzzing algorithms for FP SMT performance fuzzing. As seen in the table below, BanditFuzz maximizes the PAR-2 score of the target solver, compared to the other fuzzing algorithm within a given time budget.

Target solver	BanditFuzz	Random	Mutational	Genetic	% Improvement
Colibri	499061.5	499544.2	499442.2	499295.1	−0.10%
CVC4	144568.9	68714.2	125273.0	38972.7	15.40%
MathSAT5	36654.5	12024.9	31615.4	8208.0	15.94%
Z3	467590.0	239774.3	256973.1	251108.2	81.96%

The fuzzing algorithm that has the largest runtime separation between the target solver and the reference solvers, in the given amount of time, is declared the best fuzzing algorithm among all the algorithms we compare. We show that BanditFuzz consistently outperforms random, mutation, and evolutionary fuzzing algorithms according to these criteria.

Quantitative Evaluation via PAR-2 Margins: For each solver/input pair, we record the wallclock time. To evaluate a solver over a set of inputs, we use *PAR-2* scores. PAR-2 is defined as the sum of all successful runtimes, with unsolved inputs labelled as twice the timeout. As we are fuzzing for performance with respect to a target solver, we evaluate the returned test suite of a fuzzing algorithm based on the *PAR-2 margin* between the PAR-2 of the target solver and the input wise maximum across all of the reference solvers. More precisely,

$$\text{PAR-2Margin}(S, s_t, D) := \sum_{I \in D} \text{PAR-2}(I, s_t) - \max_{s \in S, s \neq s_t}(\text{PAR-2}(I, s))$$

for a set of solvers S and target solver $s_t \in S$, and generated input dataset D.

---

[5] Integer/Boolean constants are added for the theory of strings when appropriate (default behaviour of StringFuzz).

For example, consider a target solver S_1 against a set of reference solvers S_2, S_3, over a benchmark suite of three inputs. Let the runtimes for the solver S_1 on the three inputs be $1000.0, timeout, 100.0$, that of solver S_2 be $50.0, 30.0, 10.0$, and that of solver S_3 be $100.0, 1000.0, 1.0$, respectively. With our timeout of 2500 seconds, S_1 would have a PAR-2 of 6100, S_2 a score of 90, and S_3 a score of 1101. We define the PAR-2 margin by summing the difference between the maximum of S_2, S_3 from that of solver S_1 on each of the inputs, which in this example results in a $(1000 - 100) + (5000 - 1000) + (100 - 10) = 4990$ PAR-2 margin.

We want to remark that a perfect PAR-2 margin (i.e., the target solver fails to solve all instances and each competing solver solves all instances instantly) over a set of n inputs to be $2 \cdot n \cdot timeout$, which in the above example with three inputs and a timeout of 2500 is $15,000$ $(3 \cdot 2 \cdot 2500)$. In our experiments, we generate 100 inputs, resulting in an optimal score of 500000. Note that the fuzzing algorithm with the largest PAR-2 margin over all fuzzed inputs for a given target solver is deemed the best fuzzer for that target solver. The fuzzer that is best, as measured by PAR-2 margin, among all fuzzers across all target solvers, is considered the best fuzzer overall.

Table 2. PAR-2 Score Margins of the returned inputs for considered fuzzing algorithms for string SMT performance fuzzing. As seen in the table below, BanditFuzz aims to maximize the PAR-2 score of the target solver, compared to the other fuzzing algorithm within a given time budget.

Target solver	BanditFuzz	Random	Mutational	Genetic	Improvement
CVC4	45629.8	30815.4	30815.4	31619.4	44.15%
Z3str3	499988.6	499986.7	499987.2	499986.8	0.00%
Z3seq	499883.4	409111.0	433416.5	445097.4	12.31%

Visualization: As discussed below, the performance results of the solvers on the fuzzed inputs generated by the baseline fuzzers and BanditFuzz are visualized using *cactus plots*. A cactus plot demonstrates a solvers performance over a set of benchmarks, with the X-axis denoting the total number of solved inputs and the Y-axis denoting the solver timeout in seconds. A point (X, Y) on a cactus plot can be interpreted as the solver can solve X of the inputs from the benchmark set with each input solved within Y seconds. In our setting, cactus plots can be used to visualize the performance separation from the target solver and reference solvers.

4.3 Performance Fuzzing Results for FP SMT Solvers

In our performance fuzzing evaluation of BanditFuzz, we consider the following state-of-the-art FP SMT solvers: **Z3** v4.8.0 - a multi-theory open source SMT solver [18], **MathSAT5** v5.5.3. a multi theory SMT solver [16], **CVC4** CVC4

1.7-prerelease [git master 61095232] - a multi theory open source SMT Solver [4], and **Colibri** v2070 - A proprietary CP Solver with specialty in FP SMT [8,30].

Table 1 presents the margins of the PAR-2 scores between the target solver and the maximum of the reference solvers across the returned inputs for each fuzzing algorithm. BanditFuzz shows a notable improvement on fuzzing baselines except for when Colibri is selected as the target solver. In the case of Colibri being the target solver, all baselines observe PAR-2 margins near the maximum value of 500,000, leaving no room for BanditFuzz to improve. Having such a high margin indicates each run of a fuzzer resulted in an input where Colibri timed out, yet all other considered solvers solved it almost immediately.

Figure 2 presented the cactus plot for the experiments when Z3 was the target solver. Also, we can obtain a ranking of grammatical constructs by extrapolating the α, β values from the learned model and sampling its beta distribution to approximate the expected value of reward for the grammatical construct's corresponding action. The top three for each target solver are: Colibri – fp.neg, fp.abs, fp.isNegative, CVC4 – fp.sqrt, fp.gt, fp.geq, MathSAT5 – fp.isNaN, RNE, fp.mul, Z3 – fp.roundToIntegral, fp.div, fp.isNormal. This indicates that, e.g., CVC4's reasoning on fp.sqrt could be improved by studying Z3's implementation.

4.4 Performance Fuzzing for String SMT Solvers

In our performance fuzzing evaluation of BanditFuzz, we consider the following state-of-the-art string SMT solvers: **Z3str3** v4.8.0 [6], **Z3seq** v4.8.0 [18], and **CVC4 v1.6** [4]. We fuzz the string solvers for relative performance issues, with each considered as a target solver. Identically to the above FP experiments, each run of a fuzzer is repeated 100 times to generate 100 different inputs.

Table 2 presents the margins of the PAR-2 scores between the target solver and the maximum of the remaining solvers across the returned inputs for each fuzzing algorithm. BanditFuzz shows a substantial improvement on fuzzing baselines except for when Z3str3 is selected as the target solver. However, in this scenario, the PAR-2 margins are near the maximum value of 500000, across all fuzzing algorithms. This implies a nearly perfect input suite with Z3str3 timing out while CVC4 and Z3seq solve the input nearly instantly.

As in the previous Sect. 4.3, we can extrapolate the grammatical constructs that were most likely to cause a performance slowdown. The top three for each target solver are as follows: CVC4 – re.range, str.contains, str.to_int, Z3seq – re.in_regex, str.prefixOf, str.length, Z3str3 – str.contains, str.suffixOf, str.concat. Further, Fig. 3 presents the cactus plot for the experiments when Z3seq was the target solver. The cactus plot provides a visualization of the fuzzing objective, aiming to maximize the performance margins between Z3seq and the other solvers collectively[6]. The line for BanditFuzz for the Z3seq solver is not rendered on the plot as the inputs returned by BanditFuzz were too hard for Z3seq and were not solved in the given timeout.

---

[6] Cactus plots for Z3str3 and CVC4 solvers can be found on the BanditFuzz webpage.

Discussion of Results with Developers: We shared our tool and benchmarks with the Z3str3 string solver team. The Z3str3 team found the tool to be "invaluable" in localizing performance issues, as well as identifying classes of inputs on which Z3str3 outperforms competing string solvers such as CVC4. For example, we managed to generate a class of instances that had roughly an equal number of string constraints and integer (arithmetic over the length of strings) constraints over which Z3str3 outperforms CVC4. By contrast, CVC4 outperforms Z3str3 when inputs have many str.contains and str.concat constructs. The Z3str3 team is currently working on improving their solver based on the feedback from BanditFuzz.

5 Related Work

Fuzzers for SMT Solvers: We refer to Takanen et al. [47] and Sutton et al. [43] for a detailed overview of fuzzing. While there are many tools and fuzzers for finding bugs in specific SMT theories [7, 11, 12, 28, 28, 34], BanditFuzz is the first performance fuzzer for SMT solvers that we are aware of.

Machine Learning for Fuzzing: Bottinger et al. [9] introduce a deep Q learning algorithm for fuzzing model-free inputs, further PerfFuzz by Lemieux et al., uses bitwise mutation for performance fuzzing. These approaches would not scale to either FP SMT nor string SMT theories, given the complexity of their grammars. Such a tool would need to first learn the grammar to penetrate the parsers to begin to discover performance issues. To this end, Godefroid et al. [19] use neural networks to learn an input grammar over complicated domains such as PDF and then use the learned grammar for model-guided fuzzing. To the best of our knowledge, BanditFuzz is the first fuzzer to use RL to implement model-based mutation operators that can be used to isolate the root causes of performance issues in the programs-under-test.

While bandit MAB algorithms have been used in various aspects as fuzzing, it has not been used to implement a mutation. Karamcheti et al. [22] trained bandit algorithms to select model-less bitwise mutation operators from an array of fixed operators for greybox fuzzing. Woo et al. [48] and Patil et al. [35] used bandit algorithms to select configurations of global hyper-parameters of fuzzing software. Rebert et al. [37] used bandit algorithms to select from a list of valid inputs seeds to apply a model-less mutation procedure on. Our work differs from these methods, as we learn a model-based mutation operator implemented by an RL agent. Appelt et al. [1] combine blackbox testing with machine learning to direct fuzzing. To the best of our knowledge, our work is the first to use reinforcement learning or bandit algorithms to learn and implement a mutation operator within a grammar-based mutational fuzzing algorithm.

Delta Debugging: BanditFuzz differs significantly from delta debugging, where a bug-revealing input E is given, and the task of a delta-debugger is to minimize E to get E' while ensuring that E' exposes the same error in the program-under-test as E [2, 32, 33, 50]. BanditFuzz, on the other hand, generates and examines a set of inputs that expose performance issues in a target program by leveraging reinforcement learning. The goal of BanditFuzz is to discover patterns over the entire generated set of inputs via a historical analysis of the behavior of the program via RL. Specifically, BanditFuzz finds and ranks the language features that are the root cause of performance issues in the program-under-test.

6   Conclusions and Future Work

In this paper, we presented BanditFuzz, a performance fuzzer for FP and string SMT solvers that automatically isolates and ranks those grammatical constructs in an input that are the most likely cause of a relative performance slowdown in a target program relative to a (set of) reference programs. BanditFuzz is the first fuzzer for FP SMT solvers that we are aware of, and the first fuzzer to use reinforcement learning, specifically MAB, to fuzz SMT solvers. We compare BanditFuzz against a portfolio of baselines, including random, mutational, and evolutionary fuzzing techniques, and found that it consistently outperforms existing fuzzing approaches. In the future, we plan to extend BanditFuzz to all of SMT-LIB.

References

1. Appelt, D., Nguyen, C.D., Panichella, A., Briand, L.C.: A machine-learning-driven evolutionary approach for testing web application firewalls. IEEE Trans. Reliab. **67**(3), 733–757 (2018)
2. Artho, C.: Iterative delta debugging. Int. J. Softw. Tools Technol. Transf. **13**(3), 223–246 (2011)
3. Baldwin, S.: Compute Canada: advancing computational research. J. Phys. Conf. Ser. **341**, 012001 (2012). IOP Publishing
4. Barrett, C., et al.: CVC4. In: Gopalakrishnan, G., Qadeer, S. (eds.) CAV 2011. LNCS, vol. 6806, pp. 171–177. Springer, Heidelberg (2011). https://doi.org/10.1007/978-3-642-22110-1_14. http://www.cs.stanford.edu/barrett/pubs/BCD+11.pdf
5. Barrett, C., Fontaine, P., Tinelli, C.: The Satisfiability Modulo Theories Library (SMT-LIB). www.SMT-LIB.org (2016)
6. Berzish, M., Ganesh, V., Zheng, Y.: Z3str3: a string solver with theory-aware heuristics. In: 2017 Formal Methods in Computer Aided Design (FMCAD), pp. 55–59. IEEE (2017)
7. Blotsky, D., Mora, F., Berzish, M., Zheng, Y., Kabir, I., Ganesh, V.: StringFuzz: a fuzzer for string solvers. In: Chockler, H., Weissenbacher, G. (eds.) CAV 2018. LNCS, vol. 10982, pp. 45–51. Springer, Cham (2018). https://doi.org/10.1007/978-3-319-96142-2_6
8. Bobot-CEA, F., Chihani-CEA, Z., Iguernlala-OCamlPro, M., Marre-CEA, B.: FPA solver
9. Böttinger, K., Godefroid, P., Singh, R.: Deep reinforcement fuzzing. arXiv preprint arXiv:1801.04589 (2018)
10. Brain, M., Tinelli, C., Rümmer, P., Wahl, T.: An automatable formal semantics for IEEE-754 floating-point arithmetic. In: 2015 IEEE 22nd Symposium on Computer Arithmetic (ARITH), pp. 160–167. IEEE (2015)

11. Brummayer, R., Biere, A.: Fuzzing and delta-debugging SMT solvers. In: Proceedings of the 7th International Workshop on Satisfiability Modulo Theories, pp. 1–5. ACM (2009)
12. Bugariu, A., Müller, P.: Automatically testing string solvers. In: International Conference on Software Engineering (ICSE), 2020. ETH Zurich (2020)
13. Cadar, C., Ganesh, V., Pawlowski, P.M., Dill, D.L., Engler, D.R.: EXE: automatically generating inputs of death. ACM Trans. Inf. Syst. Secur. (TISSEC) **12**(2), 10 (2008)
14. Tinelli, C., Barrett, C., Fontaine, P.: Theory of unicode strings (draft) (2019). http://smtlib.cs.uiowa.edu/theories-UnicodeStrings.shtml
15. Cha, S.K., Woo, M., Brumley, D.: Program-adaptive mutational fuzzing. In: 2015 IEEE Symposium on Security and Privacy, pp. 725–741. IEEE (2015)
16. Cimatti, A., Griggio, A., Schaafsma, B.J., Sebastiani, R.: The MathSAT5 SMT solver. In: Piterman, N., Smolka, S.A. (eds.) TACAS 2013. LNCS, vol. 7795, pp. 93–107. Springer, Heidelberg (2013). https://doi.org/10.1007/978-3-642-36742-7_7
17. Committee, I.S., et al.: 754–2008 IEEE standard for floating-point arithmetic. IEEE Computer Society Std **2008**, 517 (2008)
18. de Moura, L., Bjørner, N.: Z3: an efficient SMT solver. In: Ramakrishnan, C.R., Rehof, J. (eds.) TACAS 2008. LNCS, vol. 4963, pp. 337–340. Springer, Heidelberg (2008). https://doi.org/10.1007/978-3-540-78800-3_24
19. Godefroid, P., Peleg, H., Singh, R.: Learn&fuzz: machine learning for input fuzzing. In: Proceedings of the 32nd IEEE/ACM International Conference on Automated Software Engineering, pp. 50–59. IEEE Press (2017)
20. Gulwani, S., Srivastava, S., Venkatesan, R.: Program analysis as constraint solving. ACM SIGPLAN Not. **43**(6), 281–292 (2008)
21. Gupta, A.K., Nadarajah, S.: Handbook of Beta Distribution and Its Applications. CRC Press, Boca Raton (2004)
22. Karamcheti, S., Mann, G., Rosenberg, D.: Adaptive grey-box fuzz-testing with Thompson sampling. In: Proceedings of the 11th ACM Workshop on Artificial Intelligence and Security, pp. 37–47. ACM (2018)
23. Koza, J.R.: Genetic programming (1997)
24. Le Goues, C., Leino, K.R.M., Moskal, M.: The Boogie verification debugger (tool paper). In: Barthe, G., Pardo, A., Schneider, G. (eds.) SEFM 2011. LNCS, vol. 7041, pp. 407–414. Springer, Heidelberg (2011). https://doi.org/10.1007/978-3-642-24690-6_28
25. Lemieux, C., Padhye, R., Sen, K., Song, D.: PerfFuzz: automatically generating pathological inputs. In: Proceedings of the 27th ACM SIGSOFT International Symposium on Software Testing and Analysis, pp. 254–265 (2018)
26. Liang, T., Reynolds, A., Tsiskaridze, N., Tinelli, C., Barrett, C., Deters, M.: An efficient SMT solver for string constraints. Form. Methods Syst. Des. **48**(3), 206–234 (2016)
27. Manes, V.J., et al.: Fuzzing: art, science, and engineering. arXiv preprint arXiv:1812.00140 (2018)
28. Mansur, M.N., Christakis, M., Wüstholz, V., Zhang, F.: Detecting critical bugs in SMT solvers using blackbox mutational fuzzing. arXiv preprint arXiv:2004.05934 (2020)
29. Heule, M., Järvisalo, M., Suda, M.: SAT race 2019 (2019). http://sat-race-2019.ciirc.cvut.cz/
30. Marre, B., Bobot, F., Chihani, Z.: Real behavior of floating point numbers. In: 15th International Workshop on Satisfiability Modulo Theories (2017)

31. Miller, C., Peterson, Z.N., et al.: Analysis of mutation and generation-based fuzzing. Technical report, Independent Security Evaluators (2007)
32. Misherghi, G., Su, Z.: HDD: hierarchical delta debugging. In: Proceedings of the 28th International Conference on Software Engineering, pp. 142–151. ACM (2006)
33. Niemetz, A., Biere, A.: ddSMT: a delta debugger for the SMT-LIB v2 format. In: Proceedings of the 11th International Workshop on Satisfiability Modulo Theories, SMT 2013), affiliated with the 16th International Conference on Theory and Applications of Satisfiability Testing, SAT 2013, Helsinki, Finland, 8–9 July 2013, pp. 36–45 (2013)
34. Niemetz, A., Preiner, M., Biere, A.: Model-based API testing for SMT solvers. In: Brain, M., Hadarean, L. (eds.) Proceedings of the 15th International Workshop on Satisfiability Modulo Theories, SMT 2017, affiliated with the 29th International Conference on Computer Aided Verification, CAV 2017, Heidelberg, Germany, 24–28 July 2017, 10 pages (2017)
35. Patil, K., Kanade, A.: Greybox fuzzing as a contextual bandits problem. arXiv preprint arXiv:1806.03806 (2018)
36. Rawat, S., Jain, V., Kumar, A., Cojocar, L., Giuffrida, C., Bos, H.: VUzzer: application-aware evolutionary fuzzing. NDSS 17, 1–14 (2017)
37. Rebert, A., et al.: Optimizing seed selection for fuzzing. In: USENIX Security Symposium, pp. 861–875 (2014)
38. Rümmer, P., Wahl, T.: An SMT-LIB theory of binary floating-point arithmetic. In: International Workshop on Satisfiability Modulo Theories (SMT), p. 151 (2010)
39. Russell, S.J., Norvig, P.: Artificial Intelligence: A Modern Approach. Pearson Education Limited, Malaysia (2016)
40. Russo, D.J., Van Roy, B., Kazerouni, A., Osband, I., Wen, Z., et al.: A tutorial on Thompson sampling. Found. Trends® Mach. Learn. 11(1), 1–96 (2018)
41. Seagle Jr., R.L.: A framework for file format fuzzing with genetic algorithms (2012)
42. Sigaud, O., Buffet, O.: Markov Decision Processes in Artificial Intelligence. Wiley, New York (2013)
43. Sutton, M., Greene, A., Amini, P.: Fuzzing: Brute Force Vulnerability Discovery. Pearson Education, Upper Saddle River (2007)
44. Sutton, R.S., Barto, A.G.: Reinforcement Learning: An Introduction. MIT Press, Cambridge (2018)
45. Sutton, R.S., Barto, A.G., et al.: Reinforcement Learning: An Introduction. MIT Press, Cambridge (1998)
46. Szepesvári, C.: Algorithms for reinforcement learning. Synt. Lect. Artif. Intell. Mach. Learn. 4(1), 1–103 (2010)
47. Takanen, A., Demott, J.D., Miller, C.: Fuzzing for Software Security Testing and Quality Assurance. Artech House, Norwood (2008)
48. Woo, M., Cha, S.K., Gottlieb, S., Brumley, D.: Scheduling black-box mutational fuzzing. In: Proceedings of the 2013 ACM SIGSAC Conference on Computer & Communications Security, pp. 511–522. ACM (2013)
49. Zalewski, M.: American fuzzy lop (2015)
50. Zeller, A., Hildebrandt, R.: Simplifying and isolating failure-inducing input. IEEE Trans. Softw. Eng. 28(2), 183–200 (2002)

Synthesis of Solar Photovoltaic Systems: Optimal Sizing Comparison

Alessandro Trindade[1]([✉]) [ID] and Lucas C. Cordeiro[2] [ID]

[1] Federal University of Amazonas, Manaus, Brazil
alessandrotrindade@ufam.edu.br
[2] University of Manchester, Manchester, UK
lucas.cordeiro@manchester.ac.uk

Abstract. In the current scenario, energy demand rises by 1.3% each year to 2040, and photovoltaic (PV) systems have emerged as an alternative to the fossil or nuclear fuel energy generation. The use of formal methods for PV systems is a new subject with significant research spanning only five years. Here we develop and evaluate an automated synthesis technique to obtain optimal sizing of PV systems based on Life Cycle Cost (LCC) analysis. The optimal solution is the lowest cost from a list of equipment that meets the electrical demands from a house, plus the replacement, operation, and maintenance costs over 20 years. We propose a variant of the counterexample guided inductive synthesis (CEGIS) approach with two phases linking the technical and cost analysis to obtain the PV sizing optimization. We advocate that our technique has various advantages if compared to off-the-shelf optimization tools available in the market for PV systems. Experimental results from seven case studies demonstrate that we can produce an optimal solution within an acceptable run-time; different software verifiers are evaluated to check performance and soundness. We also compare our approach with a commercial tool specialized in PV systems optimization. Both results are validated with commercial design software; furthermore, some real PV systems comparison are used to show our approach effectiveness.

Keywords: Formal synthesis · Software verification · Solar photovoltaic systems · Cyber-physical systems

1 Introduction

Lack of access to clean and affordable energy is considered a core dimension of poverty [19]. Progress has been made worldwide; in particular, in 2017, the number of people without electricity access fell below 1 billion for the first time [20]. The share of people without access to electricity from Africa is 58%, while 19% of the share comes from developing Asia, and 31% from Latin America [20].

Supported by Newton Fund (ref. 261881580) and FAPEAM (Amazonas State Foundation for Research Support, calls 009/2017 and PROTI Pesquisa 2018).

© Springer Nature Switzerland AG 2020
M. Christakis et al. (Eds.): NSV 2020/VSTTE 2020, LNCS 12549, pp. 87–105, 2020.
https://doi.org/10.1007/978-3-030-63618-0_6

Numbers from Brazil show the aim to electrify 270 isolated areas and 2.7 million people by 2023 [13]. There exists a close relationship between the lack of energy and the low HDI (Human Development Index) of those localities [11]. It follows that increased access to energy allows economic growth and poverty alleviation [21]. To provide electricity for all, decentralized systems led by solar photovoltaic (PV) in off-grid and mini-grid systems will be the lowest-cost solution for three-quarters of the connections needed [19].

To evaluate or to obtain the optimal sizing of a PV system, there exist various specialized tools, e.g., RETScreen [25] and HOMER [28]; and even general-purpose tools, e.g., MATLAB/Simulink [16]. However, these tools are based on simulation; they have the drawback of incomplete coverage of design-space since verification of all possible combinations, and potential failures of a system are not feasible [10].

However, the industry demands the design solution to be the optimum, considering equipment manufacturers and models available on the market and not just minimum or maximum values of current or power for the optimized items. We need to evaluate the electrical compatibility among the equipment, which can only be achieved with specialized PV optimization software. Therefore, the optimal solution is the lowest cost from a list of equipment that meets the house's electrical demands. Our analysis is based on Life Cycle Cost (LCC) [4], where the acquisition and replacement cost are considered over a specific period.

Optimization of PV systems is not a recent topic; since the 1990s, different techniques using different criteria to find ultimate combinations for design parameters, based on intuitive, numerical, and analytical methods, were proposed and developed [4]. Concerning the use of automated verification or synthesis to electrical systems, we can mention that in 2015, an automated simulation-based verification technique was applied to verify the correctness of the power system protection settings [27]. In 2017, Abate suggested the application of formal methods to verify and control the behavior of devices in a smart grid (e.g., [2]). In 2018, a verification methodology was applied to PV panels and its distributed power point tracking [12]. Lastly, in 2019, an automated verification methodology was proposed to validate the sizing of stand-alone solar PV systems [31]. However, *formal methods and its application to synthesize PV systems are not explored in literature, mainly because it requires background and experience in computer science and PV systems, which is not common.*

Here we developed a variant of the counterexample guided inductive synthesis (CEGIS) [3] technique for synthesizing optimal sizing of stand-alone PV systems. If we provide a correctness specification σ, our method uses that as a starting point and then iteratively produces a sequence of candidate solutions that satisfy σ related to power reliability. In particular, on each iteration, we synthesize the sizing of stand-alone PV systems, but that may not achieve the lowest cost. The candidate solution is then verified via software model checking with a lower bound that serves as the minimum cost of reference. If the verification step does not produce a counterexample, then the lower bound is adjusted; otherwise, we have achieved an optimal PV sizing.

Our work makes three significant contributions to advance the state-of-the-art in PV optimal sizing. First, the use of automated software verification in PV systems was uncommon in recent prior studies; we have shown that formal methods can detect various errors in PV systems designed by existing commercial tools [31]. The application of software verification to synthesize PV sizing is novel, thereby leading to more accurate results than existing commercial tools. Second, we evaluate our approach using different state-of-the-art software verifiers to obtain the best performance in our verification backend for synthesizing optimal PV systems. We compare that to HOMER Pro optimization, with the results being validated with accurate commercial design software called PVsyst. Lastly, we discuss the challenges of applying software verification to PV systems and reflect on lessons learned from this experience.

2   Background

Figure 1 illustrates how to obtain the optimal sizing of a stand-alone PV system using the manual or simulation techniques and the proposed synthesis technique. Note that the input information is the same for all the methods: weather data, price information, design requirements, as load curve and power demand, and design assumptions. However, when using automated synthesis, we also define the bound k to restrict the design-space search. Here we start with a low bound k and incrementally increase it to avoid time and memory constraints on our verification engine. Therefore, the proper choice of k is essential to this method.

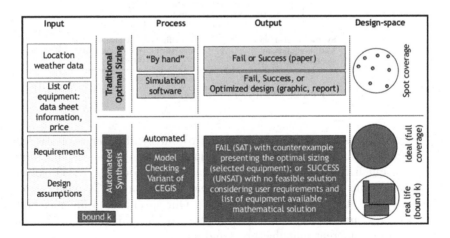

Fig. 1. Comparison of optimal sizing methods.

The techniques (manual, simulation, and automated synthesis) produce either a SUCCESS or FAIL result, thereby considering a feasible technical solution with the lowest cost. On the one hand, when done by simulation, we get a report or graphical result; on the other hand, the automated synthesis technique, which is mathematical reasoning about a model, presents a counterexample with the optimal solution stored in variables. Furthermore, the design-space coverage during the optimal sizing search is sound and complete when using synthesis.

2.1 Program Synthesis

The basic idea of program synthesis is to automatically construct a P program that satisfies a correctness specification σ. In particular, program synthesis is automatically performed by engines that use a correctness specification σ, as a starting point, and then incrementally produce a sequence of candidate solutions that partially satisfy σ [1]. As a result, a given candidate program p is iteratively refined to match σ more closely. Figure 2 illustrates the underlying architecture.

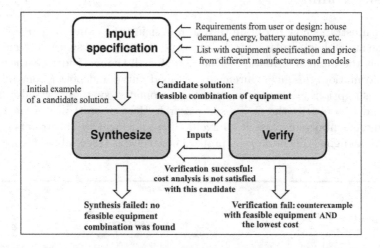

Fig. 2. CEGIS in PV system sizing.

The correctness specification σ provided to our synthesizer is of the form $\exists F.\forall x.\sigma(x, F)$, where F ranges over functions, x ranges over ground terms, and σ is a quantifier-free (QF) formula typically supported by SMT solvers. The ground terms are interpreted over some finite domain $\mathcal{D}$, where $\mathcal{D}$ can be encoded using the SMT's bit-vectors part. Our specification includes house demand, energy, and battery autonomy; we also provide equipment specifications and prices from different manufacturers and models.

In Fig. 2, the phases SYNTHESIZE and VERIFY interact via a finite set of test vectors INPUTS, which is incrementally updated. Given the correctness specification σ, the SYNTHESIZE procedure tries to find an existential witness F satisfying the specification $\sigma(x, F)$, for all x in INPUTS (as opposed to all $x \in \mathcal{D}$). If SYNTHESIZE succeeds in finding a witness F, the latter is a candidate solution to the full synthesis formula, which is passed to VERIFY to check whether it is a proper solution (*i.e.*, F satisfies the specification $\sigma(x, F)$ for all $x \in \mathcal{D}$). If this is the case, then the algorithm terminates.

One may notice that each iteration of the traditional CEGIS loop adds a new input to the finite set $INPUTS$, which is then used for synthesis. Given that the full set of inputs $\mathcal{D}$ is finite because we use bit-vector expressions, the refinement loop can only iterate over a finite number of times. However, SYNTHESIZE may conclude that no candidate solution obeying σ for the finite set $INPUTS$ exists.

In our CEGIS variant, there exist four differences related to the traditional one: (1) there exists no test vector, and every candidate is generated in the SYNTHESIZE phase and sent to the VERIFY phase; (2) if the VERIFY phase is unsuccessful, then a new candidate is generated by SYNTHESIZE and (3) the lower bound of the VERIFY phase is incremented to search for the lowest cost; as a result, (4) there exists no refinement from the VERIFY phase back to the SYNTHESIZE phase. In particular, a new counterexample is not added to the INPUT set since a failure during the VERIFY phase will only discard a given candidate, which could be feasible in the next iteration with a new lower bound.

In summary, our proposal is a technique based on CEGIS, which aims to synthesize the optimal solution of a PV system; therefore, our technique addresses an optimization problem.

2.2   Sizing Stand-Alone Solar PV Systems

A PV system is illustrated in Fig. 3. It employs the PV generator (*panel or an array*), a semiconductor device that can convert solar energy into DC electricity. For night hours or rainy days, we hold *batteries*, where power can be stored and used. The use of batteries as a storage form implies the presence of a *charge controller* [17]. The PV arrays produce DC, and therefore when the PV system contains an AC load, a DC/AC conversion is required (*inverter*). The *AC load* dictates the behavior of the AC electrical load from the house that will be fed by the system.

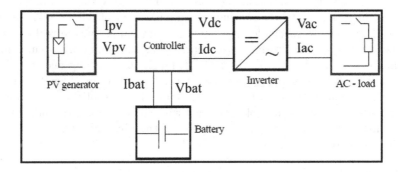

Fig. 3. Block diagram for a typical stand-alone PV system [17].

The sizing check stage can ensure that the system meets the standard project steps related to the critical period method (worst month) for solar energy system sizing [24]. It adopts an MPPT (Maximum Power Point Tracking) charge controller, which is the most common in use.

Since this paper's audience is targeted to be from the software verification area, we decided to use a higher-level explanation about the PV sizing. The sizing process involves a set of eighteen equations related to the electrical engineering area, which is detailed online.[1] Figure 4 illustrates the overview of the steps that must be taken to size a stand-alone PV system.

On the left side of Fig. 4, we describe the needed **inputs** to size a PV system. There exist requirements from the house to be electrified; in particular, we have the design assumptions, weather information from the targeted local of the PV system deployment, and a possible initial list of equipment to be used, covering all the items listed in Fig. 3. Concerning the equipment list, the designer can use a few pieces of equipment or a vast one. We can also decide not to adopt the commercial equipment list. However, the result is a PV sizing of specific power, current, or voltage values, and usually just close to original equipment, which can be found in the market. This possibility has the drawback of possible incompatibility among equipment when the real one is bought and deployed.

There exist specific steps that aim the calculation of some variables and others related to the electrical compatibility validation among equipment items, both enumerated from **i** to **xiv**, as illustrated in Fig. 4; those represent different shades of gray of the rectangle boxes. The start point is usually a candidate list of PV panels, charge controller, battery, and inverter, as indicated at the top of the flowchart. The arrows, on the right side, show a point where some specific item is validated. The diagram does not show the returning location. However, if the candidate item is not compatible with others or does not meet some requirement, it must be changed to follow the indicated flow. The last rectangle box checks the inverter electrical compatibility with the DC-bus voltage, with the required AC voltage from the outlet. Besides, the inverter specified power must be lower than the charge controller power to avoid it from burning by overcharge. At the end of the flowchart, all the items are defined, and the PV sizing is finished.

These equations model the continuous-time behavior of the PV system; they produce real numbers except for the batteries and panels, where real numbers must be converted into integer ones, considering the minimum or maximum according to each equation. The verification and simulation tools need to handle non-linear real arithmetic to produce the correct result. Our mathematical model uses floating-point arithmetic. It is just an approximation of the real numbers. However, in this work, we are not concerned with calculating the rounding error, which is negligible when considering the size of the physical quantities and the variables adopted [15].

---

[1] https://tinyurl.com/yck7dfxt.

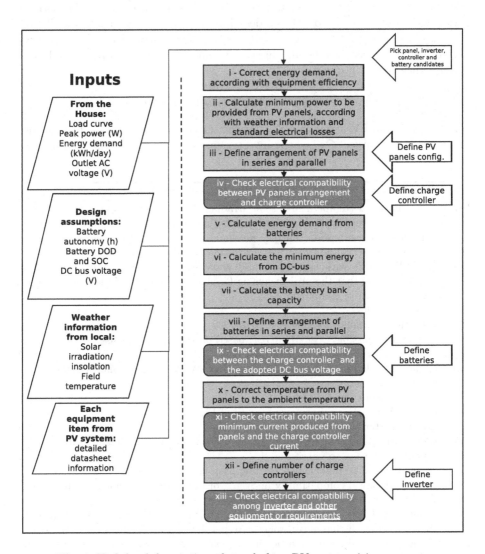

Fig. 4. High level description of stand-alone PV system sizing process.

3   Synthesizing Optimal Sizing of Stand-Alone Solar Photovoltaic Systems

The best compromise between two objectives makes the optimal sizing of PV systems: *power reliability* and *system cost* [4]. This study will rely on the critical period solar energy method [24], as described in Sect. 2.2. Our study will use an adapted Life Cycle Cost (LCC) analysis, where the acquisition cost of every item of equipment is considered, plus the installation cost, the operational and maintenance costs [4], given as,

$$LCC = C_{PV} + C_{bat} + C_{charger} + C_{inv} + C_{installation} + C_{batrep} + C_{PWO\&M} \quad (1)$$

where C_{PV} is the PV array cost, C_{bat} is the initial cost of batteries, $C_{charger}$ is the cost of the charger, C_{inv} is the inverter cost, $C_{installation}$ is the installation

---

Algorithm 1. Synthesis algorithm

Input: weather data (temperature, solar irradiance); data from panels, controllers, batteries, and inverters; design requirements (load curve, peak demand, load surge power, energy consumption, battery autonomy, AC voltage); design assumptions (SOC, DOD, criteria and objectives for technical and cost analysis)

Output: FAIL (SAT) with counterexample showing the optimal sizing; SUCCESS (UNSAT), saying that the project has no feasible solution considering the requirements and the list of equipment

 1: Initialize variables
 2: Declare the maximum possible cost $MaxCost$
 3: Calculate min possible Cost $MinCost$, based on the equipment list
 4: **for** $HintCost = MinCost$ to $MaxCost$ **do**
 5:     Declare non-deterministic variables to select PV Panel, Controller, Battery, and Inverter from list
 6:     Calculate Steps i and ii of Fig. 4
 7:     Define PV panels arrangement: Step iii of Fig. 4
 8:     Calculate Step iv of Fig. 4
 9:     Enforce electrical compatibility in Step v of Fig. 4 with statement **assume**
10:     Calculate Steps vi to viii of Fig. 4
11:     Define battery arrangement according Step ix of Fig. 4
12:     Enforce electrical compatibility in Step x of Fig. 4 with statement **assume**
13:     Correct variables to ambient temperature: Step xi of Fig. 4
14:     Enforce electrical compatibility in Step xii of Fig. 4 with statement **assume**
15:     Define number of charge controllers: Step xiii of Fig. 4
16:     Enforce electrical compatibilities in Step xiv of Fig. 4 with statement **assume** and define the inverter
17:     Non-deterministic variables hold feasible equipment and cost
18:     $F_{obj} \leftarrow N_{TP}*Panel_{Cost} + N_{TB}*Battery_{Cost} + Controller_{Cost} + Inverter_{Cost} + Installation_{Cost} + batrep_{Cost} + PWO\&M_{Cost}$
19:     Violation check with **assert**$(F_{obj} > HintCost)$
20: **end for**
21: **return** ()

---

cost, C_{batrep} is battery replacement cost at current prices, and $C_{PWO\&M}$ is operation and maintenance costs at current rates. In this study, we will use a $C_{installation}$ equivalent to 5% of total equipment cost and a $C_{PWO\&M}$ equal to U\$ 289.64/year according to Amazon State literature data [29]; and a LCC lifetime analysis of 20 years.

Algorithm 1 describes our pseudo-code to synthesize stand-alone PV systems. It uses software model checking as a backend verification engine [30]. The analytical method of optimization was adopted.

Our synthesis algorithm will synthesize constant values; it starts with the input of the manufacturer's data and prices of PV panels, batteries, charge controllers, and inverters. Moreover, we define design (house) requirements and design assumptions. The *for*-loop started in line 4 controls the lowest cost of the PV solution. In particular, it begins with a value $MinCost$ and stops when the algorithm finds a feasible solution in which the value breaks the *assertion* stated in line 18. If that happens, then our algorithm has found an optimal solution, thereby indicating that the VERIFY phase reached a satisfiable condition (SAT). The $MaxCost$ value in line 2 is just a very high value inserted as a limit to the *for*-loop, that meets one of the following requirements. (1) It will never be reached because the optimal solution will be found first (SAT result); or (2) it will be achieved when the search engine did not find a feasible solution for the optimization (UNSAT result).

Our synthesis algorithm uses non-deterministic variables to choose one specific constant from a given list of PV panels, controllers, batteries, and inverters (line 5). This procedure ensures that our synthesis engine checks all combinations of items from each equipment, and combines them to assemble a viable (candidate) PV solution, which meets user requirements. A list of forty equipment from ten different manufacturers was provided (as INPUT) to our synthesis engine to allow the choice of every item of PV sizing. Datasheet from each item was necessary to collect technical information. Moreover, the price of each item was obtained from available quotations in the market, and if the currency was not in US dollars, then it was used the exchange rate of the day to convert it to US dollars. All this data is available online.[2]

Next, we use a set of equations to calculate the sizing variables (lines 6, 7, 8, 10, 11, 13, 15). The statements *assume* (lines 9, 12, 14, and 16) ensures compatibility of the items chosen from the list of equipment: the VERIFY phase uses only items (among all the possible ones) that satisfy the statements of those lines. Line 12 is for the battery bank. Lines 9 and 14 are the charge controller voltage check. Line 16 does the inverter check and ensures the power demand and the surge power of the inverter. Therefore, our synthesis algorithm reaches line 17 with one feasible solution, and the cost of that solution is calculated in F_{obj} (line 18). This cost is the equivalent to Eq. (1).

If our algorithm does not find a feasible solution among the item of equipment that was provided for our SYNTHESIZE phase, then the result is unsatisfiable ($UNSAT$). In particular, the program finishes without finding a solution,

---

[2] https://tinyurl.com/ycgbsgkp.

indicating that it was unable to combine the specific items of equipment to create a feasible solution. The main challenge for the SYNTHESIZE phase is to find a feasible candidate solution for the constraints and user requirements. The problem for the VERIFY phase is to find the lowest acquisition cost from a list of equipment and components provided by the SYNTHESIZE phase.

Summarizing: We use four non-deterministic variables to index four matrices with complete datasheet information from an equipment item. We have four variables and four matrices: one to PV panels, one to batteries, one to the inverter, and one to the charge controller. Those non-deterministic variables are used during the search for the feasible solution and controlled by the statements **assume**. The candidate solution is proposed in the phase SYNTHESIZE of the technique. For the VERIFY phase, we performed a linear search for the lowest cost, and the result is based on FAIL or SUCCESS check from a cost that is linearly incremented in this model. The model checking is used during this VERIFY phase. If the process produces FAIL, then an optimal solution is found. If SUCCESS is presented, i.e. the property holds, there is no feasible solution from the equipment list provided by the technique. Note that the process described here is completely automated and that validation is performed by our VERIFY phase to ensure that the solution is sound. The verification engines transform the Algorithm 1 into the Boolean expressions that are passed to the solver to verify $(C \wedge \neg P)$, as described online.[3]

4   Results and Discussion

4.1   Description of the Case Studies

The proposed synthesis approach was evaluated in seven stand-alone PV system case studies. These case studies were defined based on the usual electrical load found in riverside communities in the Amazonas State, Brazil [29,31], except for case 7, which was idealized to support a few lamps and a 12k BTUs air-conditioner solution. Here we report each case study as a 4-tuple {*power peak (W); power surge (W); energy consumption (Wh/day); battery autonomy (hours)*} as follows: **1:** {342; 342; 3,900; 48}; **2:** {814; 980; 4,880; 48}; **3:** {815; 980; 4,880; 12}; **4:** {253; 722; 3,600; 48}; **5:** {263; 732; 2,500; 48}; **6:** {322; 896; 4,300; 48}; **7:** {1,586; 2,900; 14,000; 48}. This 4-tuple represents the Algorithm 1 inputs. For all cases, an estimated load curve (kWh) was defined based on the electronics consumers in each house. Our synthesis algorithm was fed with data and costs of forty equipment items from ten different manufacturers of PV systems. Three state-of-the-art verifiers, CBMC[4] v5.11 with MiniSat 2.2.1 [23], ESBMC[5] v6.0.0 [14] with the Boolector 3.0.1 solver [8], and CPAchecker[6] v1.8 [6] with

---

[3] https://tinyurl.com/yajfmavl.

[4] Command-line: $ cbmc --unwind 100 file.c --trace.

[5] Command-line: $ esbmc filename.c --incremental-bmc --boolector.

[6] Command-line: $ scripts/cpa.sh -heap 64000m -config config/bmc-incremental.properties -spec config/specification/sv-comp-reachability.spc file.c.

MathSAT 5.5.3 [9], were used as verification engines to compare the proposed approach effectiveness and efficiency.

4.2 Optimization/Simulation Tools and Assumptions

Concerning the off-the-shelf optimization/simulation tools, only HOMER Pro performs an off-grid system with battery backup analysis and includes economical analysis. Here we used HOMER Pro version 3.13.1 as a state-of-the-art optimization tool for comparison purposes. In particular, HOMER Pro has the following characteristics: (a) it is available only for MS-Windows, its annual standard subscription costs US$ 504.00 [18]; (b) it has two optimization algorithms: one algorithm simulates all of the feasible system configurations defined by the search space, and additionally, a proprietary derivative-free algorithm to search for the least-costly system; (c) it does not have LCC cost in its reports, only Net Present Cost (NPC); however, we can obtain LCC from NPC; (d) the optimization analysis defines a load curve and temperature according to data collected from online databases. However, to allow a correct comparison, the curve load and the temperature were defined the same as our synthesis approach; (e) it does not have a charge controller. During the tests, we have chosen the "load-following" option, which produces enough power to meet the demand [18] and (usually) presents a non-overestimated solution; (f) it was assumed 95% availability of the PV system. By definition, "availability" is the percentage of time at which a power system can feed the load requirements [22]. For an ordinary house electrical load, 95% is considered acceptable; (g) it was assumed a string of two batteries to match the voltage of the 24 V DC system, which was used for our automated synthesis tool; (h) it was included a generic flat-plate PV of 1 kW and generic lead-acid batteries of 1 kW (83.4 Ah capacity). During runtime, HOMER decides the size in kW of each one based on feasibility and lower cost.

To validate and compare the optimal sizing solution produced by our approach and by HOMER Pro, we use a simulation tool, called PVsyst version 6.86 [26], with plenty of commercial equipment in its data bank. We have considered a comparison for an entire year's weather data of simulation to guarantee that the proposed sizing meets the electrification requirements. PVsyst is a PC software package developed by a Swiss company used for the study, sizing, simulation and data analysis of solar PV systems. PVsyst contains design, sizing, 3D shading scene, simulation, grid, and off-grid features. It uses comprehensive irradiation data from Meteonorm,[7] and aging analysis [5]. However, it does not perform optimization; therefore, PVsyst needs the system sized to validate it. Furthermore, PVsyst does not have commercial inverter equipment and, as a result, does not consider surge power demand as the ones produced by air conditioners and refrigerators for a few seconds. PVsyst is commercial software with a 30-day test possibility and runs only in MS-Windows.

---

[7] https://meteonorm.com/en/.

4.3   Objectives and Setup

Our evaluation aims to answer three experimental goals: [EG1] (**soundness**) Does our automated synthesis approach provide correct results?; [EG2] (**performance**) How do the software verifiers compare to each other for synthesizing PV systems?; and [EG3] (**state-of-the-art**) how does our formal synthesis tool compare to a specialized simulation tool?

All experiments regarding the verification tools were conducted on an otherwise idle Intel Xeon CPU E5-4617 (8-cores) with 2.90 GHz and 64 GB RAM, running Ubuntu 16.04 LTS 64-bits. For HOMER Pro, we have used an Intel Core i5-4210 (4-cores) with 1.7 GHz and 4 GB RAM running Windows 10. The ideal scenario would be to use the same hardware configuration for the experiments. However, we faced restrictions concerning the license for the HOMER Pro tool; besides, we did not have the autonomy to change the Linux VM machine installed in our university's servers due to the internal policy. This setup has an impact on performance, which is less favorable to HOMER Pro. PVsyst used the same configuration as HOMER Pro. We perform the experiments with a predefined *time out* of 660 min.

4.4   Results

The results are presented in Table 1. The violation (SAT result) indicated in Table 1 is the *assert* of the line 18 in Algorithm 1 and suggests that an optimal solution was found. Here, CBMC was unable to produce any conclusive result; *out of memory* situations occurred in all case studies.

CPAchecker was able to synthesize optimal sizing in three out of the seven case studies (cases 1, 4, and 5): the result was produced within the time limit, which varied from 4 to 9 h. Figure 5 illustrates the result of case 5 with the optimal sizing appearing on the left side as the integer 3 for the solar panel (which is the Canadian CS6U-330P model of 330 W from the manufacturer Victron Energy), battery 0 refers to the model 12MF80 of 80 Ah from Moura, charge controller 0 refers to the model 35A-145V MPPT from Victron Energy. The inverter number 2 refers to the Epever model IP350-11 of 280 W (nominal power) and 750 W of surge power. The variables NTP, NPS, NPP, NBS, NBP, and NBTotal, also presented in the counterexample, shows the number of panels and batteries and how they are connected. Case studies 2, 3, 6, and 7 led to a *time out* result in CPAchecker, i.e., it was not solved within 11 h.

Here we used ESBMC in BMC incremental mode with Boolector; ESBMC was able to reach the optimal sizing of case studies 1, 3, 4, 5, and 6 with a FAIL/SAT response, varying from 36 min to 10 h. ESBMC, with this configuration, was unable to obtain an optimal solution in cases 2 and 7. Case 2 produced a *time out*. Moreover, case 7 resulted in a UNSAT result, i.e., ESBMC was unable to provide a feasible solution. However, this is not a bug, and it means that the available list of equipment can not produce a feasible solution that satisfies electrical compatibility or design requirements. This UNSAT situation was reached in less than one minute. These experimental results answer the *EG2*.

Table 1. Case studies and results: optimization of stand-alone PV systems.

Tools	CBMC 5.11 (MiniSat 2.2.1)	ESBMC 6.0.0 (Boolector 3.0.1)	CPAchecker 1.8 (MathSAT 5.5.3)	HOMER Pro 3.13.1
Specification	Result	Result	Result	Result
Case Study 1 Peak:342W Surge:342W E:3,900Wh/day Autonomy:48h	OM	SAT (620 min) NTP:6×330W (2P-3S) NBT:16×105Ah (2S-8P) Controller 35A/145V Inverter 700W/48V LCC: US$ 10,214.04	SAT (548 min) NTP:6×330W (2P-3S) NBT:16×105Ah (2S-8P) Controller 35A/145V Inverter 700W/1600W/48V LCC: US$ 10,214.04	(Time: 0.33 min) 2.53 kW of PV NBT:12×83.4Ah (2S-6P) 0.351kW inverter LCC: US$ 7,808.04
Case Study 2 Peak:814W Surge:980W E:4,880Wh/day Autonomy:48h	OM	TO	TO	(Time: 0.18 min) 3.71 kW of PV NBT:20×83.4Ah (2S-10P) 0.817kW inverter LCC: US$ 12,861.75
Case Study 3 Peak:815W Surge:980W E:4,880Wh/day Autonomy:12h	OM	SAT (63 min) NTP:14×150W (7P-2S) NBT:6×105Ah (2S-3P) Controller 35A/145V Inverter 1,200W/48V LCC: US$ 9,274.07	TO	Not possible
Case Study 4 Peak:253W Surge:722W E:3,600Wh/day Autonomy:48h	OM	SAT (147 min) NTP:6×330W (2P-3S) NBT:16×105Ah (2S-8P) Controller 35A/145V Inverter 280W/48V LCC: US$ 9,678.63	SAT (605 min) NTP:6×330W (2P-3S) NBT:16×105Ah (2S-8P) Controller 35A/145V Inverter 280W/48V LCC: US$ 9,678.63	(Time: 0.23 min) 2.42 kW of PV NBT:12×83.4Ah (2S-6P) 0.254kW inverter LCC: US$ 7,677.95
Case Study 5 Peak:263W Surge:732W E:2,500Wh/day Autonomy:48h	OM	SAT (36.70 min) NTP:4×330W (2S-2P) NBT:14×80Ah (2S-7P) Controller 35A/145V Inverter 280W/24V LCC: US$ 8,900.70	SAT (254.25 min) NTP:4×330W (2S-2P) NBT:14×80Ah (2S-7P) Controller 35A/145V Inverter 280W/24V LCC: US$ 8,900.70	(Time: 0.18 min) 1.59 kW of PV NBT:10×83.4Ah (2S-5P) 0.268kW inverter LCC: US$ 6,175.57
Case Study 6 Peak:322W Surge:896W E:4,300Wh/day Autonomy:48h	OM	SAT (380.93 min) NTP:6×320W (2P-3S) NBT:18×105Ah (2S-9P) Controller 35A/145V Inverter 400W/24V LCC: US$ 10,136.61	TO	(Time: 0.22 min) 3.15 kW of PV NBT:14×83.4Ah (2S-7P) 0.328kW inverter LCC: US$ 9,112.45
Case Study 7 Peak:1,586W Surge:2,900W E:14,000Wh/day Autonomy:48h	OM	UNSAT (0.48 min)	TO	(Time: 0.20 min) 12.5 kW of PV NBT:66×83.4Ah (2S-33P) 1.60kW inverter LCC: US$ 41,878.11

Legend: OM = out of memory; TO = time out; IF = internal failure; E = energy; NTP = total number of panels, NBtotal = total number of batteries, NPS = number of panels in series; NPP = number of panels in parallel, NBS = number of batteries in series; NBP = number of batteries in parallel; LCC = Life Cycle Cost.

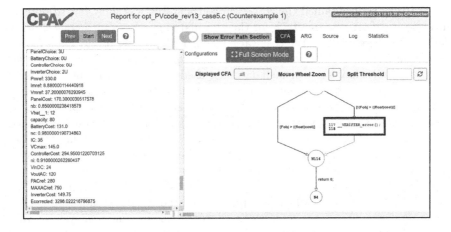

Fig. 5. Counterexample generated by CPAchecker after validation of case 5.

HOMER Pro was able to evaluate six case studies (cases 1, 2, 4, 5, 6, and 7) under 30 s; it was much faster than the proposed automated synthesis tool (cf. *EG3*). Case study 3 could not be simulated since HOMER Pro does not have the battery autonomy adjustment feature, i.e., the tool always tries to feed the given load with electricity 365 days/year. Some HOMER Pro drawbacks were also noted. (1) System equipment does not include an explicit charge controller. HOMER Pro includes a controller automatically to simulate the charge/discharge of batteries and to meet the load requirement. However, without costs or even with electrical characteristics such as maximum current and voltage, which are common during PV sizing. (2) HOMER Pro requires the inclusion of some battery specification to initiate optimization; however, it does not change the electrical specifications during simulation; the results presented are multiples of the original battery type suggested by the user. For example, it was started with an 83.4 Ah lead-acid battery, and during simulation, HOMER Pro did not try to use other capacities or types. (3) HOMER Pro does not present the optimal solution in terms of connections of PV panel arrays, just the total in terms of power, i.e., it presents neither the models and the power of each PV panel nor the total of panels in series or parallel. The cost of every equipment item used in HOMER Pro is a US-based cost, without adaptation regardless of where the equipment is installed.

We have real PV systems deployed since June 2018 in a riverside community in the State of Amazonas, Brazil, GPS coordinates 2°44′50.0″S 60°25′47.8″W, with demands of case studies 1, 4, 5, and 6, always with a 3 × 325 W (3S, total 975 W) panels and 4 × 220 Ah (2S-2P = 440 Ah) lead-acid batteries.

4.5 Comparison Between Formal Synthesis and HOMER Pro

If we compare the formal synthesis results against those of HOMER Pro, we observed some distinct effects in terms of the technical solution and cost (cf. Table 1). Concerning the performance, there exists a vast difference in favor of HOMER Pro that obtained the results in considerably less time: few seconds in the opposite of an average of 4 h for the automated synthesis technique. Particularly in the case of LCC, the cost varied from 11% to 44%, producing a higher estimation from the automated synthesis technique. However, considering that the cost of individual items of each database used to compose the optimal design is not the same among the tools, it is plausible to obtain distinct results.

On the one hand, concerning the PV panels sizing, the results presented by the automated synthesis were smaller in terms of power than the ones produced by the simulation tool. The difference varied from 19% to 65%. On the other hand, concerning the battery bank, the results were smaller in terms of HOMER Pro capacity. The difference was between 34% to 68%. The mathematical models are different and particular parameters can be tuned for each technique, and that can justify the difference, which was presented in all the case studies.

Those discrepancies are not easy to address without some real systems validation. However, we use the simulation software PVsyst to validate the optimal sizing produced, as shown in Table 2. Note that PVsyst has a pre-sizing feature, which presents a minimum recommended sizing of PV panels and batteries (only) without using manufacturers' data or models for it. This feature was used as reference mainly with HOMER Pro, where there exists no equipment brands or models (only power and capacities specification). PVsyst was used with the field-deployed and the formal synthesis sizing solutions, where brands and models were simulated in PVsyst according to the sized system.

Table 2. Optimal sizing validation with PVsyst.

CS	PVsyst (pre-sizing)	Field deployed validation	Formal synthesis sizing validation	HOMER Pro sizing validation
CS 1	P= 1,166 W B= 381 Ah (minimum)	Not correct sizing Avail. < 95% (91.06%)	No error found 100% of avail.	No error found Panels oversized in 2.16 × Batteries oversized in 1.39 ×
CS 2	P= 1,482 W B= 478 Ah (minimum)	NA There exists no real PV system available for comparison	NA (TO result in Table 1)	No error found Panels oversized in 2.6 × Batteries oversized in 1.74 ×
CS 3	Not possible to simulate (autonomy < 24h)	NA There exists no real PV system available for comparison	Only technique that produced solution	NA (autonomy < 24h)
CS 4	P= 1,078 W B= 354 Ah (minimum)	No error found 95.76% of avail.	No error found 97.37% of avail.	No error found Panels oversized in 2.24 × Batteries oversized in 1.41 ×
CS 5	P= 823 W B= 268 Ah (minimum)	No error found 100% of avail.	No error found 100% of avail.	No error found Panels oversized in 1.93 × Batteries oversized in 1.56 ×
CS 6	P= 1,299 W B= 421 Ah (minimum)	Not correct sizing Avail. < 95% (85.65%)	No error found 100% of avail.	No error found Panels oversized in 2.42 × Batteries oversized in 1.38 ×
CS 7	P= 4,263 W B= 1,384 Ah (minimum)	NA There exists no real PV system available for comparison	NA (UNSAT result in Table 1)	No error found Panels oversized in 2.9 × Batteries oversized in 1.99 ×

Legend: CS = case study; NA = sizing not available for validation; B = batteries capacity; P = panels power; Avail.= Availability (expected of 95% or greater as a design requirement).

Each simulation with PVsyst took 4 s. We were unable to validate the case study 3 using PVsyst. The battery autonomy is less than 24 h, and only the proposed synthesis technique can perform the optimal sizing (PVsyst and HOMER Pro are limited for a 24 h minimum). Case studies 2 and 7 had only HOMER Pro sizing validation. There is no deployed equivalent system in the field, and the synthesis technique did not present a solution due to *time out* and internal failures in the underlying verification engine.

Overall, those comparisons with our approach, the optimization software, and the deployed systems, with validation through simulation tool, show that the synthesis solution is sound and complete, which answers *EG1* and EG3.

Concerning the cost (LCC) present by both tools, HOMER Pro does not use the real cost for PV systems deployed in Brazil; therefore, the optimal solution presented by HOMER Pro is notoriously cheaper than our technique. However, considering that the aim is to present an optimal PV sizing solution that is feasible and closer to the market prices, our technique is more indicated.

Besides that, HOMER Pro suggests a value in kW for the inverters that are very close to the maximum load of every case study, but it is not commercial.

The proposed synthesis tool, however, presents inverters that are commercial and can be obtained off-the-shelf. Moreover, our synthesis approach considers surge power demand from the house, which is not viewed by HOMER Pro or PVsyst. This feature is a definite advantage of the formal synthesis method. HOMER Pro does not include charge controllers as a specific item of equipment in its mathematical model; only the synthesis tool presents a commercial controller and includes it during the cost analysis. The formal synthesis method, therefore, presents more reliable results than HOMER Pro.

In summary, our synthesis technique can present a solution that is far more detailed and closer to commercial conditions than the answer given by HOMER Pro. In particular, the automated synthesis method can provide all the details of every component of a PV system solution, with complete electrical information from the manufacturer datasheet, including the model of the component, nominal current, and voltage. In this respect, even the name of the manufacturer can be cited (in Table 1, it was removed to avoid unauthorized advertising). Moreover, the validation through PVsyst simulation, using the PV sizing produced by HOMER Pro and our synthesis approach, shows that our results are feasible and not as oversized as HOMER Pro results, mainly concerning PV panels.

An optimal solution from a tool is not necessarily the same optimal from other tools, mainly when the database of equipment items (with different costs) is not the same [4]. Therefore, the comparison must take this issue into account.

4.6 Threats to Validity

We have reported a favorable assessment of the proposed method. Nevertheless, we have also identified four threats to the validity of our results that constitute future work. First, improvement of the power reliability analysis: to include loss of load probability or loss of power supply probability, which can make the study more accurate. Second, improvement of the system cost analysis by adding operational and maintenance costs to the adopted LCC analysis. Third, increase the equipment and manufacturers database: this will increase the optimization complexity, but the result will also allow improved sizing. Lastly, the underlying software verifiers employed here perform bit-precise verification based on the Floating-Point (FP) theory. We could use a real arithmetic strategy to tackle these equations; however, in this study, we have exploited the FP arithmetic, approximating the real one.

5   Conclusions

Our novelty relies on a practical approach to pursue the optimal PV systems' optimal solution using contemporary formal methods. The use of formal synthesis to design PV systems has no precedent in literature; we show that our approach results, using seven case studies, are promising. Our synthesis tool can present a solution that is far more detailed and closer to commercial reality than the solution given by the commercial tool. The battery autonomy feature, together with the details of every component of a PV system solution, is advantageous for our synthesis approach; these details are essential for the PV system owner. The industry demands proximity between the result presented by optimization tools and the items of equipment for solar systems available on the market.

Our synthesis technique was developed and used open-source software verifiers and the environment, in contrast to the optimization and simulation tools used in this work. We have also observed that state-of-the-art software verifiers are doing an excellent job of solving hard verification conditions based on the underlying SAT/SMT solvers. Lastly, the use of data from real deployed systems in Brazil and the validation through PVsyst was essential to validate the comparison. We have shown that our technique has a promising result for PV system sizing optimization. Our focus for future work consists of improving the search mechanism used in the VERIFY phase of our synthesis technique to speed up the overall time. We plan to use parallel binary search [32] or even a solver that is specific to perform optimization with model checking as νZ [7].

References

1. Abate, A., et al.: Automated formal synthesis of digital controllers for state-space physical plants. In: Majumdar, R., Kunčak, V. (eds.) CAV 2017. LNCS, vol. 10426, pp. 462–482. Springer, Cham (2017). https://doi.org/10.1007/978-3-319-63387-9_23

2. Abate, A.: Verification of networks of smart energy systems over the cloud. In: Bogomolov, S., Martel, M., Prabhakar, P. (eds.) NSV 2016. LNCS, vol. 10152, pp. 1–14. Springer, Cham (2017). https://doi.org/10.1007/978-3-319-54292-8_1

3. Abate, A., David, C., Kesseli, P., Kroening, D., Polgreen, E.: Counterexample guided inductive synthesis modulo theories. In: Chockler, H., Weissenbacher, G. (eds.) CAV 2018. LNCS, vol. 10981, pp. 270–288. Springer, Cham (2018). https://doi.org/10.1007/978-3-319-96145-3_15

4. Alsadi, S., Khatib, T.: Photovoltaic power systems optimization research status: a review of criteria, constrains, models, techniques, and software tools. Appl. Sci. 8(1761), 1–30 (2018)

5. Barua, S., Prasath, R.A., Boruah, D.: Rooftop solar photovoltaic system design and assessment for the academic campus using PVsyst software. Int. J. Electron. Electr. Eng. 5(1), 76–83 (2017)

6. Beyer, D., Keremoglu, M.E.: CPACHECKER: a tool for configurable software verification. In: Gopalakrishnan, G., Qadeer, S. (eds.) CAV 2011. LNCS, vol. 6806, pp. 184–190. Springer, Heidelberg (2011). https://doi.org/10.1007/978-3-642-22110-1_16

7. Bjørner, N., Phan, A.-D., Fleckenstein, L.: νZ - an optimizing SMT solver. In: Baier, C., Tinelli, C. (eds.) TACAS 2015. LNCS, vol. 9035, pp. 194–199. Springer, Heidelberg (2015). https://doi.org/10.1007/978-3-662-46681-0_14

8. Brummayer, R., Biere, A.: Boolector: an efficient SMT solver for bit-vectors and arrays. In: Kowalewski, S., Philippou, A. (eds.) TACAS 2009. LNCS, vol. 5505, pp. 174–177. Springer, Heidelberg (2009). https://doi.org/10.1007/978-3-642-00768-2_16

9. Cimatti, A., Griggio, A., Schaafsma, B.J., Sebastiani, R.: The MathSAT5 SMT solver. In: Piterman, N., Smolka, S.A. (eds.) TACAS 2013. LNCS, vol. 7795, pp. 93–107. Springer, Heidelberg (2013). https://doi.org/10.1007/978-3-642-36742-7_7

10. Clarke, E.M., Henzinger, T.A., Veith, H.: Introduction to model checking. In: Handbook of Model Checking, pp. 1–26. Springer, Cham (2018). https://doi.org/10.1007/978-3-319-10575-8_1

11. Coelho, S., et al.: Biomass residues as electricity generation source in low HD source in regions of Brazil. In: UNESP (ed.) The XI Latin Congress of Electricity Generation and Transmission - CLAGTEE, pp. 1–8 (2015)

12. Driouich, Y., Parente, M., Tronci, E.: A methodology for a complete simulation of cyber-physical energy systems. In: IEEE Workshop on Environmental, Energy, and Structural Monitoring Systems (EESMS), pp. 1–5 (2018)

13. Empresa de Pesquisa Energética EPE: Sistemas Isolados - Planejamento Ciclo 2018–2023 (2018). http://www.epe.gov.br/sites-pt/publicacoes-dados-abertos/publicacoes. Accessed 04 Apr 2019

14. Gadelha, M., Monteiro, F., Morse, J., Cordeiro, L., Fischer, B., Nicole, D.: ESBMC 5.0: an industrial-strength C model checker. In: 33rd IEEE/ACM International Conference on Automated Software Engineering (ASE 2018), pp. 888–891. ACM, New York (2018)

15. Gadelha, M.Y.R., Cordeiro, L.C., Nicole, D.A.: An efficient floating-point bit-blasting API for verifying C programs. CoRR abs/2004.12699 (2020). https://arxiv.org/abs/2004.12699

16. Gow, J., Manning, C.: Development of a photovoltaic array model for use in power-electronics simulation studies. In: Proceedings of the 14th IEE Electric Power Applications Conference, vol. 146(2), pp. 193–200 (1999)

17. Hansen, A., Sørensen, P., Hansen, L., Bindner, H.: Models for a stand-alone PV system. No. 1219 in Denmark. Forskningscenter Risoe. Risoe-r, Forskningscenter Risoe (2001)

18. HOMER: The HOMER microgrid software (2017). http://www.homerenergy.com/software.html. Accessed 1 June 2019

19. Hussein, M., Leal Filho, W.: Analysis of energy as a precondition for improvement of living conditions and poverty reduction in sub-Saharan Africa. In: Scientific Research and Essays, vol. 7(30), pp. 2656–2666 (2012)

20. IEA: World Energy Outlook 2018. IEA, Paris (2018)

21. Karekesi, S., Lata, K., Coelho, S.: Renewable Energy - A Global Review of Technologies, Policies and Markets, chap. Traditional Biomass Energy: Improving Its Use and Moving to Modern Energy Use, pp. 231–261. Earthscan, London (2006)

22. Khatib, T., Elmenreich, W.: Optimum availability of standalone photovoltaic power systems for remote housing electrification. Int. J. Photoenergy 2014(Article ID 475080), 5 pages (2014)

23. Kroening, D., Tautschnig, M.: CBMC – c bounded model checker. In: Ábrahám, E., Havelund, K. (eds.) TACAS 2014. LNCS, vol. 8413, pp. 389–391. Springer, Heidelberg (2014). https://doi.org/10.1007/978-3-642-54862-8_26

24. Pinho, J., Galdino, M.: Manual de Engenharia para Sistemas Fotovoltaicos. CEPEL - CRESESB, Rio de Janeiro (2014)

25. Pradhan, S., Singh, S., Choudhury, M., Dwivedy, D.: Study of cost analysis and emission analysis for grid connected PV systems using RETSCREEN 4 simulation software. Int. J. Eng. Res. Tech. 4(4), 203–207 (2015)

26. PVsyst: Logiciel Photovoltaïque (2020). https://www.pvsyst.com/. Accessed 24 Apr 2020

27. Sengupta, A., Mukhopadhyay, S., Sinha, A.: Automated verification of power system protection schemes–Part I: modeling and specifications. IEEE Tran. Power Del. **30**(5), 2077–2086 (2015)
28. Swarnkar, N., Gidwani, L., Sharma, R.: An application of HOMER Pro in optimization of hybrid energy system for electrification of technical institute. In: International Conference on Energy Efficient Technologies for Sustainability (ICEETS), pp. 56–61 (2016)
29. Trindade, A.: Ferramenta de análise comparativa de projetos de eletrificação rural com fontes renováveis de energia na amazônia. In: IX Congresso sobre Geração Distribuída e Energia no Meio Rural - AGRENER GD. p. n.pag. (2013)
30. Trindade, A., Cordeiro, L.C.: Optimal sizing of stand-alone solar PV systems via automated formal synthesis. CoRR abs/1909.13139 (2019). http://arxiv.org/abs/1909.13139
31. Trindade, A.B., Cordeiro, L.C.: Automated formal verification of stand-alone solar photovoltaic systems. Solar Energy **193**(1), 684–691 (2019)
32. Trindade, A.B., Degelo, R.D.F., Junior, E.G.D.S., Ismail, H.I., Silva, H.C.D., Cordeiro, L.C.: Multi-core model checking and maximum satisfiability applied to hardware-software partitioning. IJES **9**(6), 570–582 (2017)

Verified Transformations and Hoare Logic: Beautiful Proofs for Ugly Assembly Language

Jay Bosamiya[1(✉)], Sydney Gibson[2], Yao Li[3], Bryan Parno[1],
and Chris Hawblitzel[4]

[1] Carnegie Mellon University, Pittsburgh, USA
jaybosamiya@cmu.edu
[2] Massachusetts Institute of Technology, Cambridge, USA
[3] University of Pennsylvania, Philadelphia, USA
[4] Microsoft Research, Redmond, USA

Abstract. Hand-optimized assembly language code is often difficult to formally verify. This paper combines Hoare logic with verified code transformations to make it easier to verify such code. This approach greatly simplifies existing proofs of highly optimized OpenSSL-based AES-GCM cryptographic code. Furthermore, applying various verified transformations to the AES-GCM code enables additional platform-specific performance improvements.

1 Introduction

Some of the most important code in the world is also some of the ugliest. The most commonly used implementations of cryptographic algorithms are heavily optimized, typically employing hand-crafted assembly language for maximum performance. For example, OpenSSL's implementation of AES-GCM, the cryptographic algorithm used for 91% of secure web traffic [14], contains thousands of lines of hand-optimized x86-64 assembly language code. The optimizations unroll loops, prefetch data from memory, carefully hand-schedule instructions, and interleave otherwise unrelated instructions in an effort to expose parallelism and keep the processor's functional units busy. The resulting code is extremely fast, but difficult to understand, maintain, and verify.

Recent work on EverCrypt [17] used Hoare logic to verify a variant of OpenSSL's AES-GCM x64 code. Hoare logic is a natural way to express the verification of well-structured programs. Unfortunately, the optimizations in OpenSSL's AES-GCM code obscure the natural structure of the underlying AES-GCM algorithm, making Hoare logic awkward to use directly on the optimized code. In particular, to automate the proofs, it helps to keep code units relatively small, since that keeps the proof "debug" cycle tolerable for developers. However, the interleaving of unrelated instructions makes it difficult to modularly decompose the code into smaller units with natural preconditions and

© Springer Nature Switzerland AG 2020
M. Christakis et al. (Eds.): NSV 2020/VSTTE 2020, LNCS 12549, pp. 106–123, 2020.
https://doi.org/10.1007/978-3-030-63618-0_7

postconditions. As a result, the preconditions and postconditions describe situations where natural invariants do not yet hold or have already been broken. Worse, each repeated section of code generated from loop unrolling has to be verified separately, because the instruction scheduling and interleaving cause each section to contain slightly different code with slightly different preconditions and postconditions. The ugly code leads to ugly proofs and duplicated effort.

This creates a stark trade-off. On one hand, the performance gains from carefully optimized code are enormous and valuable: the verified code based on OpenSSL's optimized code runs 6× faster than earlier verified code written in a simpler, easier-to-verify style [7]. On the other hand, the effort involved in verifying optimized code may dissuade authors of cryptographic code from attempting any formal verification.

We argue that the trade-off is not as stark as it may seem at first glance:

- First, we demonstrate how to use verified transformers to recover the elegance of Hoare logic. In this approach, the programmer uses Hoare logic to verify a clean, modular version of the code. In addition, the programmer writes (but does not directly verify) the optimized, non-modular version of the code. Our verified transformation tool then attempts to automatically discover the relationship between the clean and optimized versions and prove their equivalence. This proves that the properties established via Hoare logic for the clean code apply to the optimized code.
- Second, we manually create a clean, modular version of EverCrypt's AES-GCM code and measure its performance. To our surprise, on some CPUs, the clean code actually runs slightly *faster* on average than the original EverCrypt code. In other words, not all of OpenSSL's optimizations are equally necessary to achieving its fast performance, and the optimization that causes the most trouble for EverCrypt's verification does not appear to pay off consistently.
- Third, inspired by the observed performance difference between the clean code and EverCrypt code, we investigate the performance of alternate interleavings of the assembly language instructions for various x86-64 processor models. We develop a tool that automatically finds interleavings that are faster than both the EverCrypt code and the clean code, and we use our verified transformation tool to verify the correctness of these new interleavings. Hence, verified transformers support automated development of hyper-targeted optimized implementations while still allowing the developer to write beautiful, Hoare-style proofs.

The rest of the paper is as follows. Section 2 presents background on the Vale language and tool [5,7], which provides the operational semantics and Hoare Logic reasoning for our assembly language code. Section 3 presents our verified transformation tool and describes how it deals with subtle equivalence issues, such as assembly language status flags. Section 4 applies the tool to an important real-world case study: OpenSSL's optimized AES-GCM. Section 5 shows that our tool can verify alternate interleavings of OpenSSL's code that are faster than the original code. Section 6 compares to related work, including related verification of

cryptographic code such as Fiat-Crypto [6] and Jasmin [1,2]. Section 7 concludes
with recommendations for verifying optimized code.

All of our code and proofs are available online, under an open source license.[1]

2   Background: Vale and Assembly Language

In order to verify x64 code for AES-GCM, previous work [7,17] defined syntax
and operational semantics for x64 instructions as F⋆ [20] datatypes and functions. Below, we provide a representative sampling of these definitions.

```
// Instruction syntax and semantics, defined in F*
type reg = Rax | Rbx | Rcx | Rdx | ...
type operand =
  | OConst: n:int -> operand
  | OReg: r:reg -> operand
  | OMem: m:mem_addr -> operand
type ins =
  | Mov64: dst:operand -> src:operand -> ins
  | Add64: dst:operand -> src:operand -> ins
  ...
type code =
  | Ins: ins:ins -> code
  | Block: block:list code -> code
  ...
type state = {
  ok:bool;
  regs:reg -> nat64;
  flags:nat64;
  mem:map int nat8;
}
let eval_ins (ins:ins) =
  ...
  match ins with
  | Mov64 dst src -> ...
  | Add64 dst src -> ...
  ...
let rec eval_code (c:code) (s:state) ... =
  match c with
  | Ins ins -> Some (run (eval_ins ins) s)
  ...
```

Here, the big-step operational semantics defined by `eval_ins` and `eval_code`
evaluate the effects of assembly language instructions on some state, producing
a new state as a result. The state tracks the values in registers (`regs`), the CPU
status flags (`flags`), and the memory (`mem`). An additional state field `ok` indicates

---

[1] https://github.com/project-everest/hacl-star/tree/_vale_unstructured/vale.

whether execution has succeeded or crashed. (This description is simplified for clarity; the full F* implementation of **state** also includes multimedia (xmm) registers, a stack, and a more complex memory model.)

The previous work then used the Vale tool [5,7] to build a Hoare logic on top of the F* syntax and semantics, building the Hoare logic as verified rules on top of the operational semantics, so that the operational semantics in F* were part of the trusted computing base but the Hoare logic and the Vale tool did not need to be trusted. The Vale language uses procedures with modifies, requires, and ensures clauses to express the Hoare logic semantics of instructions like **Add64** and to build more complex procedures on top of instructions:

```
// Two example Vale procedures
procedure Add64(inout dst:dst_opr64, in src:opr64)
    modifies efl;
    requires src + dst < pow2_64;
    ensures dst == old(dst + src);

procedure Test()
    modifies efl; rax;
    requires rax < 100;
    ensures rax == old(rax + 2);
{
    Add64(rax, 1);
    Add64(rax, 1);
}
```

In this work, we leverage the distinction between operational semantics in F* and Hoare logic in Vale to define verified transformers (Sect. 3) that translate between idealized, structured code and optimized, unstructured code. Specifically, we first use Vale's Hoare logic to verify the idealized code. Since the Hoare logic rules are already built on top of the operational semantics, this gives us a proof about the idealized code in terms of the operational semantics. We then define verified transformers in terms of the x64 syntax and operational semantics, without having to modify the Hoare logic. These verified transformers prove that the operational semantics for the idealized code is equivalent to the operational semantics for the optimized code.

The transformers work by comparing the idealized code to the optimized code, where both versions of the code are expressed as an F* datatype, as in the **ins** datatype shown above. Since the code is a datatype, the transformers can inspect the code by pattern matching on the datatype. For better modularity, though, we used a slight variant of this approach: we refactored the **ins** type to be a more general dependent type that contains an arbitrary number of input and output operands and a function that computes the values for the output operands from the values from the input operands. With this, the transformer only has to match on a small number of general instructions rather than matching separately on **Mov64**, **Add64**, etc. (For the most part, only the input and output operands matter; whether an instruction adds numbers, subtracts numbers, or just moves numbers is usually irrelevant to the transformations.)

3   Verified Code Transformers

It is easier to write beautiful proofs about modular code. Our goal is to enable such proofs even for high-performance ugly code. We achieve this by designing a collection of verified code transformers which allow the developer to write proofs about the modular code and then apply one or more transformers to automatically produce the high-performance ugly code. By proving that each transformer preserves the semantics of the original code, we ensure that the results of the elegant proofs carry over to the ugly code.

Below, we describe the core workflow for a developer using these transformers (Sect. 3.1), details about their design, implementation, and verification (Sect. 3.2), as well as several transformers (Sect. 3.3) which have significantly improved the modularity of the proofs for AES-GCM, a case study we describe in Sect. 4.

3.1   Developer Workflow

To make use of verified code transformers, a developer first writes a clean, modular version of their code, and writes proofs about it. Next, they write, but prove nothing about, a performance-optimized version of their code. This can be based on existing code (e.g., OpenSSL's), their own intuition as to what will maximize performance for a particular architecture, or even an automated empirical search (see Sect. 5). Following this, the developer adds simple, high-level annotations to indicate which transformations (e.g., register re-allocation or instruction shuffling) they believe will convert their modular code into the high-performance version. At this point, the transformers take over: An untrusted tool first deduces a collection of hints necessary to apply a given transformation (e.g., which permutation should be applied to reorder the instructions). Next, a verified transformer uses the hints to validate the proposed transformation, and if successful, performs it. If unsuccessful, then the transformer indicates to the developer why it was unable to automatically perform a safe transformation.

As an example of using the workflow to verify the high-performance but ugly code foo_ugly, a developer first annotates foo_ugly with the attribute {:codeOnly} which indicates that no proofs have been written (yet) about it. Next, they mark the cleaner code foo (which they have proven against its Hoare logic spec) with the attribute {:transform T, foo_ugly}. This indicates that they wish to apply the T transformation to map foo to foo_ugly. These top-level annotations are the only ones the developer needs to supply, and the transformers automatically recursively apply themselves to internally called Vale procedures. Vale then replaces the code and proofs of foo with the result of applying the transformer (i.e., the code of foo_ugly), as well as automatically generated proofs derived from the original proof for foo and the generic proof for the transformer T, that show that the transformed code satisfies the same pre- and post-conditions as foo. Thus, any callers of foo obtain the useful Hoare conditions for foo, but they also transparently obtain the higher performance of foo_ugly.

3.2 Proving a Code Transformer Correct

To support the workflow described above, we design our code transformers with an eye towards automation and one-time verification effort. In particular, we ensure that our transformers are provably guaranteed to preserve the semantics of the original code, and we structure each transformer as a combination of an untrusted front-end that *finds* the necessary transformation steps and describes them via a series of hints, and a verified back-end that checks the proposed transformation and then performs it.

We define two blocks of code to be semantically equivalent in the standard way; i.e., if and only if starting from valid equivalent initial states, both execute to equivalent final states, i.e., roughly:

```
let semantically_equivalent (c1 c2:code) =
  (forall (s1 s2:state).
     equiv_states s1 s2 ==>
       equiv_states (eval_code c1 s1)
       (eval_code c2 s2))
```

Two states are defined to be equivalent if and only if they are pairwise equal on all of their observable projections. That is, their registers are equal, values in memory are equal, flags are equal, etc. We can then define a verified code transformer as a total function that takes code (and possibly some auxiliary data, called "hints") as input and produces code that is semantically equivalent to the original code. By allowing for untrusted hints, we follow a de Bruijn structure that allows us to use arbitrarily complicated algorithms for finding transformations, without needing to prove anything about those algorithms. Additionally, by choosing the correct representation for the hints (which can be different for each transformer), we can allow for highly expressive control over the transformer.

We describe more transformers below, but as a simple example, it is easy to see why a no-op transformer (i.e., a transformer that simply returns its input) is a verified code transformer, albeit a trivial one. It may still be practically useful, however, when integrated with a more complex transformer that might fail, since the no-op transformer can be invoked on failure and hence produce an overall total transformer. Keeping the transformers total makes it easier to stay within the pre-existing Vale framework, without needing special handling for transformed code. We show error messages that may arise during a failure via an additional field added to the internal representation of procedures, which is checked upon extraction.

The code for the transformers is completely untrusted, since their results are proven against the pre-existing Vale semantics. In addition, since the transformers prove the semantic equivalence of their results, Vale's existing correctness lemmas follow simply and immediately.

Finally, as an important security precaution, we ensure that we perform the transformations *before* Vale's verified taint analyzer runs. (The taint analyzer runs a dataflow analysis on the instructions to ensure that the code is free of basic digital side channels [5]). As a result, the taint analyzer runs directly on the final, ugly code. Hence, the transformers do not impact the results of the side-channel analysis.

3.3 Example Transformers

Our framework is extensible and many transformers can be written. Here we describe three transformers we developed to support the modularization of proofs for AES-GCM: the *generic peephole transformer* (particularly its instantiation for *movbe-elimination*) searches for a small pattern of instructions and replaces them with equivalent instructions; *control-flow lowering* transforms high-level if/else/while statements into low-level control-flow, and *instruction reordering* reorders instructions to improve run-time performance.

A Generic Peephole Transformer. A peephole transformation searches for a small pattern of instructions and replaces them with equivalent instructions. For example, a simple peephole transformation might replace all occurrences of mov {reg},0 with xor {reg},{reg}. Peephole optimizations are well studied in the compiler literature [13] and have been verified for CompCert [15]. Here, we implemented a generic peephole transformer which can safely perform such search-and-replace operations in a single pass over the code when provided with an arbitrary replacement pattern that (provably) preserves semantics. As a further convenience, the transformation recursively applies itself to all callees of that procedure too. Since such a replacement is locally semantics-preserving, and the rest of the code remains untouched, we prove that it is also globally semantics preserving.

As a concrete example, we used the peephole transformer to safely refactor pre-existing code, which relies on the movbe instruction, to work on older architectures. The movbe instruction is a recent addition to the x86-64 architecture (introduced on Atom, supported since Haswell on mainstream Intel processors). It performs an endianness change (i.e., a byte swap) while performing a mov. On earlier processor generations, this step is typically implemented via a mov and then a bswap instruction which performs an in-place endianness change. OpenSSL's version of AES-GCM (and hence the verified EverCrypt version) regularly uses movbe, which prevents it from running on older processors that otherwise support the necessary AES extensions.

Hence, we instantiated our generic peephole transformer with a pattern to replace movbe {dst},{src} with mov {dst},{src}; bswap {dst}. This transformation takes no auxiliary data, and it can be used to automatically update code to work on processor generations without movbe support, simply by adding a {:transform movbe_eliminate} attribute to the top-level procedure.

Similarly, we instantiated the peephole transformer to allow the insertion of prefetch instructions, which act as processor hints to prefetch lines of data into the cache. Our automatic optimization technique (Sect. 5) uses this transformer to improve performance.

Control-Flow Lowering. The Vale language supports only structured control flow statements (if/else and while) rather than unstructured control flow. Previously, this structured control flow was built directly into the operational semantics, and Vale's assembly language printer had to be trusted to correctly translate these statements into the right labels and conditional branches. To add flexibility and reduce the trusted computing base, we extended the operational semantics to support unstructured control flow. We then wrote a verified transformer to translate if/else and while statements into labels and branches, in the style of certified compilation [11].

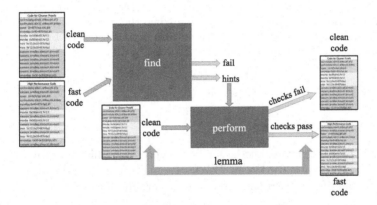

Fig. 1. Instruction-reordering transformation

This transformer is slightly different from other transformers, in that it is applied to all Vale code, rather than only code that is explicitly user-annotated with a {:transform ...} declaration. Additionally, beyond the standard guarantee of semantics-preservation provided by other transformers, this transformer also guarantees preservation of digital traces, and thus strongly ensures maintenance of digital side-channel freedom, independent of whether Vale's verified taint-analyzer is run before or after the transformer.

Instruction Reordering. Our most powerful workhorse transformer is the instruction reordering transform. As Fig. 1 illustrates, this transformer takes as input two code objects (as Vale procedures), and tries to transform one into the other, as long as it is able to do so in a safe way. These code objects correspond to the verification-friendly clean modular code, and either hand-optimized code (for example, from OpenSSL), or automatically optimized candidate code (as described in Sect. 5). To do this transformation safely, the transformer feeds both code objects into an unverified **find** function, which produces hints that a verified **perform** then validates. If validation succeeds, it applies the transformation to the first code object in order to produce the second, along with a proof of semantic equivalence. If validation fails, it returns the first code object, and provides an informative error message to the developer.

The hints that are sent from **find** to **perform** are of the form "move the 12th instruction to the start", "move the 5th group of instructions next", etc., which taken as a whole specify a permutation of the original instructions. This supports permutation past Vale procedure boundaries, which allows the clean code to remain modular, despite the lack of clean modularity in the EverCrypt code. These hints are then validated by **perform** which checks that these moves preserve the semantics of the code. It does so by decomposing moves into a series of swaps, and checking that each swap is allowed, performing it if so. If at any point a swap is disallowed, the transformer immediately stops any further processing, and sends a description of the failure to the user.

In building the transformer, we prove that a swap of two groups of instructions, say A and B, is semantics-preserving when the locations written to by A's instructions is strictly disjoint from the locations that are read by or written to by B, and vice-versa. That is, there are no read-write or write-write conflicts:

$$(\forall (X, Y) \in \{(A, B), (B, A)\}.$$
$$(\forall l \in \text{writes}(X).$$
$$(l \notin \text{reads}(Y) \land$$
$$l \notin \text{writes}(Y))))$$

Given this proof, **perform** checks for both types of conflicts, and if the checks pass, performs the proposed swap. By proceeding through a series of such swaps, we prove that if **perform** succeeds, then it produces semantically equivalent code. Hence, in combination with **find**, we have a verified transformer that can safely reorder code from a clean, modular form into a user-chosen, performance-optimized ordering.

Unfortunately, allowing swaps only when there are no read-write or write-write conflicts disallows many reorderings that are actually safe. In particular, many instructions on x86-64 affect the flags. Changing the flags is technically a write to a location in the state, and hence any two instructions that modify the flags would be prevented from moving past one another even if the value of the flags they set was never used after their execution. This is a frequent use case in Vale, since the Vale semantics conservatively model most instructions as "havocing" the flags, i.e., setting them to an unrestricted and underspecified value. To overcome this issue, we observe that two underspecified writes are safe to exchange with each other, since their result, while different, is equivalent with respect to any value that can be observed. Thus, if we consider the value of each flag to be a ternary value (e.g., true, false, or unspecified), then we can safely and provably refine our condition for safe swaps as follows: a swap that proposes to move instruction group B in front of instruction group A is semantics-preserving if all of the locations written to by A both do not belong to the locations read by B and either do not belong to the locations that are written to by B or are a constant-write for both A and B and the same constant is written; and vice-versa. That is, write-write conflicts are allowed as long as they write the same constant value:

$$(\forall(X, Y) \in \{(A, B), (B, A)\}.$$
$$(\forall l \in \text{writes}(X). \, (l \notin \text{reads}(Y) \, \wedge$$
$$(l \notin \text{writes}(Y) \, \vee$$
$$(l \in \text{constwrites}(X) \, \wedge \, l \in \text{constwrites}(Y) \, \wedge$$
$$\text{constwrites}(X)[l] = \text{constwrites}(Y)[l]))))) $$
$$\implies \text{safeswap}(A, B)$$

Note that we refer to "group of instructions" above, when performing the moves and swaps. This is because it is convenient to move certain instructions as a coherent block of code to avoid having a proposed swap be rejected by the conservative checks in `perform`. As a toy example, consider two groups of instructions `add rax, 1; adc rbx, 1` and `add rcx, 1; adc rdx, 1`. In both cases, the `add` instruction sets the carry-flag (based on its arguments), and then the add-with-carry instruction (`adc`) reads that flag as part of its addition calculation. It is easy to see that both orderings of the two groups are semantically equivalent (assuming the flags can be ignored after these instructions). However, if one were to naively try to change one into the other using a series of *instruction-only* swaps, then one runs into trouble. The `add`s set up the carry flag specifically for their immediately succeeding `adc`, and simple instruction-only swapping would lead to an ordering that consisted of two `add`s followed by two `adc`s, along the way to actually reordering them. However, if we consider them as groups, then they satisfy the constraints for the swap. A large portion of `find` is thus dedicated to automatically finding groups of instructions to move together, rather than individually. Note that this is where the separation between an unverified `find` and the verified `perform` shines: we can have arbitrarily complicated heuristics for finding good groups of instructions, without needing to write any proofs about the heuristics, since the transformation and hints they produce are validated.

4   Verifying AES-GCM

As a case study on the utility of verified code transformations, we apply them to a version of OpenSSL's implementation that was verified in prior work [17].

4.1   Background on AES-GCM

AES-GCM is a cryptographic scheme for Authenticated Encryption with Authenticated Data (AEAD). In other words, it protects the secrecy and integrity of a message (e.g., the payload of a network packet) and (optionally) protects the integrity of some additional public information (e.g., a network packet's header). AES-GCM is one of the world's main tools for protecting bulk data, particularly on the Internet, where it is used for 91% of secure traffic [14]. In many of these settings, AES-GCM is on the critical path, since it dictates how quickly data can be read/written.

Given this ubiquity, the world has devoted considerable effort to optimizing the performance of AES-GCM, both in hardware and software. On the hardware side, in 2008, Intel introduced AES-NI [9], a collection of new instructions devoted to accelerating portions of the AES-GCM computation. Even with these hardware instructions, optimal software implementations are non-trivial. For example, OpenSSL's most optimized implementation on x64 involves over 950 SLOC of Perl scripts [21], which generate 724 SLOC of assembly. Using Perl allows the code to, for example, generate assembly for unrolled loops and customize the registers used in each unrolling. The complexity of these optimizations can lead to concrete security vulnerabilities: In 2013, a performance improvement was added to OpenSSL's codebase, passed all tests, and was on its way into the mainline code when two cryptographers noticed that the optimization would allow an attacker to forge arbitrary messages [8].

lea	($in0,%r12),$in0
vpclmulqdq	\$0x01,$Hkey,$Ii,$T2
vpclmulqdq	\$0x11,$Hkey,$Ii,$Hkey
vpxor	16+8(%rsp),$Xi,$Xi
vmovdqu	0x40+8(%rsp),$Ii
vmovdqu	0x30−0x20($Xip),$Z1
movbe	0x58($in0),%r13
movbe	0x50($in0),%r12
mov	%r13,0x20+8(%rsp)
mov	%r12,0x28+8(%rsp)
vaesenc	$rndkey,$inout0,$inout0
vaesenc	$rndkey,$inout1,$inout1
vaesenc	$rndkey,$inout2,$inout2
vaesenc	$rndkey,$inout3,$inout3
vaesenc	$rndkey,$inout4,$inout4
vaesenc	$rndkey,$inout5,$inout5

(a) **A modular version of the code**

vpclmulqdq	\$0x01,$Hkey,$Ii,$T2
lea	($in0,%r12),$in0
vaesenc	$rndkey,$inout0,$inout0
vpxor	16+8(%rsp),$Xi,$Xi
vpclmulqdq	\$0x11,$Hkey,$Ii,$Hkey
vmovdqu	0x40+8(%rsp),$Ii
vaesenc	$rndkey,$inout1,$inout1
movbe	0x58($in0),%r13
vaesenc	$rndkey,$inout2,$inout2
movbe	0x50($in0),%r12
vaesenc	$rndkey,$inout3,$inout3
mov	%r13,0x20+8(%rsp)
vaesenc	$rndkey,$inout4,$inout4
mov	%r12,0x28+8(%rsp)
vmovdqu	0x30−0x20($Xip),$Z1
vaesenc	$rndkey,$inout5,$inout5

(b) **Representative snippet of OpenSSL**

Fig. 2. We write proofs about the cleaner, more modular version of the AES-GCM code (a) and then use verified code transformers to connect these proofs to the original OpenSSL code (b). AES operations are highlighted in blue, GCM in green, prefetching and processing of input data in red, and loop control checks in yellow. (Color figure online)

Conceptually, computing AES-GCM involves splitting the input into 128-bit blocks, computing AES counter-mode encryption on each block to produce a ciphertext, and finally computing the GCM message authentication algorithm on the resulting ciphertext and any additional authenticated data. A naive implementation written along these conceptual lines is relatively straightforward to verify, but results in performance that is 6× slower than OpenSSL's [17].

Indeed, in its drive for better performance, OpenSSL's implementation merges these conceptual operations so that it need only perform a single pass over the data. It also, when able, processes the input six blocks at a time, so as to make maximal use of available registers. Even at the block level, the individual instructions for performing AES steps are intermixed with those for performing the GCM steps as well as with memory manipulation steps (e.g., loading input data, transforming it into a suitable form to feed to AES, and storing results back to memory), presumably in an effort to keep the processor's functional units fully saturated. The GCM instructions for carryless multiplies and polynomial reductions are carefully ordered to improve parallelism, and various modular reduction steps are delayed to amortize their cost. Individual instructions themselves rely heavily on SIMD operations over 128-bit XMM registers.

As shown in Fig. 2b, the result is Perl code that mixes, instruction-by-instruction, conceptually different operations (shown by the various colors).

Unsurprisingly, such code is far more challenging to verify. Prior work [17] relies on SMT solvers and hence is limited in how many instructions can reasonably fit into a single procedure. As a result, they divide OpenSSL's code into smaller units demarcated with Hoare-logic pre- and postconditions. Unfortunately, the intermingled nature of the code makes it difficult to decompose the code in a clean modular fashion, since at any given instruction boundary, the invariants for one conceptual step do not yet hold or have already been broken. The result is large (~3500 LOC), inelegant proofs, despite the automation provided by the SMT solver (and a custom VC generator [7]).

4.2 Verifying AES-GCM via Code Transformations

With the power of verified code transformers at hand, we re-wrote the previously verified, OpenSSL-based AES-GCM code [17], in a clean, modular fashion. Figure 2a shows a representative snippet, where the instructions for each conceptual operation are now grouped, and even within a group, logically similar operations (e.g., vpclmulqdq) are themselves grouped together. This reordering already makes the conceptual structure of the code much simpler to see and reason about (e.g., the AES instructions are now more obviously computing six 128-bit blocks in parallel, using the same round key for each block).

Furthermore, with the ability to reorder instructions, we were able to extract the three major functional steps (AES, GCM, and input manipulation) into generic procedures that utilize Vale's *operand parameters* and *inline arguments* to customize each procedure at compile time. Hence, each procedure can be customized at its invocation point to, for example, use a particular register assignment in a given round of the AES computation, as shown in Fig. 3. This eliminates the need for custom per-round procedures and dramatically reduces the total amount of code and proofs needed.

For our case study, we applied our transformers to the inner loop of EverCrypt's AES-GCM implementation, where the proof-to-code ratio is 5.0:1 (compared to 2.6:1 in the remaining 3250 lines of proof and code). Overall, the instruction-reordering transformer enabled us to write the inner loop of AES-GCM in 450 lines of code and proof, compared with EverCrypt's version, which required 1250 lines, a nearly 3× reduction. Both versions produce the same approximately 250 lines of assembly code.

Given our clean, modular version and the original ugly EverCrypt version, the instruction-reordering transformer automatically discovered the necessary instruction permutations; the only annotation needed was to specify which transformation we desired.

We subsequently employed our peephole transformer to create custom variants of the code that can run on older platforms that do not support the movbe instruction. Also, using our peephole transformer, we show that the prefetch optimizations are indeed safe.

```
procedure Loop6x_plain(
  inline alg:algorithm, // inline argument
  inline rnd:nat, // inline argument
  ...
  out rndkey:xmm) // rndkey is an operand parameter
  ...
{
  Load128_buffer(rndkey, rcx, // rcx is base address
    16 * (rnd + 1) − 0x80, // offset from rcx
    ...);
  VAESNI_enc(inout0, inout0, rndkey);
  VAESNI_enc(inout1, inout1, rndkey);
  VAESNI_enc(inout2, inout2, rndkey);
  VAESNI_enc(inout3, inout3, rndkey);
  VAESNI_enc(inout4, inout4, rndkey);
  VAESNI_enc(inout5, inout5, rndkey);
  ...
}
...
Loop6x_plain(alg, 0, ..., xmm2);
Loop6x_plain(alg, 1, ..., xmm15);
...
Loop6x_plain(alg, 8, ..., xmm15);
```

Fig. 3. Compile-time customization of procedures in our modular AES-GCM code

Finally, since we apply the control-flow lowering transform to all Vale code, we automatically obtain provably-correct unstructured code.

5   Optimizing Code for Each Processor Generation

When writing high-performance software, micro-architectural details of a given processor can influence which style of code performs best. In particular, code that is optimized for one processor generation may not perform optimally on another generation of the same processor. Nevertheless, maintaining a different version of the code for each generation of each processor is a daunting task, and hence, even OpenSSL (which supports a wide variety of CPUs with and without various extensions like SSE2, AVX, AES-NI) typically does not go to these lengths to squeeze out additional performance. With the use of verified code transformers, however, we show that we can now safely and automatically produce code that is optimized on a per-generation basis. Hence, verification enables us to reap the rewards of higher performance, in a provably safe way, with marginal extra effort.

The key observation is that having done the work to produce a verified transformer (in particular, the instruction-reordering transformer from Sect. 3.3), we can supply it with our clean modular code and *any* unverified code that produces a performance improvement. As long as the transformer accepts that code, we can safely employ it.

Hence, we developed a genetic algorithm to search for faster instruction orderings on a given processor. The algorithm takes as input an initial code object and applies a series of random mutations (shuffling of instructions) to create the first "generation" of candidates. Candidates also are allowed to mutate with a small chance to have random prefetch instructions added. Each candidate is sanity-checked for correctness on a single input-output test pair. Candidates that pass this fast sanity-check are then automatically benchmarked on the processor. The fastest candidates then "breed" by combining portions of their mutations (along with a small chance of new random mutations appearing), to produce a new generation of candidates. This process continues looping up to a time or generation bound provided by the developer, at which time the overall fastest candidate across all the generations is returned.

To evaluate the effectiveness of this approach, we have run this algorithm on five x86-64 processors of varying generations, namely Intel's i5-2500, i7-3770, i7-7600U, and i9-9900K, and AMD's Ryzen 7 3700X. For each processor, we experimented with starting the genetic algorithm both from the original Ever-Crypt version of OpenSSL's hand-optimized assembly, and from our clean, modular version. We took the resulting optimized algorithm from each processor and automatically verified them using the transformers from our cleaned up modular version to confirm semantic equivalence. For the i5-2500 and i7-3770 processors, which do not support the movbe instruction that is used in EverCrypt, we applied the movbe-elimination transformer (Sect. 3.3) before starting optimization. We also applied it to implementations optimized for newer platforms before running them on the older non-movbe platforms. As additional context, we also include the (unverified) OpenSSL code that was the basis for the EverCrypt implementation; running this code on the i5-2500 and i7-3770 processors entailed manual modifications to replace movbe instructions. We then ran all of these implementations on all of our processors.

The results of these benchmarks are shown in Table 1. Each row of the table corresponds to a different instruction-ordering of the code, while each column corresponds to a different processor. Each cell in the table shows the minimum number of cycles it took to encrypt 4096 bytes of data, with zero bytes of additional data, across 20 million iterations. The smallest value in each column is marked in **bold**, and represents the fastest code for that processor. As the table illustrates, each processor has an optimal ordering, and this optimal ordering can give speedups on top of state-of-the-art OpenSSL or EverCrypt code by up to 27% or 13% respectively.

Table 1. Cycle counts for various reorderings on different processors. Code with ^ used the movbe-elimination transformer to run/optimize on older processors. Code with * denotes manual elimination of `movbe` from OpenSSL's interleaved variant.

Code\Tested on	i5-2500	i7-3770	i7-7600U	i9-9900K	3700X
Optimized for i5-2500	^**12957**	^12560	^2454	^**2378**	^3492
Optimized for i7-3770	^12960	^**12557**	^2454	^2382	^3456
Optimized for i7-7600U	^14340	^13917	**2450**	2476	3528
Optimized for i9-9900K	^14382	^13941	2453	**2378**	3528
Optimized for 3700X	^14127	^13696	2452	2486	**3168**
Clean	^13632	^13222	2463	2486	3420
EverCrypt	^14619	^14198	2452	2474	3492
OpenSSL	*14943	*14428	2986	2980	4032

Overall, our results show that highly targeted code implementations can give non-trivial performance improvements. Further optimizations are, of course, still possible, either via an improved automated search algorithm, or via targeted changes from performance optimization experts. Either way, the verified code transformers conveniently and automatically connect the clean, proven code with the optimized versions, ensuring that such optimizations will never violate correctness or security (unlike some previous optimizations attempts [8]).

6 Related Work

Although few projects have explored verified translations at the level of assembly language, verified transformations are well understood at higher levels. In particular, verified transformations are the basis for certified compilers such as CompCert [11], which applies repeated translations and optimizations to compiler intermediate languages. The VST project [3] built a Hoare logic on top of CompCert, so that Hoare logic proofs about high-level code imply properties about compiler-generated low-level code too. An example application of VST was a cryptographic primitive (SHA) [4], although compiler-generated cryptographic code often runs slower than hand-optimized assembly language code [5].

To support hand-optimized code, our reordering transformation must examine two existing versions of code and discover the relationship between them.

This contrasts with typical verified compilers and optimizers, which are given just one version of the code and can then decide which code to generate.

Translation validation is a pragmatic alternative to compiler verification [16]. In contrast to the latter, which aims to verify that a compiler *always* produces the correct code, this approach verifies that a *particular* compiled code correctly implements its source program. For example, Sewell et al. [19] use this approach to extend the verification of the source code of seL4, an operating system micro-kernel [10], written in C, to that of the compiled binary. The validation is based on a refinement proof between the two programs. TINA [18] takes a different approach, lifting inline assembly into C, to improve the precision of existing C analyzers, by applying translation validation to confirm that the lifted-and-recompiled code is equivalent to the original. While translation validation can leverage the general-purpose reasoning of an SMT solver, it can also suffer from the unpredictability of SMT solvers. Targeted verified translations are less general, but produce more predictable results.

Fiat-Crypto [6] and Jasmin [1,2] both support verified translation from higher-level code to lower-level code. Jasmin uses Hoare logic at a high level; its lowest is slightly higher than assembly language, although low enough to make compilation straightforward (for example, the Jasmin compiler's register allocator never spills variables to the stack). Fiat-Crypto includes high-level domain-specific optimizations for elliptic curve cryptography, relieving the programmer of having to generate low-level optimized C code. Nevertheless, for widely used algorithms like AES-GCM, cryptography developers still consider it worthwhile to develop hand-optimized assembly code, and we believe that it is valuable to verify this hand-optimized code.

Superoptimizers [12] search for fast assembly language sequences and try to automatically establish equivalence with the original source code. However, typical superoptimizers can only generate short code sequences. Our genetic algorithm and verified transformer works on much longer instruction sequences (100s of instructions), albeit only for specific types of transformations.

7   Conclusions and Future Work

Code designed to be verified is not necessarily the same as code designed to run fast. However, some simple transformations can connect the two versions of the code. We have demonstrated such transformations both to increase confidence in existing code (in particular, OpenSSL's highly interleaved AES-GCM implementation) and to point the way towards alternate implementations that can have even higher performance on some platforms. Although the performance impact of interleaving instructions is small on the most recent Intel processors, we did find significant differences in performance both on older Intel processors and on a recent AMD processor; based on this, we speculate that such differences may be even more significant on less recent and/or non-Intel processors, such as less-powerful embedded processors.

For people focused on verification, it is heartening (and surprising) that the verification-friendly version of the AES-GCM code that we developed often outperformed the original, more interleaved code on several platforms. This suggests that developers of high-performance verified code should focus on major optimizations like domain-specific algorithm optimizations, loop unrolling and careful register allocation, and worry less about the exact sequence of instructions; this sequence may be better determined by automated search algorithms, supported by verified transformation tools.

One limitation of our current verified transformations is that writes to the heap cannot be reordered relative to other heap reads and writes. We are currently exploring ways to relax this restriction. For example, we are annotating heap loads and stores with identifiers that represent disjoint regions of memory; with these annotations, a transformer can safely reorder memory operations annotated with distinct identifiers.

Acknowledgments. We thank the anonymous reviewers for valuable feedback. Work at Carnegie Mellon University was supported in part by the Department of the Navy, Office of Naval Research under Grant No. N00014-18-1-2892, and grants from the Intel Corporation and the Alfred P. Sloan Foundation.

References

1. Almeida, J.B., et al.: Jasmin: high-assurance and high-speed cryptography. In: Proceedings of the 2017 ACM SIGSAC Conference on Computer and Communications Security (2017). https://doi.org/10.1145/3133956.3134078
2. Almeida, J.B., et al.: The last mile: high-assurance and high-speed cryptographic implementations. CoRR abs/1904.04606 (2019)
3. Appel, A.W.: Verified software toolchain. In: ESOP: 20th European Symposium on Programming (2011)
4. Appel, A.W.: Verification of a cryptographic primitive: SHA-256. ACM Trans. Program. Lang. Syst. **37**(2), 7:1–7:31 (2015)
5. Bond, B., et al.: Vale: verifying high-performance cryptographic assembly code. In: Proceedings of the USENIX Security Symposium (2017)
6. Erbsen, A., Philipoom, J., Gross, J., Sloan, R., Chlipala, A.: Simple high-level code for cryptographic arithmetic - with proofs, without compromises. In: Proceedings of the IEEE Symposium on Security and Privacy (2019)
7. Fromherz, A., Giannarakis, N., Hawblitzel, C., Parno, B., Rastogi, A., Swamy, N.: A verified, efficient embedding of a verifiable assembly language. In: Proceedings of the ACM Symposium on Principles of Programming Languages (POPL) (2019)
8. Gueron, S., Krasnov, V.: The fragility of AES-GCM authentication algorithm. In: Proceedings of the Conference on Information Technology: New Generations (2014)
9. Gueron, S.: Intel® advanced encryption standard (AES) new instructions set (2012). https://software.intel.com/sites/default/files/article/165683/aes-wp-2012-09-22-v01.pdf
10. Klein, G., et al.: Comprehensive formal verification of an OS microkernel. ACM Trans. Comput. Syst. **32**(1), 2:1–2:70 (2014)
11. Leroy, X., Blazy, S., Kästner, D., Schommer, B., Pister, M., Ferdinand, C.: CompCert - a formally verified optimizing compiler. In: Embedded Real Time Software and Systems (ERTS). SEE (2016)

12. Massalin, H.: Superoptimizer - a look at the smallest program. In: Architectural Support for Programming Languages and Operating Systems (ASPLOS) (1987)

13. McKeeman, W.M.: Peephole optimization. Commun. ACM **8**, 7 (1965)

14. Mozilla: Measurement dashboard (2018). https://mzl.la/2ug9YCH

15. Mullen, E., Zuniga, D., Tatlock, Z., Grossman, D.: Verified peephole optimizations for CompCert. In: Proceedings of the 37th ACM SIGPLAN Conference on Programming Language Design and Implementation (PLDI) (2016)

16. Pnueli, A., Siegel, M., Singerman, E.: Translation validation. In: Steffen, B. (ed.) TACAS 1998. LNCS, vol. 1384, pp. 151–166. Springer, Heidelberg (1998). https://doi.org/10.1007/BFb0054170

17. Protzenko, J., et al.: EverCrypt: a fast, verified, cross-platform cryptographic provider. In: Proceedings of the IEEE Symposium on Security and Privacy (2020)

18. Recoules, F., Bardin, S., Bonichon, R., Mounier, L., Potet, M.L.: Get rid of inline assembly through verification-oriented lifting. In: Proceedings of the 34th IEEE/ACM International Conference on Automated Software Engineering (ASE 2019) (2019)

19. Sewell, T.A.L., Myreen, M.O., Klein, G.: Translation validation for a verified OS kernel. In: Proceedings of ACM PLDI (2013)

20. Swamy, N., et al.: Dependent types and multi-monadic effects in F*. In: Proceedings of the ACM Conference on Principles of Programming Languages (POPL), pp. 256–270. ACM (2016)

21. Wheeler, D.A.: SLOCCount. Software Distribution. http://www.dwheeler.com/sloccount/

MCBAT: Model Counting for Constraints over Bounded Integer Arrays

Abtin Molavi, Tommy Schneider, Mara Downing, and Lucas Bang[✉]

Harvey Mudd College, Claremont, CA 91711, USA
bang@cs.hmc.edu

Abstract. Model counting procedures for data structures are crucial for advancing the field of automated quantitative program analysis. We present an algorithm and practical tool for performing Model Counting for Bounded Array Theory (MCBAT). As the satisfiability problem for the theory of arrays is undecidable in general, we focus on a fragment of array theory for which we are able to specify an exact model counting algorithm. MCBAT applies to quantified integer array constraints in which all arrays have a finite length. We employ reductions from the theory of arrays to uninterpreted functions and linear integer arithmetic (LIA), and we prove these reductions to be model-count preserving. Once reduced to LIA, we leverage Barvinok's polynomial time integer lattice point enumeration algorithm. Finally, we present experimental validation for the correctness and scalability of our approach and apply MCBAT to a case study on automated average case analysis for array programs, demonstrating applicability to automated quantitative program analysis.

1 Introduction

Model counting is the enabling technology and theory behind automated quantitative program analyses. The ability to count the number of solutions to a constraint allows one to perform reliability analysis [14], probabilistic symbolic execution [17], quantitative information flow analysis [18,23,27,33,35], Bayesian inference [10,11,30], and compiler optimization [29]. Originally stated with respect to Boolean formulas [6], more recent advances in model counting have extended counting capabilities to the theories of linear integer arithmetic [21,34], non-linear numeric constraints [7], strings [2,3,12,22,31,32], word-level counting for bit-vectors applied to the problem of automatic inference [9], and more recent work has begun to combine theories of strings and integers [3]. This paper is the first that we are aware of to directly address model counting for constraints over arrays.

The current space of exploration in model counting is driven by the ubiquity of the types found in common programming languages–Booleans, integers, and strings. In this paper, we expand the space of model countable theories with an algorithm for counting the number of models to constraints over the theory of bounded integer arrays. Model counting for array constraints has practical value in its own right, and also has potential as a basis for future model counting

© Springer Nature Switzerland AG 2020
M. Christakis et al. (Eds.): NSV 2020/VSTTE 2020, LNCS 12549, pp. 124–143, 2020.
https://doi.org/10.1007/978-3-030-63618-0_8

algorithms for other structures that can be modeled as arrays: vectors, maps, hash tables, caches, and so on.

Model counting is a crucial step is quantitative program analysis. For instance, probabilistic symbolic execution (PSE) computes the probability of a program path by counting the number of solutions to the associated path constraints [17]. Quantitative information flow (QIF) analysis often uses PSE to compute probabilistic relationships between program inputs, outputs, observable behaviors, and sensitive information and applies information theoretic metrics to measure the security of an application, design, or protocol [18,23,27,35]. Existing PSE and QIF techniques are either limited to constraints for which there are model counters already available or require ad-hoc model counting approaches [33]. MCBAT provides another tool in the space of model counters which we believe can be useful to quantitative program analysis researchers who encounter integer arrays constraints, as integer arrays are an extremely common data structure. This paper makes the following contributions:

• **Theoretical results.** Our algorithm, MCBAT, composes several model-count preserving reductions to convert an integer array constraint to a formula over linear integer arithmetic (LIA), which can then be model counted using existing algorithms for LIA. We show that our reductions are model-count preserving.

• **Practical tool.** Our tool, also named MCBAT, implements our reductions, applies them to array constraints, and returns the model count.

• **Experimental Validation.** We validated the *correctness* of our implementation by comparing with a baseline alternative implementation that enumerates models using Z3. Both implementations agree on the number of models for all constraints in our benchmark. We evaluated the *scalability* of our algorithm on a benchmark of array formulas with positive results. Finally, we applied our model counting approach in a case study on automatic expected performance analysis.[1]

Example 1. Suppose we want to know the number of sorted integer arrays A of length 3 with array values between 0 and 10. We can express this as an array constraint:

$$\text{LENGTH}(a) = 3 \land \forall i \; 0 \le a[i] \le 10 \land \forall i \; \forall j \; (i < j \; \rightarrow A[i] \le A[j])$$

On a technical note, observe that the variable i is universally quantified in the second conjunct. It may be possible that $a[i]$ is an out-of-bounds array index. In our setting, we will take the stance that any indexing that occurs beyond the length of an array results in the same undefined value $\perp$. Now, observe that, ruling out undefined values due to out-of-bounds indexing, the original constraint is equivalent to a set of constraints with three variables a_0, a_1, and a_2 over $\mathbb{Z}$:

$$0 \le a_0 \le 10 \land 0 \le a_1 \le 10 \land 0 \le a_2 \le 10 \land a_0 \le a_1 \land a_1 \le a_2$$

This constraint, temporarily ignoring the fact that each a_i is an integer, defines a polytope volume P in $\mathbb{R}^3$ (Fig. 1), where each axis corresponds to one of the three $a_i(1)$. The number of solutions to this constraint is then the number of points in $\mathbb{Z}^3 \cap P$. While we do not spell out the details here, one can find that there are 286 integer lattice points in the volume defined by the corresponding polytope. In addition, it is easy to see that the number of models for the original constraint is the same as the number of integer lattice points.

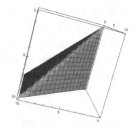

Fig. 1. Polytope defined by constraint of Example 1.

Example 2. Consider a constraint over integer array a and integer variable k.

$$\text{LENGTH}(a) = 2 \wedge (k \geq -15) \wedge \forall i \ (k \leq a[i] \leq 10 \vee k \leq -a[i] \leq 10)$$

This constraint is equivalent to a constraint with three variables $a_0, a_1, k \in \mathbb{Z}$:

$$k \geq -15 \wedge (k \leq a_0 \leq 10 \vee k \leq -a_0 \leq 10) \wedge (k \leq a_1 \leq 10 \vee k \leq -a_1 \leq 10)$$

Similar to our earlier reasoning, this constraint over three variables defines a polytope P in $\mathbb{R}^3$ (Fig. 2). Observe that integer lattice points in P correspond to integer triples (k, a_0, a_1), corresponding to the free variables k and a of the original constraint. Our procedure counts the number of possible models for all free variables in a constraint. For this example, the number of integer lattice points in this polytope, and therefore the number of models to the original constraint, is 10076.

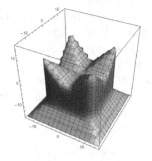

Fig. 2. Polytope defined by constraint of Example 2.

These two examples illustrate the main idea of our approach: count models for an array constraint by transforming it into an instance of lattice point counting within a polytope. While these two examples are easy to visualize, in general, a finite array constraint over integers is model-count equivalent to a set of lattice points in a multi-dimensional polytope.

1.1 Overview

We describe the syntax and semantics of bounded array theory in Sect. 2, which includes quantifiers, Boolean combinations, array terms, integer terms, and linear arithmetic operations and comparisons. In Sect. 3 we describe our model counting algorithm, MCBAT, which relies on a sequence of reductions. These reductions are syntactic transformations applied to a formula f, resulting in a new formula f' that has the same number of solutions as f. These reductions work by returning formulas that (1) contains no array indexing subexpression, (2) contains no array element assignment subexpressions, (3) are quantifier free, and (4) contains only integer expressions, via Ackermann's reduction [1]. Sects. 3 and 3.2 provide the details of these reductions and proofs that they preserve model counts. The core of our implementation, Sect. 4.2, is written in Haskell and makes calls to the polytope lattice point enumeration library Barvinok. Additionally, Sect. 4.2 describes our experimental benchmark, consisting of array constraints generated from either loop invariant synthesis or symbolic execution. We find that our implementation agrees on the number of models compared to an algorithm which uses Z3 to enumerate models. Finally, we describe a case study in which we perform automatic expected running time analysis on sorting algorithms using MCBAT.

$$
\begin{aligned}
\textit{formula}: \quad & \textit{formula} \wedge \textit{formula} \\
& | \textit{formula} \vee \textit{formula} \\
& | \textit{formula} \rightarrow \textit{formula} \\
& | \neg \textit{formula} \\
& | \forall (\textit{int-id}).(\textit{formula}) \\
& | \text{LENGTH}(\textit{array-id}, \mathbb{Z}^{\geq}) \\
& | \textit{atom} \\
\textit{atom}: \quad & \textit{term} = \textit{term} \,|\, \textit{term} < \textit{term} \,|\, \textit{array} = \textit{array} \\
\textit{array}: \quad & \textit{array-id} \,|\, \textit{array}\{\textit{term} \leftarrow \textit{term}\} \\
\textit{term}: \quad & \textit{int-id} \,|\, \mathbb{Z} \,|\, \mathbb{Z} \times \textit{term} \,|\, \textit{term} + \textit{term} \,|\, \textit{array}[\textit{term}]
\end{aligned}
$$

Fig. 3. Abstract grammar for bounded integer array theory constraints.

2   Array Theory: Background, Syntax, and Semantics

The abstract syntax of array constraints that we consider is given in Fig. 3. Our constraint language supports Boolean combinations of formulas, with the expected standard semantics, which may consist of formulas quantified over integer variables, length predicates, or atoms. The formula $\text{LENGTH}(a, n)$ denotes that the array a has length n. We often write $|a|$ for the length of array a. Atomic expressions may be equality or order comparisons between integer term expressions or equality comparisons between array expressions. Array expressions can be the name of an array (array-id) or an array store, written $a\{i \leftarrow e\}$. The notation $a\{i \leftarrow e\}$ represents an array equal to a, except possibly at index i, at which place the array $a\{i \leftarrow e\}$ has the value e. Integer terms can be the names of integer variables (int-id), integer constants, products of integer constants and terms, addition of terms, or array index expressions. The term $a[i]$ represents the value stored in the array a indexed at the index i. Note that the arithmetic that makes up the terms is Presburger arithmetic [29]. Note that our grammar here does not enforce that all arrays have a length constraint, but going forward, we will assume that every symbolic array variable a has an associated constraint of the form $\text{LENGTH}(a, n)$ where n is a positive integer.

Note that while it is *syntactically* possible to access an array outside of its bounds, this is semantically meaningless. As noted in the introduction example, we define indexing that occurs beyond the length of any array to be the undefined value $\perp$.

The semantics of our bounded array theory is that which one would expect from finite length integer arrays found in common programming languages. Our semantics for array store and select expressions departs slightly from the semantics typically employed in the SMT theory of arrays [26]. For instance, the Z3 solver treats arrays as uninterpreted functions from the *entire* set of integers to the array element type: arrays indices in Z3 are unbounded in both the positive and negative directions. Our semantics allows indexes only in the range $[0, \text{LENGTH}(a) - 1]$.

Given a bounded integer array constraint $\phi(a_1, \ldots, a_n, k_1, \ldots, k_w)$, with n symbolic array variables and w integer variables, an interpretation for ϕ is a mapping $I : \{a_1, \ldots, a_n, k_1, \ldots, k_w\} \to \mathbb{Z}^{|a_1|} \times \ldots \times \mathbb{Z}^{|a_n|} \times \mathbb{Z}^w$ such that when instantiating each free symbol of ϕ with the value defined by I, ϕ evaluates to true. We say that I models ϕ and write $I \models \phi$. The model counting problem to to determine to number of interpretations (models) for a given formula; our goal is to compute $|\{I : I \models \phi\}|$.

3   Model Counting Algorithm: MCBAT

In this section we describe MCBAT, which consists of a series of reductions to linear integer arithmetic, and then show that our reductions are model-count preserving.

3.1   The MCBAT Algorithm

We'll start by presenting an overview of MCBAT (Algorithm 1), and later provide details of important subprocedures (Algorithms 2, 3, 4, and 5).

MCBAT Input. MCBAT takes a formula in the theory of bounded arrays of the form

$$\phi(a_1, \ldots, a_n; k_1, \ldots, k_w) = \text{LENGTH}(a_1, \ell_1) \land \cdots \text{LENGTH}(a_n, \ell_n) \land \phi_A$$

where ϕ^A is a Boolean combination of quantified array formulas. Here, we've explicitly denoted the n free array-variables and the w free integer-variables. Throughout our algorithm some steps may introduce new free variables, but we ensure that the model count is preserved.

MCBAT Output. We output the number of models there are for $\phi(a_1, \ldots, a_n; k_1, \ldots, k_w)$.

Algorithm 1. MCBAT: Compute the model count for $\phi(a_1, \ldots, a_n; k_1, \ldots, k_w)$

1: **procedure** MCBAT($\phi(a_1, \ldots, a_n; k_1, \ldots, k_w)$)
2:     Decompose ϕ into a tree $\mathbf{T}$ of array formulas $\phi_1, \phi_2, \ldots, \phi_m$.
3:     Create a tree $\mathbf{T}'$ and a label-formula map $\mathbf{M}$ using $\phi_1, \phi_2, \ldots, \phi_m$ as labels.
4:     **for** ϕ_i **do**
5:         $\phi_i^{(1)}$ $\longleftarrow$ REMOVETERMSINACCESS(ϕ_i)
6:         $\phi_i^{(2)}$ $\longleftarrow$ REPLACEALLARRAYSTORES($\phi_i^{(1)}$)
7:         $\phi_i^{(3)}$ $\longleftarrow$ REMOVEQUANTS($\phi_i^{(2)}$)
8:     **end for**
9:     Construct $\mathbf{M}'$ from $\mathbf{M}$ and the formulas $\phi_1^{(3)}, \ldots, \phi_m^{(3)}$.
10:    Construct $\phi^{(4)}$ by applying the label-formula map $\mathbf{M}'$ to the Boolean tree $\mathbf{T}'$.
11:    $\phi^{(5)}$ $\longleftarrow$ ACKERMANNREDUCTION($\phi^{(4)}$)
12:    **return** BARVINOK($\phi^{(5)}$)
13: **end procedure**

High-Level Overview. MCBAT (Algorithm 1) has these main steps:

- Decompose a boolean combination of quantified array formulas into individual quantified array formulas.
- Replace index terms that occur within array access terms with auxiliary integer variables; introduce auxiliary integer constraints to capture this replacement.
- Each array-store term is replaced by equivalent constraints that do not contain array-store expressions.
- Rewrite expressions that are universally quantified over array index variables as a conjunction over all possible indices, with upper bounds enforced by each array s LENGTH predicate.
- Perform Ackermann's reduction, converting array access terms into integer terms.
- Send the resulting linear integer arithmetic constraint to BARVINOK to compute the final model count.

Separating Array Sub-formulas. We take a boolean combination of array formulas and decompose it into individual array sub-formulas. We maintain the Boolean skeleton structure of the original input formula, so that after transforming each array sub-formula, we can reconstruct the Boolean combination. Then each of the next steps is performed on individual array sub-formulas. This step is straightforward, we do not provide an algorithm.

Replacing Array Accesses. We replace index terms that occur within array access terms with auxiliary integer variables and introduce auxiliary integer constraints to capture this replacement (Algorithm 2).

Algorithm 2. Replace Array Accesses

1: **procedure** REPLACEARRAYACCESSES(ϕ)
2:    **for each** unique term t in an array access $a[t]$ **do**
3:       introduce a new universally quantified variable i_t
4:       conjunct to the antecedent of ϕ the constraint $t = i_t$
5:       replace every instance of t with i_t
6:    **end for**
7: **end procedure**

Replacing Array Stores. Next, each array-store term is replaced by equivalent constraints that do not contain array-store expressions (Algorithm 3).

REPLACEARRAYSTORES examines a statement in the theory of bounded arrays, and replaces array-stores (i.e., arrays elements of the form $a\{i \leftarrow e\}$) with "fresh" variables. Intuitively, this means that when we encounter an array store operation at index i, we mimic storing a value by using a new array variable to 'imitate' the original array everywhere except for potentially at index i where the new value is e.

Removing Universal Quantifiers. So far, we have a formula containing quantifiers where each array index term is an individual integer variable and there are no array store terms. We then rewrite expressions that are universally quantified over array index variables as a conjunction over all possible indices (Algorithm 4).

Algorithm 3. Replace Array Stores

1: **procedure** REPLACEARRAYSTORES(ϕ)
2:    **for each** array store $a\{i \leftarrow e\}$ **do**
3:       replace $a\{i \leftarrow e\}$ with the array a', then conjoin the original formula with:
4:       $\forall(j).((\neg(j = i) \rightarrow a'[j] = a[j]) \wedge (j = i \rightarrow a'[j] = e))$
5:    **end for**
6: **end procedure**

Algorithm 4. Remove Quantifiers

1: **procedure** REMOVEQUANTS(ϕ)
2:    Let ℓ denote the longest array-length.
3:    **while** ϕ is of the form $\forall(\cdot).(\phi')$ **do**
4:       $\phi \leftarrow \bigwedge_{i \in \{0,...,\ell-1\}} \phi'$
5:    **end while**
6: **end procedure**

Ackermann's Reduction. Next, we run Ackermann's reduction (Algorithm 5) [1]. Ackermann's reduction is originally phrased as a transformation on terms in the theory of uninterpreted functions. In our setting, observe that we can think of arrays as functions from $\mathbb{Z}$ to $\mathbb{Z}$ and apply the same technique. The reduction is intended to be satisfiability preserving, but here we use it as a model-count preserving reduction, and show why it is model-count preserving in the following section.

Algorithm 5. Ackermann's Reduction.

1: Input: An array theory formula ϕ^A with array access terms.
2: Output: A linear integer arithmetic formula ϕ^{LIA} that has the same model count.
3: **procedure** ACKERMANNREDUCTION(ϕ^A)
4:     Let $\text{FLAT}^{LIA} := \tau(\phi^A)$, where τ replaces the access $a[i]$ with a fresh variable a_i.
5:     Let FC^{LIA} denote the following conjunction of *functional consistency* constraints:

$$\text{FC}^{LIA} := \bigwedge_{i \in T} \bigwedge_{j \in T} i = j \rightarrow a_i = a_j$$

where T is the set of all terms used as indices in an array access.
6:     **return** ϕ^{LIA} **where** $\phi^{LIA} = \text{FC}^{LIA} \wedge \text{FLAT}^{LIA}$
7: **end procedure**

The fundamental insight behind this reduction is that we can replace any array accesses on single integer variables with new integer variables along with additional *functional consistency constraints*. For example, suppose the terms $a[x], a[y],$ and $a[z]$ occur in a constraint. (Recall that by this point, more complex array index expressions have all been replaced with fresh, individual integer variables.) We can then replace $a[x]$ with a new array value variable a_x, $a[y]$ with a_y, and $a[z]$ with a_z. But now, we need to ensure that if any two variables that were used as indices are ever equal, then the corresponding array value variables must agree. Thus, we also introduce constraints of the form $x = y \rightarrow a_x = a_y$. We introduce such functional consistency constraints for possible pairwise combinations of array index variables.

Model Count the LIA Formula. BARVINOK performs model counting by representing a linear integer arithmetic constraint ϕ on variables $X = \{x_1, \ldots, x_n\}$ as a set of symbolic polytopes $\mathscr{P} \subseteq \mathbb{R}^n$. Barvinok's polynomial-time algorithm decomposes $\mathscr{P}$ into a set of n-dimensional 'cones' $\mathscr{K}$, one per vertex of $\mathscr{P}$, computing generating functions that enumerate the set $K \cap \mathbb{Z}^n$ for each $K \in \mathscr{K}$, and then composing the generating functions in order to compute $|\mathscr{P} \cap \mathbb{Z}^n|$, i.e. the number of integer lattice points in the interior of $\mathscr{P}$ and therefore the number of models for ϕ. We have elided many details of Barvinok's algorithm, but the interested reader may consult the provided references for a thorough treatment [4, 21, 34].

3.2   Correctness

Lemma 1. *Removing access terms is model-count preserving.*

Proof Sketch. Assume an array sub-formula of the form

$$\phi = \forall(i_1, \ldots, i_n).(\phi^A),$$

where ϕ^A contains one or more instances of an array accessed by a term that includes a universally quantified variable. We need to ensure that, when performing quantifier elimination, we do not introduce array accesses that are out-of-bounds. It is straightforward to ensure that if a term is a lone universally quantified variable then that array access, $a[i_1]$, will never be indexed out-of-bounds. If the array has length ℓ, then this will occur exactly when $i_1 < 0$ or $\ell - 1 < i_1$. Thus, when we replace the quantifier $\forall i_1$ with a conjunction over all possible values of i_1, i.e., those from 0 to $\ell - 1$, we introduce new universally quantified variables and in ϕ^A replace old access terms with the new universal variables we set the new universal variable to be equal to the old access term. For example, consider ϕ^A that contains the term $a[2 \times i_3 + 1]$. Then we transform ϕ^A into $\phi'^{AP} \equiv \forall(i_1, \ldots, i_n, j).\phi'^A$ where $\phi'^A = \phi^A \wedge j = 2 \times i_3 + 1$ and each occurrence of $2 \times i_3 + 1$ is replaced by j in ϕ^A. How does this transformation affect the model count? Clearly ϕ'^A is true if and only if $j = 2 \times i_3 + 1$ so the model count is preserved. This holds in general as well, since equating two terms implies that one can substitute them for each other, or in other words, the relevant models are in correspondence.

Lemma 2. *Replacing array stores is model-count preserving.*

Proof Sketch. Next, we remove all the array stores. To do this, we replace the array stores with fresh array variables, and introduce new store-free array formulas to ensure that the fresh array variables operate as the old array stores did. If an array formula contains the array store $a\{i \leftarrow e\}$, then we replace every instance of $a\{i \leftarrow e\}$ with a fresh array variable b. Then, we append to the array formula two more constraints: $b[i] = e$ and $\forall(j).(i = j \rightarrow a[j] = b[j])$.

How does this transformation affect the model count? We're introducing a new free-variable—b—which has the potential to increase the model count. However, the number of models in our new formula will be the same as our old formula because the values of b are completely fixed for any particular values of a, i, and e. Thus, we've ensured our there is only one option for the new variable b for each set of variables that satisfies our original formula.

Lemma 3. *Removing universal quantifiers is model-count preserving.*

Proof Sketch. The next step in our algorithm is to remove the universal quantification from our formula. In particular, we remove quantification of the form $\forall(i).(\phi(i))$, replacing each $\forall$ by conjoining $\phi(i)$ over all values of i such that $\phi(i)$ does not have an array accessed out-of-bounds. If ℓ is the length of an array in $\phi(i)$, then this is $\bigwedge_{i \in \{0, \ldots, \ell-1\}} \phi(i)$.

This rule is carried out exhaustively on each array sub-formula. How does this transformation affect the model count? If a set of variables satisfies our original formula, it clearly satisfies the resulting formula because universal quantification is the same as conjunction over the integers. Moreover, no statement $\phi(i)$ with $i < 0$ or $i \geq \ell$ has any meaning because $\phi(i)$ will then include an array accessed out-of-bounds. Thus, the model count is preserved.

This step is similar to computing the *index set*, $\mathscr{I}$, of the well-known procedure for SAT-checking array constraints [8]. That computation of the index set computes the minimal set of index variables $\mathscr{I}$ that might be used within array indexing expressions so that satisfiability is maintained when replacing universal quantification with a conjunction over all variables in $\mathscr{I}$. This does not work for model counting, as we need to keep models in correspondence after each transformation.

Lemma 4. ϕ^A and ϕ^{LIA} as defined in Ackermann's reduction are equisatisfiable.

Proof Sketch. The equisatisfiable nature of Ackermann's reduction is well-known [1]. We provide a proof sketch giving us the machinery to also claim that Ackermann's reduction is model-count preserving in the next lemma.

Let I^A be a satisfying interpretation for ϕ^A (the input to Algorithm 5). We define I^{LIA}, a satisfying interpretation of ϕ^{LIA} (Algorithm 5 line 6) in the following way. For all variables v that appear in both ϕ^A and ϕ^{LIA}, let $I^{LIA}(v) := I^A(v)$. Then, for the remaining variables in ϕ^{LIA}, let $I^{LIA}(a_i) := I^A(a[i])$. The fact that I^{LIA} is a model for FLAT^{LIA} follows immediately from I^A modeling ϕ^A. Note that FLAT^{LIA} is identical to ϕ^A except that the array access $a[i]$ is replaced with the variable a_i. Since $I^{LIA}(a_i) = I^A(a[i])$, the formulas are identical after substituting variable assignments. Because we may think of array access as a function from $\mathbb{Z}$ to $\mathbb{Z}$, the conjunction of functional consistency constraints FC^{LIA} (Algorithm 5 line 5) is satisfied automatically. Thus their conjunction, ϕ^{LIA}, is satisfied by I^{LIA}.

Now we will assume that I^{LIA} models $\phi^{LIA} = FC^{LIA} \wedge \text{FLAT}^{LIA}$, and show that inverting the process above generates a model for ϕ^A. Let

$$I^A(v) := I^{LIA}(v) \quad \text{and} \quad I^A(a[i]) := I^{LIA}(a_i).$$

We must now argue that I^A models ϕ^A. Note that FC$^{LIA} \wedge$ FLAT^{LIA} implies that FC^{LIA} is true and FLAT^{LIA} is true. From the fact that FLAT$^{LIA} = \tau(\phi^A)$, we have that ϕ^A is true unless I^{LIA} is an assignment such that

$$I^{LIA}(i) = I^{LIA}(j) \wedge \neg(I^{LIA}(a_i) = I^{LIA}(a_j)) \text{ for some } i \text{ and } j.$$

However, I^{LIA} is a model of FC^{LIA} so this cannot be the case. Consequently. Ackermann's reduction preserves satisfiability.

Lemma 5. *Ackerman's reduction is model-count preserving; that is, ϕ^A and ϕ^{LIA} as defined in Ackermann's reduction have the same model count.*

Proof Sketch. Let f be the mapping from a model of ϕ^A to one of ϕ^{LIA} from Lemma 4 and let g be the mapping from a model of ϕ^{LIA} to one of ϕ^A from the same lemma. Note that $(f \circ g)(I^A) = (g \circ f)(I^A) = I^A$. Therefore, there is a bijection between the set of models of ϕ^A and those of ϕ^{LIA}. The sets have the same cardinality.

Theorem 1. *The MCBAT algorithm is model count preserving.*

Proof Sketch. By Lemmas 1 through 5, the steps to reduce a integer array formula to a formula of linear integer arithmetic are model-count preserving. By appealing to the correctness of the Barvinok algorithm [4], which we then call to produce the final count, MCBAT is a model-count preserving algorithm.

Example 3. Consider a constraint that emerges in work on array-based loop invariant synthesis by Larraz, et al. [20]. Consider a program that, given an length 10 array of integers between -10 and 10 (inclusive), partitions it into two arrays of length 5 where the first contains only nonnegative values and the second contains only negative values. The constraint that emerges from this program is shown here on the left. Applying the steps of MCBAT to this constraint eventually leads to the following mode-count-equivalent LIA formula on the right. Sending this constraint to BARVINOK give a final model count of 62661399052455.

$$
\begin{array}{l}
\text{LENGTH}(b,5) \land \\
\text{LENGTH}(c,5) \land \\
\forall(\alpha).(0 \le \alpha \le i-1 \to 0 \le b[\alpha]) \land \\
\forall(\alpha).(0 \le \alpha \le j-1 \to c[\alpha] < 0) \land \\
\forall(k).(-10 \le b[k] \le 10) \land \\
\forall(k).(-10 \le c[k] \le 10) \land \\
0 \le i \le 4 \land 0 \le j \le 4
\end{array}
\quad
\xrightarrow[\text{Reductions}]{\text{MCBAT}}
\quad
\begin{array}{l}
\bigwedge_{0 \le \alpha \le 4} -10 \le b_\alpha \le 10 \ \land \\
\bigwedge_{0 \le \alpha \le 4} -10 \le c_\alpha \le 10 \ \land \\
\bigwedge_{0 \le \alpha \le 4} \alpha \le i-1 \to 0 \le b_\alpha \ \land \\
\bigwedge_{0 \le \alpha \le 4} \alpha \le j-1 \to c_\alpha < 0 \ \land \\
0 \le i \le 4 \land 0 \le j \le 4
\end{array}
$$

4   Experiments and Implementation

4.1   The MCBAT Implementation

We implemented the MCBAT algorithm in a tool, also called MCBAT. A high level architecture of MCBAT can be seen in Fig. 4. The core MCBAT algorithm is implemented in a series of Haskell functions, eventually passing a quantifier-free linear integer arithmetic formula to the Barvinok library which returns the final model count. Array constraints may be entered directly as Haskell expressions and MCBAT also supports reading constraint files in an SMT-LIB2-like format. The complete implementation is freely available along with the source code[1]. In addition, our implementation has an associated Docker image, so that one can immediately download and run MCBAT in a virtual environment using a single terminal command.

---

[1] Note to reviewers: our implementation and experiments are ready for immediate public release upon publication of our results.

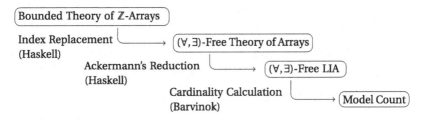

Fig. 4. High-level view of MCBAT implementation architecture.

4.2   MCBAT Experiments

In this section, we give experimental validation of MCBAT's correctness and efficiency and we then describe a case study in which model counting for the theory of arrays is used for automated expected algorithm performance computation. Overall, our experiments have demonstrated that MCBAT is

- **Correct:** MCBAT produces the same model counts compared to a straightforward enumerative approach using Z3, but much faster.
- **Efficiently scalable:** For realistic array sizes and array value domains that may be encountered in practice (up to length 400 with 32-bit array values), MCBAT produces model counts in reasonable amounts of time
- **Applicable:** We applied MCBAT to the problem of automatically computing the average case analysis of well-known array algorithms.

Validating Correctness. We verify that MCBAT computes correct model counts by comparing with a second algorithm using Z3. There is no pre-existing model counting tool for the theory of arrays that we are aware of, so our straightforward baseline comparison is to generate all possible models for an array constraint using Z3 to check satisfiability while incrementing a counter. As mentioned previously in this paper, our array semantics differ slightly from those of Z3: integer arrays in Z3 are a total map from $\mathbb{Z}$ to $\mathbb{Z}$. We accounted for this by automatically constructing additional constraints to require that for any array, $a[i] = 0$ if $i < 0$ or $i > \text{LENGTH}(a)$. Hence, the models of Z3 and MCBAT are brought into correspondence.

The constraints that we use for this comparison are from the work of Larraz, et al. on automatic generation of loop invariants using SMT for programs operating on arrays [20]. We note that model counting for constraints involving loop invariants is useful in the context of quantitative information flow analysis [18]. Note, we attempted to consistently choose array length, 5, and value range parameters, $[-5, 5]$, so that the Z3 enumerative methods would finish in reasonable time limit of 1 hour. However, three benchmarks (Par, Bin, Copy) did not even finish within one hour using Z3, so we used ranges of $[-1, 1]$ for just those benchmarks in order to complete the correctness comparison. In our experiments, both MCBAT and model enumeration via Z3 computed identical model counts, with MCBAT being significantly faster (Table 1). Consequently, we are confident that MCBAT correctly counts models.

Table 1. Experimental results in which MCBAT and model enumeration using Z3 produce identical counts, along with their running times in seconds.

ID	Description	Length	Range	Count	Z3 time (s)	MCBAT time (s)
HP	Heap property	5	$[-5,5]$	61226	813	0.02
PI	Partial initialization	5	$[-5,5]$	1331	327	0.01
Pal	Palindrome	5	$[-5,5]$	14641	360	0.01
Init	Array initialization	5	$[-5, 5]$	14641	345	0.01
Ins	Sorted insertion	5	$[-5,5]$	161051	1097	0.01
Par	Array partition	5	$[-1,1]$	2916	207	0.02
Bin	Binary search	5	$[-1, 1]$	1971	140	0.12
Copy	Array copy	5	$[-1, 1]$	6561	231	0.01
FNN	First not null	5	$[-5, 5]$	14641	349	0.01
Max	Array maximum	5	$[-5,5]$	85184	713	<0.01
FO	First occurence	5	$[-5,5]$	100000	797	0.02
SP	Sum of pairs	5	$[-5,5]$	83799	1387	0.02
Seq	Seq. initialization	5	$[-5,5]$	336596	3085	0.01
Shuf	Shuffle	5	$[-5,5]$	161051	1142	0.27
AC	JutgePaperAC	5	$[-5,5]$	100000	1002	0.04

Efficiency and Scalability. We applied MCBAT to the same benchmarks that were used to validate the correctness, but with increased array lengths and array value ranges. Considering array lengths of up to 400 and array value ranges as large as $[-2^{32}, 2^{32} - 1]$ (i.e. the range of 64-bit signed integers), the enumerative approach using Z3 is not feasible. However, MCBAT is able to compute model counts for all constraints in reasonable amounts of time (Table 2).

Note that MCBAT computes exact model counts, but in Table 2, we report only approximations of model counts in scientific notation up to two significant digits, as the exact model count would not fit in the table (e.g. the count for HP with length 400 and 64-bit integer ranges is almost an 8000 digit number.) With a 10 min timeout limit, we observe the following:

- **Sensitivity to array length.** The dominant bottleneck in our approach is array length. We see that execution time grows significantly as the length increases for a given constraint.
- **Insensitivity to value range.** The running time of MCBAT does not have a high dependence on value range. For example, for the HP benchmark, both value range settings result in extremely similar running times as a function of array length, despite there being large differences in the resulting model counts.

Table 2. McBAT run-time for benchmark constraints. Array lengths run from 10 to 400, and value ranges are $[-2^4, 2^4]$ (8-bit integers) and $[-2^{32}, 2^{32}-1]$ (32-bit integers). Times are in seconds, timeout was 10 min. Only the "first" timeout of each experiment set is show, as larger lenghts or ranges also induce a timeout.

ID	Len.	Range	Count	Time
HP	10	$[-2^4,2^4]$	5.33×10^{14}	0.084
HP	50	$[-2^4,2^4]$	2.94×10^{75}	0.413
HP	100	$[-2^4,2^4]$	2.48×10^{151}	2.853
HP	200	$[-2^4,2^4]$	1.76×10^{303}	26.803
HP	400	$[-2^4,2^4]$	8.87×10^{606}	328.46
HP	10	$[-2^{32}, 2^{32}-1]$	1.52×10^{192}	0.101
HP	50	$[-2^{32}, 2^{32}-1]$	6.59×10^{962}	0.392
HP	100	$[-2^{32}, 2^{32}-1]$	1.30×10^{1926}	3.112
HP	200	$[-2^{32}, 2^{32}-1]$	5.09×10^{3863}	31.920
HP	400	$[-2^{32}, 2^{32}-1]$	7.78×10^{7705}	377.50
PI	10	$[-2^4,2^4]$	1.41×10^{12}	0.123
PI	50	$[-2^4,2^4]$	7.74×10^{72}	2.190
PI	100	$[-2^4,2^4]$	6.52×10^{148}	32.659
PI	200	$[-2^4,2^4]$	4.63×10^{300}	598.75
PI	400	$[-2^4,2^4]$	–	t.o.
PI	10	$[-2^{32}, 2^{32}-1]$	1.34×10^{154}	0.141
PI	50	$[-2^{32}, 2^{32}-1]$	5.81×10^{924}	3.934
PI	100	$[-2^{32}, 2^{32}-1]$	1.15×10^{1888}	32.982
PI	200	$[-2^{32}, 2^{32}-1]$	–	t.o.
Pal	10	$[-2^4,2^4]$	4.64×10^{13}	0.113
Pal	50	$[-2^4,2^4]$	2.55×10^{74}	0.319
Pal	100	$[-2^4,2^4]$	2.15×10^{150}	2.358
Pal	200	$[-2^4,2^4]$	1.53×10^{302}	25.442
Pal	400	$[-2^4,2^4]$	–	t.o.
Pal	10	$[-2^{32}, 2^{32}-1]$	2.47×10^{173}	0.125
Pal	50	$[-2^{32}, 2^{32}-1]$	1.07×10^{944}	0.371
Pal	100	$[-2^{32}, 2^{32}-1]$	2.12×10^{1907}	2.330
Pal	200	$[-2^{32}, 2^{32}-1]$	8.28×10^{3833}	24.889
Pal	400	$[-2^{32}, 2^{32}-1]$	–	t.o.
Init	10	$[-2^4,2^4]$	4.64×10^{13}	9.430
Init	50	$[-2^4,2^4]$	–	t.o.
Init	10	$[-2^{32}, 2^{32}-1]$	1.34×10^{154}	243.46
Ins	10	$[-2^4,2^4]$	1.53×10^{15}	0.292
Ins	25	$[-2^4,2^4]$	1.98×10^{37}	15.507
Ins	10	$[-2^{32}, 2^{32}-1]$	4.56×10^{593}	0.265
Ins	25	$[-2^{32}, 2^{32}-1]$	4.45×10^{481}	15.160
Par	10	$[-2^4,2^4]$	1.46×10^{29}	0.099
Par	50	$[-2^4,2^4]$	4.43×10^{150}	10.106
Par	65	$[-2^4,2^4]$	1.59×10^{196}	332.75
Par	10	$[-2^{32}, 2^{32}-1]$	1.30×10^{384}	0.146
Par	50	$[-2^{32}, 2^{32}-1]$	2.44×10^{1925}	8.280
Par	65	$[-2^{32}, 2^{32}-1]$	2.32×10^{2503}	327.55
Shuf	5	$[-2^4,2^4]$	3.91×10^{7}	34.948
Shuf	5	$[-2^{32}, 2^{32}-1]$	2.14×10^{96}	36.528

ID	Len.	Range	Count	Time
Bin	10	$[-2^4,2^4]$	1.01×10^{14}	2.473
Bin	25	$[-2^4,2^4]$	2.45×10^{31}	241.96
Bin	10	$[-2^{32}, 2^{32}-1]$	5.39×10^{193}	2.524
Bin	25	$[-2^{32}, 2^{32}-1]$	3.25×10^{476}	287.01
Copy	5	$[-2^4,2^4]$	4.64×10^{13}	0.241
Copy	7	$[-2^4,2^4]$	5.50×10^{19}	5.688
Copy	10	$[-2^4,2^4]$	2.15×10^{27}	509.55
Copy	5	$[-2^{32}, 2^{32}-1]$	2.47×10^{173}	0.366
Copy	7	$[-2^{32}, 2^{32}-1]$	2.86×10^{250}	6.884
FNN	5	$[-2^4,2^4]$	1.19×10^{6}	0.129
FNN	7	$[-2^4,2^4]$	1.29×10^{9}	2.621
FNN	5	$[-2^{32}, 2^{32}-1]$	1.16×10^{77}	0.121
FNN	7	$[-2^{32}, 2^{32}-1]$	3.94×10^{115}	2.600
Max	10	$[-2^4,2^4]$	5.08×10^{15}	0.137
Max	50	$[-2^4,2^4]$	2.79×10^{75}	0.441
Max	100	$[-2^4,2^4]$	2.35×10^{151}	2.769
Max	200	$[-2^4,2^4]$	1.67×10^{303}	31.198
Max	400	$[-2^4,2^4]$	–	t.o.
Max	10	$[-2^{32}, 2^{32}-1]$	1.14×10^{93}	0.093
Max	50	$[-2^{32}, 2^{32}-1]$	4.94×10^{963}	0.382
Max	100	$[-2^{32}, 2^{32}-1]$	9.77×10^{1925}	2.750
Max	200	$[-2^{32}, 2^{32}-1]$	3.82×10^{3852}	31.263
Max	400	$[-2^{32}, 2^{32}-1]$	–	t.o.
FO	10	$[-2^4,2^4]$	1.02×10^{6}	0.329
FO	25	$[-2^4,2^4]$	1.57×10^{28}	18.845
FO	10	$[-2^{32}, 2^{32}-1]$	4.46×10^{189}	0.333
FO	25	$[-2^{32}, 2^{32}-1]$	1.33×10^{474}	16.728
SP	5	$[-2^4,2^4]$	1.20×10^{7}	0.185
SP	7	$[-2^4,2^4]$	3.27×10^{8}	0.467
SP	10	$[-2^4,2^4]$	8.91×10^{11}	2.105
SP	12	$[-2^4,2^4]$	2.89×10^{14}	5.715
SP	5	$[-2^{32}, 2^{32}-1]$	4.27×10^{95}	0.182
SP	7	$[-2^{32}, 2^{32}-1]$	2.92×10^{132}	0.463
SP	10	$[-2^{32}, 2^{32}-1]$	3.62×10^{189}	2.188
SP	12	$[-2^{32}, 2^{32}-1]$	3.92×10^{227}	5.811
Seq	5	$[-2^4,2^4]$	3.91×10^{7}	0.149
Seq	7	$[-2^4,2^4]$	4.26×10^{10}	3.967
Seq	5	$[-2^{32}, 2^{32}-1]$	2.14×10^{97}	0.145
Seq	7	$[-2^{32}, 2^{32}-1]$	7.27×10^{134}	4.007
AC	10	$[-2^4,2^4]$	2.79×10^{12}	2.218
AC	25	$[-2^4,2^4]$	1.06×10^{29}	344.31
AC	10	$[-2^{32}, 2^{32}-1]$	8.91×10^{189}	2.240
AC	25	$[-2^{32}, 2^{32}-1]$	2.65×10^{474}	367.55

Case Study: Average Runtime for Array Algorithms. We now present a case study in which we apply MCBAT to the problem of automatic average case analysis of programs that operate on integer arrays.

Consider a program P that performs operations on integer arrays, an extremely common type of program. For instance, P could be an implementation of a sorting algorithm. Suppose we wish to know what is the average behavior of P over all possible array inputs for a given array length. We can define a cost metric, for example, to be the number of basic code block executed while P runs. We perform symbolic execution on P using a small custom symbolic execution engine for integer array programs written in python. We collect the set of path constraints on symbolic array inputs while tracking the cost of every execution path. Assuming that any array of a given length is equally likely, we compute the relative likelihood of a particular path by performing model counting on the path constraints. Let p_i be the probability of path i and c_i be its cost in terms of the number of executed instructions.

$$E[Cost[P]] = \sum_{i=1}^{n} p_i c_i = \frac{\sum_{i=1}^{n} \mathsf{MCBAT}(\phi_i) \cdot c_i}{\mathsf{MCBAT}\left(\bigvee_{j=1}^{n} \phi_j\right)}$$

For our case study on automatic average case analysis of array algorithms, we implemented the following common procedures and symbolically executed them to produce a set of path constraints Φ and corresponding costs for each program P.

- **Index value check**: Check if an array hold a given value at a given index, $|a| = 10$.
- **Search for constant**: Finds the first index of a value in an array, $|a| = 10$.
- **Search for input parameter**: Finds the first index of an input parameter, $|a| = 10$.
- **Array Comparison**: Lexicographically compares two arrays, $|a| = 200$.
- **Find Max**: Finds the largest value in an array, $|a| = 12$.
- **Sorted Insert**: Performs insert step of insertion sort on a sorted array, $|a| = 14$.
- **Insertion Sort**: Performs an insertion sort on an array, $|a| = 6$.
- **Selection Sort**: Performs a selection sort on an array, $|a| = 6$.
- **Bubble Sort**: Performs a bubble sort on an array, $|a| = 6$.
- **Sorted Merge**: Merges two sorted arrays into a single sorted array, $|a| = 12$.
- **Check Sorted**: Checks whether an array is sorted, $|a| = 50$.

The path constraints were then used to compute $E[\textsc{Cost}(P)]$ using the formula above. The results of this experiment are given in Table 3.

Table 3. Case study results expected computation cost, showing number of path constraints (PC)s the expected cost, symbolic exeuction (SE) time, and time to compute expected cost.

Program	# PCs	E[Cost]	SE time (s)	E[Cost] time (s)
Index Val. Check	2	1	0.0550	12.084
Search for Constant	11	21	57.9044	9.434
Search for Param.	11	21	50.8026	309.530
Array Comparison	301	4.5	107.7987	4401.533
Sorted Insert	14	7.5	0.5920	0.957
Insertion Sort	720	18.5	71.3072	32.288
Select Max	2048	23	252.0237	320.149
Selection Sort	1359	43	653.9933	65.550
Bubble Sort	720	43	34.464S	28.385
Sorted Merge	924	22.84	240.8224	110.283
Check Sorted	50	4.44	7.5666	50.813

5   Related Work

The Theory of Arrays. In 1962, McCarthy introduced a formal theory of arrays based the two *select and store* axioms [24]. In more recent times, decision procedures for the theory of arrays have been developed and implemented, for instance in the Z3 SMT solver [25,26]. A comprehensive treatment of satisfiability checking for array constraints is given in Kroening and Strichman's "Decision Procedures: An Algorithmic Point of View" [19].

We find that the most closely related work to ours is that of Plazar, et al [28]. While their work is focused primarily on satisfiability checking of array constraints over arbitrary value types, the bounded fragment of array theory that they focus on and the resulting algorithm bear resemblances to our approaches that focus on bounded integer arrays. While the authors observe a "strong correspondence between the models to the input and transformed formulas", their algorithm, as it is not concerned with model counting, is not strong enough to fully maintain the model correspondence across transformations.

Applications of Array Constraint Procedures. SMT solving for arrays is an important component of symbolic execution for programs that operate on arrays, as in Symbolic Path Finder for Java [16]. Another useful application of satisfiability checking for arrays is the synthesis of invariants over arrays [20] by Larraz, et al., whose constraints we used as a benchmark for our experimental analysis. In this paper, we applied model counting to a case study on computing expected computational cost of functions operating on arrays. Work exists on automatic expected cost computation, based on generating functions rather than model counting algorithms, for algorithms over recursively defined data types [15].

Model Counting. Initial work in model counting applied to formulas of propositional logic. Of particular interest is the use of DPLL as a model counting procedure [6]. Recent years have seen a significant increase in interest in model counting for domains beyond propositional logic. LattE [21] and Barvinok [34] are popular model counters for the theory of linear integer arithmetic. Closely related to the theory of arrays is the theory of strings, which are also an indexable type. Recent approaches to model counting for strings make use of generating functions [22], recurrence relations [32], and automata theory [2]. Earlier work on model counting for data structures exists in which Java code that defines a data structure is symbolically executed and the resulting constraints are model counted using LattE during analysis [13]. Finally, recent theoretical results have been shown for the problem of weighted model counting for constraints containing uninterpreted functions [5].

6   Conclusions and Future Work

We presented our algorithm and practical tool, MCBAT, for performing model counting on constraints over integer arrays of bounded length. MCBAT performs a series of transformations on constraints in order to accomplish model counting, and we showed that these transformations are model-count preserving. In addition, we experimentally validated our approach and demonstrated its usefulness on a case study. It is our hope that MCBAT can be used by other researchers in applications requiring model counting for array constraints.

There are many avenues for future work. Extending our approach to higher dimensional arrays would increase the expressiveness of MCBAT, as would handling arrays of types other than integers. In addition, we would like to allow for reasoning over arrays of symbolic lengths. Finally, as arrays can be used to model vectors, hash maps, memory accesses, heaps, and so on, we model counting for arrays is a first step toward model counting for such more complex data structures.

In performing this research, we observed that in many works on model counting the fundamental insights are to (1) convert elements of satisfiability checking procedure into a model counting procedure or (2) convert elements a model enumeration procedure into a model counting procedure. This is the case with model counting algorithms that are based on DPLL, automata, and generating functions. The challenging question arises: to what degree can satisfiability checking and model enumeration algorithms be converted, perhaps automatically, into counting algorithms?

To conclude, we note that Satisfiability Modulo Theories has dramatically increased the ability to perform program analyses. SMT solvers combine decision procedures for Boolean combinations of constraints from various theories. Because there are model counting algorithms for Boolean formulas, linear integer arithmetic, strings, and now integer arrays, we look forward to a future in which Model Counting Modulo Theories combines model counting procedures for various theories to become the fundamental enabling technology behind quantitative program analysis.

References

1. Ackermann, W.: Solvable Cases of the Decision Problem. North-Holland Pub. Co., Amsterdam (1954)
2. Aydin, A., Bang, L., Bultan, T.: Automata-based model counting for string constraints. In: Kroening, D., Păsăreanu, C.S. (eds.) CAV 2015. LNCS, vol. 9206, pp. 255–272. Springer, Cham (2015). https://doi.org/10.1007/978-3-319-21690-4_15
3. Aydin, A., et al.: Parameterized model counting for string and numeric constraints. In: Proceedings of the 2018 ACM Joint Meeting on European Software Engineering Conference and Symposium on the Foundations of Software Engineering, ESEC/SIGSOFT FSE 2018, Lake Buena Vista, FL, USA, 04–09 November 2018, pp. 400–410 (2018)
4. Barvinok, A.I.: A polynomial time algorithm for counting integral points in polyhedra when the dimension is fixed. Math. Oper. Res. **19**(4), 769–779 (1994)
5. Belle, V.: Weighted model counting with function symbols. In: Proceedings of the Thirty-Third Conference on Uncertainty in Artificial Intelligence, UAI 2017, Sydney, Australia, 11–15 August 2017 (2017)
6. Birnbaum, E., Lozinskii, E.L.: The good old Davis-Putnam procedure helps counting models. J. Artif. Int. Res. **10**(1), 457–477 (1999)
7. Borges, M., Phan, Q.-S., Filieri, A., Păsăreanu, C.S.: Model-counting approaches for nonlinear numerical constraints. In: Barrett, C., Davies, M., Kahsai, T. (eds.) NFM 2017. LNCS, vol. 10227, pp. 131–138. Springer, Cham (2017). https://doi.org/10.1007/978-3-319-57288-8_9
8. Bradley, A.R., Manna, Z., Sipma, H.B.: What's decidable about arrays? In: Emerson, E.A., Namjoshi, K.S. (eds.) VMCAI 2006. LNCS, vol. 3855, pp. 427–442. Springer, Heidelberg (2005). https://doi.org/10.1007/11609773_28
9. Chakraborty, S., Meel, K., Mistry, R., Vardi, M.: Approximate probabilistic inference via word-level counting, November 2015
10. Chavira, M., Darwiche, A.: On probabilistic inference by weighted model counting. Artif. Intell. **172**(6), 772–799 (2008)
11. De Salvo Braz, R., O'Reilly, C., Gogate, V., Dechter, R.: Probabilistic inference modulo theories. In: Proceedings of the Twenty-Fifth International Joint Conference on Artificial Intelligence, IJCAI 2016, pp. 3591–3599. AAAI Press (2016)
12. Eiers, W., Saha, S., Brennan, T., Bultan, T.: Subformula caching for model counting and quantitative program analysis. In: Proceedings of The 34th IEEE/ACM International Conference on Automated Software Engineering ASE (2019)
13. Filieri, A., Frias, M.F., Păsăreanu, C.S., Visser, W.: Model counting for complex data structures. In: Fischer, B., Geldenhuys, J. (eds.) SPIN 2015. LNCS, vol. 9232, pp. 222–241. Springer, Cham (2015). https://doi.org/10.1007/978-3-319-23404-5_15
14. Filieri, A., Pasareanu, C.S., Visser, W.: Reliability analysis in symbolic pathfinder. In: 35th International Conference on Software Engineering, ICSE 2013, San Francisco, CA, USA, 18–26 May 2013, pp. 622–631 (2013)
15. Flajolet, P., Salvy, B., Zimmermann, P.: Automatic average-case analysis of algorithm. Theor. Comput. Sci. **79**(1), 37–109 (1991)
16. Fromherz, A., Luckow, K.S., Pasareanu, C.S.: Symbolic arrays in symbolic pathfinder. ACM SIGSOFT Softw. Eng. Notes **41**(6), 1–5 (2016)
17. Geldenhuys, J., Dwyer, M.B., Visser, W.: Probabilistic symbolic execution. In: Proceedings of the 2012 International Symposium on Software Testing and Analysis, ISSTA 2012, pp. 166–176. ACM, New York (2012)

18. Klebanov, V.: Precise quantitative information flow analysis - a symbolic approach. Theor. Comput. Sci. **538**, 124–139 (2014)
19. Kroening, D., Strichman, O.: Decision Procedures: An Algorithmic Point of View, 1st edn. Springer, Heidelberg (2008). https://doi.org/10.1007/978-3-540-74105-3
20. Larraz, D., Rodríguez-Carbonell, E., Rubio, A.: SMT-based array invariant generation. In: Giacobazzi, R., Berdine, J., Mastroeni, I. (eds.) VMCAI 2013. LNCS, vol. 7737, pp. 169–188. Springer, Heidelberg (2013). https://doi.org/10.1007/978-3-642-35873-9_12
21. Loera, J.A.D., Hemmecke, R., Tauzer, J., Yoshida, R.: Effective lattice point counting in rational convex polytopes. J. Symb. Comput. **38**(4), 1273–1302 (2004)
22. Luu, L., Shinde, S., Saxena, P., Demsky, B.: A model counter for constraints over unbounded strings. In: Proceedings of the 35th ACM SIGPLAN Conference on Programming Language Design and Implementation, PLDI 2014, pp. 565–576. ACM, New York (2014)
23. Malacaria, P., Khouzani, M.H.R., Pasareanu, C.S., Phan, Q., Luckow, K.S.: Symbolic side-channel analysis for probabilistic programs. In: 31st IEEE Computer Security Foundations Symposium, CSF 2018, Oxford, United Kingdom, 9–12 July 2018, pp. 313–327 (2018)
24. McCarthy, J.: Towards a mathematical science of computation. In: Colburn, T.R., Fetzer, J.H., Rankin, T.L. (eds.) Information Processing. SCS, vol. 14, pp. 21–28. Springer, Dordrecht (1962). https://doi.org/10.1007/978-94-011-1793-7_2
25. de Moura, L., Bjørner, N.: Z3: an efficient smt solver. In: Ramakrishnan, C.R., Rehof, J. (eds.) TACAS 2008. LNCS, vol. 4963, pp. 337–340. Springer, Heidelberg (2008). https://doi.org/10.1007/978-3-540-78800-3_24
26. de Moura, L.M., Bjørner, N.: Generalized, efficient array decision procedures. In: Proceedings of 9th International Conference on Formal Methods in Computer-Aided Design, FMCAD 2009, 15–18 November 2009, Austin, Texas, USA pp. 45–52 (2009)
27. Phan, Q., Malacaria, P., Pasareanu, C.S., d'Amorim, M.: Quantifying information leaks using reliability analysis. In: 2014 International Symposium on Model Checking of Software, SPIN 2014, Proceedings, San Jose, CA, USA, 21–23 July 2014, pp. 105–108 (2014)
28. Plazar, Q., Acher, M., Bardin, S., Gotlieb, A.: Efficient and complete fd-solving for extended array constraints, pp. 1231–1238, August 2017
29. Pugh, W.: Counting solutions to Presburger formulas: how and why. In: Proceedings of the ACM SIGPLAN 1994 Conference on Programming Language Design and Implementation, PLDI 1994, pp. 121–134. ACM, New York (1994)
30. Sang, T., Bearne, P., Kautz, H.: Performing bayesian inference by weighted model counting. In: Proceedings of the 20th National Conference on Artificial Intelligence, AAAI 2005, vol. 1, pp. 475–481. AAAI Press (2005)
31. Sherman, E., Harris, A.: Accurate string constraints solution counting with weighted automata. In: Proceedings of The 34th IEEE/ACM International Conference on Automated Software Engineering ASE (2019)
32. Trinh, M.-T., Chu, D.-H., Jaffar, J.: Model counting for recursively-defined strings. In: Majumdar, R., Kunčak, V. (eds.) CAV 2017. LNCS, vol. 10427, pp. 399–418. Springer, Cham (2017). https://doi.org/10.1007/978-3-319-63390-9_21
33. Tsiskaridze, N., Bang, L., McMahan, J., Bultan, T., Sherwood, T.: Information leakage in arbiter protocols. In: Lahiri, S.K., Wang, C. (eds.) ATVA 2018. LNCS, vol. 11138, pp. 404–421. Springer, Cham (2018). https://doi.org/10.1007/978-3-030-01090-4_24

34. Verdoolaege, S., Seghir, R., Beyls, K., Loechner, V., Bruynooghe, M.: Counting integer points in parametric polytopes using Barvinok's rational functions. Algorithmica **48**(1), 37–66 (2007)
35. Visser, W., Pasareanu, C.S.: Probabilistic programming for Java using symbolic execution and model counting. In: Proceedings of the South African Institute of Computer Scientists and Information Technologists, SAICSIT 2017, Thaba Nchu, South Africa, 26–28 September 2017, pp. 35:1–35:10 (2017)

Verification of an Optimized NTT Algorithm

Jorge A. Navas, Bruno Dutertre$^{(\boxtimes)}$, and Ian A. Mason

Computer Science Laboratory, SRI International, Menlo Park, CA 94025, USA
{jorge.navas,bruno.dutertre,ian.mason}@sri.com

Abstract. The Number Theoretic Transform (NTT) is an efficient algorithm for computing products of polynomials with coefficients in finite fields. It is a common procedure in lattice-based key-exchange and signature schemes. These new cryptographic algorithms are becoming increasingly important because they are *quantum resistant*. No quantum algorithm is known to break these lattice-based algorithms, unlike older schemes such as RSA or elliptic curve cryptosystems.

Many implementations and optimizations of the NTT have been proposed in the literature. A particular efficient variant is due to Longa and Naehrig. We have implemented several of these variants, including an improved version of the Longa and Naehrig algorithm. An important concern is to show that numerical overflows do not happen in such algorithms. We report on several attempts at automatically verifying the absence of overflows using static analysis tools. Off-the-shelf tools do not work on the NTT code. We present a specialized abstract-interpretation method to solve the problem.

1 Introduction

We present an experiment in verification of an optimized implementation of the Number Theoretic Transform (NTT). This transform is a key procedure in lattice-based cryptography, one of the most promising approach to developing quantum-resistant replacement for today's public-key cryptography. Current schemes are based on the hardness of factoring or discrete logarithms and will be broken if or when quantum computers become practical.

We first give an overview of the NTT and its application to computing products of polynomials. We then discuss several optimizations that attempt to reduce the cost of modular operations. A particular efficient method is due to Longa and Naehrig [29]. We propose to further improve their algorithm, but correctness of this improvement requires showing that no integer overflow is possible (when implemented using 32bit integers).

We discuss our attempts at proving that no such overflow occurs by using different software verification tools and methods. Because the procedures use combinations of array manipulation, arithmetic, shift, and bit-masking, they are difficult to prove correct with off-the-shelf tools. We present a specialized abstract

© Springer Nature Switzerland AG 2020
M. Christakis et al. (Eds.): NSV 2020/VSTTE 2020, LNCS 12549, pp. 144–160, 2020.
https://doi.org/10.1007/978-3-030-63618-0_9

interpretation method that can solve this problem. The method is implemented in SeaHorn [24] and uses the Crab abstract interpretation library [12]. We also describe an alternative technique that relies on source-code transformation.

2   The Number Theoretic Transform

Lattice-based cryptography is based on the hardness of problems such as finding a short vector in an integer lattice. Commonly used lattices are defined by matrices $A \in \mathbb{Z}_q^{n \times m}$ where q is a prime number and $\mathbb{Z}_q$ denotes the ring of integers modulo q. Efficient implementations use lattices with a special structure that allows large random matrices to be replaced by random polynomials in $\mathbb{Z}_q[X]/(X^n+1)$. One of the most common operations is computing the product of two such polynomials: given $f = a_0 + \ldots + a_{n-1}X^{n-1}$ and $g = b_0 + \ldots + b_{n-1}X^{n-1}$, their product is the polynomial $h = c_0 + \ldots + c_{n-1}X^{n-1}$ defined by

$$c_i = \left(\sum_{j+k=i} a_j b_k - \sum_{j+k=n+i} a_j b_k \right) \bmod q. \tag{1}$$

The Number Theoretic Transform (NTT) is a specialization of the Fast Fourier Transform for computing such products. It starts with a number ω that is a primitive n-th root of unity in $\mathbb{Z}_q$. This means that $\omega^n = 1 \pmod{q}$ and that $\omega^m \neq 1 \pmod{q}$ when $0 < m < n$. Such an ω exists as long as n divides $q - 1$ (for q prime). Let $a = (a_0, \ldots, a_{n-1})$ be a vector of n elements in $\mathbb{Z}_q$, and let $f = a_0 + \ldots + a_{n-1}X^{n-1}$, then the *forward transform* of a, denoted by $\mathrm{NTT}(a)$, is the vector $\tilde{a} = (\tilde{a}_0, \ldots, \tilde{a}_{n-1})$ such that

$$\tilde{a}_i = \sum_{j=0}^{n-1} a_j \omega^{ji} \bmod q \; = \; f(\omega^i)$$

The NTT is a bijection from $\mathbb{Z}_q^n$ to $\mathbb{Z}_q^n$. Its inverse INTT is given by $\mathrm{INTT}(\tilde{a}) = (b_0, \ldots, b_{n-1})$ where

$$b_i = n^{-1} \sum_{j=0}^{n-1} \tilde{a}_j \omega^{-ji} \bmod q \; = \; n^{-1} f(\omega^{-i}),$$

and we have $\mathrm{INTT}(\mathrm{NTT}(a)) = a$.

The vector c defined by Eq. 1 is the *negative wrapped convolution* of a and b. A standard method for computing c is shown Fig. 1. It requires an additional parameter ψ such that $\psi^2 = \omega \pmod{q}$ (thus, ψ is a $2n$-th primitive root of unity). The procedure first multiplies a and b by powers of ψ to form vectors $\hat{a} = (a_0, a_1\psi, \ldots, a_{n-1}\psi^{n-1})$ and $\hat{b} = (b_0, b_1\psi, \ldots, b_{n-1}\psi^{n-1})$. It then computes $\mathrm{NTT}(\hat{a})$ and $\mathrm{NTT}(\hat{b})$, multiplies the results component-wise, applies the inverse transform, and multiplies the result by powers of ψ^{-1}. This method is presented

Input: $f = a_0 + a_1 X + \ldots + a_{n-1} X^{n-1}$
          $g = b_0 + b_1 X + \ldots + b_{n-1} X^{n-1}$

Output: $h = c_0 + c_1 X + \ldots + c_{n-1} X^{n-1}$ such that $h = f.g$.

Procedure:
$$\hat{a} := (a_0, a_1\psi, \ldots, a_{n-1}\psi^{n-1})$$
$$\hat{b} := (b_0, b_1\psi, \ldots, b_{n-1}\psi^{n-1})$$
$$\tilde{a} := \text{NTT}(\hat{a})$$
$$\tilde{b} := \text{NTT}(\hat{b})$$
$$\tilde{c} := (\tilde{a}_0 \tilde{b}_0, \ldots, \tilde{a}_{n-1}\tilde{b}_{n-1})$$
$$\hat{c} := \text{INTT}(\tilde{c})$$
$$c := (\hat{c}_0, \hat{c}_1\psi^{-1}, \ldots, \hat{c}_{n-1}\psi^{-(n-1)})$$

Fig. 1. NTT-based product of polynomials in $\mathbb{Z}_q[X]/(X^n + 1)$.

by Winkler [38] and it is a basic procedure in many implementations of lattice-based cryptographic algorithms (e.g. [29, 33, 35]).

A direct computation of products using Eq. 1 has cost $O(n^2)$. The main benefit of the NTT is to reduce this cost to $O(n \log n)$, since both NTT and INTT can be implemented in $O(n \log n)$. This reduction is significant in lattice-based cryptography because the polynomials are dense and n is relatively large (e.g., $n = 1024$ or $n = 512$ are commonly used).

In the rest of this paper, we fix the parameter q to 12289, which is the prime used in existing schemes such as Bliss [18, 19] and New Hope [1]. With this choice of q, NTT with n as large as 2048 are possible, but we are mostly interested in the case $n = 1024$, which is used by Bliss and New Hope.

2.1 Basic NTT Implementation

Two possible implementations of the NTT are shown in Fig. 2. The two procedures operate on an array **a** of **n** elements, where **n** is a power of two. Each function uses an auxiliary array **p** of pre-computed constants. For both functions, elements of **p** are powers of ω modulo q (so they can be stored as 16bit integers). On entry to either function, array **a** contains a vector of **n** integers in the range $[0, q)$. On exit, the array **a** stores NTT(a) in *bit-reversed order*: the i-th coefficient of NTT(a) is stored in **a**$[j]$ where j is obtained by writing i in binary and reversing the bits. For example, if $n = 2^6 = 64$ and $i = 5$ then $j = \mathsf{bitrev}(i) = \mathsf{bitrev}(0b000101) = 0b101000 = 40$. Implementations of the inverse NTT are very similar to these two procedures.

Variants of the procedures in Fig. 2 take input in bit-reversed order and produce results in the standard order. Many optimizations of the basic algorithms are possible. A simple one is to omit multiplications by **w** in lines 15 and 32 when **j=0**. But the most expensive operation involved in NTT computations is the reduction modulo q that occurs in the inner loops of both procedures. On typical Intel/AMD processors, the integer division instructions with 32bit operands commonly have a latency about 10 times larger than an integer multiply on the same size [20]. Thus many optimizations focus on removing integer divisions or replacing them with more efficient arithmetic. Harvey [26] presents several such optimizations for the inner loops of NTT and INTT. Other optimizations avoid pre-multiplications by powers of ψ and post-multiplications by powers ψ^{-1} by adjusting the pre-computed constants in the array p [34,35].

```
1   #define Q 12289
2
3   void ntt_ct_std2rev(int32_t *a, uint32_t n, const uint16_t *p) {
4       uint32_t j, s, t, u, d;
5       int32_t x, w;
6
7       d = n;
8       for (t = 1; t < n; t <<= 1) {
9           d >>= 1;
10          u = 0;
11          for (j = 0; j < t; j++) {
12              w = p[t + j]; // w_t^bitrev(j)
13              u += 2 * d;
14              for (s = u; s < u + d; s++) {
15                  x = a[s + d] * w;
16                  a[s + d] = (a[s] - x) % Q;
17                  a[s] = (a[s] + x) % Q;
18              }
19          }
20      }
21  }
22
23  void ntt_gs_std2rev(int32_t *a, uint32_t n, const uint16_t *p) {
24      uint32_t j, s, t;
25      int32_t w, x;
26
27      for (t = n >> 1; t > 0; t >>= 1) {
28          for (j = 0; j < t; j++) {
29              w = p[t + j]; // w_t^j
30              for (s = j; s < n; s += t + t) {
31                  x = a[s + t];
32                  a[s + t] = ((a[s] - x) * w) % Q;
33                  a[s] = (a[s] + x) % Q;
34              }
35          }
36      }
37  }
```

Fig. 2. Two example NTT implementations. The top procedure follows Cooley-Tukey [7] and the bottom procedure uses the Gentleman-Sande variant [21].

One should note that compiler optimizations replace integer divisions by more efficient instruction sequences when the divisor is a known constant. In our case, $q = 12289$, and the unsigned 32bit division by q can be removed by using the equality $x \bmod q = x - \lfloor x/q \rfloor = x - \lfloor 2863078533x/2^{45} \rfloor$, which holds when $0 \le x < 2^{32}$. In this equation, 2863078533 is $2^{45}/q$ suitably rounded. This optimization is applied by both GCC and Clang when compiling for x86-64. The resulting machine code uses three instructions but it is much more efficient than a single DIV instruction. These division tricks are explained in Chap. 10 of Warren's Hacker's Delight [37].

2.2   Longa and Naehrig's Reduction

Another type of optimization replaces reduction modulo q by a related operation that is cheaper to compute, such as Montgomery's reduction [32]. Instead of computing $x \bmod q$, the Montgomery reduction returns $y \equiv \alpha x \pmod{q}$ for some fixed constant α (i.e., α is the inverse of 2^{32} modulo q). One can easily correct for the extra factor α by adjusting the constants in array p. Although this reduction removes division by q, it is more expensive than the compiler optimization trick presented previously (Montgomery's reduction uses two multiplications).

```
1   // single reduction
2   static int32_t red(int32_t x) {
3       return 3 * (x & 4095) - (x >> 12);
4   }
5
6   // reduction of x * y using 64bit arithmetic
7   static int32_t mul_red(int32_t x, int32_t y) {
8       int64_t z;
9       z = (int64_t) x * y;
10      x = z & 4095;
11      y = z >> 12;
12      return 3 * x - y;
13  }
```

Fig. 3. Longa-Naehrig reduction for $q = 12289 = 3.2^{12} + 1$

Longa and Naehrig [29] introduce a different reduction. To support NTT computations, the prime number q must have primitive $2n$-roots of unity where n is a power of two. This implies that $q - 1$ is divisible by a power of two: we have $q - 1 = k2^m$ where k is an odd number. In our case $q = 12289$ so $m = 12$ and $k = 3$. Then the Longa-Naehrig reduction of an integer x is defined as

$$\mathsf{red}(x) = k \times (x \bmod 2^m) - \lfloor x/2^m \rfloor. \tag{2}$$

This reduction can be efficiently implemented using shift and mask. Figure 3 shows two functions that implement $\mathsf{red}(x)$ and $\mathsf{red}(xy)$ for 32bit signed integers. A key property is $\mathsf{red}(x) = kx \pmod{q}$ and we also have bounds such as

$$|\mathsf{red}(wx)| \le k|x| + (q - k) \quad \text{if } 0 \le w < q \tag{3}$$

By using this reduction, Longa and Naehrig propose the procedure shown[1] in Fig. 4. As before, the input is an array a of n integers in standard order and the array elements are assumed to be in the range $[0, q)$. The NTT is computed in place and the result is stored in a in bit-reversed order. Array p contains precomputed constants also in the range $[0, q)$. These are powers of ω appropriately scaled to cancel the factor k introduced by the reduction (i.e., replacing $\omega^j \bmod q$ by $(k^{-1}\omega^j) \bmod q$). This procedure mirrors the basic implementation in Fig. 2,

---

[1] We have modified the original slightly.

except for line 15. This line performs an additional reduction. It is there to prevent numerical overflows by reducing the magnitude of all elements in the array. Because of this extra reduction, the result of the procedure is not quite the NTT but a scaled version. This scaling can be corrected later by adapting the inverse NTT calculation [29].

```
1   void ntt_red_ct_std2rev(int32_t *a, uint32_t n, const uint16_t *p) {
2     uint32_t j, s, t, u, d;
3     int32_t x, y, w;
4
5     d = n;
6     for (t = 1; t < n; t <<= 1) {
7       d >>= 1;
8       u = 0;
9       for (j = 0; j < t; j++) {
10        w = p[t + j]; // w_t^bitrev(j)
11        u += 2 * d;
12        for (s = u; s < u + d; s++) {
13          y = a[s];
14          x = mul_red(a[s + d], w);
15          if (t == 128) { y = red(y); x = red(x); }
16          a[s] = y + x;
17          a[s + d] = y - x;
18        }
19      }
20    }
21  }
```

Fig. 4. Example NTT procedure that uses the Longa-Naehrig reduction.

We are interested in verifying NTT procedures that use the Longa-Naehrig reductions. In particular, we revise the procedure of Fig. 4 to avoid the extra reduction of line 15. To do this, we replace the constant coefficients stored in array p, by equivalent coefficients that are smaller in absolute value. We just allow these coefficients to be negative, so that they are all in the interval $[-(q-1)/2, (q-1)/2]$ instead of $[0, q-1]$. This ensures that the elements of a do not grow as fast during execution. Our revised procedure is the same as in Fig. 4, except that elements of p have type int16_t and that line 15 is removed.

We have implemented this procedure and several variants that all use the Longa-Naehrig reduction. The example in Fig. 4 takes an input array in standard order and produces an output in bit-reversed order. Variants take input in bit-reversed order and produce output in standard order. Other variants use the Gentleman-Sande method instead of the Cooley-Tukey method, and some combine NTT/INTT and multiplication by powers of ψ. All these examples are available in our software repository hosted on GitHub [15].

A critical issue is showing that no numerical overflows occur in these procedures. One can try to estimate how large the coefficients grow by using inequalities such as (3), but this is tedious and error-prone and it is difficult to get sufficiently precise bounds. Instead, we explore the use of static analysis tools.

3 Verification

To show that the NTT does not overflow, we first make assumptions on its input. As shown in Fig. 5, we use an approach common to software model checkers: elements of array a are non-deterministic values (obtained by calling external function int32_nd). These values are then constrained to be in the range $[0, 12289)$ by using an "assume" statement. All the tools that we have tried support this approach. We also annotate the mul_red procedure with assertions to prove the absence of integer overflows. The bounds on z at line 20 are calculated to ensure that $\mathsf{red}(z)$ fits in a signed 32bit integer. In the general case, where $q - 1 = k2^m$, these bounds are as follows:

$$-2^{31+m} + 2^m(q - k) \leq z \leq 2^{31+m} + 2^m - 1.$$

```
1   #define Q 12289
2   extern int32_t int32_nd(void);
3   int main(void) {
4     int32_t nd_a[16];
5     int i;
6
7     for(i = 0; i < 16; i++) {
8       int32_t x = int32_nd();
9       assume(x >= 0 && x < Q);
10      nd_a[i] = x;
11    }
12
13    // call NTT procedure using on nd_a
14    return 0;
15  }
16
17  static int32_t mul_red(int32_t x, int32_t y) {
18    int64_t z;
19    z = (int64_t) x * y;
20    assert(-8796042698752 <= z && z <= 8796093026303);
21    x = z & 4095;
22    y = z >> 12;
23    return 3 * x - y;
24  }
```

Fig. 5. Test harness and assertion

3.1 Out-of-the-Box Verification Techniques

We have attempted to prove the assertion at line 20 of Fig. 5 using state-of-the-art software-verification techniques and tools:

- Bounded model-checking: CBMC [6],
- Symbolic execution: SAW/Crucible [17].
- Infinite-state model checking: CPAChecker [3] and SeaHorn [24] with IC3-PDR [27].
- Abstract interpretation: SeaHorn with Abstract Interpretation.

With default backend solvers, CBMC and Crucible work on a scaled-down version of the problem with $n = 16$, but they fail when $n = 1024$ (we stopped them after more than 24 h of computation). The infinite-state model checkers all time-out without finding an adequate inductive invariant (these tools use a default timeout of 900 s). The SeaHorn abstract interpreter finishes within seconds but cannot prove the property.

These results are not too surprising because the Longa-Naehrig reduction involves a mixture of logical and arithmetic operations that is not easy for general-purpose tools to reason about. Moreover, these computations are stored in an array and involve complex indexing that makes things even harder. We do not believe that increasing the timeout would help the infinite-state model checkers.

CBMC and Crucible use bit-precise reasoning, which is adequate for the Longa-Naehrig reduction, but the SAT or SMT problems they generate become very hard when we increase n to 1024. With CBMC, we have managed to verify an NTT transform with $n = 1024$ but that takes several hours of computation. To perform this proof, we used the CaDiCaL SAT solver[2] instead of the default[3]. In this verification, CBMC produces a problem with more than five million Boolean variables and 25 million clauses. CaDiCal 1.2.1 can show that this problem is unsatisfiable (and thus that our assertions have no counterexamples) in 9026 s. CBMC needs 287 s to generate the SAT instance.

3.2   Proofs by Abstract Interpretation

A more scalable solution is to devise specialized techniques based on abstract interpretation. Since we have to compute safe bounds on the value of array elements, we choose the interval abstract domain [8] as the numerical domain. However, the bitwise operations used by the Longa-Naehrig reduction cause difficulties for this domain. We solve this problem by defining a custom transfer function to model the effect of lines 10-12 in Fig. 3.

Specialized Transfer Function. The interval domain abstracts the set of possible values of a variable as an interval. The abstract values are either non-empty intervals with finite or infinite bounds, or a special symbol $\bot$ denoting error:

$$\mathcal{I} = \{[a, b] \mid a \in \mathbb{Z} \cup \{-\infty\}, b \in \mathbb{Z} \cup \{+\infty\}, a \leq b\} \cup \{\bot\}$$

The greatest element is $[-\infty, +\infty]$ and the least element is $\bot$. The concretization function $\gamma_{\mathcal{I}}$ is defined in the natural way: $\gamma_{\mathcal{I}}(\bot) = \emptyset$ and $\gamma_{\mathcal{I}}([a, b]) = \{x \in \mathbb{Z} \mid a \leq x \leq b\}$. The ordering between intervals is defined as $[a, b] \sqsubseteq_{\mathcal{I}} [c, d] \Leftrightarrow (a \geq c) \wedge (b \leq d)$. The least upper bound of two intervals is defined as $[a, b] \sqcup_{\mathcal{I}} [c, d] = [\min(a, c), \max(b, d)]$. The transfer functions for addition $(+_{\mathcal{I}})$ and subtraction

---

[2] http://fmv.jku.at/cadical/.
[3] By default, CBMC relies on MiniSAT 2.2.1.

$(-_\mathcal{I})$ are defined as $[a, b] +_\mathcal{I} [c, d] = [a + c, b + d]$ and $[a, b] -_\mathcal{I} [c, d] = [a - d, b - c]$, respectively.

The transfer function for the Longa-Naehrig reduction, red, is defined as follows for finite intervals:

$$\mathsf{red}_\mathcal{I}([a, b]) = \Big[\mathsf{red}(\max(b \,\&\, {\sim}4095, a)), \mathsf{red}(\min(a \mid 4095, b)) \Big] \tag{4}$$

The operators $\&$ and $\mid$ are the usual bitwise *and* and bitwise *or*, and $\sim$ is bitwise *negation*. Generalizing to infinite bounds is straightforward. We denote the interval domain extended with $\mathsf{red}_\mathcal{I}$ as $\mathcal{I}_{red}$.

Lemma 1. ($\mathsf{red}_\mathcal{I}$ is sound). $\{\mathsf{red}(x) \mid x \in \gamma_\mathcal{I}([a, b])\} \subseteq \mathsf{red}_\mathcal{I}([a, b])$.

Proof. If we write $x = 4096d + r$ where $0 \le r < 4096$ (by Euclidean division), then we have $\mathsf{red}(x) = 3r - d$. If $a \le x \le b$, the smallest value of $\mathsf{red}(x)$ is obtained by setting d as large as possible and r as small as possible. Let x_0 denote the largest integer such that $x_0 \le b$ and $x_0 \bmod 4096 = 0$, then x_0 is equal to $b \,\&\, {\sim}4095$. Either $a \le x_0$, in which case the minimum of red in $[a, b]$ is reached at x_0, or $a > x_0$, in which case the minimum is reached at a. Similarly, to find the maximum of red in $[a, b]$ we must make d as small as possible and r as large as possible. Let $x_1 = a \mid 4095$ then x_1 is the smallest integer such that $x_1 \ge a$ and $x_1 \bmod 4096 = 4095$. The maximum of red is reached either at point x_1 if $x_1 \le b$ or at b otherwise.

Arrays and Loops. Abstract interpretation tools (such as our SeaHorn analyzer [24]) use abstract domains to represent arrays and compute fixed points for loops using techniques such as widening. By default, SeaHorn uses a simple array domain $\mathcal{A}(\mathcal{D})$ [4] that models each memory region offset separately with a *synthetic* variable in the underlying numerical domain $\mathcal{D}$. The synthetic variables are *smashed* into a single *summary* variable if an array write occurs at an index that cannot be determined constant during analysis. Once an array is smashed, all the array writes are modeled as weak updates.

Such an array domain is not precise enough for our problem. To understand why, let us focus on ntt_ct_std2rev in Fig. 2. The abstract array representing a gets first "smashed" because it is accessed at non-constant indices. After one loop iteration, all elements of a are then represented by a summary variable a_{sum}. Lines 16-17 perform operations: a[s + d] = a[s] - x; a[s] = a[s] + x;, which make a_{sum} both increase and decrease by x. Eventually, widening must be applied, which loses the lower and upper bounds of a_{sum} (i.e., the final abstraction is $[-\infty, +\infty]$).

More precise array abstractions [10, 16, 22, 25] together with a more precise widening strategy (e.g., widening with thresholds [28]) could potentially help. A simpler approach is loop unrolling. Once we fix n, all the loops and arrays in our NTT examples are statically bounded, so all the loops can be fully unrolled. After unrolling, the loss of precision due to the array smashing abstraction and the widening operator disappear and $\mathcal{A}(\mathcal{I}_{red})$ can prove that the assertion holds.

SeaHorn Results. We have modified SeaHorn to support the analysis method just described. SeaHorn extends the LLVM compiler infrastructure with verification techniques based on software model checking and abstract interpretation. The SeaHorn abstract interpreter is called Crab [12]. Crab does not analyze directly LLVM bitcode but instead, it analyzes a control-flow graph (CFG) language[4] from which equation systems are extracted. These equations are solved using a chaotic iteration strategy [2] based on Bourdoncle's weak topological ordering. Crab implements general-purpose numerical domains such as intervals [8], congruences [23], zones [30], octagons [31], and polyhedra [11]. Crab also implements combination methods such as direct and reduced products [9].

We have added the transfer function for red to Crab's interval domain and we leverage LLVM to fully unroll all the loops. On the resulting loop-free code, Crab with domain $\mathcal{A}(\mathcal{I}_{red})$ can prove that all the assertions hold.

Table 1. SeaHorn results without inlining

Program	Description	Num checks	Time (s)
intt_red1024	inv CT/std2rev, $\psi = 1014$	2026	900
intt_red1024b	inv CT/rev2std, $\psi = 1014$	2026	972
ntt_red1024	CT/std2rev, $\psi = 1014$	2026	923
ntt_red1024b	CT/rev2std, $\psi = 1014$	2026	836
ntt_red1024c	CT/std2rev	1974	1151
ntt_red1024d	CT/rev2std	1974	1258
ntt_red1024e	GS/std2rev, $\psi = 1014$	8194	8265
ntt_red1024f	GS/rev2std, $\psi = 1014$	8194	8115

Experimental results are shown in Tables 1 and 2. Table 1 shows verification time when functions are not inlined. Table 2 shows results after all functions are inlined. All experiments were carried out on 2.6 GHz 6-Core Intel Core i7 MacOS laptop with 32 GB of memory. The examples in the table are variant implementations of the forward and inverse NTT using both the Cooley-Tukey (CT) and the Gentleman-Sande (GS) variants. All the functions are safe; no numerical overflow can occur. In most tests, we used a fixed value for ψ and ω (i.e., $\psi = 1014$ and $\omega = 8209$). In such cases, the array p contains explicit constants. In examples ntt_red1024c and ntt_red1024d, we treat array p symbolically. We initialize it with non-deterministic values in the range $[-6144, 6144]$ (i.e., $[-q/2, +q/2]$). The results show then that our NTT procedures do not suffer integer overflows as long as all elements of p are in this range, which implies no overflow for any choice of ω.

Without inlining, SeaHorn can prove all properties with runtimes of the order of tens of minutes to a few hours. Inlining reduces the runtimes to seconds. It

---

[4] Translation from LLVM bitcode to Crab CFG is implemented by a SeaHorn component called Clam [5].

Table 2. SeaHorn results after inlining

Program	Description	Num checks	Time (s)
intt_red1024	inv CT/std2rev, $\psi = 1014$	8188	9
intt_red1024b	inv CT/rev2std, $\psi = 1014$	8188	9
ntt_red1024	CT/std2rev, $\psi = 1014$	8188	9
ntt_red1024b	CT/rev2std, $\psi = 1014$	8188	9
ntt_red1024c	CT/std2rev	8194	9
ntt_red1024d	CT/rev2std	8194	11
ntt_red1024e	GS/std2rev, $\psi = 1014$	8188	10
ntt_red1024f	GS/rev2std, $\psi = 1014$	8188	10

might be surprising that inlining has such an impact since the analyzed program contain a small number of functions: test harness, forward or inverse NTT, and Longa-Naehrig reduction. However, after loop unrolling, the reduction function is called hundreds of times. This imposes a very high overhead in the Crab inter-procedural analysis because each time the analysis calls or returns from a function, array abstract operations such as projection and meet must be called. The use of the inter-procedural analysis also explains why the number of checks is lower in Table 1 than in Table 2. Crab implements inter-procedural analysis in a classical top-down analysis with memoization. It does not re-analyze a function if it is safe to do so, in which case the assertions in this functions are counted only once. For comparison, we managed to prove the first example of both tables with CBMC and CaDiCaL but the verification took more than two and a half hours of CPU time.

Verification by Source-Code Transformation. We now examine an alternative approach that does not build on a specialized tool such as SeaHorn. Instead, we can perform abstract interpretation by transforming the source code to operate in the abstract domain. This idea is illustrated in Fig. 6. The figure shows an NTT procedure converted to work in the abstract domain (i.e., intervals) rather than in the concrete domain (i.e., 32 bit integers).

We implement the interval domain as sketched in the figure, namely, we represent an interval by a pair of 64bit signed integers, which is sufficient for our application. We implement the usual transfer functions for arithmetic operators such as, the functions add and sub used in Fig. 6. We also add specialized transfer function to handle the Longa-Naehrig reduction. For example, function red_scale in the figure is the transfer for the operation mul_red(x, y) of Fig. 3 in the case where one argument is a constant and the other is an interval. In other words, red_scale(w, a) computes an interval $[l, h]$ such that $\forall x : l_a \leq x \leq h_a \Rightarrow l \leq \mathsf{red}(wx) \leq h$, where w is a scalar constant and a is the interval $[l_a, h_a]$.

As shown in Fig. 6, input to the abstract NTT function is now in the abstract domain and consists of an array a of n intervals. We also instrument the abstract function with code to print the abstract interpretation results at every main iteration and to check that all the intervals are included in $[-2^{31}, 2^{31} - 1]$ (which implies that all intermediate results fit in signed 32bit integers). To show that no integer overflow is possible, we just execute the abstract procedure on a suitable array of input intervals such as follows:

```
1   interval_t *a[1024];
2   for (int i=0; i<1024; i++) {
3     a[i] = interval(0, Q-1);
4   }
5   abstract_ntt_red_ct_std2rev(a, 1024, ntt_red1024_omega_powers_rev);
```

This method is not fully general but it works in our context because all computations are bounded. We replace the concrete array a of 32bit integers by an array of intervals. All other variables in the procedure (i.e., loop counters, array indices, and bounds) remain concrete. Executing the abstract program computes safe bounds on the value of the concrete array element a[i]. We check that these bounds on a[i] are compatible with our concrete implementation using 32bit arithmetic.

Although the source-code transformation could be automated, we currently rewrite the code by hand. The interval domain and transfer functions are implemented as a separate library. This analysis method is simple (it requires only a C compiler) and it is very efficient and scalable. Table 3 shows verification runtimes for the same examples as before. All runtimes are now less than 1 s.

Table 3. Verification using source-code transformation

Program	Description	Time (s)
intt_red1024	inv CT/std2rev, $\psi = 1014$	0.02
intt_red1024b	inv CT/rev2std, $\psi = 1014$	0.02
ntt_red1024	CT/std2rev, $\psi = 1014$	0.02
ntt_red1024b	CT/rev2std, $\psi = 1014$	0.02
ntt_red1024c	CT/std2rev	0.56
ntt_red1024d	CT/rev2std	0.58
ntt_red1024e	GS/std2rev, $\psi = 1014$	0.21
ntt_red1024f	GS/rev2std, $\psi = 1014$	0.19

4   Discussion and Future Work

To prove the absence of overflows in NTT procedures, we use on loop unrolling and abstract interpretation. By taking advantage of the special structure of the forward and inverse NTT transform, we have developed two scalable verification methods. One is implemented in the SeaHorn analyzer and makes aggressive use of existing LLVM optimizations. The other approach rewrites the source code to operate in the abstract domain and requires only a C compiler. These techniques rely on a key property, namely, all NTT computations are bounded once we fix the parameter n. A second major ingredient is the definition of special transfer functions to handle the Longa-Naehrig reduction in the interval domain.

Our most general results (examples ntt_red1024c and ntt_ref1024d) are that the Longa-Naehrig procedures we analyze are safe for $n = 1024$ as long as the constants in array p are all within the interval $[-(q-1)/2, (q-1)/2]$. This result no longer holds for $n = 2048$. However, these bounds on p[i] are not precise.

```
1   // abstract domain
2   typedef struct interval_s {
3     int64_t min;
4     int64_t max;
5   } interval_t;
6
7   // basic operations
8   extern interval_t *add(const interval_t *a, const interval_t *b);
9   extern interval_t *sub(const interval_t *a, const interval_t *b);
10
11  // Reduction:
12  // red_scale(w, a) returns an interval [l, h]
13  // such that l <= red(w * x) <= h for any x in a
14  extern interval_t *red_scale(int64_t w, const interval_t *a);
15
16  // abstract version of ntt_red_ct_std2rev
17  void abstract_ntt_red_ct_std2rev(interval_t **a, uint32_t n,
18        const int16_t *p) {
19    uint32_t j, s, t, u, d;
20    interval_t *x, *y, *z;
21    int64_t w;
22
23    d = n;
24    for (t = 1; t < n; t <<= 1) {
25      show_intervals("ct_std2rev", t, a, n);
26
27      d >>= 1;
28      u = 0;
29      for (j = 0; j < t; j++) {
30        w = p[t + j]; // w_t^bitrev(j) extended to 64 bits
31        u += 2 * d;
32        for (s = u; s < u + d; s++) {
33          x = a[s + d];
34          y = a[s];
35        z = red_scale(w, x);
36          a[s + d] = sub(y, z);
37        a[s] = add(y, z);
38        }
39      }
40    }
41
42    show_intervals("ct_std2rev", t, a, n);
43  }
```

Fig. 6. Abstract NTT procedure. Array a is an array of intervals. Functions red_scale, add, and sub operate on intervals. Function show_intervals prints intermediate results and checks for overflows.

The actual value of p[i] depends on i and the parameters ψ and n, and all elements of p are powers of $\omega = \psi^2 \bmod q$. For a fixed n there are n possible choices for parameter ψ. We can then exhaustively enumerate all possible values for ψ, construct the corresponding constant table p, and verify the NTT procedures for this p. Our abstract-interpretation approach is fast enough to enable this exhaustive analysis. With this method, we can show that the NTT procedures based on the Longa-Naehrig reduction are safe (for 32bit arithmetic) not just for $n = 1024$ but also for $n = 2048$. We can also show that no arithmetic overflow occurs under weaker assumptions than discussed in this paper. In particular, we can relax the assumption that input elements in array a are between 0 and $q - 1$. For $n = 1024$, the procedures remain safe for input in larger intervals.

In our verification, we have mostly considered fully automated verification tools. In principle, other tools—such as, Frama-C [13]—that support analysis of C code by deductive methods could also be used. However, the main issue with using such tools in our applications is finding program annotations to show that the procedures are correct. This amounts to finding appropriate inductive loop invariants for the NTT procedures. We do not know automated methods for finding such invariants other than the interval abstraction we propose. Alternatives may include hand calculation using inequalities such as 3, but it is difficult to derive precise enough bounds by hand. It is also unclear whether the default SMT solvers used by Frama-C can handle the bit-shift and bit-mask operations involved in the Longa-Naehrig reduction.

All our analysis so far has focused on soundness, namely, the absence of integer overflow. We are also interested in automated methods to prove functional correctness of different NTT implementations. An avenue we would like to explore is showing that the NTT procedure is linear, which we hope can be done with automated tools. If we can prove that, then it will be enough to test the NTT on a finite set of input vectors (i.e., a basis of $\mathbb{Z}_q[X]/(X^n + 1)$) to prove that it is correct everywhere.

The NTT procedures that we discussed, and the verification examples and tools are available in an open-source software repository hosted on GitHub [15]. Our verification work was motivated by our implementation of Bliss, which is also available there [14]. SeaHorn, Crab, and Clam are also open-source and also hosted on GitHub [5,12,36].

5 Conclusion

We have presented an experiment in verifying that an optimized implementation of the NTT is free of integer overflows. Although this implementation consists of a few lines of code, it is very challenging for current software verification technology because it mixes array manipulation and bitwise operations. Combining static loop unrolling with a specialized abstract interpretation method solves the problem. The technical foundations of our work are not novel since the techniques used here are well-known. We believe that verification of NTT algorithms is a good domain to demonstrate the usefulness of verification tools. We look forward to better abstractions and algorithms to verify this kind of algorithms in a more efficient way.

Acknowledgments. This work benefited from many discussions with Tancrède Lepoint. The work was partially supported by NSF Grants CCF-1816936 and CCF-1817204.

References

1. Alkim, E., Ducas, L., Pöppelmann, T., Schwabe, P.: Post-quantum key exchange - a new hope. In: USENIX Security Symposium, pp. 327–343 (2016)
2. Amato, G., Scozzari, F.: Localizing widening and narrowing. In: Logozzo, F., Fähndrich, M. (eds.) SAS 2013. LNCS, vol. 7935, pp. 25–42. Springer, Heidelberg (2013). https://doi.org/10.1007/978-3-642-38856-9_4
3. Beyer, D., Keremoglu, M.E.: CPAChecker: a tool for configurable software verification. In: Gopalakrishnan, G., Qadeer, S. (eds.) CAV 2011. LNCS, vol. 6806, pp. 184–190. Springer, Heidelberg (2011). https://doi.org/10.1007/978-3-642-22110-1_16
4. Blanchet, B., et al.: Design and implementation of a special-purpose static program analyzer for safety-critical real-time embedded software. In: Mogensen, T., Schmidt, D., Sudborough, I.H. (eds.) The Essence of Computation: Complexity, Analysis, Transformation (2002)
5. Clam: Crab for LLVM Abstraction Manager. https://github.com/seahorn/crab-llvm
6. Clarke, E., Kroening, D., Lerda, F.: A tool for checking ANSI-C programs. In: Jensen, K., Podelski, A. (eds.) TACAS 2004. LNCS, vol. 2988, pp. 168–176. Springer, Heidelberg (2004). https://doi.org/10.1007/978-3-540-24730-2_15
7. Cooley, J.W., Tukey, J.W.: An algorithm for the machine calculation of complex Fourier series. Math. Comput. **19**(90), 297–301 (1965)
8. Cousot, P., Cousot, R.: Static determination of dynamic properties of programs. In: ISOP 1976, pp. 106–130 (1976)
9. Cousot, P., Cousot, R.: Systematic design of program analysis frameworks. In: POPL, pp. 269–282 (1979)
10. Cousot, P., Cousot, R., Logozzo, F.: A parametric segmentation functor for fully automatic and scalable array content analysis. In: POPL, pp. 105–118. ACM (2011)
11. Cousot, P., Halbwachs, N.: Automatic discovery of linear restraints among variables of a program. In: Aho, A.V., Zilles, S.N., Szymanski, T.G. (eds.) POPL 1978, pp. 84–96. ACM Press (1978)
12. CoRnucopia of ABstractions: A language-agnostic library for abstract interpretation. https://github.com/seahorn/crab
13. Cuoq, P., Kirchner, F., Kosmatov, N., Prevosto, V., Signoles, J., Yakobowski, B.: Frama-C: a software analysis perspective. In: Eleftherakis, G., Hinchey, M., Holcombe, M. (eds.) SEFM 2012. LNCS, vol. 7504, pp. 233–247. Springer, Heidelberg (2012). https://doi.org/10.1007/978-3-642-33826-7_16
14. BLISS Implementation: Bimodal Lattice Signature Schemes. https://github.com/SRI-CSL/Bliss
15. An Implementation of the Number Theoretic Transform. https://github.com/SRI-CSL/NTT

16. Dillig, I., Dillig, T., Aiken, A.: Fluid updates: beyond strong vs. weak updates. In: Gordon, A.D. (ed.) ESOP 2010. LNCS, vol. 6012, pp. 246–266. Springer, Heidelberg (2010). https://doi.org/10.1007/978-3-642-11957-6_14

17. Dockins, R., Foltzer, A., Hendrix, J., Huffman, B., McNamee, D., Tomb, A.: Constructing semantic models of programs with the software analysis workbench. In: Blazy, S., Chechik, M. (eds.) VSTTE 2016. LNCS, vol. 9971, pp. 56–72. Springer, Cham (2016). https://doi.org/10.1007/978-3-319-48869-1_5

18. Ducas, L.: Accelerating Bliss: the geometry of ternary polynomials. Cryptology ePrint Archive, Report 2014/874 (2014). http://eprint.iacr.org/2014/874

19. Ducas, L., Durmus, A., Lepoint, T., Lyubashevsky, V.: Lattice signatures and bimodal Gaussians. In: Canetti, R., Garay, J.A. (eds.) CRYPTO 2013. LNCS, vol. 8042, pp. 40–56. Springer, Heidelberg (2013). https://doi.org/10.1007/978-3-642-40041-4_3

20. Fog, A.: Instruction tables: instruction latencies, throughputs and micro-operation breakdowns for Intel, AMD and VIA CPUs (2020). www.agner.org/optimize

21. Gentleman, W.M., Sande, G.: Fast Fourier transforms–for fun and profit. In: AFIPS 1966, pp. 563–578 (1966). https://doi.org/10.1145/1464291.1464352

22. Gopan, D., Reps, T., Sagiv, M.: A framework for numeric analysis of array operations. In: POPL, pp. 338–350. ACM (2005)

23. Granger, P.: Static analysis of arithmetical congruences. Int. J. Comput. Math. **30**, 165–190 (1989)

24. Gurfinkel, A., Kahsai, T., Komuravelli, A., Navas, J.A.: The SeaHorn verification framework. In: Kroening, D., Păsăreanu, C.S. (eds.) CAV 2015. LNCS, vol. 9206, pp. 343–361. Springer, Cham (2015). https://doi.org/10.1007/978-3-319-21690-4_20

25. Halbwachs, N., Péron, M.: Discovering properties about arrays in simple programs. In: PLDI, pp. 339–348. ACM (2008)

26. Harvey, D.: Faster arithmetic for number-theoretic transforms. J. Symb. Comput. **60**, 113–119 (2014). https://doi.org/10.1016/j.jsc.2013.09.002

27. Komuravelli, A., Gurfinkel, A., Chaki, S.: SMT-based model checking for recursive programs. Formal Methods Syst. Des. **48**(3), 175–205 (2016). https://doi.org/10.1007/s10703-016-0249-4

28. Lakhdar-Chaouch, L., Jeannet, B., Girault, A.: Widening with thresholds for programs with complex control graphs. In: Bultan, T., Hsiung, P.-A. (eds.) ATVA 2011. LNCS, vol. 6996, pp. 492–502. Springer, Heidelberg (2011). https://doi.org/10.1007/978-3-642-24372-1_38

29. Longa, P., Naehrig, M.: Speeding up the number theoretic transform for faster ideal lattice-based cryptography. In: Foresti, S., Persiano, G. (eds.) CANS 2016. LNCS, vol. 10052, pp. 124–139. Springer, Cham (2016). https://doi.org/10.1007/978-3-319-48965-0_8

30. Miné, A.: A new numerical abstract domain based on difference-bound matrices. In: Danvy, O., Filinski, A. (eds.) PADO 2001. LNCS, vol. 2053, pp. 155–172. Springer, Heidelberg (2001). https://doi.org/10.1007/3-540-44978-7_10

31. Miné, A.: The octagon abstract domain. High.-Order Symb. Comput. **19**(1), 31–100 (2006)

32. Montgomery, P.L.: Modular multiplication without trial division. Math. Comput. **44**(170), 519–521 (1985)

33. Pöppelmann, T., Güneysu, T.: Towards efficient arithmetic for lattice-based cryptography on reconfigurable hardware. In: Hevia, A., Neven, G. (eds.) LATIN-CRYPT 2012. LNCS, vol. 7533, pp. 139–158. Springer, Heidelberg (2012). https://doi.org/10.1007/978-3-642-33481-8_8

34. Pöppelmann, T., Oder, T., Güneysu, T.: High-performance ideal lattice-based cryptography on 8-bit ATxmega microcontrollers. In: Lauter, K., Rodríguez-Henríquez, F. (eds.) LATINCRYPT 2015. LNCS, vol. 9230, pp. 346–365. Springer, Cham (2015). https://doi.org/10.1007/978-3-319-22174-8_19
35. Roy, S.S., Vercauteren, F., Mentens, N., Chen, D.D., Verbauwhede, I.: Compact ring-LWE cryptoprocessor. In: Batina, L., Robshaw, M. (eds.) CHES 2014. LNCS, vol. 8731, pp. 371–391. Springer, Heidelberg (2014). https://doi.org/10.1007/978-3-662-44709-3_21
36. SeaHorn verification framework. https://github.com/seahorn/seahorn
37. Warren, H.S.: Hacker's Delight, 2nd edn. Addison-Wesley, Boston (2013)
38. Winkler, F.: Polynomial Algorithms in Computer Algebra. Texts and Monographs in Symbolic Computation. Springer, Heidelberg (1996). https://doi.org/10.1007/978-3-7091-6571-3

NSV 2020

Can We Avoid Rounding-Error Estimation in HPC Codes and Still Get Trustworthy Results?

Fabienne Jézéquel[1,2(✉)], Stef Graillat[1], Daichi Mukunoki[3], Toshiyuki Imamura[3], and Roman Iakymchuk[1,4]

[1] Sorbonne Université, CNRS, LIP6, Paris, France
{fabienne.jezequel,stef.graillat,roman.iakymchuk}@sorbonne-universite.fr
[2] Université Panthéon-Assas, Paris, France
[3] RIKEN Center for Computational Science, Kobe, Japan
{daichi.mukunoki,imamura.toshiyuki}@riken.jp
[4] Fraunhofer ITWM, Kaiserslautern, Germany

Abstract. Numerical validation enables one to ensure the reliability of numerical computations that rely on floating-point operations. Discrete Stochastic Arithmetic (DSA) makes it possible to validate the accuracy of floating-point computations using random rounding. However, it may bring a large performance overhead compared with the standard floating-point operations. In this article, we show that with perturbed data it is possible to use standard floating-point arithmetic instead of DSA for the purpose of numerical validation. For instance, for codes including matrix multiplications, we can directly utilize the matrix multiplication routine (GEMM) of level-3 BLAS that is performed with standard floating-point arithmetic. Consequently, we can achieve a significant performance improvement by avoiding the performance overhead of DSA operations as well as by exploiting the speed of highly-optimized BLAS implementations. Finally, we demonstrate the performance gain using Intel MKL routines compared against the DSA version of BLAS routines.

Keywords: BLAS · Discrete Stochastic Arithmetic (DSA) · Floating-point arithmetic · Numerical validation · Rounding errors

1 Introduction

Numerical simulations rely on finite precision arithmetic. This means that each elementary operation (like addition or multiplication) is potentially subject to rounding errors. The existence of rounding errors may cause a catastrophic consequence when meaningless results are computed owing to their accumulation, in particular in large-scale computation on supercomputers. In addition, there is a reproducibility issue: as floating-point computations are non-associative, different results may be computed even with the same code and the same input if the order of the computation is changed. As a consequence, it makes it difficult for us to

© Springer Nature Switzerland AG 2020
M. Christakis et al. (Eds.): NSV 2020/VSTTE 2020, LNCS 12549, pp. 163–177, 2020.
https://doi.org/10.1007/978-3-030-63618-0_10

distinguish bugs from rounding errors in software development. Therefore, we can see a strong motivation for analyzing the numerical quality of computed results. Moreover, the recent advances in mixed-precision techniques with precision reduction [3,12], which intend to achieve better speed as well as energy efficiency, assist the importance of understanding the effect of rounding errors.

Several approaches exist for addressing issues caused by rounding errors. Backward error analysis [13,21] provides error bounds on the computed solutions of linear problems. This approach is used for instance to verify the numerical quality of solutions of linear systems in linear algebra libraries and in particular in the LAPACK library [2]. Interval arithmetic [1,16], which briefly consists in performing floating-point operations on intervals instead of scalars, provides guaranteed error bounds on computed results. However, a naive application of interval arithmetic in a code may result in a gross overestimation of the errors. Therefore, interval arithmetic is usually used together with a special algorithm for each numerical method.

Numerical validation can also be performed with a probabilistic approach based on several executions of the program to control. While interval arithmetic ensures the number of correct digits, probabilistic methods estimate it. One of the advantages of the probabilistic approach is that it is applicable for any floating-point computations without any changes in the algorithms. This study focuses on a probabilistic method for numerical validation, discrete stochastic arithmetic (DSA), which estimates rounding errors using random rounding. DSA is implemented in the CADNA library [6,15], which can control the numerical quality of codes using half, single, double and/or quadruple precision, as well as in the SAM library [11], which can be used in arbitrary precision codes. Other tools rely on a probabilistic approach to control rounding errors: MCALIB [9], Verificarlo [5], and Verrou [10]. While DSA is a synchronous method and requires three executions of each operation, the other tools rely on an asynchronous approach which requires more executions (at least 50 for MCALIB). Another advantage of DSA is its ability to detect numerical instabilities during the execution.

In this article, we consider the common situation when the input data are affected by rounding and/or measurement errors. We address, at the same time, the problem of numerical quality of computed results, the performance overhead of existing numerical validation methods, as well as the development cost induced by their application to HPC codes. Thus, we respond to these three challenging issues with the following contributions.

- We study numerical validation in case of perturbed data in HPC codes on examples of key Basic Linear Algebra Subprograms (BLAS) routines. These routines often appear in HPC codes consuming significant part of their execution time.
- In case of perturbed data, we propose an alternative approach that uses the standard floating-point arithmetic, instead of DSA, to perform efficient computations and still obtain trustworthy results.
- This novel approach shows outstanding performance as well as simplifying performance optimization as we directly rely on existing user-implemented

codes or highly-optimized vendor-provided implementations. Hence, this approach is suitable for high-performance computations.

The remaining part of this paper is organized as follows. Section 2 introduces the principles of DSA and describes its implementations. Section 3 presents the error induced by perturbed data. Section 4 proposes the utilization of the standard floating-point arithmetic in numerical validation. Then, we demonstrate our approach on matrix-vector multiplication (GEMV) and matrix-matrix multiplication (GEMM) using Intel MKL compared against DSA with the reference BLAS code: Sect. 5 is devoted to the accuracy comparison, while Sect. 6 presents the performance evaluation. Section 7 discusses the pros and cons of the proposed approach. Finally, conclusions are given in Sect. 8.

2   Discrete Stochastic Arithmetic (DSA)

2.1   DSA in a Nutshell

The CESTAC method [19] enables one to estimate the rounding error propagation which occurs with floating-point arithmetic. This probabilistic method uses a random rounding mode: at each elementary operation, the result is rounded up (towards $+\infty$) or down (towards $-\infty$) with the probability of 50%. Hence, with this random rounding mode, the same program run several times provides different results. Therefore, the computer's deterministic arithmetic is replaced by a stochastic arithmetic, where each arithmetic operation is performed N times before the next one is executed. The CESTAC method supplies us with N samples $R_1, \ldots, R_N$ of the computed result R. The value of the computed result $\overline{R}$ is then chosen as the mean value of $\{R_i\}$ and, if no overflow occurs, its number of correct digits (*i.e.* its number of digits not affected by rounding errors) can be estimated [4, 19] as

$$C_R = \log_{10}\left(\frac{\sqrt{N}\,|\overline{R}|}{\sigma\tau_\beta}\right) \text{ with } \overline{R} = \frac{1}{N}\sum_{i=1}^{N} R_i, \ \sigma^2 = \frac{1}{N-1}\sum_{i=1}^{N}\left(R_i - \overline{R}\right)^2. \quad (1)$$

τ_β is the value of Student's distribution for $N - 1$ degrees of freedom and a confidence level $1 - \beta$. In practice, $\beta = 5\%$ and $N = 3$. Therefore the number of correct digits is estimated within a $1 - \beta = 95\%$ confidence interval. It has been shown [4, 19] that $N = 3$ is in some reasonable sense the optimal sample size. The estimation with $N = 3$ is more reliable than with $N = 2$ and increasing N does not significantly improve the quality of the estimation.

If both operands in a multiplication or the divisor in a division have no correct digits, the validity of C_R is compromised [4]. Therefore, the CESTAC method requires, during the execution of the user code, a dynamical control of multiplications and divisions, which is a so-called *self-validation* of the method. In order to estimate the accuracy of such operands, the method is implemented in a synchronous way: the N values R_i are computed simultaneously. This self-validation has also led to the concept of *computational zero* [18]. A computed result is a computational zero, denoted by @.0, if $\forall i, R_i = 0$ or $C_R \leq 0$. This means that a computational zero is either a mathematical zero or a number without any significance, *i.e.* numerical noise. Relational operators that take into account rounding errors have been defined as follows and called *discrete stochastic relations* [4]. Let $X = (X_1, \ldots, X_N)$ and $Y = (Y_1, \ldots, Y_N)$ be two results computed using the CESTAC method,

$$X = Y \text{ if and only if } X - Y = @.0;$$
$$X > Y \text{ if and only if } \overline{X} > \overline{Y} \text{ and } X - Y \neq @.0;$$
$$X \geq Y \text{ if and only if } \overline{X} \geq \overline{Y} \text{ or } X - Y = @.0.$$

Discrete Stochastic Arithmetic (DSA) [19,20] is the joint use of the CESTAC method, the concept of computational zero, and the discrete stochastic relations.

2.2   The CADNA Library

CADNA[1] [6,15] is a library which implements DSA in C, C++, or Fortran codes. Thus, classic floating-point variables are replaced by the corresponding stochastic variables, which are composed of three floating-point values and an integer to store the accuracy. The library contains the definition of all arithmetic operations and order relations for the stochastic types. The rounding error that affects any stochastic variable can be estimated with the probability of 95%. Only the correct digits of a stochastic variable are printed, or "@.0" for numerical noise. Because all operators are redefined for stochastic variables, CADNA requires only a few modifications in a program: essentially in the declarations of variables and in input/output statements.

During the execution of the user code, CADNA can detect numerical instabilities. Such instabilities can occur for instance if a mathematical function or a branching statement involves numerical noise. A numerical instability is also reported in the case of a cancellation, *i.e.* the subtraction of two very close values which generates a sudden loss of accuracy. When numerical instabilities are detected, dedicated CADNA counters are incremented. At the end of the run, the value of these counters together with appropriate warning messages are printed. Because of the composition of stochastic variables, CADNA requires 4x memory storage compared to the original code. Its cost in execution time depends on the code to control and on the instability detection level chosen by the user. If self-validation of DSA is activated, arithmetic compute- and memory-bound benchmarks described in [6] run about 10 times slower with CADNA.

3   Error Induced by Perturbed Data

In the sequel, we assume to work with a binary floating-point arithmetic adhering to IEEE 754 floating-point standard [14]. The relative rounding error unit

---

[1] http://cadna.lip6.fr.

is denoted by **u**. For the IEEE 754 *binary64* format (hereafter referred to as "double-precision"), we have $\mathbf{u} = 2^{-53}$ and for the *binary32* format (hereafter referred to as "single-precision") $\mathbf{u} = 2^{-24}$.

Let us consider a function f and let us denote by x its input data. Let $y = f(x)$. Let us denote by $\widehat{f}$ the numerical evaluation of f on a computer. Usually, $\widehat{f} \neq f$ because of the finite precision of the computer arithmetic. Therefore, the computed result is often not y, but $\widehat{y} = \widehat{f}(x)$. The forward error is the difference between the exact solution y and the computed solution $\widehat{y}$.

The backward analysis tries to seek for Δx such that $\widehat{y} = f(x + \Delta x)$. The quantity Δx is said to be the backward error associated with $\widehat{y}$. It measures the distance between the problem that is solved and the initial problem.

Let us denote by C the condition number of the problem. It is defined as

$$C := \lim_{\varepsilon \to 0^+} \sup_{|\Delta x| \leq \varepsilon} \left[\frac{|f(x + \Delta x) - f(x)|}{|f(x)|} \bigg/ \frac{|\Delta x|}{|x|} \right]. \tag{2}$$

If the algorithm is backward-stable (*i.e.* the backward error is of the order of the rounding unit **u**) then one has the following *rule of thumb* [13],

$$|f(x) - \widehat{f}(x)|/|f(x)| \lesssim C\mathbf{u}. \tag{3}$$

If the input data is perturbed, *i.e.* the input data is not x but $\widehat{x} = x(1 + \delta)$, then, by definition of the condition number (2), one computes $\widehat{f}(\widehat{x})$ with

$$|f(x) - \widehat{f}(\widehat{x})|/|f(x)| \lesssim C(\mathbf{u} + |\delta|). \tag{4}$$

If $|\delta| \gg \mathbf{u}$, then $C|\delta| \gg C\mathbf{u}$. In this case, the rounding error generated by $\widehat{f}$ is negligible w.r.t. $C|\delta|$.

4   Combining DSA and Standard Floating-Point Arithmetic

In this section we show how numerical validation can be performed if standard floating-point arithmetic is used instead of DSA operations. For the sake of simplicity, in the sequel, we consider a BLAS routine that is executed in a code controlled using DSA. However, the approach described here is the same if several computation routines are used continuously. We assume that the BLAS routine is executed with input data affected by rounding errors and/or by measurement errors. We compare the results provided by the CADNA routine and its classic floating-point version.

Let us denote by D the input data of the BLAS routine. Note that BLAS is divided into three levels: BLAS-1 for scalar-vector and vector-vector operations; BLAS-2 for matrix-vector computations; BLAS-3 for matrix operations. Thus, D can correspond to a few arrays: a few vectors for BLAS-1 routines; a matrix and a few vectors for BLAS-2; a few matrices for BLAS-3. Because the code uses the CADNA library, D is composed of stochastic variables: each array element of D is a triplet. Let us assume that the result of the BLAS routine is an array: a matrix in the case of a matrix multiplication; a vector in the case of a matrix-vector multiplication or scalar-/ and vector-vector operations. We describe, first, the case when a CADNA routine is used, then our approach which consists in replacing a call to the CADNA routine by three calls to a classic BLAS routine:

Fig. 1. Execution flow with a call to CADNA routines.

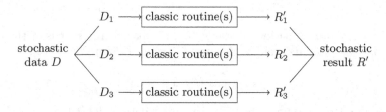

Fig. 2. Execution flow with three calls to classic BLAS routines.

– On the one hand, the CADNA version of the BLAS routine is executed: every arithmetic operation is performed three times with the random rounding mode. The result R is a stochastic array. The associated execution flow is represented in Fig. 1 in the general case when one CADNA routine is used or several CADNA routines are executed continuously.

– On the other hand, three input data D_1, D_2, D_3 are created from the triplets of the stochastic data D. Indeed each array element D^i is a triplet (D_1^i, D_2^i, D_3^i). This is followed by three executions of a classic BLAS routine (a user or a vendor implementation) providing three results R'_1, R'_2, R'_3, each of them being a classic floating-point array. A stochastic array R' is created from these three arrays R'_1, R'_2, R'_3: each array element R'^i is a triplet $(R_1'^i, R_2'^i, R_3'^i)$. This array R' can be used in the CADNA routines in the next parts of the code. Figure 2 illustrates the associated execution flow. In this approach, we can clearly benefit from highly-optimized vendor routines to speed up the entire DSA process.

Section 5 compares the accuracy of R and R', while Sect. 6 presents the performance comparison between the CADNA and pure BLAS routines. The C++ codes developed for our experiments are available[2].

---

[2] http://www.lip6.fr/Fabienne.Jezequel/ARTICLES/CODES_NSV2020.tar.gz.

5 Accuracy Comparison

5.1 Experimental Setup

In this section, we compare the accuracy of results provided by the CADNA version and the classic version of BLAS routines for matrix (xGEMM) and matrix-vector (xGEMV) multiplications. The numerical experiments have been carried out with stochastic data randomly generated between -10^E and $+10^E$, where the choice of E depends on the test case. In the experiments described in Sects. 5.2 and 5.3, E is set to 20 (resp. 3) if computations are carried out in double-precision (resp. single-precision). Each stochastic value $x = \{x_i\}$ $(i = 1, 2, 3)$ is initialized as $x_1 = x_2 = x_3 = \alpha 10^e$, where α is a random variable uniformly distributed between -1 and 1 and e is an integer randomly generated in $\{0, \ldots, E\}$. This initialization ensures the generation of data with different orders of magnitude.

Table 1. Accuracy comparison of matrix multiplication.

	(a) Double-precision					(b) Single-precision			
δ	accuracy of R		accuracy difference between R and R'		δ	accuracy of R		accuracy difference between R and R'	
	mean	min-max	mean	max		mean	min-max	mean	max
1.e-14	13.9	9-15	2.5e-2	2	1.e-6	5.6	1-7	2.3e-1	2
1.e-13	12.8	8-15	5.8e-3	1	1.e-5	4.8	0-7	1.9e-2	2
1.e-12	11.9	7-14	4.2e-4	1	1.e-4	3.7	0-6	2.8e-3	1
1.e-11	10.9	6-13	2.4e-5	1	1.e-3	2.8	0-5	2.8e-4	1

We assume that the input data is affected by measurement errors and/or rounding errors due to previous computation. To simulate such errors, we use the *data_st* CADNA function that enables one to perturb a stochastic value with a relative or an absolute error set by the user. In this paper, according to the chosen error δ, each stochastic value $x = \{x_i\}$ $(i = 1, 2, 3)$ is perturbed following this equation:

$$\widehat{x}_i = x_i(1 + \beta_i \delta) \text{ for } i = 1, 2 \text{ and } \widehat{x}_3 = x_3, \tag{5}$$

where β_i is a random variable uniformly distributed between -1 and 1.

5.2 Matrix Multiplication

We present here results obtained with the multiplication of square matrices of size $n = 500$. In accordance with Sect. 4, we denote by R the stochastic matrix computed with the CADNA routine and by R' the stochastic matrix built from the three matrices computed with the classic floating-point routine. In both cases, the accuracy of each element of the resulting matrix is estimated by CADNA according to Eq. 1. For $i = 1, \ldots, n^2$, CADNA computes the number of correct digits C_{R^i} (resp. $C_{R'^i}$) in the element R^i (resp. R'^i) of the array R (resp. R'). As a remark, superscripts are used here to avoid confusion with the triplet composing a stochastic variable. Table 1 reports:

- the relative data perturbation δ;
- the mean value, the minimum and the maximum of the accuracy of the n^2 results that are computed by the CADNA routine;
- the mean value and the maximum of the difference between the accuracy of the results obtained with the CADNA routine and the accuracy of those computed with the classic routine. For $i = 1, \ldots, n^2$, this difference Δ^i is evaluated as $\Delta^i = |C_{R^i} - C_{R'^i}|$.

It has been observed that the minimum and the maximum accuracy are the same with both approaches. Table 1(a) presents results computed in double-precision with data randomly generated between -10^{20} and 10^{20}, while Table 1(b) shows results computed in single-precision with data randomly generated between -10^3 and 10^3. We recall that the best possible accuracy is 15 digits in double-precision and 7 digits in single-precision.

Table 2. Accuracy comparison of matrix-vector multiplication.

	(a) Double-precision						(b) Single-precision			
δ	accuracy of R		accuracy difference between R and R'			δ	accuracy of R		accuracy difference between R and R'	
	mean	min-max	mean	max			mean	min-max	mean	max
1.e-14	13.9	12-15	4.6e-2	1		1.e-6	5.5	3-7	3.2e-1	2
1.e-13	12.7	11-14	7.0e-3	1		1.e-5	4.8	2-6	2.4e-2	1
1.e-12	11.8	10-13	0	0		1.e-4	3.7	1-5	7.0e-3	1
1.e-11	10.9	9-12	0	0		1.e-3	2.8	0-4	1.0e-3	1

As the order of magnitude of the perturbation δ increases, the mean accuracy decreases by 1 digit. A low difference can be observed between the accuracy of the results obtained with the CADNA routine and the accuracy of those computed with the classic routine. The order of magnitude of the mean value of this difference decreases as the order of magnitude of δ increases. If the perturbation is sufficiently high (10^{-13} in double-precision, 10^{-4} in single-precision), maximum accuracy difference is 1 digit. As expected, a high perturbation in single-precision induces a low accuracy on the results: if $\delta = 10^{-3}$ the mean accuracy is less than 3 digits.

5.3 Matrix-Vector Multiplication

The same accuracy comparison as in Sect. 5.2 is performed for the multiplication of a square matrix of size 1000 with a vector. On the one hand, the matrix-vector multiplication is performed with a CADNA routine. On the other hand, it is performed three times with a classic routine. Like in Sect. 5.2, the minimum and the maximum accuracy are the same with both approaches. Table 2(a) presents results computed in double-precision with data randomly generated between

-10^{20} and 10^{20}, while Table 2(b) represents results computed in single-precision with data randomly generated between -10^3 and 10^3.

Like in Sect. 5.2, as the order of magnitude of δ increases, the mean accuracy decreases by 1 digit. The mean value of the accuracy difference remains low and it decreases as the perturbation δ increases: in double-precision, all the results have the same accuracy if δ is greater than or equal to 10^{-12}. Like in Sect. 5.2, in single precision a high perturbation results in a poor accuracy.

6   Performance Comparison

6.1   Experimental Setup

The run times of the execution flows described in Figs. 1 and 2 are compared for different matrix sizes. Section 6.2 presents the performance obtained for matrix multiplication and Sect. 6.3 for matrix-vector multiplication. In both sections, we compare the execution time of a code using CADNA with that of various implementations of our proposed approach: they perform three matrix or matrix-vector multiplications and array copies. We analyze the performance of:

- "CADNA": a sequential code that performs with CADNA a naive matrix or matrix-vector multiplication;
- "naive seq": a sequential code that implements our approach (described in Fig. 2) using the same naive algorithm with classic floating-point arithmetic;
- "naive OMP": an implementation of our proposed approach that relies on a naive algorithm with classic floating-point arithmetic parallelized using OpenMP;
- "MKL seq": an implementation of our proposed approach using a sequential MKL BLAS routine;
- "MKL OMP": an implementation of our proposed approach that relies on a parallel MKL BLAS routine, which underneath uses OpenMP.

By "naive algorithm", we mean a non-optimized algorithm based on nested loops. In naive OMP and MKL OMP, the array copies are also parallelized using OpenMP, but they are not parallelized in the other cases. In this section, we present the execution times of double-precision codes. As a remark, the same trends are observed in single-precision. However, as mentioned in Sect. 5, single-precision may not be suitable for computation with perturbed data because they induce low accuracy results.

Except with the CADNA routine, array copies are required to split the stochastic data into three classic floating-point data, and then to merge the three classic floating-point resulting arrays into a stochastic array, as shown in Fig. 2. In our evaluations, to point out the array copy cost w.r.t. the BLAS routine execution time, those array copies are performed before and after the BLAS routine execution. This is the worst case that maximizes the array copy cost in the total execution time. However, if standard floating-point operations (or classic BLAS routines) are continuously used, those array copies are required only before and after them. As the stochastic type in double-precision is a structure consisting of three 64-bit floating-point values and two 32-bit integer values (one for storing the accuracy and one for memory alignment), it has 4 times memory footprint than the standard 64-bit floating-point operation. The array copy corresponds to the conversion between array-of-structures (the stochastic type) and structure-of-arrays (three standard floating-point values).

The evaluation environment is as follows. The platform for performance measurements is an Intel Core i7-8650U processor clocked at 1.9 GHz with 4 cores, 8 MB cache. The operating system is Linux Ubuntu 18.04.4. The codes are compiled with gcc version 8.3.0 and optimized with the `-O3` flag. We use the `-frounding-math` option to disable transformations and optimizations that assume default floating-point rounding behavior. The MKL version is 2019.5.281. The CADNA version is cadnac-3.1.5 and for performance evaluation, instability detection is deactivated. In parallel codes that rely on OpenMP, the number of threads is set to 4.

6.2 Matrix Multiplication (Compute-Bound)

Figure 3 presents the execution time of the different implementations as previously described. A log scale is used for the y-axis to improve the readability of the obtained results. Figure 3 also shows the time spent in matrix multiplications and in array copies if the matrix size is 2000. We can observe that despite the memory copies the codes using three classic matrix multiplications perform better than the CADNA routine. Most of their total execution time is spent in matrix multiplications.

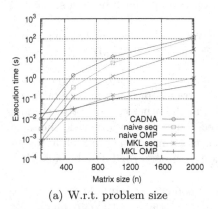
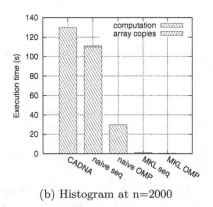

(a) W.r.t. problem size   (b) Histogram at n=2000

Fig. 3. Execution time including matrix multiplications and array copies.

The performance ratio between the CADNA routine and the sequential code that performs three naive matrix multiplications ("naive seq") decreases from 4 to 1.2 as the matrix size increases from 100 to 2000. The performance ratio can be explained by the following two differences. First, the CADNA routine performs the random rounding at each operation. Second, the CADNA routine accesses the matrix values from a structure, that is indirect memory access.

Table 3. Execution time (in seconds) of CADNA and the proposed method with MKL OMP on a matrix multiplication.

	(a) Core i7-8650U (1.9 GHz, 4 cores), n=2000				(b) Dual-socket Xeon Gold 6126 (2.6 GHz, 12 cores×2), n=5000		
	CADNA	Proposed w/ MKL OMP	Speedup		CADNA	Proposed w/ MKL OMP	Speedup
Comp	130	0.393	331x	Comp	2520	0.563	4476x
Copy	–	0.0495	–	Copy	–	0.0889	–
Total	130	0.4425	294x	Total	2520	0.652	3865x

As expected, the OpenMP naive matrix multiplication provides better performance than the sequential one. The MKL sequential matrix multiplication performs even better. From a certain matrix size, the MKL parallel implementation using OpenMP outperforms all the other codes. In particular, if the matrix size is 2000, we can notice a performance ratio of 294 between the CADNA routine and the MKL OMP code that performs three matrix multiplications using OpenMP and array copies. Table 3 summarizes the speedup against CADNA with our proposed method with MKL OMP. Herein, we also show another result with n = 5000 on 24 cores with dual-socket Intel Xeon Gold 6126 (2.6 GHz with 12 cores) with the MKL library 2019.1.144 (the codes were compiled with Intel icpc 19.0.1.144). This table shows that the performance gain increases on large scale and that the array copy cost becomes visible against the computation cost, in particular on many-cores that can efficiently perform the computation.

6.3   Matrix-Vector Multiplication (Memory-Bound)

Figure 4 shows the execution time of the different implementations as previously described. It can be observed that the matrix-vector multiplication with CADNA performs better than the sequential codes which execute three floating-point matrix-vector multiplications and array copies. In the sequential codes that use classic floating-point arithmetic the main part of the execution time is spent in array copies. If we consider computation time only, the performance ratio between the CADNA routine and the code that performs three sequential matrix-vector multiplications decreases from 4 to 3 as the matrix size increases from 100 to 10000. Like for matrix multiplication, accessing values from a structure is more costful, especially for small problems. From a certain matrix size, thanks to the parallel array copies, the OpenMP codes that use classic floating-point arithmetic perform better than the CADNA code.

As a remark, we note that the array copy cost shown in this example is the worst case, which is the situation when classic GEMV routines are used only once

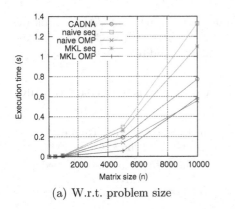
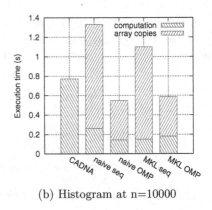

(a) W.r.t. problem size   (b) Histogram at n=10000

Fig. 4. Execution time including matrix-vector multiplications and array copies.

and the ratio between the memory reference in one array copy and that in the routine is approximately 1. In this case, three matrix copies are performed before and after the classic GEMV executions. If standard floating-point operations (or classic BLAS routines) are continuously used, the array copy cost arises only before and after them.

7   Discussion: Pros and Cons of the Proposed Approach

7.1   Pros: Performance and Applicability

The proposed approach includes two performance advantages and one regarding the applicability as follows.

- The performance gain by avoiding DSA operations. On compute-bound operations, the overhead caused by random rounding may be eliminated. On memory-bound operations, in the cases we can ignore the array copy cost (*i.e.* when we use classic routines continuously), the overhead of CADNA is reduced by a factor of 3.
- The possible performance gain by directly relying on existing optimized codes. The demonstration on matrix-multiplication in Sect. 6.2 is a typical example that gains high-performance from a vendor optimized library.
- Avoiding the translation of an existing code to the CADNA version for numerical validation. Previously, when the target code included some portions where CADNA could not be applied (for example, relying on external libraries or including some intrinsic instructions for optimization), we needed to prepare an alternative code.

Those advantages can be more pronounced on many-core processors. While CADNA supports OpenMP, the performance overhead can be larger than single-thread due to the existence of some private sections [8]. CADNA for CUDA is also available, but it is observed that the overhead (especially on compute-bound operations) becomes higher than that on CPUs [7].

7.2   Cons: Instability Detection and Accuracy

Instability Detection. With perturbed data, if a CADNA routine is replaced by three calls to a classic routine, the result accuracy can still be correctly estimated by CADNA. In particular, the user can be informed that the result is numerical noise (*i.e.* no correct digit). However, numerical instabilities are not detected if a classic floating-point routine is used instead of a CADNA routine.

As an example, we consider the multiplication in double-precision of two matrices A and B of size 10. The first row of A is $[1, 1, 1, 1, 1, -1, -1, -1, -1, -1]$: its first half is set to 1, while the second half is -1. The other lines of A are randomly generated between -10^{20} and 10^{20}, as described in Sect. 5.1. All the elements of the matrix B are set to 1. Then A and B are perturbed with a relative error $\delta = 10^{-12}$. We denote by C the matrix product obtained using CADNA and by C' the matrix product computed by three calls to a classic routine according to the execution flow described in Fig. 2. In both resulting matrices, each element of the first line is numerical noise and can be displayed by CADNA as "@.0". Let us focus on the first element of C and C'. The associated triplets are:

$$C_{1,1} = \{\text{-1.1590728377086634e-13},$$
$$+4.9227288911879442\text{e-13},$$
$$+0.0000000000000000\text{e+00}\},$$

$$C'_{1,1} = \{\text{-1.1790568521589528e-13},$$
$$+4.9327208984079348\text{e-13},$$
$$+0.0000000000000000\text{e+00}\}.$$

Each triplet is composed of values that have no common digit. The differences between $C_{1,1}$ and $C'_{1,1}$ are due to the random rounding mode of CADNA. One advantage of the CADNA routine is the instability detection. Here, the user is informed that 10 catastrophic cancellations occurred (*i.e.* subtractions of close values affected by rounding errors).

Accuracy Improvement. CADNA may improve the accuracy of results thanks to the detection of numerical noise. Such improvement is not possible if a CADNA routine is replaced by three calls to a classic routine. As an example, let us consider the linear system $Ax = b$ with

$$A = \begin{pmatrix} 21 & 130 & 0 & 2.1 \\ 13 & 80 & 4.74\ 10^8 & 752 \\ 0 & -0.4 & 3.9816\ 10^8 & 4.2 \\ 0 & 0 & 1.7 & 9\ 10^{-9} \end{pmatrix}, \quad b = \begin{pmatrix} 153.1 \\ 849.74 \\ 7.7816 \\ 2.6\ 10^{-8} \end{pmatrix}.$$

Its exact solution is $x_{exact} = (1, 1, 10^{-8}, 1)^T$.

A and b are perturbed with a relative error $\delta = 10^{-6}$. Then the linear system is solved using Gaussian elimination with partial pivoting. The result x obtained using CADNA and the result x' computed by three calls to a classic routine are displayed by CADNA as:

$$x = \begin{pmatrix} 0.100\text{E}+001 \\ 0.999\text{E}+000 \\ 0.999999\text{E}-008 \\ 0.999999\text{E}+000 \end{pmatrix} \quad \text{and} \quad x' = \begin{pmatrix} @.0 \\ @.0 \\ @.0 \\ 0.999999\text{E}+000 \end{pmatrix}.$$

The numerical quality of the first three elements of x is rather satisfactory, whereas these elements are numerical noise in x'. Pivoting implies to choose at several steps of Gaussian elimination a suitable value for the pivot that will be used in subsequent computation. Among several matrix elements, the one having the greatest absolute value is selected with a test such as: if ($|A_{i,j}| > p_{max}$). During the Gaussian elimination, a matrix element is numerical noise: it has no correct digits. With CADNA this non-significant element in A is not chosen as a pivot. Without CADNA, this element cannot be detected as non-significant. As its absolute value is high, it is chosen as a pivot and numerical noise is propagated in subsequent computation. With CADNA, the following list of three numerical instabilities is provided:

```
1 UNSTABLE BRANCHING(S)
1 UNSTABLE INTRINSIC FUNCTION(S)
1 LOSS(ES) OF ACCURACY DUE TO CANCELLATION(S)
```

A catastrophic cancellation occurred and generated a non-significant element used as an argument in the absolute value function. This numerical noise also caused an unstable test for the pivot selection.

8   Conclusion

This paper proposed an alternative approach for numerical validation on perturbed data, which can rely on the standard floating-point arithmetic instead of DSA operations. If the input data includes a perturbation with an order of magnitude greater than the relative rounding error unit, we can replace the DSA operations, which execute each floating-point operation three times with random rounding, by three executions with the standard floating-point arithmetic. It brings almost no accuracy difference in the results. This proposed approach contributes a significant performance improvement, in particular on compute-bound operations on many-core processors as it can directly rely on existing user-implemented codes or even highly-optimized vendor libraries. On the other hand, we lose the instability detection and the possibility of accuracy improvement, which were available on the DSA implementation CADNA. The same conclusions would be valid with a parallel code using MPI for communication. CADNA enables one to control the numerical quality of HPC codes that rely on MPI [17]. If in such a code computation-intensive routines are executed with perturbed data, the CADNA-MPI routines can be replaced by optimized floating-point MPI routines. Because the experiments presented in this article use synthetic input data, as a perspective we plan to apply our approach to real-life examples with realistic data sets.

Acknowledgements. This research was partially supported by the European Union's Horizon 2020 research, innovation programme under the Marie Skłodowska-Curie grant agreement via the Robust project No. 842528 and the Japan Society for the Promotion of Science (JSPS) KAKENHI Grant No. 19K20286.

References

1. Alefeld, G., Herzberger, J.: Introduction to Interval Analysis. Academic Press, Cambridge (1983)
2. Anderson, E., et al.: LAPACK Users' Guide, 3rd edn. SIAM, Philadelphia (1999)
3. Carson, E., Higham, N.J.: Accelerating the solution of linear systems by iterative refinement in three precisions. SIAM J. Sci. Comput. **40**(2), A817–A847 (2018)
4. Chesneaux, J.M., Vignes, J.: Les fondements de l'arithmétique stochastique. Comptes Rendus de l'Académie des Sciences - Series I - Mathematics **315**, 1435–1440 (1992)
5. Denis, C., de Oliveira Castro, P., Petit, E.: Verificarlo: checking floating point accuracy through Monte Carlo Arithmetic. In: ARITH'23, Silicon Valley, USA (2016)
6. Eberhart, P., Brajard, J., Fortin, P., Jézéquel, F.: High performance numerical validation using stochastic arithmetic. Reliable Comput. **21**, 35–52 (2015)
7. Eberhart, P., Landreau, B., Brajard, J., Fortin, P., Jézéquel, F.: Improving CADNA performance on GPUs. In: IPDPSW, Vancouver, Canada, pp. 1016–1025 (2018)
8. Eberhart, P., Brajard, J., Fortin, P., Jézéquel, F.: Estimation of round-off errors in OpenMP codes. In: Maruyama, N., de Supinski, B.R., Wahib, M. (eds.) IWOMP 2016. LNCS, vol. 9903, pp. 3–16. Springer, Cham (2016). https://doi.org/10.1007/978-3-319-45550-1_1
9. Frechtling, M., Leong, P.H.W.: MCALIB: measuring sensitivity to rounding error with Monte Carlo programming. ACM TOPLAS **37**(2), 1–25 (2015)
10. Févotte, F., Lathuilière, B.: Debugging and optimization of HPC programs in mixed precision with the Verrou tool. In: CRE at SC 2018, Dallas, USA (2018)
11. Graillat, S., Jézéquel, F., Wang, S., Zhu, Y.: Stochastic arithmetic in multiprecision. Math. Comput. Sci. **5**(4), 359–375 (2011)
12. Haidar, A., et al.: The design of fast and energy-efficient linear solvers: on the potential of half-precision arithmetic and iterative refinement techniques. In: Shi, Y., et al. (eds.) ICCS 2018. LNCS, vol. 10860, pp. 586–600. Springer, Cham (2018). https://doi.org/10.1007/978-3-319-93698-7_45
13. Higham, N.: Accuracy and Stability of Numerical Algorithms, 2nd edn. SIAM, Philadelphia (2002)
14. IEEE Computer Society: IEEE Standard for Floating-Point Arithmetic. IEEE Standard 754-2008 (2008)
15. Jézéquel, F., Chesneaux, J.M.: CADNA: a library for estimating round-off error propagation. Elsevier CPC **178**(12), 933–955 (2008)
16. Kulisch, U.: Advanced Arithmetic for the Digital Computer. Springer, Wien (2002). https://doi.org/10.1007/978-3-7091-0525-2
17. Montan, S., Denis, C.: Numerical verification of industrial numerical codes. In: ESAIM: Proceedings, vol. 35, pp. 107–113 (2012)
18. Vignes, J.: Zéro mathématique et zéro informatique. Comptes Rendus de l'Académie des Sciences - Series I - Mathematics **303**, 997–1000 (1986)
19. Vignes, J.: A stochastic arithmetic for reliable scientific computation. Math. Comput. Simul. **35**(3), 233–261 (1993)
20. Vignes, J.: Discrete Stochastic Arithmetic for validating results of numerical software. Numer. Algorithms **37**(1–4), 377–390 (2004)
21. Wilkinson, J.H.: Rounding Errors in Algebraic Processes, vol. 32. HMSO, Richmond (1963)

An Efficient Floating-Point Bit-Blasting API for Verifying C Programs

Mikhail R. Gadelha[1]($\boxtimes$) (iD), Lucas C. Cordeiro[2](iD), and Denis A. Nicole[3]

[1] SIDIA Instituto de Ciência e Tecnologia, Manaus, Brazil
`mikhail.gadelha@sidia.com`
[2] University of Manchester, Manchester, UK
`lucas.cordeiro@manchester.ac.uk`
[3] University of Southampton, Southampton, UK
`dan@ecs.soton.ac.uk`

Abstract. We describe a new SMT bit-blasting API for floating-point (FP) programs and evaluate it using different off-the-shelf SMT solvers during the verification of several C programs. The new FP API is part of the SMT backend in ESBMC, a state-of-the-art bounded model checker for C and C++. For the evaluation, we compared our FP API against the native FP APIs in Z3 and MathSAT. We show that Boolector, when using our new FP API, outperforms the solvers with native support for FP, correctly verifying more programs in less time. Experimental results also show that our FP API implemented in ESBMC is on par with other state-of-the-art software verifiers. Furthermore, when verifying programs with FP arithmetic, our new FP API produced no wrong answers.

Keywords: Floating-point arithmetic · Satisfiability modulo theories · Software verification

1 Introduction

Many software verification tools operate by converting their input (e.g., a program source code) into a format understandable by an automated theorem prover, encoding high-level program properties (e.g., arithmetic overflow) and algorithms (e.g., bounded model checking) into low-level equations (e.g., SMT). The encoding process of a program usually involves several intermediate steps, designed to generate a formula that can be efficiently solved by the theorem provers. In this domain, the analysis of programs with floating-point arithmetic has received much attention, primarily when safety depends on the correctness of these programs. Due to, in essence, an exception thrown by an invalid floating-point conversion, the Ariane 5 rocket exploded mid-air in 1996 [38]. Floating point verification is a complex problem because the semantics may change beyond code level, including the optimization performed by compilers [42].

There exist various static analysis tools that are able to examine floating-point computations [7,8,19,20,27,50,54]. For example, Astrée is a static analysis

© Springer Nature Switzerland AG 2020
M. Christakis et al. (Eds.): NSV 2020/VSTTE 2020, LNCS 12549, pp. 178–195, 2020.
https://doi.org/10.1007/978-3-030-63618-0_11

tool that considers all possible rounding errors when verifying C programs with floating-point numbers [7]. It has been applied to verify embedded software in flight controllers by Airbus. CBMC [19] is also another notable example of a software model checking tool, which implements a bit-precise decision procedure for the theory of floating-point arithmetic [9]. It has been applied to verify industrial applications from the automotive industry, which rely on floating-point reasoning [53]. CBMC is also the main verification engine employed by other software verifiers that efficiently verify C programs with floating-point numbers such as PeSCo [51] and VeriAbs [17]. To our knowledge, there exists no other study that shows a thorough comparative evaluation of software verifiers and SMT solvers concerning the verification of C programs that contain floating-points.

Here we present the new floating-point technology developed in one bounded model checker, ESBMC [28], and evaluate it using a large set of floating-point benchmarks [5]. In particular, we evaluate a new floating-point API on top of our SMT backend that extends the floating-point feature to all solvers supported by ESBMC (including Boolector [12] and Yices [24] that currently do not support the SMT FP logic [11]). For evaluation, we used the benchmarks of the 2020 International Competition on Software Verification (SV-COMP) [5], from the floating-point sub-category. The five different solvers supported by ESBMC were evaluated (Z3 [23], Yices [24], Boolector [12], MathSAT [18], and CVC4 [3]) and ESBMC is able to evaluate more benchmarks within the usual time and memory limits (15 min and 15 GB, respectively) when using Boolector. In particular, results show that Boolector can solve more floating-point problems using the new floating-point API than MathSAT or Z3, which have native floating-point APIs. Our experimental results also show that our floating-point API implemented in ESBMC is competitive to other state-of-the-art software verifiers, including CBMC [19], PeSCo [51], and VeriAbs [17].

2   Floating-Point Arithmetic

The manipulation of real values in programs is a necessity in many fields, e.g., scientific programming [42]. The set of real numbers, however, is uncountable, and some numbers cannot be represented with finite precision, e.g., irrational numbers. Over the years, computer manufacturers have experimented with different machine representations for real numbers [31]. The two fundamental ways to encode a real number are the fixed-point representation, and the floating-point representation, in particular, the IEEE floating-point standard (IEEE 754-2008 [34]), which has been formally accepted by many processors [32].

Each encoding can represent a range of real numbers depending on the word-length and how the bits are distributed. A fixed-point representation of a number usually consists of an integer component, a fractional component, using a 2-complement encoding. In contrast, the floating-point representation consists of an exponent component, a significand component, and a bit for the sign. Floating-point has a higher dynamic range than fixed-point (e.g., a float in C has 24 bits of precision, but can have values up to 2^{128}), while fixed-point can have higher precision than floating-point [46]. Furthermore, the IEEE floating-point standard defines values that have no equivalent in a fixed-point or real encoding, e.g., positive and negative infinities. IEEE floating-points are of the following kinds: *zeroes, NaNs, infinities, normal, denormal (or subnormal)* [34].

Definition 1 *(Infinities). Both +inf and -inf are defined in the standard. These floating-points represent overflows or the result of non-zero floating-point divisions by zero (Annex F of the C language specification [35]).*

Definition 2 *(Zeroes). Both +0 and -0 are defined in the standard. Most of the operations will behave identically when presented with +0 or -0 except when extracting the sign bit or dividing by zero (usual rules about signedness apply and will result in either +inf or -inf). Equalities will even be evaluated to true when comparing positive against negative zeroes.*

Definition 3 *(NaNs). The **N**ot **a** **N**umber special values represent undefined or unrepresentable values, e.g., $\sqrt{-1}$ or 0.f/0.f. As a safety measure, most of the operations will return NaN if at least one operator is NaN, as a way to indicate that the computation is invalid. NaNs are not comparable: except for the not equal operator (!=), all other comparisons will evaluate to false (even comparing a NaN against itself). Furthermore, casting NaNs to integers is undefined behavior.*

Definition 4 *(Normal). A non-zero floating-point that can be represented within the range supported by the encoding.*

Definition 5 *(Denormal (or subnormal)). A non-zero floating-point representing values very close to zero, filling the gap between what can be usually represented by the encoding and zero.*

The IEEE standard also defines five kinds of exceptions: *invalid operation, overflow, division by zero, underflow,* and *inexact*, which raised under specific conditions [34].

Exception 1 *(Invalid Operation). This exception is raised when the operation produces a NaN as a result.*

Exception 2 *(Overflow). This exception is raised when the result of an operation is too large to be represented by the encoding. The default value returned depend on the rounding mode.*

Exception 3 *(Division By Zero). It is raised by $x/\pm 0$, for $x \neq 0$. By default, these operations return $\pm inf$.*

Exception 4 *(Underflow). Raised when the result is too small to be represented by the encoding. The default result depend on the rounding mode and can either be a denormal floating-point or zero.*

Exception 5 (Inexact). *This exception is raised when the encoding cannot represent the result of an operation unless it is rounded. By default, these operations will round the result.*

The standard defines five rounding modes. Given a real number x, a rounded floating-point $r(x)$ will be rounded using: *Round Toward Positive (RTP)*, *Round Toward Negative (RTN)*, *Round Toward Zero (RTZ)*, *Round to Nearest ties to Even (RNE)*, and *Round to Nearest ties Away from zero (RNA)*:

Mode 1 (RTP). *$r(x)$ is the least floating-point value $\geq x$.*

Mode 2 (RTN). *$r(x)$ is the greatest floating-point value $\leq x$.*

Mode 3 (RTZ). *$r(x)$ is the floating-point with the same sign of x, such that $|r(x)|$ is the greatest floating-point value $\leq |x|$.*

Mode 4 (RNE). *$r(x)$ is the floating-point value closest to x; if two floating-point values are equidistant to x, $r(x)$ is the one which the least significant bit is zero.*

Mode 5 (RNA). *$r(x)$ is the floating-point value closest to x; if two floating-point values are equidistant to x, $r(x)$ is the one further away from zero.*

The standard also defines some arithmetic operations (add, subtract, multiply, divide, square root, fused multiply-add, remainder), conversions (between formats, to and from strings), and comparisons and total ordering. In particular, the standard defines how floating-point operations are to be encoded using bit-vectors. Table 1 shows four primitive types usually available in the x86 family of processors that follow the standard; each type is divided into three parts: one bit for the sign, an exponent, and a significant part which depends on the bit length of the type. The significands also include a hidden bit: a 1 bit that is assumed to be the leading part of the significand, unless the floating-point is denormal. In Annex F of the C language specification [35], fp32 and fp64 are defined as `float` and `double`. The standard does not define any types for fp16, and compilers usually implement two formats: `__fp16` as defined in the ARM C language extension (ACLE) [1] and `_Float16` as defined by the ISO/IEC 18661-3:2015 standard [36]. While `__fp16` is only a storage and interchange format (meaning that it is promoted when used in arithmetic operations), `_Float16` is

Table 1. IEEE floating-point types.

Name	Common name	Size (exponent + significand)
fp16	Half precision	16 (5 + 10)
fp32	Single precision	32 (8 + 23)
fp64	Double precision	64 (11 + 52)
fp128	Quadruple precision	128 (15 + 112)

an actual type, and arithmetic operations are performed using half-precision. The standard only weakly specifies how an fp128 (**long double** in C) should be implemented, and compilers implement it using an 80-bit long double extended precision format [32].

Floating-points are represented as $(-1)^{sig} \times sgn \times 2^{exp}$. Here, $1 \leq sgn \leq 2$ and 2^{exp} is the scaling factor [48]. Regular floating-points are encoded assuming that the leading hidden bit is 1 and the exponent is in the range $[-exp_{max} + 1, exp_{max} - 1]$, e.g., the number 0.125 is represented as $\langle 0011000000000000 \rangle$ in the floating-point format. Denormals are encoded assuming that the leading hidden bit is zero and the exponent is $-exp_{max}$. Zeros are represented as an all-zero bit-vector (except for the *sig* bit if the zero is negative). Finally, a bit-vector with the exponent equal to exp_{max} and significand all zero is an infinity. In contrast, a bit-vector with an exponent equal to exp_{max} and significand not zero is a NaN.

3 A Floating-Point Bit-Blasting API for Verifying C Programs

When ESBMC was created, all floating-point types and operations were encoded using fixed-points [4, 16]. A fixed-point number is represented in ESBMC as two bit-vectors, one signed bitvector for the integer part and one unsigned bitvector for the fractional part. For example, the number 0.125 is represented as $\langle 0000.0010 \rangle$ (assuming it is 8 bits long) in the fixed-point format. Fixed-point arithmetic is performed similarly to bit-vector arithmetic, except that the operations are applied separately to the integral and fractional parts and concatenated at the end (overflow in the fractional parts are treated accordingly).

However, the lack of proper floating-point encoding meant that ESBMC was unable to accurately verify an entire class of programs, such as the famous floating-point "issue" [55] illustrated in Fig. 1.

```
1 int main()
2 {
3     double x = 0.1;
4     double y = 0.2;
5     double w = 0.3;
6     double z = x + y;
7     assert(w == z);
8     return 0;
9 }
```

Fig. 1. The assertion in line 7 does not hold when using floating-point arithmetic.

The assertion in line 7 does not hold if the program is encoded using radix-2 floating-point arithmetic. The assertion violation arises from the fact that floating-points in the IEEE standard are represented as whole numbers multiplied by a power of two, so the only numbers that use a prime factor of the base two that can be correctly expressed as fractions. Since in binary (or base 2) the only prime factor is 2, only $\frac{1}{2}, \frac{1}{4}, \frac{1}{8}, \ldots$ would be correctly expressed as decimals, so the constants 0.1, 0.2, 0.3 (or $\frac{1}{10}, \frac{1}{5}, \frac{1}{3}$) in the program are only approximations. In the program in Fig. 1, the decimal representation of the floating-point constants (following the IEEE-754 standard binary format) are:

- x is 0.1000000000000000055511151231257827021181583404541015625
- y is 0.200000000000000011102230246251565404236316680908203125
- w is 0.299999999999999988897769753748434595763683319091796875
- z is 0.3000000000000000444089209850062616169452667236328125

The discrepancy happens in the C program because the closest floating-point to 0.3 is smaller than the real 0.3 but the closest floating-point to 0.2 is greater than the real 0.2, so adding the floating-points 0.1 and 0.2 results in a floating-point slightly greater than the constant floating-point 0.3, i.e., in floating-point arithmetic (0.1 + 0.2) > 0.3.

To address this limitation, ESBMC was extended to support floating-point arithmetic [29] but was only able to encode it using SMT solvers that offered native support for the floating-point theory, i.e., Z3 and MathSAT. A floating-point is represented in ESBMC following the IEEE-754 standard for the size of the exponent and significand precision. For example, a half-precision floating-point (16 bits) has 1 bit for the sign, 5 bits for the exponent, and 11 bits for the significand (1 hidden bit) [34].

The work described in this paper, namely a new floating-point API in our SMT backend, is the natural evolution of our research: the support of floating-point arithmetic for the remaining SMT solvers in ESBMC (Boolector [45], Yices [24], and CVC4 [3]). The new floating-point API works by converting all floating-point types and operations to bit-vectors (a process called bit-blasting), thus extending the support for floating-point arithmetic to any solver that supports bit-vector arithmetic [30].

3.1   Bit-Blasting Floating-Point Arithmetic

The SMT FP logic is an addition to the SMT standard, first proposed in 2010 by Rümmer and Wahl [52]. The current version of the theory largely follows the IEEE standard 754-2008 [34]. It formalizes floating-point arithmetic, ±infinity and ±zero, NaNs, relational and arithmetic operators, and five rounding modes: round nearest with ties choosing the even value, round nearest with ties choosing away from zero, round towards positive infinity, round towards negative infinity and round towards zero.

There exist some functionalities from the IEEE standard that are not yet supported by the FP logic as described by Brain et al. [11]; however, when encoding C programs using the FP logic, most of the process is a one-to-one conversion, as we described in our previous work [29].

Encoding programs using the SMT floating-point theory has several advantages over a fixed-point encoding. However, the main one is the correct modeling of ANSI-C/C++ programs that use the IEEE floating-point arithmetic. ESBMC ships with models for most of the current C11 standard functions [35]; floating-point exception handling, however, is not yet supported.

The encoding algorithms, however, can be very complex, and it is not uncommon to see the SMT solvers struggling to support every corner case [25,47]. Currently, various SMT solvers support the SMT floating-point theory, e.g., Z3 [23], MathSAT [18], CVC4 [3], Colibri [40], Solonar [49], and UppSAT [56]; ESBMC implements the floating-point encoding for all of them using their native API. Regarding the support from the solvers, Z3 implements all operators, MathSAT implements all but two: `fp.rem` (remainder operator) and `fp.fma` (fused multiply-add) and CVC4 implements all but the conversions to other sorts.

The three solvers offer two (non-standard) functions to reinterpret floating-points to and from bit-vectors: `fp_as_ieeebv` and `fp_from_ieeebv`, respectively. These functions can be used to circumvent any lack of operators, and only require the user to write the missing operators. Note that this is different from converting floating-points to bit-vectors and vice-versa: converting to bit-vectors follows the rounding modes defined by the IEEE-754 standard while reinterpreting floating-point as bit-vectors returns the bit-vector format of the floating-point. We use these functions to implement the fused multiply-add operator for MathSAT.

The implementation of the floating-point API is based on the encoding of IEEE-754 [44], however, before we can discuss the algorithms in the floating-point API, we first need to describe the basic operations performed by most of them, the four-stage pipeline [10]: unpack, operate, round, and pack.

1. *Unpack stage*: the floating-point is split into three bit-vectors, one for the sign, one for the exponent, and one for the significand. In our floating-point API, the unpack operation also adds the hidden bit to the significand, and unbiases the exponent. It offers an option to normalize subnormals exponents and significands if requested.
2. *Operate stage*: in this stage, conversion and arithmetic operations are performed in the three bit-vectors. Depending on the operation, the bit-vectors need to be extended, e.g., during a fused multiply-add operation, the significand has length 2 * `sb` + 3, and the exponent has length `eb` + 2.
3. *Round stage*: since the previous stage was performed using extended bit-vectors, this stage needs to round the bit-vectors back to the nearest representable floating-point of the target format. Here, *guard* and *sticky* bits in the significand are used to determine how far the bit-vector is from the nearest representable, and the rounding mode is used to determine in which direction the floating-point will be rounded. The exponent bit-vector is also checked for under- or overflow when rounding, to create the correct floating-point. For example, infinity might be created if the exponent is too large for the target format, or ±zero might be created if the target format cannot hold a very small subnormal.
4. *Pack stage*: in the final stage, the three bit-vectors are concatenated to form the final floating-point.

The four-stage pipeline will be used when performing operations with the floating-points. We grouped the operations into seven groups: sorts constructors, rounding modes constructors, value constructors, classification operators, comparison operators, conversion operators, and arithmetic operators.

In the three constructors groups (sorts, rounding modes, and value), the floating-points are encoded using bit-vectors:

Sorts Constructors. The sorts follow the definitions in Table 1 for the bit-vector sizes. We do not support the 80-bit long double extended precision format used in some processors [32]; instead, we use 128 bits for quadruple precision.

Rounding Mode Constructors. The floating-point API supports all rounding modes described in Sect. 2, even though the C standard does not support RNA [35]. These are encoded as 3-bits long bit-vectors.

Value Constructors. Floating-point literals, ±infinity, ±zero and NaN can be created. For the later, the same NaN is always created (positive, the significand is $000\ldots01$). All values are bit-vectors with total length `1 + eb + sb`, where `eb` is the number of exponent bits and `sb` is the number of significand bits. All algorithms in the floating-point API assume one hidden-bit in the significand.

The remaining four operators groups use at least one of the pipeline stages to reason about floating-points:

Classification Operators. Algorithms to classify normals, subnormals, zeros (regardless of sign), infinities (regardless of sign), NaNs, and negatives and positives. The operators work by unpacking the floating-point and comparing the bit-vectors against the definitions.

Comparison Operators. The operators "greater than or equal to", "greater than", "less than or equal to", "less than", and "equality" are supported. The first three are written in terms of the last two. All of them evaluate to false if one of their arguments is NaN, which is done using the NaN classification operator.

Conversion Operators. The floating-point API can convert:

- Floating-points to signed bit-vectors and floating-points to unsigned bit-vectors: converts the floating-point to bit-vectors always rounding towards zero. These operations generate a free variable if it can not represent the floating-point using the target bit-vector, i.e., if the floating-point is out-of-range, ±NaN or ±infinity. Minus zero is converted to zero.
- Floating-points to another floating-point: converts the floating-point to a different format using a rounding mode. ±NaN, ±infinity, and ±zero are always convertible between floating-points, but converting between formats might create ±infinity if the target format can not represent the original floating-point.
- Signed bit-vectors to floating-points and unsigned bit-vectors to floating-points: converts bit-vectors to the nearest representable floating-point, using a rounding mode. It might create ±infinity if the target format can not represent the original bit-vector.

Arithmetic Operators. The floating-point API implements:

- *Absolute value operator*: sets the sign bit of the floating-point to 0.
- *Negation operator*: flips the sign bit of the floating-point.
- *Addition operator*: the significands are extended by 3 bits to perform the addition. The exponent is extended by 2 bits to check for overflows. The algorithm first aligns the significands, then it adds them.
- *Subtraction operator*: negates the right-hand side of the expression and uses the addition operator, i.e., $x - y = x + (-y)$.
- *Multiplication operator*: the length of the significand bit-vectors are doubled before multiplying them, and the exponents are added together. The final sign bit is the result of xor'ing the sign of both operands of the multiplication.
- *Division operator*: the length of both significand and exponent are extended by 2 bits. After that, bit-vector subtractions are used to calculate the target significand and exponent.
- *Fused multiply-add*: the significand is extended to length 2 * sb + 3 to accommodate both the multiplication and the addition, and the exponent is extended by 2 bits. The first two operands are multiplied, and the result is aligned with the third operand before adding them.
- *Square root operator*: neither the significand nor the exponent is extended since the result always fits the original format and can never underflow or overflows as per the operator definition. Here, $\sqrt{x} = l * 2^d$, where the final exponent d is half the unbiased exponent minus the leading zeros, and l is calculated using a restorative algorithm [44, Chap. 10].

All operators but the absolute value and negation handle particular values ($\pm$NaN, $\pm$infinity, and $\pm$zero) before performing the operations. For example, in the multiplication operator, if the left-hand side argument is positive infinity, the result is NaN if the right-hand side argument is 0; otherwise, the result is an infinity with the right-hand side argument sign. Furthermore, all arithmetic operations in the floating-point API that take more than one floating-point as an argument assume that the floating-points have the same format. This assumption is not a problem when converting C programs, as type promotion rules already ensure this pre-condition [35].

4   Experimental Evaluation

Our experimental evaluation consists of three parts. In Sect. 4.1, we present the benchmarks used to evaluate the implementation of our floating-point API. In Sect. 4.2, we compare the verification results of the new floating-point API in ESBMC using several solvers. In Sect. 4.3, we compare the best solver found in Sect. 4.2 against all the tools that competed in the *ReachSafety-Floats* subcategory in SV-Comp 2020. We answer two research questions:

> **RQ1 (Soundness and completeness)** Is our floating-point API sound and complete?
>
> **RQ2 (Performance)** How does the implementation of our floating-point API compare to other software verifiers?

4.1 Experimental Setup

We evaluate our approach using the verification tasks in SV-COMP 2020 [5]. We considered 466 benchmarks for the sub-category *ReachSafety-Floats*, described as *"containing tasks for checking programs with floating-point arithmetics"*.

The *ReachSafety-Floats* sub-category is part of the *ReachSafety* category. In this category, a function call is checked for reachability; the property is formally defined in the competition as G ! call(__VERIFIER_error()) or *"The function __VERIFIER_error() is not called in any finite execution of the program"*.

We have implemented our floating-point API in ESBMC. We run ESBMC on each benchmark in that sub-category once per solver, with the following set of options: --no-div-by-zero-check, which disables the division by zero check (an SV-COMP requirement); --incremental-bmc, which enables the incremental BMC; --unlimited-k-steps, which removes the upper limit of iteration steps in the incremental BMC algorithm; --floatbv, which enables SMT floating-point encoding; --32, which assumes a 32 bits architecture; and --force-malloc-success, which forces all dynamic allocations succeed to (also an SV-COMP requirement). We also disable pointer safety checks and array bounds check (--no-pointer-check, --no-bounds-check) as, per the competition definition, these benchmarks only have reachability bugs. Finally, in order to select an SMT solver for verification, the options --boolector, --z3, --cvc, --mathsat, and --yices are used.

All experiments were conducted on our mini cluster at the University of Manchester, UK. The compute nodes used are equipped with Intel(R) Xeon(R) CPU E5-2620 v4 @ 2.10 GHz and 180 GB of RAM, where nine instances of ESBMC were executed in parallel. For each benchmark, we set time and memory limits of 900 s and 15 GB, respectively, as per the competition definitions. However, we do not present the results as scores (as it is done in SV-COMP) but show the number of correct and incorrect results and the verification time.

4.2 Floating-Point API Evaluation

Figure 2 shows the number of correctly verified programs out of the 466 benchmarks from the *ReachSafety-Floats* sub-category, using several solvers and how long it took to complete the verification. There exists no case where ESBMC reports an incorrect result.

Boolector (lingeling, fp2bv) reports the highest number of correct results (421), followed by MathSAT using their native floating-point API (414). This evaluation produced a slightly better result than our previous one of these solvers, where MathSAT was able to solve floating-point problems quickly but suffered slowdowns in programs with arrays [29]. MathSAT (fp2bv) presented the fewest number of correct results (329).

The results show that Z3 with its native floating-point API and Z3 with our fp2bv API produce very similar results: 390 and 387, respectively; this result is expected since our fp2bv API is heavily based on the bit-blasting performed by Z3 when solving floating-points. The number of variables and clauses generated in the CNF format, when using Z3 with its native floating-point API, is 1%–2% smaller than the number generated when using our fp2bv API. The smaller number explains the slightly better results: we assume this is the result of optimizations when Z3 performs the bit-blasting internally.

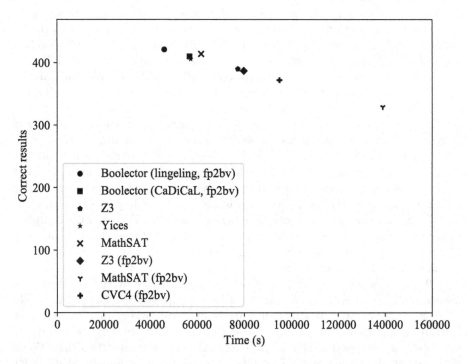

Fig. 2. *ReachSafety-Floats* results for each solver, using the incremental BMC. The "fp2bv" next to the solver name means that our floating-point API was used to bit-blast floating-point arithmetic.

MathSAT results show that their API can solve 85 more benchmarks than MathSAT (fp2bv) within time and memory limits. These benchmarks contain chains of multiplications. They thus require a high computational effort during the propositional satisfiability search. Given that we replace all higher-level operators by bit-level circuit equivalents (bit-blasting), we end up destroying structural word-level information in the problem formulation. Therefore, these results lead us to believe that the MathSAT ACDL algorithm is somehow optimized for FP operations; unfortunately, MathSAT is a free but closed source tool, so we cannot confirm this.

The total verification time for each solver is also illustrated in Fig. 2, and again Boolector (lingeling, fp2bv) was the faster solver, thereby solving all programs in 46100 s. It is followed by Boolector (CaDiCal, fp2bv) with 56900, and Yices (fp2bv) with 57400 s. Overall, Boolector (lingeling, fp2bv) presented the best results. It correctly verified more programs while also being the faster solver, almost 20% faster than the second faster solver, which is also Boolector but with a different SAT solver (CaDiCaL).

> ESBMC produced no incorrect result in this evaluation, which partially answers **RQ1:** although we can not formally prove that our algorithm is sound and complete, empirical evidence suggests it.

4.3   Comparison to Other Software Verifiers

We compare the implementation of our floating-point API with other software verifiers: 2LS [39], CBMC [37], CPA-Seq [6], DIVINE [2], PeSCo [51], Pinaka [15], Symbiotic [14], VeriAbs [17]. Figure 3 illustrates the *ReachSafety-Floats* results from our best approach against tools that participated in SV-COMP 2020. In particular, we have used the binary and scripts of these tools that are available at the SV-COMP 2020 website under "Participating Teams".[1] Overall, VeriAbs achieved the highest number of correct results (435) in 53600 s followed by Pinaka (422) with 27800 s, ESBMC (421) with 46100 s, and CBMC (420) with 49200 s.

VeriAbs can verify C programs with floating-points via abstraction using SAT solvers. In particular, VeriAbs replaces loops in the original code by abstract loops of small known bounds; it performs value analysis to compute loop invariants and then applies an iterative refinement using k-induction. The VeriAbs tool uses CBMC as its backend to prove properties and find errors, which thus allows VeriAbs to verify C programs with floating-points. By contrast, ESBMC uses an iterative technique and verifies the program for each unwind bound until it exhausts the time or memory limits. Intuitively, ESBMC can either find a counterexample with up to k loop unwinding or fully unwinds all loops using the same unwinding bound to provide a correct result. ESBMC also relies on SMT solvers to check the satisfiability of the verifications conditions that contain floating-point arithmetic.

Pinaka verifies C programs using CBMC, but it relies on an incremental SAT solving coupled with eager state infeasibility checks. Additionally, Pinaka extends CBMC to support Breadth-First Search and Depth-First Search as state exploration strategies and partial and full incremental modes. We have not evaluated the SMT incremental mode implemented in ESBMC since this feature is currently supported for the SMT solver Z3 only. Other SMT solvers do

---

[1] https://sv-comp.sosy-lab.org/2020/systems.php.

support incremental solving, but ESBMC does not provide support for incremental solving for other SMT solvers yet.

CBMC [19] implements a bit-precise decision procedure for the theory of floating-point arithmetic [9]. Both VeriAbs and Pinaka rely on CBMC to verify the underlying C program using that decision procedure. ESBMC originated as a fork of CBMC in 2008 with an improved SMT backend [22] and support for the verification of concurrent programs using an explicit interleaving approach [21]. CBMC uses SAT solvers as their primary engine but offers support for the generation of an SMT formula for an external SMT solver. ESBMC supports SMT solvers directly, through their APIs, along with the option to output SMT formulae. The main difference between CBMC and ESBMC relies on the encoding and checking of the verification conditions that contain floating-point arithmetic.

> These results answer our **RQ2**: our floating-point API is on par with other state-of-the-art tools. VeriAbs and Pinaka implement several heuristics to simplify the check for satisfiability using CBMC, while ESBMC used an incremental approach produced close results. ESBMC was also slightly faster and provided a few more results than CBMC, which lead us to believe that our tool would also greatly benefit VeriAbs and Pinaka if used as backend.

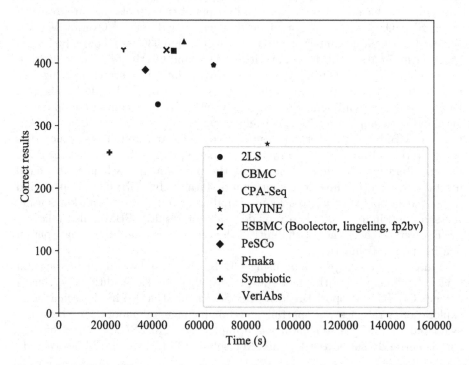

Fig. 3. *ReachSafety-Floats* results from our best approach against tools from SV-COMP 2020.

5   Related Work

Several symbolic execution tools try to verify programs with floating-point arithmetic by employing different strategies. CoverMe [27] reformulates floating-point constraints as mathematical optimization problems. It uses a specially built solver called XSat [26] to check for satisfiability. Pex [54] uses a similar approach and reasons for floating-point constraints as a search problem, and they are solved by using meta-heuristics search methods. FPSE [8] models floating-point arithmetic by using an interval solver over real arithmetic combined with projection functions.

HSE [50] extends KLEE [13] to execute the program and convert floating-points into bit-vectors symbolically. It then uses SMT solvers to reason about satisfiability. Astrée is a static analysis tool that considers all possible rounding errors when verifying C programs with floating-point numbers [7]. It has been applied to verify embedded software in flight controllers by Airbus.

Bounded model checkers have also been applied to verify programs with floating-point arithmetic: CBMC [19] and 2LS [53] convert floating-point operations to bit-vectors and use SAT solvers to reason about satisfiability. CPBPV [20] uses bounded model checking combined with their FPCS [41] interval solver to generate tests that violate output constraints in the program.

Brain et al. [10] describe an approach called SymFPU for handling the theory of floating-point by reducing it to the theory of bit-vectors. In particular, the authors describe a library of encodings, which can be included in SMT solvers to add support for the theory of floating-point by taking into account floating-point reasoning and the fundamentals of circuit design. Brain et al. have integrated SymFPU into the SMT solver CVC4 and evaluate it using a broad set of benchmarks; they conclude that SymFPU+CVC4 can substantially outperform all previous systems despite using a straightforward bit-blasting approach for floating-point problems. We could not compare our approach against SymFPU because of bugs in the CVC4 C API; we contacted the author, and we will create bug reports about the issues we identified.

Fluctuat [33] is another software verification tool capable of analyzing all possible program behaviors using both real and finite precisions and characterizing the differences between them. In particular, Fluctuat implements an abstract-interpretation based error analysis of finite precision for C and Ada programs using zonotopic abstract domains. It produces as output bounds for all program variable values in C and Ada, considered both with a real and a finite floating-point semantics, for all possible program path executions given the sets of program inputs and parameters.

PRECiSA (Program Round-off Error Certifier via Static Analysis) implements a static analysis technique to verify round-off error bounds of floating-point computations based on a sound overapproximation [43]. In particular, it statically computes a symbolic estimation of floating-point round-off errors and a proof certificate that ensures its correctness. PRECiSA evaluates this symbolic estimation based on concrete inputs to produce formally verified numerical error bounds. It has been applied to verify various floating-point programs at NASA.

6   Conclusions

We have described our new SMT floating-point API, which bit-blasts floating-point arithmetic and extends the floating-point support for SMT solvers that only support bit-vector arithmetic. The floating-point API was implemented in the SMT backend of ESBMC. Our experimental results show that Boolector (with lingeling as SAT solver) presented the best results: the highest number of correct results within the shortest verification time. We also show that our floating-point API implemented in ESBMC is on par with other state-of-the-art software verifiers. VeriAbs and Pinaka implement several heuristics to simplify the check for satisfiability using CBMC, while ESBMC, with a straightforward incremental approach, produced close results.

ESBMC was already extensively used to verify digital systems [4,16]. However, these projects were limited to fixed-point arithmetic; supporting floating-point encoding will allow researchers to expand their scientific community activities. The extensive evaluation performed during the development of these technologies also identified areas to be improved in the solvers and other verification tools. In particular, we submitted patches to Z3 to optimize the generation of unsigned less-than operations during the bit-blast of floating-points[2] (accepted, part of Z3 4.6.1). We reported bugs to both CBMC[3] and MathSAT, concerning floating-point arithmetic issues, which were confirmed by the developers.

References

1. ARM: ARM C Language Extensions 2.1 (2016). IHI 0053D
2. Baranová, Z., et al.: Model checking of C and C++ with DIVINE 4. In: D'Souza, D., Narayan Kumar, K. (eds.) ATVA 2017. LNCS, vol. 10482, pp. 201–207. Springer, Cham (2017). https://doi.org/10.1007/978-3-319-68167-2_14
3. Barrett, C., et al.: CVC4. In: Gopalakrishnan, G., Qadeer, S. (eds.) CAV 2011. LNCS, vol. 6806, pp. 171–177. Springer, Heidelberg (2011). https://doi.org/10.1007/978-3-642-22110-1_14
4. Bessa, I., Ismail, H., Palhares, R., Cordeiro, L.C., Filho, J.E.C.: Formal non-fragile stability verification of digital control systems with uncertainty. IEEE Trans. Comput. **66**(3), 545–552 (2017)
5. Beyer, D.: Advances in automatic software verification: SV-COMP 2020. In: Biere, A., Parker, D. (eds.) TACAS 2020. LNCS, vol. 12079, pp. 347–367. Springer, Cham (2020). https://doi.org/10.1007/978-3-030-45237-7_21
6. Beyer, D., Keremoglu, M.E.: CPACHECKER: a tool for configurable software verification. In: Gopalakrishnan, G., Qadeer, S. (eds.) CAV 2011. LNCS, vol. 6806, pp. 184–190. Springer, Heidelberg (2011). https://doi.org/10.1007/978-3-642-22110-1_16
7. Blanchet, B., et al.: A static analyzer for large safety-critical software. In: Programming Language Design and Implementation, pp. 196–207 (2004)
8. Botella, B., Gotlieb, A., Michel, C.: Symbolic execution of floating-point computations: research articles. Softw. Test. Verif. Reliab. **16**(2), 97–121 (2006)

---

[2] https://github.com/Z3Prover/z3/pull/1501.
[3] https://github.com/diffblue/cbmc/issues/1944.

9. Brain, M., D'Silva, V., Griggio, A., Haller, L., Kroening, D.: Deciding floating-point logic with abstract conflict driven clause learning. Formal Methods Syst. Des. **45**(2), 213–245 (2014)
10. Brain, M., Schanda, F., Sun, Y.: Building better bit-blasting for floating-point problems. In: Vojnar, T., Zhang, L. (eds.) TACAS 2019. LNCS, vol. 11427, pp. 79–98. Springer, Cham (2019). https://doi.org/10.1007/978-3-030-17462-0_5
11. Brain, M., Tinelli, C., Ruemmer, P., Wahl, T.: An automatable formal semantics for IEEE-754 floating-point arithmetic. In: Symposium On Computer Arithmetic, pp. 160–167 (2015)
12. Brummayer, R., Biere, A.: Boolector: an efficient SMT solver for bit-vectors and arrays. In: Kowalewski, S., Philippou, A. (eds.) TACAS 2009. LNCS, vol. 5505, pp. 174–177. Springer, Heidelberg (2009). https://doi.org/10.1007/978-3-642-00768-2_16
13. Cadar, C., Dunbar, D., Engler, D.: KLEE: unassisted and automatic generation of high-coverage tests for complex systems programs. In: Symposium On Operating Systems Design And Implementation, pp. 209–224 (2008)
14. Chalupa, M., Vitovská, M., Jonáš, M., Slaby, J., Strejček, J.: Symbiotic 4: beyond reachability - (competition contribution). In: Legay, A., Margaria, T. (eds.) TACAS 2017. LNCS, vol. 10206, pp. 385–389. Springer, Heidelberg (2017). https://doi.org/10.1007/978-3-662-54580-5_28
15. Chaudhary, E., Joshi, S.: Pinaka: symbolic execution meets incremental solving - (competition contribution). In: Beyer, D., Huisman, M., Kordon, F., Steffen, B. (eds.) TACAS 2019. LNCS, vol. 11429, pp. 234–238. Springer, Cham (2019). https://doi.org/10.1007/978-3-030-17502-3_20
16. Chaves, L., Bessa, I., Cordeiro, L.C., Kroening, D., Filho, E.B.D.L.: Verifying digital systems with MATLAB. In: Symposium On Software Testing And Analysis, pp. 388–391 (2017)
17. Chimdyalwar, B., Darke, P., Chauhan, A., Shah, P., Kumar, S., Venkatesh, R.: VeriAbs: verification by abstraction (competition contribution). In: Legay, A., Margaria, T. (eds.) TACAS 2017. LNCS, vol. 10206, pp. 404–408. Springer, Heidelberg (2017). https://doi.org/10.1007/978-3-662-54580-5_32
18. Cimatti, A., Griggio, A., Schaafsma, B.J., Sebastiani, R.: The MathSAT5 SMT solver. In: Piterman, N., Smolka, S.A. (eds.) TACAS 2013. LNCS, vol. 7795, pp. 93–107. Springer, Heidelberg (2013). https://doi.org/10.1007/978-3-642-36742-7_7
19. Clarke, E., Kroening, D., Lerda, F.: A tool for checking ANSI-C programs. In: Jensen, K., Podelski, A. (eds.) TACAS 2004. LNCS, vol. 2988, pp. 168–176. Springer, Heidelberg (2004). https://doi.org/10.1007/978-3-540-24730-2_15
20. Collavizza, H., Michel, C., Ponsini, O., Rueher, M.: Generating test cases inside suspicious intervals for floating-point number programs. In: Constraints In Software Testing Verification And Analysis, pp. 7–11 (2014)
21. Cordeiro, L.C., Fischer, B.: Verifying multi-threaded software using SMT-based context-bounded model checking. In: International Conference on Software Engineering, pp. 331–340 (2011)
22. Cordeiro, L.C., Fischer, B., Marques-Silva, J.: SMT-based bounded model checking for embedded ANSI-C software. In: Automated Software Engineering, pp. 137–148 (2009)
23. de Moura, L., Bjørner, N.: Z3: an efficient SMT solver. In: Ramakrishnan, C.R., Rehof, J. (eds.) TACAS 2008. LNCS, vol. 4963, pp. 337–340. Springer, Heidelberg (2008). https://doi.org/10.1007/978-3-540-78800-3_24

24. Dutertre, B.: Yices 2.2. In: Biere, A., Bloem, R. (eds.) CAV 2014. LNCS, vol. 8559, pp. 737–744. Springer, Cham (2014). https://doi.org/10.1007/978-3-319-08867-9_49

25. Erkök, L.: Bug in floating-point conversions (2018). https://github.com/Z3Prover/z3/issues/1564. Accessed Jan 2020

26. Fu, Z., Su, Z.: XSat: a fast floating-point satisfiability solver. In: Chaudhuri, S., Farzan, A. (eds.) CAV 2016. LNCS, vol. 9780, pp. 187–209. Springer, Cham (2016). https://doi.org/10.1007/978-3-319-41540-6_11

27. Fu, Z., Su, Z.: Achieving high coverage for floating-point code via unconstrained programming. In: Programming Language Design And Implementation, pp. 306–319 (2017)

28. Gadelha, M.R., Monteiro, F., Cordeiro, L., Nicole, D.: ESBMC v6.0: verifying C programs using k-induction and invariant inference. In: Beyer, D., Huisman, M., Kordon, F., Steffen, B. (eds.) TACAS 2019. LNCS, vol. 11429, pp. 209–213. Springer, Cham (2019). https://doi.org/10.1007/978-3-030-17502-3_15

29. Gadelha, M.Y.R., Cordeiro, L.C., Nicole, D.A.: Encoding floating-point numbers using the SMT theory in ESBMC: an empirical evaluation over the SV-COMP benchmarks. In: Cavalheiro, S., Fiadeiro, J. (eds.) SBMF 2017. LNCS, vol. 10623, pp. 91–106. Springer, Cham (2017). https://doi.org/10.1007/978-3-319-70848-5_7

30. Gadelha, M.R., Menezes, R., Monteiro, F.R., Cordeiro, L.C., Nicole, D.: ESBMC: scalable and precise test generation based on the floating-point theory - (competition contribution). In: Wehrheim, H., Cabot, J. (eds.) FASE 2020. LNCS, vol. 12076, pp. 525–529. Springer, Cham (2020). https://doi.org/10.1007/978-3-030-45234-6_27

31. Gerrity, G.W.: Computer representation of real numbers. IEEE Trans. Comput. **C–31**(8), 709–714 (1982)

32. Goldberg, D.: What every computer scientist should know about floating point arithmetic. ACM Comput. Surv. **23**(1), 5–48 (1991)

33. Goubault, E., Putot, S.: Robustness analysis of finite precision implementations. In: Shan, C. (ed.) APLAS 2013. LNCS, vol. 8301, pp. 50–57. Springer, Cham (2013). https://doi.org/10.1007/978-3-319-03542-0_4

34. IEEE: IEEE Standard For Floating-Point Arithmetic (2008). IEEE 754-2008

35. ISO: C11 Standard (2011). ISO/IEC 9899:2011

36. ISO: C++ Standard (2015). ISO/IEC 18661-3:2015

37. Kroening, D., Tautschnig, M.: CBMC – C bounded model checker. In: Ábrahám, E., Havelund, K. (eds.) TACAS 2014. LNCS, vol. 8413, pp. 389–391. Springer, Heidelberg (2014). https://doi.org/10.1007/978-3-642-54862-8_26

38. Lions, J.L.: ARIANE 5 flight 501 failure. Technical report, Inquiry Board (1996)

39. Malík, V., Martiček, Š., Schrammel, P., Srivas, M., Vojnar, T., Wahlang, J.: 2LS: memory safety and non-termination. In: Beyer, D., Huisman, M. (eds.) TACAS 2018. LNCS, vol. 10806, pp. 417–421. Springer, Cham (2018). https://doi.org/10.1007/978-3-319-89963-3_24

40. Marre, B., Bobot, F., Chihani, Z.: Real behavior of floating point numbers. In: SMT Workshop (2017)

41. Michel, C., Rueher, M., Lebbah, Y.: Solving constraints over floating-point numbers. In: Walsh, T. (ed.) CP 2001. LNCS, vol. 2239, pp. 524–538. Springer, Heidelberg (2001). https://doi.org/10.1007/3-540-45578-7_36

42. Monniaux, D.: The pitfalls of verifying floating-point computations. ACM Trans. Program. Lang. Syst. **30**(3), 12:1–12:41 (2008)

43. Moscato, M., Titolo, L., Dutle, A., Muñoz, C.A.: Automatic estimation of verified floating-point round-off errors via static analysis. In: Tonetta, S., Schoitsch, E., Bitsch, F. (eds.) SAFECOMP 2017. LNCS, vol. 10488, pp. 213–229. Springer, Cham (2017). https://doi.org/10.1007/978-3-319-66266-4_14

44. Muller, J.M., et al.: Handbook of Floating-Point Arithmetic, 1st edn. Birkhäuser, Boston (2010)

45. Niemetz, A., Preiner, M., Biere, A.: Boolector 2.0 system description. J. Satisfiab. Boolean Model. Comput. **9**, 53–58 (2014)

46. Nikolić, Z., Nguyen, H.T., Frantz, G.: Design and implementation of numerical linear algebra algorithms on fixed point DSPs. Eur. Assoc. Signal Process. **2007**(1), 1–22 (2007)

47. Noetzli, A.: Failing precondition when multiplying 4-bit significand/4-bit exponent floats (2018). https://github.com/CVC4/CVC4/issues/2182. Accessed Jan 2020

48. Patterson, D.A., Hennessy, J.L.: Computer Organization and Design - The Hardware/Software Interface, 4th edn. Academic Press, Cambridge (2012)

49. Peleska, J., Vorobev, E., Lapschies, F.: Automated test case generation with SMT-solving and abstract interpretation. In: Bobaru, M., Havelund, K., Holzmann, G.J., Joshi, R. (eds.) NFM 2011. LNCS, vol. 6617, pp. 298–312. Springer, Heidelberg (2011). https://doi.org/10.1007/978-3-642-20398-5_22

50. Quan, M.: Hotspot symbolic execution of floating-point programs. In: Symposium on Foundations of Software Engineering, pp. 1112–1114 (2016)

51. Richter, C., Wehrheim, H.: PeSCo: predicting sequential combinations of verifiers - (competition contribution). In: Beyer, D., Huisman, M., Kordon, F., Steffen, B. (eds.) TACAS 2019. LNCS, vol. 11429, pp. 229–233. Springer, Cham (2019). https://doi.org/10.1007/978-3-030-17502-3_19

52. Rümmer, P., Wahl, T.: An SMT-LIB theory of binary floating-point arithmetic. In: SMT Workshop (2010)

53. Schrammel, P., Kroening, D., Brain, M., Martins, R., Teige, T., Bienmüller, T.: Incremental bounded model checking for embedded software (extended version). Formal Aspects Comput. **29**(5), 911–931 (2017)

54. Tillmann, N., de Halleux, J.: Pex–white box test generation for.NET. In: Beckert, B., Hähnle, R. (eds.) TAP 2008. LNCS, vol. 4966, pp. 134–153. Springer, Heidelberg (2008). https://doi.org/10.1007/978-3-540-79124-9_10

55. Wiffin, E.: 0.30000000000000004.com (2012). https://0.30000000000000004.com/. Accessed Apr 2020

56. Zeljić, A., Backeman, P., Wintersteiger, C.M., Rümmer, P.: Exploring approximations for floating-point arithmetic using UppSAT. In: Galmiche, D., Schulz, S., Sebastiani, R. (eds.) IJCAR 2018. LNCS (LNAI), vol. 10900, pp. 246–262. Springer, Cham (2018). https://doi.org/10.1007/978-3-319-94205-6_17

Rigorous Enclosure of Round-Off Errors in Floating-Point Computations

Rémy Garcia[(✉)], Claude Michel, and Michel Rueher

Université Côte d'Azur, CNRS, I3S, Nice, France
{remy.garcia,claude.michel,michel.rueher}@i3s.unice.fr

Abstract. Efficient tools for error analysis of programs with floating-point computations are available. Most of them provide an over-approximation of the floating-point errors. The point is that these approximations are often too coarse to evaluate the effective impact of the error on the behaviour of a program. Some of these tools compute an under-approximation of the maximal error. But, these under-approximations are either not rigorous or not reachable. In this paper, we introduce a new approach to rigorously enclose the maximal error by means of an over-approximation of the error and an under-approximation computed by means of rational arithmetic. Moreover, our system, called FErA, provides input values that exercise the under-approximations. We outline the advantages and limits of our framework and compare our approach with state-of-the-art methods for over-approximating errors as well as the ones computing under-approximation of the maximal error. Preliminary experiments on standard benchmarks are promising. FErA not only computes good error bounds on most benchmarks but also provides an effective lower bound on the maximal error.

Keywords: Floating-point numbers · Round-off error · Constraints over floating-point numbers · Optimization

1 Introduction

Floating-point computations involve errors due to rounding operations that characterize the distance between the intended computations over the reals and the actual computations over the floats. An error occurs at the level of each basic operation when its result is rounded to the nearest representable floating-point number. The final error results from the combination of the rounding errors produced by each basic operation involved in an expression and some initial errors linked to input variables and constants. Such errors impact the precision and the stability of computations and can lead to an execution path over the floats that is significantly different from the expected path over the reals. A faithfull account of these errors is mandatory to capture the actual behaviour of critical programs with floating-point computations.

This work was partially supported by ANR COVERIF (ANR–15–CE25–0002).

M. Christakis et al. (Eds.): NSV 2020/VSTTE 2020, LNCS 12549, pp. 196–212, 2020.
https://doi.org/10.1007/978-3-030-63618-0_12

Efficient tools exist for error analysis that rely on an over-approximation of the errors in programs with floating-point computations. For instance, Fluctuat [10,11] is an abstract interpreter that combines affine arithmetic and zonotopes to analyze the robustness of programs over the floats, FPTaylor [23,24] uses symbolic Taylor expansions to compute tight bounds of the error, and PRECiSA [21,27] is a more recent tool that relies on static analysis. Other tools compute an under-approximation of errors to find a lower bound of the maximal absolute error, e.g., FPSDP [16] which relies on semidefinite programming or, S3FP [2] that uses guided random testing to find inputs causing the worst error. Over-approximations and under-approximations of errors are complementary approaches for providing better enclosures of the maximal error. However, none of the available tools compute both an over-approximation and an under-approximation of errors. Such an enclosure would be very useful to give insights on the maximal absolute error, and how far computed bounds are from it. It is important to outline that approximations do not capture the effective behaviour of a program: they may generate *false positives*, that is to say, report that an assertion might be violated even so in practice none of the input values can exercise the related case. To get rid of *false positives*, computing maximal errors, i.e., the greatest reachable absolute errors, is required. Providing an enclosure of the maximal error, and even finding it, is the goal of the work presented in this paper.

The kernel of our approach is a branch-and-bound algorithm that not only provides an upper bound of the maximal error of a program with floating-point operations but also a reachable error exercised by computed input values. This is a key issue in real problems. This branch-and-bound algorithm is embedded in a solver over the floats [1,18–20,30] extended to constraints over errors [9]. The resulting system, called FErA (**F**loating-point **Er**ror **A**nalyzer), provides not only a sound over-approximation of the maximal error but also a reachable under-approximation with input values that exercise it. FErA uses rational arithmetic because we want to provide a correct lower and upper bound of the errors. A consequence of this choice is that FErA only handles basic arithmetic operators (namely $+, -, \times, /$). To our knowledge, our tool is the first one that combines upper and lower bounding of maximal round-off errors. A key point of FErA is that both bounds relies on each other for improvement.

Maximizing an error can be very expensive because the errors are unevenly distributed. Even on a single operation, such a distribution is cumbersome and finding input values that exercise it often resort to an enumeration process. A combination of floating-point operations often worsen this behaviour, but may, in some cases, soften it thanks to error compensations. One advantage of our approach is that the branch-and-bound is an anytime algorithm, i.e., it always provides an enclosure of the maximal error alongside input values exercising the lower bound.

```
z = (3*x+y)/w;

if (z - 10 <= δ) {
    proceed();
} else {
    raiseAlarm();
}
```

Example 1. Simple program

1.1 Motivating Example

Consider the piece of code in Example 1 that computes $z = (3 * x + y)/w$ using 64-bit floating-point numbers with $x \in [7, 9]$, $y \in [3, 5]$, and $w \in [2, 4]$.

The computation of z precedes a typical condition of a control-command code where the then-branch is activated when $z <= 10$. When $z - 10$ is lower than a given tolerance δ, values supported by z are considered as safe and related computations can be done. Otherwise, an alarm must be raised. As $z - 10$ satisfies Sterbenz property [25] when $z \approx 10$, only the error on the computation of z impacts the conditional. Such a conditional is typically known as an *unstable test*, where the flow over $\mathbb{F}$ can diverge from the one over $\mathbb{R}$ [28]. Now, assume that δ is set to $5.32e-15$. The issue is to know whether this piece of code behaves as expected, i.e., to know whether the error on z is small enough to avoid raising the alarm when the value of z is less than or equal to 10 on real numbers.

Table 1. Absolute error bound

	FPTaylor	PRECiSA	Fluctuat	FErA
Example 1	5.15e−15	5.08e−15	6.28e−15	4.96e−15

Table 1 reports the error values given by FPTaylor [23,24], PRECiSA [21,27], Fluctuat [10,11], and our tool FErA. Fluctuat compute a bound greater than δ whereas FErA, FPTaylor, and PRECiSA compute a bound lower than δ. Results from Fluctuat suggest that the alarm might inappropriately be raised.

FErA computes a round-off error upper bound of $4.96e-15$ in about 0.185 s. It also computes a lower bound on the largest absolute error of $3.55e-15$ exercised by the following input values:

$x = 8.99999999999996624922$ $e_x = -8.8817841970012523239e-16$

$y = 4.99999999999994848565$ $e_y = -4.4408920985006261616e-16$

$w = 3.19999999999998419042$ $e_w = +2.2204460492503130808e-16$

$z = 10.0000000000000035527$ $e_z = -3.5527136788005009293e-15$

```
z = (3*x+y)/w;

if (z <= 10 + δ) {
    proceed ();
} else {
    proceedWithError ();
}
```

Example 2. Simple program without alarm

In other words, our sound optimizer not only guarantee that errors can never raise an alarm, but it also provides an enclosure of the largest absolute error. Such an enclosure having a ratio of 1.4 shows that the round-off error bound of FErA is close to the actual errors.

Now, replace the piece of code by the one from Example 2 and assume δ is set to $3.55e-15$. The only change is that no alarm is raised when the error is greater than δ but the procedure proceedWithError is activated.

The issue here is to know if there exist at least one case where proceedWithError is reached when z is less than or equal to 10 on real numbers. FErA computes an enclosure on the largest absolute error of $[3.55e-15, 4.96e-15]$ with input values exercising the lower bound. So, it ensures that there exist at least one case when proceedWithError is taken with an error bigger than δ. FPTaylor, PRECiSA, and Fluctuat are unable to do so as none of them compute a reachable lower bound on the largest absolute error.

The rest of the paper is organized as follows: Section 2 introduces notations and definitions. Section 3 recalls the constraint system for round-off error analysis and explains how the filtering works. Section 4 formally introduces the branch-and-bound algorithm and its main properties. Section 5 describes in more detail related works for computing a lower bound on the maximal error and their pitfalls. Section 6 illustrates the capabilities of FErA on well-known examples and provides preliminary experiments on a set of standard benchmarks.

2 Notation and Definitions

Our system for round-off error analysis focuses on the four classical arithmetic operations: $+, -, \times, /$ for which the error can be computed exactly using rational numbers [9]. As usual, a constraint satisfaction problem, or CSP, is defined by a triple $\langle X, D, C \rangle$, where X denotes the set of variables, D, the set of domains, and C, the set of constraints. The set of floating-point numbers is denoted $\mathbb{F}$, the set of rational numbers is denoted $\mathbb{Q}$, and the set of real numbers is denoted $\mathbb{R}$. For each floating-point variable x in X, the domain of values of x is represented by the interval $\mathbf{x} = [\underline{\mathbf{x}}, \overline{\mathbf{x}}] = \{x \in \mathbb{F} \mid \underline{\mathbf{x}} \leq x \leq \overline{\mathbf{x}}\}$, where $\underline{\mathbf{x}}$ (resp. $\overline{\mathbf{x}}$) denotes the interval lower (resp. upper) bound, while the domain of errors of x is represented by the interval $\mathbf{e_x} = [\underline{\mathbf{e_x}}, \overline{\mathbf{e_x}}] = \{e_x \in \mathbb{Q} \mid \underline{\mathbf{e_x}} \leq e_x \leq \overline{\mathbf{e_x}}\}$. $\mathbf{x}_\mathbb{F}$ (respectively, $\mathbf{x}_\mathbb{Q}$ and $\mathbf{x}_\mathbb{R}$) denotes a variable that takes its values in $\mathbb{F}$ (respectively, $\mathbb{Q}$ and $\mathbb{R}$).

A variable is instantiated when its domain of values is reduced to a degenerate interval, i.e., a singleton.

3   A Constraint System for Round-Off Error

The branch-and-bound algorithm at the kernel of our framework is based on a constraint system on errors that we briefly introduce in this section.

3.1   Computing Rounding Errors

The IEEE 754 standard [14] requires correct rounding for the four basic operations of floating-point arithmetic. The result of such an operation over the floats must be equal to the rounding of the result of the equivalent operation over the reals. More formally, $z = x \odot y = round(x \cdot y)$ where z, x, and y are floating-point numbers, $\odot$ is one of the four basic arithmetic operations on floats, namely, $\oplus$, $\ominus$, $\otimes$, $\oslash$, while $\cdot$ are the equivalent operations on reals, namely, $+$, $-$, $\times$, $/$; $round$ being the rounding function. This property is used to bound the error introduced by each elementary operation on floats by $\pm\frac{1}{2}ulp(z)$[1] when the rounding mode is set to round to the "nearest even" float, the most frequently used rounding mode.

The deviation of a computation over the floats takes root in each elementary operation. So, it is possible to rebuild the final deviation of an expression from the composition of errors due to each elementary operation involved in that expression. Let us consider a simple operation like the subtraction as in $z = x \ominus y$: input variables, x and y, can come with errors attached due to previous computations. For instance, the deviation on the computation of x, e_x, is given by $e_x = x_{\mathbb{R}} - x_{\mathbb{F}}$ where $x_{\mathbb{R}}$ and $x_{\mathbb{F}}$ denote the expected results, respectively, on reals and on floats.

The computation deviation due to a subtraction can be formulated as follows: for $z = x \ominus y$, e_z, the error on z, is equal to $(x_{\mathbb{R}} - y_{\mathbb{R}}) - (x_{\mathbb{F}} \ominus y_{\mathbb{F}})$.

As $e_x = x_{\mathbb{R}} - x_{\mathbb{F}}$ and $e_y = y_{\mathbb{R}} - y_{\mathbb{F}}$, we have

$$e_z = ((x_{\mathbb{F}} + e_x) - (y_{\mathbb{F}} + e_y)) - (x_{\mathbb{F}} \ominus y_{\mathbb{F}})$$

So, the deviation between the result on reals and the result on floats for a subtraction can be computed by the following formula:

$$e_z = e_x - e_y + ((x_{\mathbb{F}} - y_{\mathbb{F}}) - (x_{\mathbb{F}} \ominus y_{\mathbb{F}}))$$

where $(x_{\mathbb{F}} - y_{\mathbb{F}}) - (x_{\mathbb{F}} \ominus y_{\mathbb{F}})$ characterizes the error produced by the subtraction operation itself. Lets $e_\ominus$ denotes the error produced by the subtraction operation. The formula can then be denoted by:

$$e_z = e_x - e_y + e_\ominus$$

that combines deviations from input values and the deviation introduced by the elementary operation.

---

[1] $ulp(z)$ is the distance between z and its successor (noted z^+).

$$\text{Addition: } z = x \oplus y \rightarrow e_z = e_x + e_y + e_\oplus$$
$$\text{Subtraction: } z = x \ominus y \rightarrow e_z = e_x - e_y + e_\ominus$$
$$\text{Multiplication: } z = x \otimes y \rightarrow e_z = x_\mathbb{F} e_y + y_\mathbb{F} e_x + e_x e_y + e_\otimes$$
$$\text{Division: } z = x \oslash y \rightarrow e_z = \frac{y_\mathbb{F} e_x - x_\mathbb{F} e_y}{y_\mathbb{F}(y_\mathbb{F} + e_y)} + e_\oslash$$

Fig. 1. Computation of deviation for basic operations

Computation deviations for all four basic operations are given in Fig. 1. For each of these formulae, the error computation combines deviations from input values and the error introduced by the current operation. Note that, for the multiplication and division, this deviation is proportional to the input values.

All these formulae compute the difference between the expected result on reals and the actual one on floats for a basic operation. Our constraint solver over the errors relies on these formulae.

3.2   A CSP with Three Domains

As in a classical *CSP*, to each variable x is associated $\mathbf{x}$ its domain of values. The domain $\mathbf{x}$ denotes the set of possible values that this variable can take. When the variable takes values in $\mathbb{F}$, its domain of values is represented by an interval of floats:

$$\mathbf{x}_\mathbb{F} = [\underline{\mathbf{x}_\mathbb{F}}, \overline{\mathbf{x}}_\mathbb{F}] = \{x_\mathbb{F} \in \mathbb{F}, \underline{\mathbf{x}_\mathbb{F}} \leq x_\mathbb{F} \leq \overline{\mathbf{x}}_\mathbb{F}\}$$

where $\underline{\mathbf{x}_\mathbb{F}} \in \mathbb{F}$ and $\overline{\mathbf{x}}_\mathbb{F} \in \mathbb{F}$

Errors require a specific domain associated with each variable of a problem. Since the arithmetic constraints processed here are reduced to the four basic operations, and since those four operations are applied on floats, i.e., a finite subset of rationals, this domain can be defined as an interval of rationals with bounds in $\mathbb{Q}$:

$$\mathbf{e}_x = [\underline{\mathbf{e}}_x, \overline{\mathbf{e}}_x] = \{e_x \in \mathbb{Q}, \underline{\mathbf{e}}_x \leq e_x \leq \overline{\mathbf{e}}_x\}$$

where $\underline{\mathbf{e}}_x \in \mathbb{Q}$ and $\overline{\mathbf{e}}_x \in \mathbb{Q}$.

The domain of errors on operations, denoted by $e_\odot$, that appears in the computation of deviations (see Fig. 1) is associated with each *instance* of an arithmetic operation of a problem.

3.3   Projection Functions

The filtering process of FErA is based on classical projection functions that reduce the domains of the variables. Domains of values can be reduced by means of standard floating-point projection functions defined in [19] and extended in [1, 18]. However, dedicated projections are required to reduce domains of errors.

Addition

$$\mathbf{e}_z \leftarrow \mathbf{e}_z \cap (\mathbf{e}_x + \mathbf{e}_y + \mathbf{e}_\oplus)$$
$$\mathbf{e}_x \leftarrow \mathbf{e}_x \cap (\mathbf{e}_z - \mathbf{e}_y - \mathbf{e}_\oplus)$$
$$\mathbf{e}_y \leftarrow \mathbf{e}_y \cap (\mathbf{e}_z - \mathbf{e}_x - \mathbf{e}_\oplus)$$
$$\mathbf{e}_\oplus \leftarrow \mathbf{e}_\oplus \cap (\mathbf{e}_z - \mathbf{e}_x - \mathbf{e}_y)$$

Subtraction

$$\mathbf{e}_z \leftarrow \mathbf{e}_z \cap (\mathbf{e}_x - \mathbf{e}_y + \mathbf{e}_\ominus)$$
$$\mathbf{e}_x \leftarrow \mathbf{e}_x \cap (\mathbf{e}_z + \mathbf{e}_y - \mathbf{e}_\ominus)$$
$$\mathbf{e}_y \leftarrow \mathbf{e}_y \cap (-\mathbf{e}_z + \mathbf{e}_x + \mathbf{e}_\ominus)$$
$$\mathbf{e}_\ominus \leftarrow \mathbf{e}_\ominus \cap (\mathbf{e}_z - \mathbf{e}_x + \mathbf{e}_y)$$

Multiplication

$$\mathbf{e}_z \leftarrow \mathbf{e}_z \cap (\mathbf{x}_F \mathbf{e}_y + \mathbf{y}_F \mathbf{e}_x + \mathbf{e}_x \mathbf{e}_y + \mathbf{e}_\otimes)$$
$$\mathbf{e}_x \leftarrow \mathbf{e}_x \cap \left(\frac{\mathbf{e}_z - \mathbf{x}_F \mathbf{e}_y - \mathbf{e}_\otimes}{\mathbf{y}_F + \mathbf{e}_y} \right)$$
$$\mathbf{e}_y \leftarrow \mathbf{e}_y \cap \left(\frac{\mathbf{e}_z - \mathbf{y}_F \mathbf{e}_x - \mathbf{e}_\otimes}{\mathbf{x}_F + \mathbf{e}_x} \right)$$
$$\mathbf{e}_\otimes \leftarrow \mathbf{e}_\otimes \cap (\mathbf{e}_z - \mathbf{x}_F \mathbf{e}_y - \mathbf{y}_F \mathbf{e}_x - \mathbf{e}_x \mathbf{e}_y)$$
$$\mathbf{x}_F \leftarrow \mathbf{x}_F \cap \left(\frac{\mathbf{e}_z - \mathbf{y}_F \mathbf{e}_x - \mathbf{e}_x \mathbf{e}_y - \mathbf{e}_\otimes}{\mathbf{e}_y} \right)$$
$$\mathbf{y}_F \leftarrow \mathbf{y}_F \cap \left(\frac{\mathbf{e}_z - \mathbf{x}_F \mathbf{e}_y - \mathbf{e}_x \mathbf{e}_y - \mathbf{e}_\otimes}{\mathbf{e}_x} \right)$$

Division

$$\mathbf{e}_z \leftarrow \mathbf{e}_z \cap \left(\frac{\mathbf{y}_F \mathbf{e}_x - \mathbf{x}_F \mathbf{e}_y}{\mathbf{y}_F (\mathbf{y}_F + \mathbf{e}_y)} + \mathbf{e}_\oslash \right)$$
$$\mathbf{e}_x \leftarrow \mathbf{e}_x \cap \left((\mathbf{e}_z - \mathbf{e}_\oslash)(\mathbf{y}_F + \mathbf{e}_y) + \frac{\mathbf{x}_F \mathbf{e}_y}{\mathbf{y}_F} \right)$$
$$\mathbf{e}_y \leftarrow \mathbf{e}_y \cap \left(\frac{\mathbf{e}_x - \mathbf{e}_z \mathbf{y}_F + \mathbf{e}_\oslash \mathbf{y}_F}{\mathbf{e}_z - \mathbf{e}_\oslash + \frac{\mathbf{x}_F}{\mathbf{y}_F}} \right)$$
$$\mathbf{e}_\oslash \leftarrow \mathbf{e}_\oslash \cap \left(\mathbf{e}_z - \frac{\mathbf{y}_F \mathbf{e}_x - \mathbf{x}_F \mathbf{e}_y}{\mathbf{y}_F (\mathbf{y}_F + \mathbf{e}_y)} \right)$$
$$\mathbf{x}_F \leftarrow \mathbf{x}_F \cap \left(\frac{(\mathbf{e}_\oslash - \mathbf{e}_z) \mathbf{y}_F (\mathbf{y}_F + \mathbf{e}_y) + \mathbf{y}_F \mathbf{e}_x}{\mathbf{e}_y} \right)$$
$$\mathbf{y}_F \leftarrow \mathbf{y}_F \cap [\min(\underline{\delta}_1, \underline{\delta}_2), \max(\overline{\delta}_1, \overline{\delta}_2)]$$

with

$$\delta_1 \leftarrow \frac{\mathbf{e}_x - (\mathbf{e}_z - \mathbf{e}_\oslash) \mathbf{e}_y - \sqrt{\Delta}}{2(\mathbf{e}_z - \mathbf{e}_\oslash)}$$

$$\delta_2 \leftarrow \frac{\mathbf{e}_x - (\mathbf{e}_z - \mathbf{e}_\oslash) \mathbf{e}_y + \sqrt{\Delta}}{2(\mathbf{e}_z - \mathbf{e}_\oslash)}$$

$$\Delta \leftarrow [0, +\infty) \cap ((\mathbf{e}_z - \mathbf{e}_\oslash) \mathbf{e}_y - \mathbf{e}_x)^2 + 4(\mathbf{e}_z - \mathbf{e}_\oslash) \mathbf{e}_y \mathbf{x}_F$$

Fig. 2. Projection functions of arithmetic operation

The projections on the domains of errors are defined through an extension over intervals of the formulae of Fig. 1. Since these formulae are written on reals, they can naturally be extended to intervals. The projections functions for the four basic arithmetic operations are detailed in Fig. 2. Since no error is involved in comparison operators, their projection functions only handle domains of values. So, projection functions on the domain of errors support only arithmetic operations and assignment, where the computation error from the expression is transmitted to the assigned variable. All these projection functions are used to reduce the domains of the variables until a fixed point is reached. For the sake of efficiency, but also to get rid of potential slow convergences, the fixed point computation is not computed and the algorithm stops when domain reduction is lower than 5%.

3.4   Links Between Domains of Values and Domains of Errors

Strong connections between the domain of values and the domain of errors are required to propagate reductions between these domains.

A first relation between the domain of values and the domain of errors on operations is based upon the IEEE 754 standard, that guarantees that basic arithmetic operations are correctly rounded.

$$\mathbf{e}_{\odot} \leftarrow \mathbf{e}_{\odot} \cap \left[-\frac{\min((\underline{z} - \underline{z}^{-}), (\overline{z} - \overline{z}^{-}))}{2}, +\frac{\max((\underline{z}^{+} - \underline{z}), (\overline{z}^{+} - \overline{z}))}{2} \right]$$

where z^{-} and z^{+} denote respectively, the greatest floating-point number strictly inferior to z and the smallest floating-point number strictly superior to z. This equation sets a relation between the domain of values and the domain of errors on operations. More precisely, it states that operation errors can never be greater than the greatest half-ulp of the domain of values of the operation result. Note that the contrapositive of this property offers another opportunity to connect the domain of values and the domain of errors. Indeed, since the absolute value of an operation error is less than the greatest half-ulp of the domain of values of the operation result, the smallest values of the domain of the result cannot be the support of a solution if $\inf(|e_{\odot}|) > 0$. In other words, these small values near zero cannot be associated to an error on the operation big enough to be in $e_{\odot}$ domain if their half-ulp is smaller than $\inf(|e_{\odot}|)$.

Finally, these links are refined by means of other well-known properties of floating-point arithmetic like the Sterbenz property of the subtraction [25] or the Hauser property on the addition [13]. Both properties give conditions under which these operations produce exact results, the same being true for the well-known property that states that $2^{k} \times x$ is exactly computed, provided that no overflow occurs.

3.5   Constraints over Errors

A dedicated function, $err(x)$, is used to express constraints over errors. For instance, $abs(err(x)) \geq \epsilon$, denotes a constraint on the error linked to variable x that must be, in absolute value, greater or equal to ϵ. It should be noted that since errors are taking their values in $\mathbb{Q}$, this constraint is over rationals.

Note that when a constraint mixes errors and floating-point variables, the latter are automatically promoted to rationals.

4   A Branch-and-Bound Algorithm to Maximize the Error

We use a branch-and-bound algorithm (see Algorithm 1) to maximize a given absolute error from a CSP. Such an error characterizes the greatest possible deviation between the expected computation over the reals and the actual computation over the floats. Note that the algorithm can easily be changed to maximize a signed error.

The branch-and-bound algorithm takes as inputs a CSP $\langle X, C, D \rangle$, and e, an error to maximize. This error results from floating-point computations along a given path in a program. It computes a lower bound, or primal, e^*, i.e., the maximal error computed so far and an upper bound, or dual, $\bar{e}$ of the maximal error e, i.e., the current best over-approximation of the error. Primal and dual bounds the maximal error: $e^* \leq e \leq \bar{e}$. Both of those bounds are expressed in absolute value. The computed primal e^* is a reachable error exercised by computed input values. These values and the computed bounds are returned by our algorithm. S is the ordered set of couples (e, sol) where e and sol are, respectively, an error and its corresponding input values. A box B is the cartesian product of variable domains. For the sake of clarity, a box B can be used as exponent, e.g., $\mathbf{x}^B$ indicates that an element $\mathbf{x}$ is in box B. L is the set of boxes left to compute.

Stopping Criteria. The primary aim of the branch-and-bound algorithm is to compute the maximal error. This is achieved when the primal is equal to the dual. However, such a condition may be difficult to meet.

A first issue comes from the dependency problem which appears on expressions with multiples occurrences. Multiple occurrences of variables is a critical issue in interval arithmetic since each occurrence of a variable is considered as a different variable with the same domain. This dependency problem results in overestimations in the evaluation of the possible values that an expression can take. For instance, let $y = x \times x$ with $x \in [-1, 1]$, classical interval arithmetic yields $[-1, 1]$ whereas the exact interval is $[0, 1]$. Such a drawback arise in projection functions for computing errors that contains multiple occurrences like in multiplication and division. It can leads to unnecessary over-approximation of resulting intervals. A direct consequence of this problem is that the dual is overestimated and therefore can not be achieve.

A second issue comes from the bounding of errors on operations by the half of an ulp. An operation error is bounded by $\frac{1}{2}\mathrm{ulp}(z)$ where z is the result of an operation. Such a bound is highly dependent on the distribution of floating-point numbers. Consider an interval of floating-point numbers $(2^n, 2^{n+1})$, every floating-point number is separated from the next one by the same distance. In other words, every floating-point number in this interval will have the same ulp. When the domain of the result of an operation is reduced to such an interval, the bounds of $e_\odot$ are fixed and can no longer be improved by means of projection functions. This can be generalized across all operations of a CSP. Once all operation errors are fixed, then bounds cannot be tighten without enumerating values. In other words, provided that there is no multiple occurrences, the dual can no longer be lowered at this point. That is why, we stop processing a box when all the related domains are reduced to such an interval.

Algorithm 1: branch-and-bound — maximization of error

Input	:	$\langle X, C, D \rangle$ — triple of variables, constraints, and domains
		$e \in [-\infty, +\infty]$ — error to maximize
Output	:	$(e^*, \bar{e}, S)$
Data	:	$L \leftarrow \{ \prod_{x \in X} x \mid x = (\mathbf{x}, \mathbf{e_x}) \}$ — set of boxes
		$\bar{e} \leftarrow +\infty$ — dual bound
		$e^* \leftarrow -\infty$ — primal bound
		$\bar{e}^S \leftarrow -\infty$ — upper bound of sidelined boxes
		$S \leftarrow \varnothing$ — stack of solutions

1   **while** $L \neq \varnothing$ **and** $e^* < \bar{e}$ **do**

     /* Box selection: select a box B in the set of boxes L */

2   select $B \in L$; $L \leftarrow L \setminus B$

3 $\bar{e}^B_{old} \leftarrow \bar{e}^B$

4 $B \leftarrow \Phi(X, C \wedge e > e^*, B)$

5   **if** $\bar{e}^B_{old} = \bar{e}$ **and** $(B = \varnothing$ **or** $\bar{e}^B < \bar{e})$ **then**

6   **if** $B \neq \varnothing$ **then**

7 $\bar{e} \leftarrow \bar{e}^B$

8   **else**

9 $\bar{e} \leftarrow -\infty$

10 $\bar{e} \leftarrow \max \left(\{ \bar{e}^{B_i} \mid \forall B_i \in L \} \cup \{ \bar{e}, \bar{e}^S \} \right)$

11   **if** $B \neq \varnothing$ **then**

12   **if** $\bar{e}^B > e^*$ **then**

13   **if** $isBound(B)$ **then**

14 $(e^B, sol^B) \leftarrow (e^B, B)$

15   **else**

16 $(e^B, sol^B) \leftarrow primalComputation(B, X)$

17   **if** $e^B > e^*$ **then**

18 $e^* \leftarrow e^B$

19   push (e^B, sol^B) onto S

20 $L \leftarrow L \setminus \{ B_i \in L \mid \bar{e}^{B_i} \leq e^* \}$

21   **if** $\bar{e}^B > \bar{e}^S$ **and** $\bar{e}^B > e^*$ **then**

             /* Variable selection: select a variable x in box B */

22   **if** $(select(\mathbf{x}^B, \mathbf{e_x}^B) \in B \mid \underline{\mathbf{x}}^B < \overline{\mathbf{x}}^B)$ **and** $\neg isSidelined(B)$ **then**

                 /* Domain splitting: split the domain of values of x

                     in subdomains   */

23 $B_1 \leftarrow B$

24 $B_2 \leftarrow B$

25 $\mathbf{x}^{B_1} \leftarrow \left[\underline{\mathbf{x}}^B, \frac{\underline{\mathbf{x}}^B + \overline{\mathbf{x}}^B}{2} \right]$

26 $\mathbf{x}^{B_2} \leftarrow \left[\left(\frac{\underline{\mathbf{x}}^B + \overline{\mathbf{x}}^B}{2} \right)^+, \overline{\mathbf{x}}^B \right]$

27 $L \leftarrow L \cup \{ B_1, B_2 \}$

28   **else**

29 $\bar{e}^S \leftarrow \max(\bar{e}^S, \bar{e}^B)$

30 **return** $(e^*, \bar{e}, S)$

Box Management. The algorithm manages a list L of boxes to process whose initial value is $\{ B = (D, e^B \in [-\infty, +\infty]) \}$ where D is the cross product of the domains of the variable as defined in the problem and e^B their associated error. It also manages the global primal and dual with $e^* = -\infty$, $\bar{e} = +\infty$ as initial values. A box can be in three different states: *unexplored, discarded* or *sidelined. unexplored* boxes are boxes in L that still require some computations. A *discarded* box is a box whose associated error e^B is such that $\bar{e}^B \leq e^*$. In other words, such a box does not contain any error value that can improve the computation of the maximal error. It is thus removed from L. *sidelined* boxes are boxes that fullfil the property described in the stopping criteria paragraph. These boxes cannot improve maximal error computation unless if the algorithm resorts to enumeration (provided there are no multiple occurrences). As sidelined boxes are still valid boxes, the greatest over-approximation of such boxes, $\bar{e}^S$, is taken into account when updating the dual bound. Solving stops when there are no more boxes to process or when the primal e^* and the dual $\bar{e}$ are equal, i.e., when the maximal error is found.

The main loop of the branch-and-bound algorithm can be subdivided in several steps: box selection, filtering, dual updating, primal updating, and box splitting.

Box Selection. We select the box B in the set L with the greatest upper bound of the error to provide more opportunities to improve both $\bar{e}$ and e^*. Indeed, the global $\bar{e}$ has its support in this box which also provides the odds of computing a better reachable error e^*. Once selected, the box B is removed from L.

Filtering. A filtering process (see Sect. 3), denoted Φ, is then applied to B to reduce the domains of values and the domains of errors. Note that this filtering is applied to the initial set of constraints enhanced with constraints on known bounds of e, i.e., $e^* \leq e$ and $\bar{e} \geq e$. If $\Phi(B) = \varnothing$, the selected box does not contain any solution; either because it contradicts one of the initial constraints or because of constraints over e known bounds. In both cases, the algorithm discards box B and directly jumps to the next loop iteration.

Dual Update. Once B has been filtered, if the error upper bound of the current box was support of the dual $\bar{e}$ and is no longer, then $\bar{e}$ is updated. $\bar{e}$ is updated with the maximum among the upper bound of errors of the current box, of remaining boxes in L, and of sidelined boxes.

Primal Update. A non empty box may contain a better primal than the current one. A *generate-and-test* procedure, `primalComputation`, attempts to compute a better one in the following way: each variable is, in turn, randomly set to a value that belongs to its domain. Note that the error distribution is such that a randomly instantiation of variables has a great chance to provide an improved error. The enumeration goes through two steps. A variable is first assigned with a floating-point value chosen randomly in its domain of values. Then, another random value chosen within the domain of its associated error is assign to the error associated to that variable. We exploit the fact that if the derivative sign does not change on the associated error domain, then the maximum distance between the hyperplan defined by the result over the floats and the related function over the reals is at one of the extrema of the associated error domain. When all variables from a function f representing a program have been instantiated, an evaluation of f is done exactly over $\mathbb{Q}$ and in machine precision over $\mathbb{F}$. The error is exactly computed by evaluating $f_{\mathbb{Q}} - f_{\mathbb{F}}$ over $\mathbb{Q}$. The computed error can be further improved by a local search. That is to say, by exploring floating-point numbers around the chosen input values and evaluating again the expressions. This process is repeated a fixed number of times until the error can not be further improved, i.e., a local maximum has been reached. If the computed error is better than the primal, then e^* is updated. Each new primal bound is added to S alongside the input values exercising it.

Box Splitting. A box is not split up but is discarded when its error upper bound is less than or equal to $\overline{e}^S$, the upper bound of sidelined boxes, or e^*. Discarding such a box speeds up solving time, since none of the errors contained in this box can improve the primal or the dual. Splitting occurs if and only if there exist at least one of the variables within B that is not instantiated and if the box is not sidelined. Otherwise, the box is sidelined and if $\overline{e}^B$ is strictly greater than $\overline{e}^S$, the latter is updated. The next variable to split on is selected in a lexicographic order. The bisection generates two sub-boxes that are added to L.

Note that Algorithm 1 always terminates and gives an enclosure of the maximal error: in the worst case, all boxes will be split up to degenerated boxes. Each degenerated box whose associated error e^B is lower than the primal will be discarded. If $e^* \leq e^B \leq \overline{e}$ holds, e^B will be used to update e^* and $\overline{e}$ before discarding the corresponding degenerated box. As a result, since the set of floating-point numbers is a finite set, the branch-and-bound requires a finite number of iterations to explore completely the initial box and thus, terminates.

5   Related Work

Different tools exist for computing an over-approximation of errors of floating-point computations. Fluctuat [10,11], is an abstract interpreter which combines affine arithmetic and zonotopes to analyze the robustness of programs over floats. FPTaylor [23,24] uses symbolic Taylor expansions and global optimization to compute tight bounds of the error. It represents errors in Taylor series by a first order and a second order term. A branch-and-bound algorithm is used to compute an approximation of the symbolic first order error term, and the second order error term is computed in Taylor expansions. This branch-and-bound is very different from the one used by FErA. First, it considers only one term of the error representation used by FPTaylor whereas FErA branch-and-bound uses the whole error. Second, it does not compute a lower bound on the largest absolute error but only over-approximate errors. FPTaylor is also able to produce proof certificates to verify the validity of its computed bounds. Such a certificate can be externally checked in HOL Light [12]. PRECiSA [21,27] is a static analyzer that also computes a certificate of proof that can be used to formally prove the round-off error bounds of a program. PRECiSA uses a branch-and-bound algorithm to compute concrete bounds of round-off errors. In other words, PRECiSA computes symbolic error expressions to represent round-off errors that are given to a branch-and-bound algorithm. Certificate of proof produced by PRECiSA are validated by the PVS theorem prover [22]. Gappa [8] verifies properties on floating-point programs, and in particular computes bounds on round-off errors. Gappa works with an interval representation of floating-point numbers and applies rewriting rules for improving computed results. It is also able to generate formal proof of verified properties, that can in turn be checked in Coq [26]. Real2Float [17] uses semidefinite programming for estimating bounds on error. It decomposes an error into an affine part with respect to the error variable and a higher-order part. Bounds on the higher-order part are computed in the same way as FPTaylor. For the affine part, a relaxation procedure based on semidefinite programming is employed. Rosa [6,7] uses affine arithmetic and an SMT solver to estimates round-off errors. It computes errors in a symbolic form that is given to the SMT solver to find concrete bounds on expressions. Daisy [4,5,15] is another tool by the authors of Rosa. It also relies on affine arithmetic and an SMT solver to bound round-off errors. Moreover, it also include features from FPTaylor, such as optimization-based absolute error analysis, and Fluctuat, such as interval subdivision. Most of these tools handle both transcendental functions and arithmetic operators. As said before, FErA only handles basic arithmetic operators (namely $+, -, \times, /$) because we want to provide a correct lower and upper bounds of the errors.

FPSDP [16] is a tool based on semidefinite programming that only computes under-approximation of largest absolute errors. In contrast to our approach FPSDP computes an under-approximation of the maximal error. The point is that this under-approximation might not be reachable. For instance, considers the benchmark `rigidBody1` (see Table 2). Here, FPSDP yields $3.55e{-}13$ whereas FErA, Gappa, Daisy, and FPTaylor upper bound is $2.95e{-}13$. Fluctuat and Rosa compute an upper bound of $3.22e{-}13$ and PRECiSA an upper bound of $3.23e{-}13$. The only upper bound greater than $3.55e{-}13$ is the one computed by Real2Float, about $5.33e{-}13$. Thus, the under-approximation of the maximal error provided by FPSDP is not reachable. S3FP [2] relies on random sampling and shadow values executions to find input values maximizing an error. It computes the error as the difference between the execution of a program done in a higher precision, acting as $\mathbb{R}$, and a lower precision, acting as $\mathbb{F}$. S3FP starts with an initial configuration that is cut into smaller configurations. Then, it selects a configuration and randomly instantiates variables to evaluate the program in both precisions. This process is repeated a finite number of time to improve the lower bound. Depending on the size of input intervals, S3FP can get stuck on a local maximum. To avoid this problem it uses a standard restart process. S3FP is the closest to our primal computation procedure. Both rely on random generation of input values to compute a lower bound of errors. However, as S3FP does all computations over $\mathbb{F}$, the resulting error suffers from rounding issues and thus, mights underestimate or overestimate the actual error. Such a computed error is unreachable. Furthermore, S3FP is highly reliant on the parametrized

Table 2. Experimental results for absolute round-off error bounds (bold indicates the **best approximation**, italic indicates the *second best*, and red indicates the worst one). Grey rows indicate solving time for each tool, in seconds. S3FP and e^* columns show lower bound on the maximal error, whereas other columns show an upper bound. TO indicates a time out at 10 min

	Fluctuat	Gappa	PRECiSA	Real2Float	Daisy	Rosa	FPTaylor	S3FP	FErA filtering	e^*	$\bar{e}$
carbonGas	1.17e-08	*6.03e-09*	7.09e-09	2.21e-08	3.91e-08	1.60e-08	**4.96e-09**	4.2e-09	4.24e-08	2.95e-09	7.01e-09
	0.123s	3.445s	0.034s	6.887s	37.750s	37.581s	0.320s		0.017s		0.345s
verhulst	4.80e-16	*2.84e-16*	5.14e-16	4.66e-16	3.72e-16	4.67e-16	**2.47e-16**	2.4e-16	4.19e-16	2.19e-16	2.86e-16
	0.108s	0.619s	0.023s	4.675s	28.250s	15.762s	0.290s		0.016s		0.034s
predPrey	2.35e-16	*1.67e-16*	2.09e-16	2.51e-16	1.75e-16	1.98e-16	**1.59e-16**	1.5e-16	1.84e-16	1.03e-16	*1.67e-16*
	0.107s	2.166s	0.020s	7.269s	29.500s	33.220s	0.410s		0.011s		0.084s
rigidBody1	*3.22e-13*	**2.95e-13**	3.23e-13	5.33e-13	**2.95e-13**	*3.22e-13*	**2.95e-13**	2.7e-13	2.95e-13	1.95e-13	**2.95e-13**
	2.794s	2.359s	0.033s	3.230s	27.983s	7.505s	0.280s		0.018s		1.659s
rigidBody2	*3.65e-11*	**3.61e-11**	3.65e-11	6.48e-11	**3.61e-11**	*3.65e-11*	**3.61e-11**	3.0e-11	3.61e-11	2.52e-11	**3.61e-11**
	5.090s	3.657s	0.370s	3.698s	32.683s	10.377s	0.310s		0.022s		3.298s
doppler1	*1.27e-13*	1.61e-13	2.09e-13	7.64e-12	4.19e-13	2.68e-13	**1.22e-13**	1.0e-13	4.96e-13	7.34e-14	1.56e-13
	8.347s	5.542s	0.044s	26.821s	30.817s	24.298s	1.450s		0.021s		0.752s
doppler2	*2.35e-13*	2.86e-13	3.07e-13	8.85e-12	1.05e-12	6.45e-13	**2.23e-13**	1.9e-13	1.33e-12	1.12e-13	3.36e-13
	8.244s	5.634s	0.044s	26.731s	34.000s	24.073s	1.730s		0.034s		0.356s
doppler3	*7.12e-14*	8.75e-14	9.50e-14	4.07e-12	1.68e-13	1.01e-13	**6.62e-14**	5.7e-14	1.92e-13	4.09e-14	9.00e-14
	9.028s	5.476s	0.044s	26.057s	32.250s	31.442s	1.330s		0.023s		0.341s
turbine1	3.09e-14	2.41e-14	2.52e-14	2.46e-11	8.65e-14	5.99e-14	**1.67e-14**	1.1e-14	2.16e-13	1.05e-14	*1.76e-14*
	7.555s	9.816s	0.144s	127.911s	32.950s	31.400s	0.450s		0.016s		8.514s
turbine2	2.59e-14	3.32e-14	3.01e-14	2.07e-12	1.31e-13	7.67e-14	**2.00e-14**	1.4e-14	3.04e-13	1.32e-14	*2.36e-14*
	5.562s	7.395s	0.132s	22.225s	30.183s	14.890s	0.560s		0.025s		2.803s
turbine3	1.34e-14	0.35	1.83e-14	1.70e-11	6.23e-14	4.62e-14	**9.57e-15**	6.2e-15	1.56e-13	4.76e-15	*1.10e-14*
	7.342s	11.256s	0.193s	150.653s	31.050s	31.224s	0.520s		0.026s		2.766s
sqroot	6.83e-16	5.35e-16	**4.29e-16**	1.28e-15	5.71e-16	6.18e-16	*5.02e-16*	4.7e-16	5.78e-16	3.33e-16	5.33e-16
	0.120s	7.937s	0.035s	13.840s	28.000s	8.414s	0.320s		0.032s		2.989s
sine	7.41e-16	6.95e-16	7.48e-16	6.03e-16	1.13e-15	*5.18e-16*	**4.44e-16**	2.9e-16	7.41e-16	2.24e-16	7.41e-16
	0.126s	40.351s	0.132s	13.138s	27.933s	14.265s	0.450s		0.027s		12.927s
sineOrder3	1.09e-15	6.54e-16	1.23e-15	1.19e-15	1.45e-15	9.96e-16	**5.94e-16**	4.1e-16	1.11e-15	3.28e-16	*6.36e-16*
	0.117s	3.177s	0.021s	4.241s	25.867s	6.974s	0.290s		0.021s		1.388s
kepler0	1.03e-13	1.09e-13	1.10e-13	1.20e-13	1.04e-13	*8.28e-14*	**7.47e-14**	5.3e-14	1.18e-13	5.43e-14	9.81e-14
	12.611s	12.187s	0.230s	2.120s	28.033s	11.113s	0.690s		0.037s		TO
kepler1	3.51e-13	4.68e-13	4.03e-13	4.67e-13	4.81e-13	4.14e-13	**2.86e-13**	1.6e-13	4.94e-13	1.41e-13	*3.10e-13*
	252.468s	19.785s	0.683s	93.202s	28.933s	134.149s	1.710s		0.031s		51.303s
kepler2	2.24e-12	2.40e-12	*1.66e-12*	2.09e-12	2.46e-12	2.15e-12	**1.58e-12**	8.4e-13	2.43e-12	6.08e-13	1.83e-12
	33.600s	39.048s	31.235s	59.881s	30.483s	72.847s	0.580s		0.027s		157.558s

partitioning of the initial configuration. It cannot discard configurations where no improvement of the lower bound is possible. In contrast, FErA selects boxes to explore on the basis of their upper bounds to try finding a better lower bound.

6   Experimentation

In this section, we provide preliminary experiments of FErA on a subset of benchmarks (comprising of $+, -, \times, /$ operators) from the FPBench [3] suite, a common standard to compare verification tools over floating-point numbers. Table 2 compares results from Fluctuat [10,11] (version 3.1390 with subdivisions), Gappa [8] (version 1.3.5 with advanced hints), PRECiSA [21,27] (version 2.1.1), Real2Float [17] (version 0.7), Daisy [4,5,15] (master branch, commit 8f26766), Rosa [6,7] (master branch, commit 68e58b8), FPTaylor [23,24] (master branch, commit 147e1fe with Gelpia [23] optimizer), S3FP [2] and FErA.

Benchmarks computation is done on a 2.8 GHz Intel Core i7–7700HQ with 16 GB of RAM, running under macOs Catalina (10.15.4). Results from S3FP are taken from [23], as authors state in [2] that the available tool only works on single-precision floating-point numbers.

Note that all state-of-the-art tools provide an over-approximation of errors, except S3FP, which compute a lower bound on largest absolute errors. For FErA, column *filtering* gives the over-approximation computed by a single filtering while column e^* and column $\bar{e}$ provide respectively the best reachable error and over-approximation of the error computed by FErA. Bold and italic are used to rank, respectively, the best and second best over-approximation while red indicates the worst ones. Lines in grey give the time in second to compute these bounds.

On these benchmarks, FErA classified as best twice and as second six times. Note that it never provides the worst result. In almost all cases, the computed reachable error e^* is in the same order of magnitude than $\bar{e}$. The lack of dedicated handling of multiple occurrences in FErA is underlined by the computed dual of the `sine` bench. Here, the splitting process used in the branch-and-bound is not sufficient to lower the dual value. FErA solves most of the problems in a reasonable amount of time with the exception of `kepler0`. Indeed, Kepler benchs are the problems with the biggest number of input variables and FErA performs better on small sized problems. Still, FErA as an anytime algorithm provides bounds computed so far for `kepler0`.

7 Conclusion

This paper addresses a critical issue in program verification: computing an enclosure of the maximal absolute error in floating-point computations. To compute this enclosure, we introduce an original approach based on a branch-and-bound algorithm using the constraint system for round-off error analysis from [9].

The splitting process takes advantage of an efficient filtering and the known enclosure of the error to speed up the optimization process.

Alongside a rigorous enclosure of maximal errors, the algorithm provides input values exercising the lower bound. Knowing such bounds of the maximal error is very useful to get rid of false positives, a critical issue in program verification and validation.

Preliminary experiments on a set of standard benchmarks are very promising and compare well to other available tools.

Further works include a better understanding and a tighter computation of round-off errors to smooth the effects of the dependency problem, experimentations with different search strategies dedicated to floating-point numbers [29] to improve the resolution process, as well as devising a better local search to speed up the primal computation procedure.

References

1. Botella, B., Gotlieb, A., Michel, C.: Symbolic execution of floating-point computations. Softw. Test. Verif. Reliab. **16**(2), 97–121 (2006)
2. Chiang, W., Gopalakrishnan, G., Rakamaric, Z., Solovyev, A.: Efficient search for inputs causing high floating-point errors. In: ACM SIGPLAN Symposium on Principles and Practice of Parallel Programming, PPoPP 2014, Orlando, FL, USA, 15–19 February 2014, pp. 43–52 (2014)
3. Damouche, N., Martel, M., Panchekha, P., Qiu, C., Sanchez-Stern, A., Tatlock, Z.: Toward a standard benchmark format and suite for floating-point analysis. In: 9th International Workshop on Numerical Software Verification (NSV2017), pp. 63–77 (2017)
4. Darulova, E., Horn, E., Sharma, S.: Sound mixed-precision optimization with rewriting. In: Gill, C., Sinopoli, B., Liu, X., Tabuada, P. (eds.) Proceedings of the 9th ACM/IEEE International Conference on Cyber-Physical Systems, ICCPS 2018, Porto, Portugal, 11–13 April 2018, pp. 208–219. IEEE Computer Society/ACM (2018)
5. Darulova, Eva, Izycheva, Anastasiia, Nasir, Fariha, Ritter, Fabian, Becker, Heiko, Bastian, Robert: Daisy - framework for analysis and optimization of numerical programs (Tool paper). In: Beyer, Dirk, Huisman, Marieke (eds.) TACAS 2018. LNCS, vol. 10805, pp. 270–287. Springer, Cham (2018). https://doi.org/10.1007/978-3-319-89960-2_15
6. Darulova, E., Kuncak, V.: Sound compilation of reals. In: The 41st Annual ACM SIGPLAN-SIGACT Symposium on Principles of Programming Languages, POPL 2014, San Diego, CA, USA, 20–21 January 2014, pp. 235–248. ACM (2014)
7. Darulova, E., Kuncak, V.: Towards a compiler for reals. ACM Trans. Program. Lang. Syst. **39**(2), 8:1–8:28 (2017)
8. Daumas, M., Melquiond, G.: Certification of bounds on expressions involving rounded operators. ACM Trans. Math. Softw. **37**(1), 2:1–2:20 (2010)
9. Garcia, R., Michel, C., Pelleau, M., Rueher, M.: Towards a constraint system for round-off error analysis of floating-point computation. In: 24th International Conference on Principles and Practice of Constraint Programming : Doctoral Program. Lille, France, August 2018
10. Goubault, E., Putot, S.: Static analysis of numerical algorithms. In: Yi, K. (ed.) SAS 2006. LNCS, vol. 4134, pp. 18–34. Springer, Heidelberg (2006). https://doi.org/10.1007/11823230_3
11. Goubault, E., Putot, S.: Static analysis of finite precision computations. In: Jhala, R., Schmidt, D. (eds.) VMCAI 2011. LNCS, vol. 6538, pp. 232–247. Springer, Heidelberg (2011). https://doi.org/10.1007/978-3-642-18275-4_17
12. Harrison, J.: HOL light: an overview. In: Berghofer, S., Nipkow, T., Urban, C., Wenzel, M. (eds.) TPHOLs 2009. LNCS, vol. 5674, pp. 60–66. Springer, Heidelberg (2009). https://doi.org/10.1007/978-3-642-03359-9_4
13. Hauser, J.R.: Handling floating-point exceptions in numeric programs. ACM Trans. Program. Lang. Syst. **18**(2), 139–174 (1996)
14. IEEE: 754–2008 - IEEE Standard for floating point arithmethic (2008)
15. Izycheva, A., Darulova, E.: On sound relative error bounds for floating-point arithmetic. In: Stewart, D., Weissenbacher, G. (eds.) 2017 Formal Methods in Computer Aided Design, FMCAD 2017, Vienna, Austria, 2–6 October 2017, pp. 15–22. IEEE (2017)

16. Magron, V.: Interval enclosures of upper bounds of roundoff errors using semidefinite programming. ACM Trans. Math. Softw. **44**(4), 41:1–41:18 (2018)
17. Magron, V., Constantinides, G.A., Donaldson, A.F.: Certified roundoff error bounds using semidefinite programming. ACM Trans. Math. Softw. **43**(4), 34:1–34:31 (2017)
18. Marre, B., Michel, C.: Improving the floating point addition and subtraction constraints. In: Cohen, D. (ed.) CP 2010. LNCS, vol. 6308, pp. 360–367. Springer, Heidelberg (2010). https://doi.org/10.1007/978-3-642-15396-9_30
19. Michel, C.: Exact projection functions for floating point number constraints. In: AI&M 1–2002, Seventh International Symposium on Artificial Intelligence and Mathematics (7th ISAIM), Fort Lauderdale, Floride, US (2002)
20. Michel, C., Rueher, M., Lebbah, Y.: Solving constraints over floating-point numbers. In: Walsh, T. (ed.) CP 2001. LNCS, vol. 2239, pp. 524–538. Springer, Heidelberg (2001). https://doi.org/10.1007/3-540-45578-7_36
21. Moscato, M., Titolo, L., Dutle, A., Muñoz, C.A.: Automatic estimation of verified floating-point round-off errors via static analysis. In: Tonetta, S., Schoitsch, E., Bitsch, F. (eds.) SAFECOMP 2017. LNCS, vol. 10488, pp. 213–229. Springer, Cham (2017). https://doi.org/10.1007/978-3-319-66266-4_14
22. Owre, S., Rushby, J.M., Shankar, N.: PVS: a prototype verification system. In: Kapur, D. (ed.) CADE 1992. LNCS, vol. 607, pp. 748–752. Springer, Heidelberg (1992). https://doi.org/10.1007/3-540-55602-8_217
23. Solovyev, A., Baranowski, M.S., Briggs, I., Jacobsen, C., Rakamarić, Z., Gopalakrishnan, G.: Rigorous estimation of floating-point round-off errors with symbolic Taylor expansions. ACM Trans. Program. Lang. Syst. **41**(1), 2:1–2:39 (2018)
24. Solovyev, A., Jacobsen, C., Rakamarić, Z., Gopalakrishnan, G.: Rigorous estimation of floating-point round-off errors with symbolic Taylor expansions. In: Bjørner, N., de Boer, F. (eds.) FM 2015. LNCS, vol. 9109, pp. 532–550. Springer, Cham (2015). https://doi.org/10.1007/978-3-319-19249-9_33
25. Sterbenz, P.H.: Floating Point Computation. Prentice-Hall, Upper Saddle River (1974)
26. The Coq Development Team: The Coq proof assistant reference manual, version 8.11.2 (2020). https://coq.inria.fr
27. Titolo, L., Feliú, M.A., Moscato, M., Muñoz, C.A.: An abstract interpretation framework for the round-off error analysis of floating-point programs. VMCAI 2018. LNCS, vol. 10747, pp. 516–537. Springer, Cham (2018). https://doi.org/10.1007/978-3-319-73721-8_24
28. Titolo, L., Muñoz, C.A., Feliú, M.A., Moscato, M.M.: Eliminating unstable tests in floating-point programs. In: Mesnard, F., Stuckey, P.J. (eds.) LOPSTR 2018. LNCS, vol. 11408, pp. 169–183. Springer, Cham (2019). https://doi.org/10.1007/978-3-030-13838-7_10
29. Zitoun, H.: Search strategies for solving constraint systems over floats for program verification. Université Côte d'Azur, Theses, October 2018
30. Zitoun, H., Michel, C., Rueher, M., Michel, L.: Search strategies for floating point constraint systems. In: Beck, J.C. (ed.) CP 2017. LNCS, vol. 10416, pp. 707–722. Springer, Cham (2017). https://doi.org/10.1007/978-3-319-66158-2_45

Towards Numerical Assistants
Trust, Measurement, Community, and Generality for the Numerical Workbench

Pavel Panchekha[1](✉) and Zachary Tatlock[2]

[1] University of Utah, Salt Lake City, UT, USA
pavpan@cs.utah.edu
[2] Paul G. Allen School, University of Washington, Seattle, WA, USA
ztatlock@cs.washington.edu

Abstract. The last few years have seen an explosion of work on tools that address numerical error in scientific, mathematical, and engineering software. The resulting tools can provide essential guidance to expert non-experts: scientists, mathematicians, and engineers for whom mathematical computation is essential but who may have little formal training in numerical methods. It is now time for these tools to move into practice.

Practitioners need a "numerical workbench" that not only succeeds as a research artifact but as a daily tool. We describe our experience adapting Herbie, a tool for numerical error repair, from a research prototype to a reliable workhorse for daily use. In particular, we focus on how we worked to increase user trust and use internal measurement to polish the tool. Looking more broadly, we show that community development and an investment in the generality of our tools, such as through the FPBench project, will better support users and strengthen our research community.

Floating-point rounding error is a problem for scientific, mathematical, and engineering software. Rounding error can destroy the utility of such software by rendering results meaningless; at the same time, few programmers—let alone programmers with expertise in the scientific, mathematical, or engineering domain in question—have the specialized numerical training necessary to account for and avoid rounding error.

The last few years have seen renewed interest from the broader programming languages community addressing this issue, with important progress in input generation [Kne17], error evaluation [SJRG15, TFMM18, TZPT19a], verification [ID17], tuning [DV19, DHS18, RGt13, CBB+17], and debugging [BHH12, SSPLT18, BZ13]. Herbie [PSSWT15] and FPBench [DMP+16] are our contribution to this effort. A unifying theme is the marriage of traditional programming language techniques with numerical notions of error, stability, and correctness. Tools cannot replace human expertise, but that expertise is rarely taught and thinly spread; tools can provide non-experts some recourse when numerical problems crop up.

© Springer Nature Switzerland AG 2020
M. Christakis et al. (Eds.): NSV 2020/VSTTE 2020, LNCS 12549, pp. 213–220, 2020.
https://doi.org/10.1007/978-3-030-63618-0_13

In this presentation, we briefly reflect on our past efforts and future plans towards building a "numerical workbench" of tools to help empower more programmers to confidently and effectively develop numerical software.

1   Trust and Measurement in Herbie

Herbie is a tool for rearranging and rephrasing mathematical expressions to minimize floating-point error. For example, a developer may be interested in evaluating the expression $\sqrt{x+1} - \sqrt{x}$, but concerned about error. They can pass the expression to Herbie (via Herbie's graphical user interface), and Herbie will output the rearrangement $1/(\sqrt{x+1} + \sqrt{x})$, which has much less rounding error [Ham87]. Herbie is aimed at expert non-experts: people with extensive training in some domain, and a need for mathematical computation to support their work, but without specific training in mathematical computation and numerical methods. Herbie is freely available online:

https://herbie.uwplse.org

Since we first published Herbie in 2015 [PSSWT15], we have been maintaining and improving Herbie to help these expert non-experts; we will soon release Herbie 1.4, and have had yearly releases since publication. We've found that maintenance has required few changes to the core algorithms, but extensive work on *trust* and *measurement*, work that often seemed orthogonal to Herbie's goal but was necessary to support our users.

Trust. Our users know that floating-point arithmetic is tricky, but they are rightly worried that replacing hand-written mathematical expressions with Herbie's suggestions will introduce bugs or make the code less maintainable; one textbook [Kne17] recommends keeping the original expression in a comment in case the code needs edits. We have thus built infrastructure for generating HTML reports with error charts, an interactive tester, and a derivation of the output expression from the input expression.[1] These reports reassure users, and also help us fix bugs and understand regressions.

Trust also stems from predictability. For example, Herbie can introduce if statements to select between alternative programs, and the branch conditions compare a variable to a constant:

$$\exp(x) - 1 \mapsto \left| \begin{array}{l} \textbf{if} \quad -10^{-4} < x < 10^{-4} \\ \textbf{then } x(1 + \frac{x}{2}(1 + \frac{x}{3})) \\ \textbf{else } \exp(x) - 1 \end{array} \right.$$

Prior to Herbie 1.2, that constant was always selected from among the 256 randomly-sampled input points Herbie was using to evaluate rounding error. As a result, each Herbie run would yield a different if statement, with the

---

[1] We recommend the reader try out the Herbie web demo, at https://herbie.uwplse.org/demo/, to see a report for themselves.

constants chosen often differing by factors of two. Users found this suspicious: if the branch is important, why is the branch condition seemingly-unimportant? We added a binary search step to refine the constant by sampling more points, ensuring that constants differed by less than 3% across runs. This change didn't affect our metrics–the more-accurate constant was no different on the evaluation points—but gained trust with users.

We have likewise made changes to simplify Herbie's output expressions, even at the cost of a slight accuracy penalty. If users do not *trust* that Herbie is accurate, they will not use it, at much larger cost to accuracy.

Measurement. After its initial publication, Herbie was, in the parlance of John D. Cook, a "software exoskeleton" [Coo]: a research prototype optimized to support quick development and experimentation, but featuring little coherence and several hacky kludges. That made it a poor fit for users: many bugs, confusing behavior, and poor explainability. Improving this state of affairs meant focusing our efforts on measurement and internal controls.

Doing so required first constructing a "theory of Herbie", giving each component a clear role and specification instead of evaluating Herbie end-to-end. For example, Herbie's regime inference component generates `if` statements that select between different floating-point expressions based on input ranges. That provides a clear measure of success: the resulting `if` statement is more accurate than any individual (branch-free) candidate program. Investigating the cases where it was not lead us to improve regime inference (by, for example, specially handling input points with equal outputs), even when end-to-end Herbie was performing well. Likewise, we developed an "oracle" for regime inference (evaluating each candidate program and selecting the one closest to a high-precision evaluation) to quantify how much accuracy regime inference was leaving on the table. Separating components according to their roles discovered new bugs, focused our efforts where they mattered, and improved Herbie's internal organization by enforcing a separation of concerns.

Measurement's other role was forcing us to consider alternative ways to evaluate Herbie's results. For example, comparison against Daisy [BPDT18] meant rectifying Herbie's average accuracy with Daisy's worst-case error analysis. The differences between the two lead to a better understanding of what "average accuracy" was really measuring: the size of the input space where the expression produced a meaningful answer. This realization led to a better understanding of Herbie's individual components. For example, regime inference could now be phrased as the union of input spaces, making its importance more clear.

Finally, measurement and trust build on one another. For example, we performed experiments to better establish Herbie's defaults. Our experiments showed that Herbie's default of 2048 randomly sampled inputs wasn't enough to find subtle errors while at the same time was overkill for finding simple errors, where even a hundred samples sufficed. We lowered the default, but not to the minimum possible: generality meant adding a generous safety margin, and Herbie now uses 256 sample points during search. But to ensure that subtle errors weren't ignored, we added a re-sampling stage with 8000 sample points for post-search validation. Here, better measuring the defaults made Herbie faster while increasing its trustworthiness.

2   Community and Generality in FPBench

FPBench [DMP+16] is a set of standards, benchmarks, and tools for studying the behavior of numerical kernels. Initially, we developed FPBench to enable interoperability between tools like Herbie [PSSWT15], Daisy [ID17], and Salsa [DM17]. These efforts proved successful [BPDT18] and several groups began adopting FPBench's interchange format and using its benchmarks for evaluating new tools [CR19, STF+19, JPV18, YCMJ17, ZMRM18]. As adoption has grown, we have discovered new challenges in supporting more diverse tools, especially with respect to multi-format, multi-precision (MPMF) computation and data structure support; newer versions of the FPBench standards and tools are adding features to address these challenges based on user feedback, discussion across the community, and early prototypes from the core FPBench development team.

Community Support. Herbie is but one tool—practitioners ultimately need a complete workbench of tools, from design-time tools like Herbie to additional tools for input generation, debugging, repair, and verification to support their work. As an academic community, we have neither the coordination nor the budget to develop the complete workbench as a single, integrated tool. Thus, better supporting our users has meant developing standards and formats for combining tools, and ensuring that other researchers can make use of our work.

This need was the catalyst for the FPBench project [DMP+16]. Originally developed so that Herbie and Salsa [Mar09, DMC15, DM17] could share benchmarks, FPBench has grown into a standard format for expressing multi-precision, multi-format numerical computations. FPBench collects benchmarks from multiple research groups, adds standard metadata, and provides tools for compilation to other languages (including the input formats to other community tools) and for standard program transformations (such as loop unrolling). FPBench binds the community more tightly making it easier for users to try out multiple research tools.

Supporting users also means making it easier for users to discover new research tools and try them out with minimal investment. The FPBench community page (https://fpbench.org/community.html), maintained by Mike Lam, attempts a comprehensive listing of floating-point research tools, along with brief summaries about what they do, making it easy for non-experts to explore and understand the space. And some of these tools, including Herbie, offer a web-based demo tool, reducing the cost for users to try them out. We make it easy to launch these tools from the FPBench benchmarks page (https://fpbench.org/benchmarks.html) so users can immediately try a tool without even having to come up with example inputs.

These investments in a cohesive community of floating-point researchers helps users by surfacing useful tools and allowing those tools to interoperate, and has also helped us as researchers compare and contrast multiple tools [BPDT18], uncover bugs in Herbie, and bring in a continuous stream of users that file bugs, make improvements, and suggest features that make Herbie more practical.

Generality. Trust and measurement make a tool better; users then apply that tool to new problems and expanded domains. One clear example has been interest in applying Herbie to new number systems. Herbie was initially developed to support rearrangement of double-precision formulas; while it has always supported single-precision as well, that support has been fragile. Meanwhile, new number systems such as posits [GY17] have become increasingly prominent. Researchers thus reached out to see if Herbie could better support posits, bfloat16, and other novel number systems being developed. Herbie 1.3 thus introduced a split between types (such as real numbers) and representations (such as double-precision), and added a plugin system to define new representations via their bit representation and real values.

However, supporting new number requires strengthening Herbie's other components. For example, Herbie uses random sampling to evaluate the error of expressions; this requires establishing a ground-truth, correct result for an expression at a point. Herbie uses arbitrary-precision arithmetic for this, and that requires choosing a sufficient precision. Herbie originally used a hand-tuned algorithm that worked well in double-precision but turned out to fail disastrously for lower precision, returning incorrect ground-truth values and corrupting Herbie's results. This leads us to switch to a slower but provably-sound interval-analysis technique [LB90]. As a benefit, the technique is not only sound but also more easily measurable and generalizes to arbitrary number representations.

Users would also like to apply Herbie to expressions besides pure floating-point expressions, most importantly matrix operations. This too requires flexibility, most importantly allowing users to define new rewrite rules for Herbie to use. While Herbie always operated from a library of rewrite rules, its internal algorithms were quite brittle, and tweaking the set of rules used was frequently necessary, making user-extensibility difficult. Our work on Egg [WWF+20] was motivated by the need to build easy, efficient, and extensible tools for operating with large libraries of rewrite rules, and involved a breakthrough in congruence-closure data structures that made Herbie's internal algorithms 60× faster, with gains continuing as we improve this library.

3   The Future

The growth of machine learning, robotics, and high-performance computing are making numerical errors a growing concern. In machine learning, for example, a growing interest in custom hardware and new number representations [Int18, Joh18] means numerical techniques need to be ported or reimagined for new number representations. Tools must expand in scope from short expressions to matrix and tensor computations. Trust, measurement, and generality remain key themes but must be extended to new domains.

Trust requires that the rise of new precisions and formats, and the rise of multi-precision, multi-format computation is accompanied by clear semantics and standard formats. Yet existing languages usually do not offer this, relegating the precise meaning of a floating-point computation to ad-hoc interpretations of IEEE-754. In FPBench, we are attempting to standardize on a format general enough to incorporate many proposed number systems [TZPT19b], and we are working on making Herbie's core support multiple precisions. The work is, however, rough going: a careful split between the real-number and floating-point semantics has to be brought in, and mixed-precision computations raise complex issues even at the level of type-checking programs.

Measurement also requires that FPBench expand to support new applications. Beyond the mixed-precision support added in FPBench 1.2, matrix and tensor computations must be given expression, given their clear centrality in modern numerical work. In FPBench 2.0 we hope to add the `tensor` and `for` constructs for regular loop structures and tabular data structures. Supporting these in analysis tools, however, will be its own challenge, since tensors introduce new exceptional cases (array out of bounds), new data types (indices), and new scaling challenges (thousands of variables). It is unclear how tools will adapt.

Finally, the rapidly evolving numerical environment also raises the burden of *generality*. Herbie, at its publication and still, relies on a core of hand-crafted rules combined together with a general-purpose search algorithm. As programs get more complex, crafting these rules is a challenge, and more and more special cases (triangular matrices, tridiagonal matrices, ...) mean that user extensibility becomes essential. We have been simplifying Herbie's core to rely more on components which support such generalization, transitioning more of Herbie to equivalence graphs and trading our custom evaluation algorithm for a traditional, interval-analysis based approach. We hope generality and simplicity can insulate us from change, but that remains to be seen.

Conclusion. Future programmers will face a vastly more complex numerical space, with novel number representations, new applications, and less support from the numerical methods literature. They will thus rely on a constellation of tools that help them evaluate error, improve their programs, and debug issues. Our experience building and maintaining Herbie suggests that many of these tools are on the cusp of user-friendliness, and that investment in trust, measurement, and generality will pay off for both researchers and the users of these tools. Furthermore, investing in community infrastructure will enable better research and greater impact for the whole community.

Acknowledgments. Herbie and FPBench are the result of many years of work from stellar contributors including Alex Sanchez-Stern, Bill Zorn, David Thien, Oliver Flatt, Brett Saiki, Jason Qiu, Ian Briggs, Heiko Becker, Eva Darulova, Max Willsey, James Wilcox, and many others. This work was supported by the Applications Driving Architectures (ADA) Research Center, a JUMP Center co-sponsored by SRC and DARPA.

References

[BHH12] Benz, F., Hildebrandt, A., Hack, S.: A dynamic program analysis to find floating-point accuracy problems. In: PLDI 2012, pp. 453–462. ACM (2012)

[BPDT18] Becker, H., Panchekha, P., Darulova, E., Tatlock, Z.: Combining tools for optimization and analysis of floating-point computations. In: FM, pp. 355–363 (2018)

[BZ13] Bao, T., Zhang, X.: On-the-fly detection of instability problems in floating-point program execution. SIGPLAN Not. **48**(10), 817–832 (2013)

[CBB+17] Chiang, W.F., Baranowski, M., Briggs, I., Solovyev, A., Gopalakrishnan, G., Rakamaric, Z.: Rigorous floating-point mixed-precision tuning. In: POPL, pp. 300–315 (2017)

[Coo] Cook, J.D.: Software exoskeletons. https://www.johndcook.com/blog/2011/07/21/software-exoskeletons/. Accessed 5 June 2020

[CR19] Claude, M., Rueher, M.: Dedicated search strategies for finding critical counterexamples in programs with floating point computations. In: 2019 IEEE International Conference on Artificial Intelligence Testing (AITest), pp. 138–139 (2019)

[DHS18] Darulova, E., Horn, E., Sharma, S.: Sound mixed-precision optimization with rewriting. In: ICCPS, pp. 208–219 (2018)

[DM17] Damouche, N., Martel, M.: Salsa: an automatic tool to improve the numerical accuracy of programs. In: AFM (2017)

[DMC15] Damouche, N., Martel, M., Chapoutot, A.: Formal methods for industrial critical systems. In: 20th International Workshop, FMICS 2015, Oslo, Norway, 22–23 June 2015, pp. 31–46 (2015)

[DMP+16] Damouche, N., Martel, M., Panchekha, P., Qiu, C., Sanchez-Stern, A., Tatlock, Z.: Toward a standard benchmark format and suite for floating-point analysis. In: Bogomolov, S., Martel, M., Prabhakar, P. (eds.) NSV 2016. LNCS, vol. 10152, pp. 63–77. Springer, Cham (2017). https://doi.org/10.1007/978-3-319-54292-8_6

[DV19] Darulova, E., Volkova, A.: Sound approximation of programs with elementary functions. In: Dillig, I., Tasiran, S. (eds.) CAV 2019. LNCS, vol. 11562, pp. 174–183. Springer, Cham (2019). https://doi.org/10.1007/978-3-030-25543-5_11

[GY17] Gustafson, J., Yonemoto, I.: Beating floating point at its own game: Posit arithmetic. Supercomput. Front. Innov. **4**, 71–86 (2017)

[Ham87] Hamming, R.: Numerical Methods for Scientists and Engineers, 2nd edn. Dover Publications, New York (1987)

[ID17] Izycheva, A., Darulova, E.: On sound relative error bounds for floating-point arithmetic. In: FMCAD, pp. 15–22 (2017)

[Int18] Intel. BFLOAT16 - Hardware Numerics, : White Paper, Document Number: 338302–001US. Revision 1.0

[Joh18] Johnson, J.: Rethinking floating point for deep learning. CoRR, abs/1811.01721 (2018)

[JPV18] Jacquemin, M., Putot, S., Védrine, F.: A reduced product of absolute and relative error bounds for floating-point analysis. In: Podelski, A. (ed.) SAS 2018. LNCS, vol. 11002, pp. 223–242. Springer, Cham (2018). https://doi.org/10.1007/978-3-319-99725-4_15

[Kne17] Kneusel, R.T.: Arbitrary precision floating-point. Numbers and Computers, pp. 265–292. Springer, Cham (2017). https://doi.org/10.1007/978-3-319-50508-4_9

[LB90]   Lee, V.A., Boehm, H.-J.: Optimizing programs over the constructive reals. In: PLDI 1990 (1990)

[Mar09] Martel, M.: Program transformation for numerical precision. In: PEPM 2009, pp. 101–110. ACM (2009)

[PSSWT15] Panchekha, P., Sanchez-Stern, A., Wilcox, J.R., Tatlock, Z.: Automatically improving accuracy for floating point expressions. In: PLDI (2015)

[RGt13] Rubio-González, C., et al.: Precimonious: tuning assistant for floating-point precision. In: SC, pp. 1–12. IEEE (2013)

[SJRG15] Solovyev, A., Jacobsen, C., Rakamaric, Z., Gopalakrishnan, G.: Rigorous estimation of floating-point round-off errors with symbolic Taylor expansions. In: FM (2015)

[SSPLT18] Sanchez-Stern, A., Panchekha, P., Lerner, S., Tatlock, Z.: Finding root causes of floating point error. In: PLDI, pp. 256–269 (2018)

[STF+19] Salvia, R., Titolo, L., Feliú, M.A., Moscato, M.M., Muñoz, C.A., Rakamarić, Z.: A mixed real and floating-point solver. In: Badger, J.M., Rozier, K.Y. (eds.) NFM 2019. LNCS, vol. 11460, pp. 363–370. Springer, Cham (2019). https://doi.org/10.1007/978-3-030-20652-9_25

[TFMM18] Titolo, L., Feliú, M.A., Moscato, M., Muñoz, C.A.: An abstract interpretation framework for the round-off error analysis of floating-point programs. VMCAI 2018. LNCS, vol. 10747, pp. 516–537. Springer, Cham (2018). https://doi.org/10.1007/978-3-319-73721-8_24

[TZPT19a] Thien, D., Zorn, B., Panchekha, P., Tatlock, Z.: Toward multi-precision, multi-format numerics. In: 2019 IEEE/ACM 3rd International Workshop on Software Correctness for HPC Applications (Correctness), pp. 19–26 (2019)

[TZPT19b] Thien, D., Zorn, B., Panchekha, P., Tatlock, Z.: Toward multi-precision, multi-format numerics. In: Laguna, I., Rubio-González, C. (ed) 2019 IEEE/ACM 3rd International Workshop on Software Correctness for HPC Applications (Correctness), Denver, CO, USA, 18 November 2019, pp. 19–26. IEEE (2019)

[WWF+20] Willsey, M., Wang, Y.R., Flatt, O., Nandi, C., Panchekha, P., Tatlock, Z.: egg: Easy, efficient, and extensible e-graphs (2020)

[YCMJ17] Yi, X., Chen, L., Mao, X., Ji, T.: Automated repair of high inaccuracies in numerical programs. In: 2017 IEEE International Conference on Software Maintenance and Evolution (ICSME), pp. 514–518 (2017)

[ZMRM18] Zitoun, H., Michel, C., Rueher, M., Michel, L.: Sub-domain selection strategies for floating point constraint systems. In: 24th International Conference on Principles and Practice of Constraint Programming Doctoral Program CP 2018, July 2018

Combining Zonotope Abstraction and Constraint Programming for Synthesizing Inductive Invariants

Bibek Kabi[1], Eric Goubault[1], Antoine Miné[2], and Sylvie Putot[1(✉)]

[1] LIX, Ecole Polytechnique, CNRS, Institut Polytechnique de Paris, Palaiseau, France
putot@lix.polytechnique.fr
[2] Sorbonne Université, CNRS, Laboratoire d'Informatique de Paris 6, Paris, France

Abstract. We propose to extend an existing framework combining abstract interpretation and continuous constraint programming for numerical invariant synthesis, by using more expressive underlying abstract domains, such as zonotopes. The original method, which relies on iterative refinement, splitting and tightening a collection of abstract elements until reaching an inductive set, was initially presented in combination with simple underlying abstract elements: boxes and octagons. The novelty of our work is to use zonotopes, a sub-polyhedric domain that shows a good compromise between cost and precision. As zonotopes are not closed under intersection, we had to extend the existing framework, in addition to designing new operations on zonotopes, such as a novel splitting algorithm based on paving zonotopes by sub-zonotopes and parallelotopes. We implemented this method on top of the APRON library, and tested it on programs with non-linear loops that present complex, possibly non-convex, invariants. We present some results demonstrating both the interest of this splitting-based algorithm to synthesize invariants on such programs, and the good compromise presented by its use in combination with zonotopes with respect to its use with both simpler domains such as boxes and octagons, and more expressive domains such as polyhedra.

1 Introduction

Proving loop invariants is a key ingredient in the verification of safety properties on programs. The classic method to prove that a set is indeed an invariant is to look for an *inductive invariant* which implies it, i.e., a state property that is stable by an iteration of the loop. Notably, the set of program states reachable from the initial states is the least (i.e. most precise) inductive invariant. Generally, this set is difficult to compute, so that we settle for an over-approximation, as any such over-approximation is also an invariant. Inductive invariants play a special role in program verification because they can be checked by running a single loop iteration and checking its stability, even for unbounded loops. A key

© Springer Nature Switzerland AG 2020
M. Christakis et al. (Eds.): NSV 2020/VSTTE 2020, LNCS 12549, pp. 221–238, 2020.
https://doi.org/10.1007/978-3-030-63618-0_14

```
x=[0.9,1.1];y=[0.9,1.1];
while (True) {
    xnew=2x/(0.2 + x^2 + y^2 +
        1.53x^2y^2);
    ynew=2y/(0.2 + x^2 + y^2 +
        1.53x^2y^2);
    x=xnew;y=ynew;
}
```

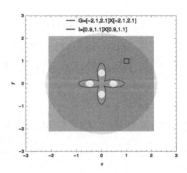

Fig. 1. (a) Example program; (b) Non-inductive invariants for the program. (Color figure online)

issue is that not all invariants are inductive, and it is often necessary, given a target invariant property to prove, to first strengthen it into an inductive invariant. We illustrate the main results of this work on the program (taken from online additional material of [1]) in Fig. 1(a), with initial values of variables (x, y) in the box $I \stackrel{\text{def}}{=} [0.9, 1.1]^2$ and the effect of a loop iteration on a set X of possible variable values $(x, y) \in X$ given by the function $F : \mathcal{P}(\mathbb{R}^2) \to \mathcal{P}(\mathbb{R}^2)$ defined as the loop body of Fig. 1(a). The box $T = [-2.1, 2.1]^2$, shown in blue in Fig. 1(b), is a valid invariant: T includes all the states reachable at the loop head, i.e., $\bigcup_{n \in \mathbb{N}} F^n(I) \subseteq T$. However, T is not an inductive invariant as $F(T) \not\subseteq T$: indeed, F maps the box T to a circle, that goes a bit outside the box T. Consider the four-petal flower shape towards the center shown in Fig. 1(b): its interior is not reachable from the initial box I, and it contains the four small circles in white which are the inverse image by F of the four parts of the circle that go beyond box T. To prove that T is an invariant for executions beginning in I, we need to infer an inductive invariant G that is included in T, and precise enough to express that the small circles inside each petal of T are not reachable states. But all such invariants have a complex shape, that cannot be represented in classical abstract domains. The idea of [1], inspired from contraint programming approaches, is to synthetize an inductive invariant as a collection of abstract elements, that are iteratively split and refined. In set-based constraint programming, these elements are generally boxes. Previous work [1] was limited to abstract domains that are closed by intersection (such as polyhedra or octagons) and required a non-standard operation: split. In this article, we extend this work to other abstract domains such as zonotopes. We show that their use in this context provides an interesting trade-off between expressiveness and efficiency, by comparing their use with that of boxes, octagons, and polyhedra. For example, on the program of Fig. 1, Figs. 2(a)–2(d) show the inductive invariant G within T as found by our algorithm in combination with box, octagon, polyhedron and zonotope abstract domains. Inference with intervals (resp. octagons, polyhedra, and zonotopes) takes 646.8 (resp. 8850.8, 126.8, and 35.6) seconds and produces

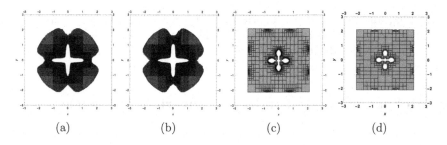

Fig. 2. Inductive invariant obtained by our algorithm using (a) boxes; (b) octagons; (c) polyhedra and (d) zonotopes.

an inductive invariant composed of 129781 (resp. 129767, 2368, and 488) parts. Less expressive domains such as boxes and octagons rely heavily on splitting, hence output a large set of elements and are slower in total, in spite of a smaller cost of manipulating a single abstract element. In particular, in polyhedra and zonotopes, the image by the loop body in the abstract domain, of a box on the left corner in Figs. 2(c)–2(d) is within the collection of elements, thus proven invariant, whereas it will not be the case in the box or octagon abstract domains, ultimately leading by splitting to the refinement of Figs. 2(a)–2(b).

Zonotopes are a cost-effective, versatile, and precise abstract domain [2] that can represent restricted forms of polyhedra as Minkowski sums of line segments. They feature more lightweight algorithms than general polyhedra, while being more expressive than other sub-polyhedra domains (e.g., octagons). They are particularly well suited to approximate non-linear functions. Yet, zonotopes do not form a lattice and do not enjoy an exact intersection, which is required in [1]. We thus need to adapt this approach, in addition to defining split and meet operators, intersection tests, and inclusion tests specifically for zonotopes.

Related Work. Garg et al. [3] developed a learning paradigm for loop invariant synthesis known as ICE, where the learner synthesizes invariants and the teacher verifies them using a constraint solver such as SMT. Thakur et al. [4] discussed a method based on abstract interpretation and SMT solving for searching inductive invariants. Essentially, the recent line of work dedicated to synthesizing invariants combines abstract interpretation and constraint-based techniques (SAT/SMT solvers). The idea of using SAT/SMT is similar to ours, except that we focus on other classes of algorithms, those used in continuous constraint programming, and we work on geometric entities, such as boxes and zonotopes, instead of logical formulas.

Contribution. Our contributions are as follows: firstly, we extend the method of [1] to domains not closed under intersection; secondly, we introduce new zonotope operators: split, inclusion and intersection tests; finally, we present a prototype, extending the Taylor1+ zonotope abstract domain [5] in the Apron library [6], and adapting the algorithm of [1]. Section 2 recalls the algorithm from [1]; Sect. 3.1 recalls the zonotope domain, introduces our new operators, and discusses how to handle domains that are not intersection-closed; Sect. 4 presents our experimental evaluation; Sect. 5 concludes and discusses future works.

2   Refinement-Based Inductive Invariant Inference

We now recall the algorithm from [1] to tighten an invariant into an inductive invariant, by splitting and tightening a collection of abstract elements.

We assume without loss of generality that variables are real-valued (which includes integers and non-special float values). A program environment is a subset of $\mathbb{R}^n$, where n is the number of variables. The concrete semantics of a program is the collecting semantics of [7]: it is given as the least fixpoint of a function $F : \mathcal{P}(\mathbb{R}^n) \rightarrow \mathcal{P}(\mathbb{R}^n)$ over an initial environment $I \subseteq \mathbb{R}^n$; typically, when a program consists of just one loop, F is the transfer function for one loop iteration.

We also assume here that we are given a target invariant $T \subseteq \mathbb{R}^n$. The goal of this article is to infer an inductive invariant $G \subseteq \mathbb{R}^n$ that proves that T is indeed an invariant. This requires finding G such that: $I \subseteq G$ (G includes the initial states), $F(G) \subseteq G$ (induction), and $G \subseteq T$ (invariant entailment).

As a first step, we replace computations in $\mathcal{P}(\mathbb{R}^n)$ with computations in an abstract domain $\mathcal{D}^\sharp \subseteq \mathcal{P}(\mathbb{R}^n)$ of tractable subsets of $\mathbb{R}^n$, such as boxes, octagons, polyhedra, or zonotopes. The abstract version of F, overapproximating the concrete semantics, is denoted by $F^\sharp : \mathcal{D}^\sharp \rightarrow \mathcal{D}^\sharp$.

Instead of generating an inductive invariant in $\mathcal{D}^\sharp$, as classically done in abstract interpretation based analyzers, we are going to look for one in the much more expressive *disjunctive completion* of $\mathcal{D}^\sharp$, i.e. in $\mathcal{P}(\mathcal{D}^\sharp)$. More precisely, we are going to synthetize finite collections $G^\sharp \subseteq \mathcal{D}^\sharp$ of abstract elements, $G^\sharp = \{S_1, \ldots, S_n\}$ that satisfies: $I \subseteq \underset{i}{\cup} S_i$, $\forall k : F^\sharp(S_k) \subseteq \underset{i}{\cup} S_i$, and $\underset{i}{\cup} S_i \subseteq T$, which implies that $\underset{i}{\cup} S_i$ is an inductive invariant. To simplify, we assume that both the initial state I and the target invariant T are exactly expressible in $\mathcal{D}^\sharp$.

Search Algorithm. The algorithm of [1] we are building upon in this article maintains a finite collection $G^\sharp \subseteq \mathcal{D}^\sharp$ that forms a candidate inductive invariant. It is initialized with the (non-inductive) target invariant: $G^\sharp = \{T\}$. We ensure at all times that $I \subseteq \underset{i}{\cup} S_i \subseteq T$, and iteratively refine $G^\sharp$ until it becomes inductive, i.e., until $\forall k : F^\sharp(S_k) \subseteq \underset{i}{\cup} S_i$. While $G^\sharp$ is not inductive, we iterate the following steps, adding, removing, and updating elements in $G^\sharp$:

- pick an element $S_k \in G^\sharp$ with $F^\sharp(S_k) \not\subseteq \underset{i}{\cup} S_i$, i.e., preventing inductiveness;
- either discard S_k from $G^\sharp$, split it into two elements that are added back to $G^\sharp$, or tighten (i.e., shrink) it.

To decide the action to perform, it is useful to classify an abstract element S_k in relation to the other elements in $G^\sharp$ and their image by $F^\sharp$. We say that S_k is:

- *doomed* if $F^\sharp(S_k) \cap (\bigcup_i S_i) = \emptyset$; such an element will always prevent inductiveness and must be discarded;
- *benign* if $F^\sharp(S_k) \subseteq \bigcup_i S_i$, i.e., it does not prevent inductiveness and does not need to be changed;
- *necessary* if $S_k \cap I \neq \emptyset$, i.e., it cannot be discarded, to keep ensuring that $I \subseteq \bigcup_i S_i$ always holds;
- *useful* if $S_k \cap (\bigcup_i F^\sharp(S_i)) \neq \emptyset$, i.e., at least an element from $G^\sharp$ relies on S_k to be benign.

Remark 1. Note that, to decide if an abstract element is *necessary* or *useful*, the algorithm requires a test for checking intersection. This test must be an exact one because discarding a necessary or useful element can result in a failure.

The algorithm first selects a non-benign element S_k. It is discarded if it is either doomed or not useful, unless it is necessary. Otherwise, it is generally split. By spliting S_k, we can hope to isolate the part that is doomed, and is ultimately discarded, from the part that is benign, and kept in the final inductive invariant. To guide our choice, a useful quantitative measure is that of coverage:

$$\text{coverage}(S_k) := \frac{\text{vol}(F^\sharp(S_k) \cap (\bigcup_i S_i))}{\text{vol}(F^\sharp(S_k))} \tag{1}$$

where $\text{vol}(X)$ is the volume of a set X. Intuitively, the coverage measure denotes how much the image of S_k lies in the candidate invariant, i.e., how much it is inductive. Note that, for this to make sense, it is important to rely on the fact that the S_i do not overlap (except maybe on common borders that have a null volume). The algorithm systematically picks the element $S_k \in G^\sharp$ with least coverage in priority, as it requires the most urgent action.

Remark 2. In [1], elements with a very low coverage are systematically discarded, as unlikely to become benign. However, it is possible that an abstract element may intersect every inductive invariant, in which case discarding this element will result in a failure. So, in the current work, we only discard an abstract element if it has a coverage of 0, i.e., it is doomed.

Tightening. Any part of an S_k that does not intersect any $F^\sharp(S_i)$ is not useful and can safely be discarded, improving the likelihood that S_k becomes benign, without making other benign elements non-benign. An additional tightening step can help the search algorithm by replacing S_k with: $\bigcup_i (S_k \cap F^\sharp(S_i)) \cup (S_k \cap I)$ suitably overapproximated to an element representable in the abstract domain.

Data Structure. To compute the coverage, and in particular $\text{vol}(F^\sharp(S_k) \cap (\bigcup_i S_i))$, it is useful to identify which elements $S_i \in G^\sharp$ each image $F^\sharp(S_k)$ may intersect. To do this efficiently, we maintain a partition $B^\sharp \subseteq \mathcal{D}^\sharp$ of the target space T, as well as a map post $: G^\sharp \to \mathcal{P}(B^\sharp)$ to denote which parts of $B^\sharp$ intersect the image of each abstract element $S_k \in G^\sharp$: $\text{post}(S_k) := \{P \in B^\sharp \mid F^\sharp(S_k) \cap P \neq \emptyset\}$. Moreover, we ensure that any element in $B^\sharp$ completely contains at most one element in $G^\sharp$. We maintain a *contents-of* function cnt : $B^\sharp \rightarrow (G^\sharp \cup \{\emptyset\})$ indicating which abstract element of $G^\sharp$, if any, is contained in each element of $B^\sharp$: $\forall S_i \in G^\sharp, \exists! B_j \in B^\sharp, \text{cnt}(B_j) = S_i$; moreover, $S_i \subseteq B_j$. Assuming that $B^\sharp$ is available, then the coverage function can be optimized by only considering the relevant parts from $B^\sharp$:

$$\text{coverage}(S_k) := \frac{\sum \{\text{vol}(F^\sharp(S_k) \cap \text{cnt}(P)) \mid P \in \text{post}(S_k)\}}{\text{vol}(F^\sharp(S_k))} \tag{2}$$

$B^\sharp$ is initialized to $\{T\}$ (as $G^\sharp$) and it is split the same way $G^\sharp$ is. However, elements in $B^\sharp$ are not tightened, so that $B^\sharp$ remains a partition of T. The maps cnt and post can be efficiently maintained when the elements from $B^\sharp$ and $G^\sharp$ are split, removed, or tightened, as detailed in [1].

Remark 3. The coverage information is first used to decide which S_i in $G^\sharp$ require urgent action. Then, it is used to decide whether to split or discard. As this is only a heuristic, an exact volume computation is not mandatory to ensure correctness. [1] relies on the volume of bounding boxes as it is easy to compute for the domains considered there. As bounding boxes and volume computations are expensive for zonotopes, we will introduce another heuristic that does not rely on computing volumes.

Testing whether an abstract element is benign, i.e. maintains inductiveness, requires inclusion checking: S_k is benign if, whenever $F^\sharp(S_k)$ intersects some partition $P \in B^\sharp$, the intersection is included in $cnt(P) \in G^\sharp$. We also need to check that $F^\sharp(S_k)$ is included within the candidate invariant T. Formally:

$$S_k \text{ is benign} \iff \forall P \in \text{post}(S_k) : P \cap F^\sharp(S_k) \subseteq \text{cnt}(P) \wedge F^\sharp(S_k) \subseteq T \tag{3}$$

Unlike coverage computation, this inclusion check must be exact to ensure that we indeed have an inductive invariant, i.e., that our method is sound.

The algorithm is parameterized by a choice of abstract domain $\mathcal{D}^\sharp$. In addition to an abstract version $F^\sharp$ of F, already provided by abstract interpretation, it requires a split operator, a meet operator for tightening, tests to check intersection and inclusion. Such operators have been proposed for boxes and octagons in [1]. In the following, we will provide these operators for zonotopes and also adapt the coverage operation from [1] by replacing the volume operator.

3   Zonotope Abstraction and Constraint Solving

We now adapt the algorithm introduced in Sect. 2 to use in combination with the abstract domain of zonotopes. We first introduce zonotopes as a classical abstract domain, then describe the new operations that were designed for the specific use here.

3.1   Affine Forms and Zonotopes

Zonotopes are based on affine arithmetic [8], an extension of interval arithmetic expressing dependencies between variables. More precisely, the set of values of a program variable x is abstracted by an affine expression of the form $\hat{x} := \alpha_0{}^x + \sum_{i=1}^{n} \alpha_i{}^x \varepsilon_i$, where ε_i are symbolic variables, called noise symbols, whose values are restricted to $[-1, 1]$. Linear dependencies between program variables can be expressed by sharing noise symbols. The set of possible values of all the variables x_k when the noise symbols vary in $[-1, 1]$ is a zonotope, i.e., a center-symmetric polytope (a bounded polyhedron) with center-symmetric faces. Compared to other restrictions of polyhedra, such as octagons or templates, the directions of zonotopic faces are not fixed *a priori*, providing some flexibility in the analysis. Zonotopes have already proved to be a simple and tractable set representation for program analysis [2,5].

Consider a tuple of affine forms $\hat{x}_i$ for p variables x_i over n noise symbols ε_j, $\hat{x}_i = \alpha_0{}^{x_i} + \sum_{k=1}^{n} \alpha_k{}^{x_i} \varepsilon_k$. This defines a matrix $A \in M(n+1, p)$ whose (j, i) entry, for $i = 1, \ldots, p$, $j = 0, \ldots, n$ is $A_{j,i} = \alpha_j^{x_i}$. The zonotope concretization is

$$\gamma(A) = \left\{ A^{\mathrm{T}} \begin{pmatrix} 1 \\ e \end{pmatrix} \mid e \in \mathbb{R}^n, \|e\|_\infty \leq 1 \right\} \subseteq \mathbb{R}^p \qquad (4)$$

For $n = 3$ and $p = 2$, the zonotope (the center symmetric polygon in blue) in Fig. 3(a) is the concretisation (joint range) of the affine forms $X = (\hat{x}, \hat{y})$ with $\hat{x} = 18 + 2\varepsilon_1 + 1\varepsilon_2 + 3\varepsilon_3$, $\hat{y} = 12 + 1\varepsilon_2 + 5\varepsilon_3$, that is, $A^{\mathrm{T}} = \begin{pmatrix} 18 & 2 & 1 & 3 \\ 12 & 0 & 1 & 5 \end{pmatrix}$. In what follows, we note $A_+ \in \mathcal{M}(n, p)$ the submatrix of $A \in \mathcal{M}(n+1, p)$, without its first column, that corresponds to the center of the zonotope. Each column of A_+ defines a generator of the zonotope, and we also represent zonotope A as $(c, g_1, \ldots g_n)$, i.e., as its center c and its collection of generators $g_1, \ldots, g_n$. For the example above, we would write $A = ((18, 12), (2, 0), (1, 1), (3, 5))$. This zonotope is spanned by the generators drawn in its center in Fig. 3(a). The Minkowski sum of the line segments described by those vectors is the zonotope itself.

3.2   Zonotope Operators

Inclusion. The best known methods for inclusion tests are known to have exponential time (in terms of the number of generators) for zonotopes [2]. Lemma 1 below is an extension of Lemma 4 from [2], which transforms the inclusion test into an infinite number of simple inequalities, that in turn translate into an exponential number of linear programs to be solved. We show below how to further decrease the number of linear programs to solve, so as to go from an exponential to a polynomial number.

Lemma 1. *For two zonotopes given by matrices $X \in \mathcal{M}(n_X + 1, p)$ and $Y \in \mathcal{M}(n_Y + 1, p)$, let $u = \{u_1, \ldots, u_k\}$ be vectors in $\mathbb{R}^p$ such that each face in $\gamma(Y)$ has a vector in u that is normal to it. Then $\gamma(X) \subseteq \gamma(Y)$ if and only if*

$$\left| \langle u_i, c_x - c_y \rangle \right| \leq \|Y_+ u_i\|_1 - \|X_+ u_i\|_1, \forall i = 1, \ldots, k \tag{5}$$

where c_x, c_y are the centers of the zonotopes $\gamma(X)$, $\gamma(Y)$ respectively

Remark 4. For a zonotope of dimension p with n generators, the upper bound on the number of faces, and thus on vectors u_i, is $2\binom{n}{p-1}$. Thus, the complexity of the inclusion test is $2\binom{n}{p-1} \times \mathcal{O}(np)$ which improves on the exponential bound of [2]. Indeed, the authors proved in [2] that $\gamma(X) \subseteq \gamma(Y)$, if and only if (5) is satisfied for all $u \in \mathbb{R}^p$. Lemma 1 shows that it is sufficient to check the inequality (5) for only a finite (polynomial in p) number of u. We can use singular value decomposition to compute the vectors u.

Meet. As observed in [2], zonotopes are closed under linear transformation and under the Minkowski sum, but the set-theoretic intersection of zonotopes is not always a zonotope [2]. Inspired from previous works in [9,10] on zonotope and polyhedron intersection, a zonotope-zonotope intersection can be over-approximated by sequential computation of intersection of the zonotope and the half-spaces.

Several methods have been proposed to compute an over-approximation (e.g., in [10–12]) of the intersection of a zonotope and a linear space geometrically. Ghorbal et al. [13] proposed a method based on functional interpretation of the intersection of a zonotope with a guard. It computes a simple yet sufficiently precise over-approximation by using constrained affine sets: the constraints produced by the tests in a program are interpreted over the noise symbols of the affine forms.

Computing the meet of a zonotope with another one as the sequence of meet of the zonotope with the faces of the other can be imprecise, as the meet with linear space is an over-approximation, and imprecision will accumulate quickly. Hence, the need for a zonotope meet that can take into account all faces of the second argument at once. There are methods which directly focus on meets between zonotopes by set representations based on collections of sets. For instance, Althoff et al. [14] and Tommaso et al. [15] introduced zonotope bundles, defined as the intersection of a set of zonotopes. Note that the intersection is not computed explicitly. Rather the zonotopes are stored in a list and all operations are performed on individual zonotopes. These methods can be accurate, but the related cost increases with the number of sets required, which can be large.

Here we introduce a new geometric meet operation on zonotopes based on the following observation. Let $\mathfrak{Z}_1$ (resp. $\mathfrak{Z}_2$) be a zonotope represented by matrix M_1 (resp. M_2) and let x be a point in the intersection of $\mathfrak{Z}_1$ and $\mathfrak{Z}_2$. Then, there exists $e \in [-1, 1]^p$ (resp. $e' \in [-1, 1]^p$) such that $x = M_1^{\mathrm{T}} \begin{pmatrix} 1 \\ e \end{pmatrix}$ and $x = M_2^{\mathrm{T}} \begin{pmatrix} 1 \\ e' \end{pmatrix}$.

For any $\alpha \in [0,1]$, trivially, $x = \alpha x + (1-\alpha)x$, therefore:

$$\mathfrak{z}_1 \cap \mathfrak{z}_2 \subseteq \left\{ \alpha M_1^{\mathrm{T}} \begin{pmatrix} 1 \\ e \end{pmatrix} + (1-\alpha) M_2^{\mathrm{T}} \begin{pmatrix} 1 \\ e' \end{pmatrix}, ||e||_\infty \leq 1, ||e'||_\infty \leq 1 \right\}.$$

The right hand side of the inclusion above is the zonotope obtained as the Minkowski sum of zonotope $\mathfrak{z}_1$ (scaled by coefficient α) with zonotope $\mathfrak{z}_2$ (scaled by coefficient $1-\alpha$), up to some translation.

Note that the meet operator introduces new directions of faces. As we will see, this gives more flexibility to our splitting operator, that uses a tiling to pave the zonotope obtained after the meet into sub-zonotopes. This approach only provides an over-approximation of the intersection. Therefore, when using the algorithm of [1], we will not apply the tightening at each step, but only at the initial step. While this does not prevent the convergence of the algorithm, the resulting invariant set may be larger than with tightening at each step. The aim of the method being to prove efficiently that an initial target region is actually invariant by computing an inner inductive invariant, we did not consider tightening at each step a key feature.

Intersection Test. In the generic algorithm of Sect. 2, we need to know when two abstract elements intersect. Consider a zonotope $\mathfrak{z}_1$ given by its center c_1 and generators $g_1, \ldots, g_k$, and $\mathfrak{z}_2$ given by c_2 and $h_1, \ldots, h_m$. As observed in [16], $\mathfrak{z}_1 \cap \mathfrak{z}_2 \neq \emptyset$ if and only if the point $c_1 - c_2$ is included in the zonotope centered at the origin, with generators $g_1, \ldots, g_k, h_1, \ldots, h_m$. This is a simple linear satisfiability problem.

Splitting. A zonotope can be viewed as the affine projection of a n-dimensional unit cube, n being the number of noise symbols, onto a p-dimensional space, p being the number of variables. Our first idea was thus to use a split operation on the unit cube in order to define a splitting operation on the resulting zonotope. However, this splitting method does produce overlapping zonotopes. The resulting algorithm was cumbersome and inefficient.

Another natural way to split zonotopes, without overlapping this time, is to use the property that zonotopes can be tiled, using generally more than 2 sub-zonotopes. These tiles are more precisely parallelotopes, as we describe below.

Consider a zonotope $\mathfrak{z}(V)$ on a set of generators $V = (v_1, \ldots, v_n) \in \mathbb{R}^{p.n}$. A zonotopal tiling of $\mathfrak{z}(V)$ is a set of tiles $\{Z_1, Z_2, \ldots, Z_M\}$ constructed from the vectors in V such that $\bigcup_{i=1}^{M} Z_i = \mathfrak{z}(V)$. Provided with a sign vector $\sigma \in \{+, -, 0\}^n$ we can define a zonotope:

$$\mathfrak{z}(\sigma) := \sum_{\{i|\ \sigma_i = 0\}} [-v_i, +v_i] + \sum_{\{i|\ \sigma_i = +\}} v_i - \sum_{\{i|\ \sigma_i = -\}} v_i \tag{6}$$

where $\mathfrak{z}((0,0,\ldots,0))$ is the largest zonotope obtainable, i.e., $\mathfrak{z}(V)$ and for all other sign vectors we obtain zonotopes which are contained in $\mathfrak{z}(V)$. The zero entries of σ characterize the shape of $\mathfrak{Z}(\sigma)$ and the non-zero entries describe how $\mathfrak{Z}(\sigma)$ will be translated with respect to the origin. Thus, given a set of vectors $V \in \mathbb{R}^{p \cdot n}$, which generates $\mathfrak{Z} := \mathfrak{Z}(V)$, we can associate a zonotopal tiling $\mathfrak{Z}(\sigma) \subseteq \mathfrak{Z}(V)$ with every sign vector $\sigma \in \{+, -, 0\}^n$. One such special kind of tiling is known as a parallelotope tiling, i.e., a tiling formed from all linearly independent subsets of $\{v_1, v_2, \ldots, v_n\}$.

In total, there are 2^n vertices in an n-dimensional hypercube, which can be projected with the generator matrix into the zonotope. All the extremal points of the zonotopes are projected hypercube vertices, but not all projected vertices are extremal in the zonotope. The parallelotopes in our tiling also have, as extremal points, projected vertices from the hypercube, some of which are internal points in the zonotope. Enumerating the parallelotopes tiles reduces to an enumeration of a set of hyper-cube vertices. We develop below an algorithm for tiling, which enumerate only the vertices characterizing the sub-zonotopes tiling a given zonotope. We use ideas issued from matroid theory established by Bohne-Dress theorem [17,18], i.e., there is a close connection between a zonotope and the signs of its vectors since they abstract combinatorial facts about the structure of the zonotope. Thus, the key objective of the algorithm is to enumerate the vertices of the tiles as sign vectors of the so-called hyperplane arrangement [19] corresponding to a zonotope, that we are going to define now.

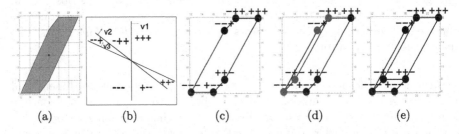

| (a) | (b) | (c) | (d) | (e) |

Fig. 3. (a) Zonotope concretization $\gamma(A)$; (b) Arrangement of hyperplanes; (c) Sign vectors; (d) Sign vectors after fixing the first generator to '-'; (e) All parallelotopic tiles.(Color figure online)

Hyperplane Arrangements. A finite family $\mathcal{A} = \{h_j : j = 1, \ldots, m\}$ of hyperplanes in $\mathbb{R}^p$ is called an arrangement of hyperplanes. Any hyperplane partitions the space $\mathbb{R}^p$ into three sets: $h_j^+ = \{x \mid v_j^T x > b_j\}$, $h_j^0 = \{x \mid v_j^T x = b_j\}$ and $h_j^- = \{x \mid v_j^T x < b_j\}$. For each point x in $\mathbb{R}^p$, there is a sign vector $\sigma(x) \in \{+, -, 0\}^n$ giving its relative location with respect to the hyperplane arrangement, defined as follows:

$$\sigma(x)_j = +, \text{if } x \in h_j^+ \quad \text{or} \quad -, \text{if } x \in h_j^- \quad \text{or} \quad 0, \text{if } x \in h_j^0 \tag{7}$$

The set of points with a given sign vector is an open polyhedron, whose faces of every dimension (including full dimensional p-dimensional cells partitioning the polyhedron) are determined by the intersection of some sets of the form h_j^0, h_j^- and h_j^+, hence are in one to one correspondence with sign vectors. Such a set is a cell if the corresponding sign vectors do not have zero entries. For a zonotope $3 = 3(V)$ generated by the columns of V, we define the associated central arrangement $\mathcal{A} = \mathcal{A}(V)$ of n hyperplanes in $\mathbb{R}^p$, each having v_j as its normal vector : $\mathcal{A}(V) = \{h_j^0 \mid j = 1, 2, \ldots, n\}$ where $h_j^0 = \{x \in \mathbb{R}^p \mid v_j^T x = 0\}$ for $j = 1, 2, \ldots, n$. There is a duality relation between a zonotope and its corresponding hyperplane arrangement. Every d-dimensional open polyhedron in $\mathcal{A}$ determined by its sign vectors corresponds to a $p-d$-dimensional region of a zonotope where $d \le p$; e.g., a full-dimensional open polyhedron corresponds to the vertices of the zonotope.

We denote by $\Sigma = \Sigma(V)$ a set of sign vectors of cells of the arrangement where each vector corresponds to a cell. For example, Fig. 3(b) illustrates an arrangement of 3 hyperplanes in $\mathbb{R}^2$ for the vectors that define the generators of the zonotope in Fig. 3(a). Each cell (region between two adjacent hyperplanes) is represented by a sign vector of dimension 3 and corresponds to an extremal point of the zonotope as shown in Fig. 3(c). Furthermore, two extreme points in 3 are adjacent in 3 if and only if the associated cells are adjacent, i.e., if and only if their sign vectors are different in exactly one component. Finding the sign vectors is a cell enumeration problem. We use here a reverse search algorithm [19] that has a time complexity of $\mathcal{O}(n\, p\, LP(n, p)\, |\Sigma|)$ to compute $\Sigma = \Sigma(V)$ for any given rational $p \times n$ matrix V, where $LP(n, p)$ is the time to solve a linear programming problem with n inequalities in p variables.

Definition 1. *Let $\sigma \in \{+, -, 0\}^n$ a sign vector. Fixing a single-element $j \in 1, \ldots, n$ means setting $\sigma_j \in \{+, -\}$ and defines a sub-zonotope*

$$3(V \setminus j^{\{+,-\}}) := \sum_{\{i \ne j \mid \sigma_i = 0\}} [-v_i, +v_i] + \sum_{\{i \ne j \mid \sigma_i = +\}} v_i - \sum_{\{i \ne j \mid \sigma_i = -\}} v_i + \sigma_j v_j$$
(8)

Freeing a single-element $j \in 1, \ldots, n$ means setting $\sigma_j = 0$ and defines a larger zonotope

$$3(\hat{V}/j^{\{+,-\}}) := \sum_{\{i \ne j \mid \sigma_i = 0\}} [-v_i, +v_i] + \sum_{\{i \ne j \mid \sigma_i = +\}} v_i - \sum_{\{i \ne j \mid \sigma_i = -\}} v_i + [-v_j, +v_j] \quad (9)$$

By Definition 1, we know that a sub-zonotope is obtained by fixing the sign of any one of the generators of a zonotope. Thus a parallelotopic tile is a zonotope with p free generators and $n-p$ fixed generators (p is the number of variables and n is the number of generators). Note that a sub-zonotope has some of its vertices in common with the vertices of the original zonotope and some inner vertices. Incrementally, if we keep fixing the sign of the generators until we enumerate the first parallelotopic tile then we have enumerated a sufficient number of inner vertices corresponding to the extremal points of each sub-zonotope to construct the remaining parallelotopic tiles. This is true by induction.

Algorithm. Figure 4 illustrates a recursive algorithm for computing all the parallelotopic tiles characterizing a given p dimensional zonotope $\mathbf{3} = \mathbf{3}(c, v_1, v_2, \ldots, v_n)$. First, it checks if the input is already a tile i.e., $n = p$, then it returns the singleton containing the zonotope itself, otherwise it arbitrarily chooses a sign to fix the first generator. Fixing v_1 will produce a sub-zonotope defined by: $\mathbf{3}_{sub} = \mathbf{3}((\sigma_1, 0, \ldots, 0))$ computed according to (6) where σ_1 is either '+' or '−'. Then we make a recursive call of the tiling function on $\mathbf{3}_{sub}$ which computes its tiling and stores the result in T. The remaining step consist in finding all the adjacent parallelotopic tiles of $\mathbf{3}_{sub}$. First, we compute the sign vectors (Σ') of $\mathbf{3}_{sub}$ and prepend to them the sign of the first generator (σ_1) and add all the non-existent sign vectors to Σ. This corresponds to the extremal points of $\mathbf{3}_{sub}$ which are not extremal points of $\mathbf{3}$. We know that the first generator was fixed by computing $\mathbf{3}_{sub}$. Now, we free it and for each subset of generators $v_2 \ldots v_n$ of length $p-1$ we compute the parallelotopes for the p free generators $\{1\} \cup S$.

> **procedure** TILINGS($\mathbf{3}$)
>   **if** $n = p$ **then**
>   return $\{\mathbf{3}\}$
>   **else**
>   Compute $\Sigma = \Sigma(V)$
>   Compute $\mathbf{3}_{sub} = \mathbf{3}((\sigma_1, 0, \ldots, 0))$
> $T = $ TILINGS($\mathbf{3}_{sub}$)
> $\Sigma' = \Sigma(V')$ where V' are the generators of $\mathbf{3}_{sub}$
>   Prepend σ_1 to Σ', and add to Σ
>   // Find all tiles adjacent to $\mathbf{3}_{sub}$
>   **for** S in $2^{\{2,\ldots,n\}}$ of length $p - 1$ **do**
>   Find parallelotopic tiles for S in Σ
>   Add to T
>   return T

Fig. 4. Algorithm to compute the tilings of the zonotope $\mathbf{3} = \mathbf{3}(c, v_1, v_2, \ldots, v_n)$ defined by center c and the generators $v_1, v_2, \ldots, v_n = V$.

Example 1. Fixing to '−' the first generator of the zonotope $\mathbf{3}(V)$ of Fig. 3(c), defined by $V = ((2,0), (1,1), (3,5))$ and center $(18, 12)$, we obtain the parallelotopic tile $\mathbf{3}(V \setminus 1^-)$ shown in Fig. 3(d), where the extremal points are marked in red. The center of this tile is computed as $\left(18, 12\right) + (-1)\left(2, 0\right) + 0\left(1, 1\right) + 0\left(3, 5\right)$. Now, we shall be using this tile to generate the others.

The generator $\left(2, 0\right)$ was fixed in order to generate the parallelotopic tile. Now, we free this generator (v_1) and for each subset of generators v_2, v_3 of length $p-1$ we compute the parallelotopes. Consider the free generator combination (v_1, v_2) with the vector v_3 fixed. We search for the sign vectors of $\mathbf{3}(V)$ in which each individual fixed generator has the same sign. For instance the sign vectors: $(+, -, -), (-.-, -), (-, +, -), (+, +, -)$ characterize a parallelotope as shown in Fig. 3(e). Similarly, we can find the tile with vectors (v_1, v_3) free and v_2 fixed.

3.3 Coverage Operation

Consider a set of zonotopes $G^\sharp$ in Fig. 5(a) partitioning an inductive invariant. Figure 5(b) illustrates the set of partitions $B^\sharp$ which covers the whole invariant space. Consider the zonotope partition noted P in Fig. 5(b). Recall from Sect. 2 that the *contents-of* function corresponding to P (i.e., $\text{cnt}(P)$) will return the parallelotope S_k marked in Fig. 5(a). The image of the zonotopes in Fig. 5(a) by a loop iteration is shown in edgeform color red in Fig. 5(c). We superimposed the images and the partitions to show which parts of $B^\sharp$ intersect the image of a zonotope $S_k \in G^\sharp$. That is the map post.

As discussed in Sect. 2 in the current work we only apply tightening during the first iteration. So, the benign test in Eq. (3) can be reduced to

$$S_k \text{is benign} \iff \forall P \in \text{post}(S_k) : \text{cnt}(P) \neq \emptyset \wedge F^\sharp(S_k) \subseteq T \qquad (10)$$

i.e., a zonotope S_k is benign if $F^\sharp(S_k)$ is included within the candidate invariant, and if, when $F^\sharp(S_k)$ intersects some zonotope $P \in B^\sharp$, we have that $\text{cnt}(P)$ is not the emptyset. For instance, consider the zonotope S_k shown in Fig. 5(a) (the parallelotope labeled as S_k) and its image under $F^\sharp$, the zonotope labeled as $F^\sharp(S_k)$ shown in Fig. 5(c). The sub-parallelotopes numbered 1, 2, up to 5 in Fig. 5(c) are thus in $\text{post}(S_k)$. Thus, the benign test for S_k consists in checking whether these partitions contain zonotopes from $G^\sharp$, and whether the image of S_k is entailed within the initial invariant, which are true here.

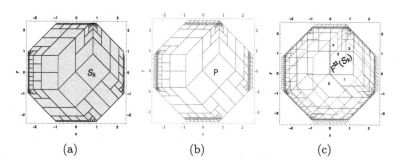

(a)	(b)	(c)

Fig. 5. (a) Set of zonotopes $G^\sharp$ partitioning an inductive invariant; (b) Partitions $B^\sharp$; (c) Map post (Color figure online)

Recall that, to compute coverage, we actually only need some approximation (with bounded ratio), so we use an heuristic measure instead of computing volume: we count the number of zonotopes $P \in B^\sharp$ which intersect $F^\sharp(S_k)$, i.e., $\#\{P | P \in \text{post}(S_k)\}$ and then, among these zonotopes, we count the ones for which $\text{cnt}(P) \neq \emptyset$, i.e., we compute $\#\{P | \text{cnt}(P) \neq \emptyset, P \in \text{post}(S_k)\}$. Our heuristic measure is thus:

$$\text{coverage}(S_k) := \frac{\#\{P | \text{cnt}(P) \neq \emptyset, P \in \text{post}(S_k)\}}{\#\{P | P \in \text{post}(S_k)\}} \qquad (11)$$

4   Experiments

A prototype analyzer was written in OCaml for the algorithm of [1] using the box and octagon abstract domains available in the Apron library [6]. We adapted this prototype analyzer, as described in Sect. 3, in order to use the zonotopic abstract domain implementation Taylor1+ [5] and polyhedra abstract domain New Polka from Apron. We added the operations split, intersection, coverage measure and the new inclusion test of Sect. 3 in Taylor1+[1]. This adapted version is available online[2].

We have chosen hard non-linear problems[3] from various articles on non-linear numeric invariant inference. Most of these examples belong to SV-COMP benchmarks[4], e.g., Sine, Square root, Newton, Newton2, Filter. In Table 1, we compare on some small but challenging loops the results of the algorithm applied to boxes, octagons, polyhedra and zonotopes. For each abstract domain, we give the number of iterations and time until a first inductive invariant is found, and the number of elements that compose this invariant. For each example, we highlight in bold in Table 1 the entries corresponding to the smallest number of elements, iterations, or execution time.

Table 1. Experimental results with tightening applied only during first iteration.

Program	Boxes			Octagons			Zonotopes			Polyhedra		
	#elems.	#iters.	time(s)	#elems.	#iters.	time(s)	#elems.	#iters.	time(s)	#elems.	#iters.	time(s)
Octagon	752	2621	0.1042	752	2756	0.6115	**1**	**1**	**0.0001**	1	1	**0.0001**
Filter	238	1310	**0.1029**	74	736	0.2105	**38**	**222**	0.5020	42	312	0.2554
Filter2	14	58	0.0034	7	13	0.0013	8	16	0.0045	**1**	**1**	**0.0009**
Arrow-Hurwicz	1784	1643	0.4033	369	931	0.5147	**15**	**38**	**0.0235**	134	484	1.0059
Harm	87	438	**0.0112**	88	448	0.0647	60	254	0.5143	**53**	**243**	0.2442
Harm-reset	87	438	**0.0204**	88	446	0.1478	60	268	0.9717	**53**	**253**	0.3867
Harm-saturated	23	15	**0.0011**	24	16	0.0112	9	14	0.0157	**5**	**9**	0.0124
Sine	240	1448	0.4395	154	348	0.1102	**21**	**33**	**0.0547**	136	286	1.1145
Square root	7	10	0.0005	4	4	0.0016	**1**	**1**	**0.0001**	4	4	0.0066
Newton	200	102	0.1097	158	76	0.1785	**11**	**17**	**0.0197**	64	26	2.0660
Newton2	1806	499	6.6861	709	430	2.2207	**8**	**6**	**0.0193**	12	12	2.7498
Corner	129781	1847	646.8494	129767	1847	8850.8766	**488**	**999**	**35.6245**	2368	4248	126.7980

Example *Octagon* in Table 1 corresponds to the motivational example from [1]. Its loop body performs a 45-degree rotation around the origin, with a slight inward scaling. The initial element obtained after the first tightening step is already inductive with zonotopes. The classical abstract semantics for addition and subtraction on octagons is too coarse to prove this is an inductive invariant, explaining why the analyzer had to iterate a lot, contrarily to the zonotopic case.

---

[1] https://github.com/bibekkabi/taylor1plus.

[2] https://github.com/bibekkabi/Prototype_analyzerwithApron.

[3] https://github.com/bibekkabi/Prototype_analyzerwithApron/tree/master/ NSV_files.

[4] https://github.com/sosy-lab/sv-benchmarks/tree/master/c/floats-cdfpl.

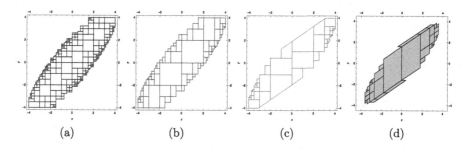

Fig. 6. Inductive invariant for *Filter* example (a) 238 boxes 1310 iterations, 0.1029 s; (b) 74 octagons, 736 iterations, 0.2105 s; (c) 42 polyhedra, 312 iterations, 0.2554 s; (d) 38 zonotopes, 222 iterations, 0.5020 s.

Filter is a second-order digital filter taken from [1]. The candidate invariant provided to the algorithm is $[-4, 4]$ which is not inductive. Figures 6(a), 6(b), 6(c), and 6(d) compare the result of the algorithm on the *Filter* program using intervals, octagons, polyhedra and zonotopes. The natural inductive invariants for such filters are ellipsoids. The inductive invariant found within each abstraction is indeed an approximation of an ellipsoid. It is composed of fewer zonotopes and polyhedra than boxes and, to a lesser extent, octagons, and requires fewer iterations to be synthesized. For *Filter2* from [20], our inductive invariant shows that x and y remain within $[-0.2, 1]^2$.

We analyzed the *Arrow-Hurwicz* loop taken from [20] as a two variable program. The algorithm with boxes, octagons, polyhedra and zonotopes was able to verify that the variables remain within the bound $[-1.73, 1.73]^2$. The analysis with zonotopes was faster and generated far fewer abstract elements compared to other domains.

Harm is an harmonic oscillator program from [20]. Its loop body is close to the identity. The programs *Harm-reset* and *Harm-saturated* add some non-determinism in the loop body. The polyhedra require fewer elements and iterations, but more time, compared to boxes and octagons. On simple cases, the use of complicated abstractions is not competitive, as expected.

For the lead-lag controllers (programs *Lead-lag*, *Lead-lag-reset* and *Lead-lag-saturated* from [21]), none of the abstract domains could find an inductive invariant before timeout. The case of the dampened oscillators [21] fails similarly.

Sine, *Square root*, *Newton*, *Newton2* (taken from [22]) and *Corner* (Fig. 1(a)) are programs with non-linear loop bodies. *Sine* and *Square root* compute the corresponding mathematical functions through Taylor expansions, while *Newton* and *Newton2* perform one step and two steps of Newton solving respectively. Zonotopes are the fastest on all these examples: they require much fewer iterations and elements compared to intervals, octagons and polyhedra.

For example, Figs. 7(a), 7(b), 7(c) and 7(d) compare the result of the algorithm on the *Sine* program using intervals, octagons, polyhedras and zonotopes.

Our zonotope-based method is better when aiming to prove as fast as possible that the initial invariant holds, strengthening it into an inductive invariant.

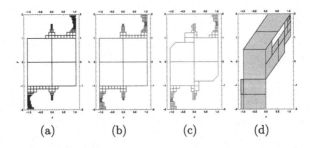

Fig. 7. Inductive invariant for *Sine* example (a) 240 boxes 1448 iterations, 0.4395 s; (b) 154 octagons, 348 iterations, 0.1102 s; (c) 136 polyhedras, 286 iterations, 1.1145 s; (d) 21 zonotopes, 33 iterations, 0.0547 s.

Indeed, with a better interpretation of non affine operations, less splitting steps are needed before getting an inductive invariant. For example, zonotopes enabled us to prove the initial invariant as inductive for the *Square root* program.

These experiments confirm that zonotopes provide a very interesting trade-off between a general purpose abstraction, that stand the comparison with simpler abstractions on basic linear examples, but are also faster and more flexible for the abstraction of more complex, non affine behaviors. In particular, the fact that they allow representing inductive invariants with fewer elements will be even more crucial for the scalability of the approach to higher dimension programs.

5   Conclusion and Future Work

In this paper, we investigated the use of constraint-solving inspired algorithms for inferring inductive invariants. The algorithm works by iteratively splitting and tightening a set of abstract elements until an inductive invariant is found. Our main contribution was to extend the type of abstract elements this algorithm can rely on, in particular when there is no natural bisection method. We instantiated it to the case of zonotopes, and demonstrated that they provide a good trade off, in particular on non-linear programs, and scale up much better than the same algorithm based on simpler domains, such as boxes. Future work includes the use of such techniques to infer invariants of continuous systems and higher dimensional programs.

Acknowledgments. This work is being supported by project ANR-15-CE25-0002-01 COVERIF

References

1. Miné, A., Breck, J., Reps, T.: An algorithm inspired by constraint solvers to infer inductive invariants in numeric programs. In: Thiemann, P. (ed.) ESOP 2016. LNCS, vol. 9632, pp. 560–588. Springer, Heidelberg (2016). https://doi.org/10.1007/978-3-662-49498-1_22

2. Goubault, E., Putot, S.: A Zonotopic framework for functional abstractions. Formal Methods Syst. Des. **47**(3), 302–360 (2016). https://doi.org/10.1007/s10703-015-0238-z

3. Garg, P., Löding, C., Madhusudan, P., Neider, D.: ICE: a robust framework for learning invariants. In: Biere, A., Bloem, R. (eds.) CAV 2014. LNCS, vol. 8559, pp. 69–87. Springer, Cham (2014). https://doi.org/10.1007/978-3-319-08867-9_5

4. Thakur, A., Lal, A., Lim, J., Reps, T.: PostHat and all that: automating abstract interpretation. Electron. Notes Theoret. Comput. Sci. **311**, 15–32 (2015)

5. Ghorbal, K., Goubault, E., Putot, S.: The Zonotope abstract domain Taylor1+. In: Bouajjani, A., Maler, O. (eds.) CAV 2009. LNCS, vol. 5643, pp. 627–633. Springer, Heidelberg (2009). https://doi.org/10.1007/978-3-642-02658-4_47

6. Jeannet, B., Miné, A.: APRON: a library of numerical abstract domains for static analysis. In: Bouajjani, A., Maler, O. (eds.) CAV 2009. LNCS, vol. 5643, pp. 661–667. Springer, Heidelberg (2009). https://doi.org/10.1007/978-3-642-02658-4_52

7. Cousot, P., Cousot, R.: Abstract interpretation: a unified lattice model for static analysis of programs by construction or approximation of fixpoints. In: Proceedings of POPL, pp. 238–252. ACM (1977)

8. Stolfi, J., De Figueiredo, L.H.: Self-validated numerical methods and applications. In: Monograph for 21st Brazilian Mathematics Colloquium, IMPA (1997)

9. Le, V.T.H., Stoica, C., Alamo, T., Camacho, E.F., Dumur, D.: Zonotope-based set-membership estimation for multi-output uncertain systems. In: IEEE International Symposium on Intelligent Control (ISIC), pp. 212–217. IEEE (2013)

10. Tabatabaeipour, S.M., Stoustrup, J.: Set-membership state estimation for discrete time piecewise affine systems using Zonotopes. In: European Control Conference (ECC), pp. 3143–3148. IEEE (2013)

11. Girard, A., Le Guernic, C.: Zonotope/hyperplane intersection for hybrid systems reachability analysis. In: Egerstedt, M., Mishra, B. (eds.) HSCC 2008. LNCS, vol. 4981, pp. 215–228. Springer, Heidelberg (2008). https://doi.org/10.1007/978-3-540-78929-1_16

12. Combastel, C., Zhang, Q., Lalami, A.: Fault diagnosis based on the enclosure of parameters estimated with an adaptive observer. IFAC Proc. Volumes **41**(2), 7314–7319 (2008)

13. Ghorbal, K., Goubault, E., Putot, S.: A logical product approach to Zonotope intersection. In: Touili, T., Cook, B., Jackson, P. (eds.) CAV 2010. LNCS, vol. 6174, pp. 212–226. Springer, Heidelberg (2010). https://doi.org/10.1007/978-3-642-14295-6_22

14. Althoff, M., Krogh, B.H.: Zonotope bundles for the efficient computation of reachable sets. In: 50th IEEE Conference on Decision and Control and European Control Conference, pp. 6814–6821. IEEE (2011)

15. Dreossi, T., Dang, T., Piazza, C.: Parallelotope bundles for polynomial reachability. In: Proceedings of the 19th International Conference on Hybrid Systems: Computation and Control, pp. 297–306. ACM (2016)

16. Guibas, L.J., Nguyen, A., Zhang, L.: Zonotopes as bounding volumes. In: Proceedings of the ACM-SIAM Symposium on Discrete Algorithms, pp. 803–812 (2003)

17. Bailey, G.D.: Tilings of Zonotopes: Discriminantal Arrangements. University of Minnesota, Oriented Matroids and Enumeration (1997)

18. Richter-Gebert, J., Ziegler, G.M.: Zonotopal tilings and the Bohne-Dress theorem. Contemp. Math. **178**, 211 (1994)

19. Ferrez, J.A., Fukuda, K., Liebling, T.M.: Solving the fixed rank convex quadratic maximization in binary variables by a parallel Zonotope construction algorithm. Eur. J. Oper. Res. **166**(1), 35–50 (2005)
20. Adjé, A., Gaubert, S., Goubault, E.: Coupling policy iteration with semi-definite relaxation to compute accurate numerical invariants in static analysis. In: Gordon, A.D. (ed.) ESOP 2010. LNCS, vol. 6012, pp. 23–42. Springer, Heidelberg (2010). https://doi.org/10.1007/978-3-642-11957-6_3
21. Roux, P., Garoche, P.-L.: Practical policy iterations. Formal Methods Syst. Des. **46**(2), 163–196 (2015). https://doi.org/10.1007/s10703-015-0230-7
22. D'Silva, V., Haller, L., Kroening, D., Tautschnig, M.: Numeric bounds analysis with conflict-driven learning. In: Flanagan, C., König, B. (eds.) TACAS 2012. LNCS, vol. 7214, pp. 48–63. Springer, Heidelberg (2012). https://doi.org/10.1007/978-3-642-28756-5_5

Author Index

Printed in the United States
By Bookmasters